# A FEMINIST
# MYTHOLOGY

ALSO AVAILABLE FROM BLOOMSBURY

*Anarchafeminism*, Chiara Bottici
*Rust*, Jean-Michel Rabaté
*Notes from the Crawl Room: A Collection of Philosophical Horrors*,
A.M. Moskovitz

# A FEMINIST MYTHOLOGY

## CHIARA BOTTICI

Translated by Sveva Scaramuzzi
and Claudia Corriero

BLOOMSBURY ACADEMIC
LONDON • NEW YORK • OXFORD • NEW DELHI • SYDNEY

BLOOMSBURY ACADEMIC
Bloomsbury Publishing Plc
50 Bedford Square, London, WC1B 3DP, UK
1385 Broadway, New York, NY 10018, USA
29 Earlsfort Terrace, Dublin 2, Ireland

BLOOMSBURY, BLOOMSBURY ACADEMIC and the Diana logo are
trademarks of Bloomsbury Publishing Plc

First published in 2016 in Italy as *Per tre miti, forse quattro* by Chiara Bottici

First published in Great Britain 2022

A catalogue record for this book is available from the British Library.

A catalog record for this book is available from the Library of Congress.

ISBN: HB:     978-1-3500-9596-0
       PB:     978-1-3500-9597-7
       ePDF:   978-1-3500-9595-3
       eBook:  978-1-3500-9598-4

Typeset by RefineCatch Ltd, Bungay, Suffolk
Printed and bound in Great Britain

To find out more about our authors and books, visit www.bloomsbury.com
and sign up for our newsletters.

To my matternalist mothers

# Contents

# Preface: a myth and a half

## Jean-Michel Rabaté

Why is it that Bocaccio decided to place his one hundred stories within the historical context of a terrible plague ravaging Florence? Was it to give urgency? Poignancy? To spice up the impeccable delivery of his tales with the threat of death? Or was it because he himself had been privy to these catastrophic events and needed to leave a trace as a witness? The *Decameron* has been quoted a good deal recently, and it seems that the coronavirus pandemic has elicited similar effects of random contagion and panicked isolation. In times of plague, we need stories or video games, we crave diversion from films, get hooked on silly YouTube home videos and gaze for hours at unspeakably boring exchanges on social media. Facing the glut of trashy images and 'entertainment', it is clear that our need for good storytelling has never been greater. By 'good', I mean not only entertaining, but also strong, gripping and thoughtful. Chiara Bottici would have to agree because these are the main qualities of her compelling stories, and also because she has renewed and refreshed time-honoured models.

Bottici follows after Bocaccio both in alphabetical order and temporal sequence, and is inscribed in a long tradition, which might be called that of the 'story-teller', a term defined with great sharpness by Walter Benjamin, who distinguishes it from the art of the novelist. Indeed, one of the best-known archetypes of the story-teller is feminine. Who could forget Scheherazade, whose diligent narratives impel the dynamics of the *1,001 Nights?* This masterpiece of Arabic literature synthesized several older folklores, blending together Persian, Indian, Greek and

Turkish tales. We all love the wonderful idea of having Scheherazade deflect the king's murderous jealousy by keeping him interested, night after night, and may forget that she would begin a new story every night, stop in the middle, and resume the following evening. No doubt, Scheherazade's art is that of calculated interruption, a temporal scansion that is not only a survival device but also implies wit and literary acumen, for she has to choose the moment in her tale at which to pause and bring about another cliffhanger. And it is not by chance that 'Sherazade and her Phantom'[1] begins the initial part of Bottici's storytelling – 'Two Myths and a Half' – and thereby triggers an entire feminist mythology, which is first, and foremost, an art of interruption.

Walter Benjamin had found the same breathless urgency and response to an imminent threat in Kafka's way of writing: 'In the stories which Kafka left us, narrative art regains the significance it had in the mouth of Scheherazade: to postpone the future.'[2] Or again about the story-teller: 'Death is the sanction of everything that the storyteller can tell. He has borrowed his authority from death.'[3] Here, the story-teller is generic, which often means masculine: *der Erzähler.* Why not have *die Erzählerin* in the feminine? This has been Bottici's gamble. Sure, in many cases, women were thought to be excellent listeners but not necessarily narrators. Bocaccio had warned us, when he mentions that his hundred stories will bring comfort to all those who have been afflicted by the plague, but more so to women:

> Who will deny that my comfort should be given, for all that it may be worth, to gentle ladies much rather than to men? Within their soft bosoms, betwixt fear and shame, they harbor secret fires of love, and how much of strength concealment adds to those fires, they know who have proved it. Moreover, restrained by the will, the caprice, the commandment of fathers, mothers, brothers, and husbands, confined most part of their time within the narrow compass of their chambers, they live, so to say, a life of vacant ease,

---

[1] The spelling chosen by Chiara Bottici, 'Sherazade', is musically closer to the Italian language than the more common spelling 'Sheherazade', which was imported into English through a German transliteration.

[2] Walter Benjamin, *Illuminations,* trans. Harry Zohn (New York: Schocken, 1968), 129.

[3] Benjamin, *Illuminations,* 94.

and, yearning and renouncing at the same moment, meditate diverse matters which cannot all be cheerful.[4]

Women need to be cheered up! Moreover, one important condition for ladies to be good listeners is to be able to feel desire – a thwarted and impossible desire, no doubt, but one that gives access to depths of empathy and sensibility. Bocaccio's sympathy with the plight of his female contemporaries is obvious—we can also remember that he outdid (in terms of numbers only) the stories of his *Decameron* when he wrote his *On famous women*. Working his way from Eve to Queen Joanna of Sicily, he chalked up 104 vignettes. These include a brief biography of Queen Europa of Crete, who happens to be one of the mythological women presented in these pages.

However, Bottici's stories are not variations on traditional themes, since they all spring from original observations but aim to recreate myths – myths about women and for women. How can we understand this term? Indeed, what is a myth at all? And first and foremost, how can we count myths? Are they not all compilations of divergent stories, some of which are contradictory, to be then streamlined into convenient but misleadingly linear summaries? Claude Lévi-Strauss gave us usable models in his structural analysis of the Oedipus legends before he began systematically exploring the myths of the Brazilian tribes that he transcribed and interpreted.[5] In his work, Lévi-Strauss breaks down the myths into individual motifs and then sorts those so as to be able to compare and classify them. From there, he creates a general grid that gives meaning to his scattered 'bundles of relationships'. For the

---

[4] G. Bocaccio, *Decameron,* trans. J. M. Rigg, 1903, online version at oaks.nvg.org › decameron. The original Italian text reads: 'E chi negherà questo, quantunque egli si sia, non molto piú alle vaghe donne che agli uomini convenirsi donare? Esse dentro a' dilicati petti, temendo e vergognando, tengono l'amorose fiamme nascose, le quali quanto piú di forza abbian che le palesi coloro il sanno che l'hanno provate: e oltre a ciò, ristrette da' voleri, da' piaceri, da' comandamenti de' padri, delle madri, de' fratelli e de' mariti, il piú del tempo nel piccolo circuito delle loro camere racchiuse dimorano e quasi oziose sedendosi, volendo e non volendo in una medesima ora, seco rivolgendo diversi pensieri, li quali non è possibile che sempre sieno allegri.'

[5] See Claude Lévi-Strauss, 'The Structural Study of Myth', in *Structural Anthropology,* trans. Claire Jacobson and Brooke Grundfest Schoep (New York: Basic Books, 1963), 206–31.

Oedipus myth, he begins with a series of discrete events that he manages to place in a general structure capable of connecting them. His myth becomes, as he says, an orchestra score. This practice links back to Bottici's work in that she too makes abundant use of variants. Like Lévi-Strauss, she has to elaborate more comprehensive categories like 'problems in blood relationships', 'autochthonous origins of humanity' or 'feminist mythology', the latter generating an utopia like the vision of a 'city of women', but also a 'bestiarium', and even an 'herbarium'.

Here one might pick up on another reference to an old Italian philosopher. Bottici's work on the political imagination takes its place in a sequence of Italian authors like Dante, Giordano Bruno, Giambattista Vico or Benedetto Croce, all of whom insist on the power of the imagination and its ability to link literature and culture, politics and myth, history and the humanities.[6] Dante would be the true precursor, for as Erich Auerbach demonstrated in his magnificent first book, this universal poet has to be understood as a realist of myth. His well-named *Comedy* gives us a picture of earthly life in which 'the human world in all its breadth and wealth is gathered into the structure of the hereafter'.[7] Here is what Auerbach describes so cogently:

> Doctrine and fantasy, history and myth are woven into an almost inextricable skein; often an almost unconscionable amount of time and effort is required to fathom the content of a single line; but once one has succeeded in surveying the whole, the hundred cantos, with the radiant *terza rima,* their perpetual binding and loosing, reveal the dreamlike lightness and remoteness of a perfection that seems to hover over us like a dance of unearthly figures.[8]

Vico offers the next key here, because his entire philosophy is founded upon a rehabilitation of myth, a concern that he felt inevitable

---

[6] See Chiara Bottici, *A Philosophy of Political Myth* (Cambridge: Cambridge University Press, 2007); Chiara Bottici and Benoît Challand, *Imagining Europe: Myth, Memory, and Identity,* (Cambridge: Cambridge University Press, 2013); and *Imaginal Politics: Images Beyond Imagination and the Imaginary* (New York, Columbia University Press, 2019).
[7] Erich Auerbach, *Dante, Poet of the Secular World,* trans. Ralph Manheim (New York: New York Review Books, 2007), 133.
[8] Ibid.

after the Cartesian revolution had launched scientific modernity.[9] Whereas Descartes had no patience with the legends of the past and wanted to usher in a calculating epistemology that would – thanks to a mathematical, scientific approach – get rid of all mythologies, Vico situates his 'new science' at the exact opposite point. As Vico repeats, and Bottici echoes in her *A Philosophy of Political Myth*, we can leave exact numbers to God; in the domain of history, his main field of reference, deeds and actions have been performed by men and women, hence their truth relies upon a certain way of doing things.[10] It follows that poetic tropes are different ways of conveying historical truth. Any myth, no matter how wild, fanciful or whimsical its details, will contain a 'true story', the meaning of which will emerge only once it has been interpreted: 'We find that *mythos* was defined as *vera narratio,* or true narration.'[11] Of course, by 'true', Vico does not mean literally true, but metaphorically so: 'The first poets attributed to physical bodies the being of animate substances, endowed with limited powers of sense and emotion like their own. In this way, they created myths about them; and every such metaphor is a miniature myth.'[12] This leads to the remarkably astute notion that original metaphors are metaphors of the body. Bottici's work, especially in the 'Herbarium' section, confirms that insight: we discover a whole city in which, after the introduction of a new fashion, the town folk's eyesight and hearing are significantly altered – the rest I leave to the narrator.

Such constant metamorphoses in Bottici's work are not just hidden allusions to Greek and Latin mythology, although one might say that there is still some life in Ovid's recreation of a classical pantheon in beautiful dactylic hexameters. Some of us have not forgotten the relatively abrupt opening ('*In nova fert animus mutatas dicere formas / corpora* . . .' – 'I intend to speak of forms changed into new / bodies'), and know how influential these retellings of myths have been for culture in Europe – and beyond. Vico's original position as an interpreter entails

---

[9] See also Bottici's reference to Vico's *Scienza Nuova* in her *A Philosophy of Political Myth* (Cambridge: Cambridge University Press, 2007), 108–10.
[10] Ibid, 169–70.
[11] Giambattista Vico, *New Science,* 3rd ed., trans. David Marsh (London: Penguin, 2001), 157.
[12] Ibid, 159.

that one has to grapple with some form of ignorance, out of which a creative process will be born, not only for the poet but also for the audience. Having explained how primitive humanity made itself the measure of the universe, and primitive people reduced the entire world to their own body, Vico outlines a method:

> Now rational metaphysics teaches us that man becomes all things through understanding, *homo intelligendo fit omnia*. But with perhaps greater truth, this imaginative metaphysics shows that man becomes all things by not understanding, *homo non intelligendo fit omnia*. For when man understands, he extends his mind to comprehending things; but when he does not understand, he makes them out of himself and, by transforming himself, becomes them.[13]

Vico makes us grasp that human imagination recreates the world and makes sense of it, and that, given such a principle, one can understand social interactions. For instance, he makes a lot of the question of proper names, for as he sees the origins of Rome, at first only the founding fathers had names; the runaway slaves that flocked to the city seeking protection took their masters' names. Only later, after much struggle, were they granted their own names. Similarly, the name of a major god like Jupiter condenses several principles at once: *jus,* the root of 'justice', and *pater,* the 'father'. Poetic metaphors converge with mythical metamorphoses to make sense of history, a history of class conflict and appropriation that impressed Karl Marx when he read him, and whom he quotes in *Capital*.

If both Marx and Vico believed that men make history, what about the history that women make, and what about the accompanying mythologies? This is Bottici's pointed question, for her relentless investigation of the feminine as myth or myth-making process suggests that there is an urgent task here, which begins by adumbrating a different canon. Such a canon would be somehow linked with the concept of hesitation around the number of myths presented: we may recall here that the first three parts of this book are the English translation of a work originally published in Italian with the title of *Per tre miti, forse*

---

[13] Ibid, 160.

*quattro*: *Through Three, Maybe Four, Myths*. This hesitation in counting reminds us of Jacques Lacan's tempering Vico's optimism facing a sayable truth. As Lacan repeats, he always tells the truth, but not all of – the truth can only be 'half-said' (*mid-dite*).[14] This half-saying can make us think about generating 'half-myths', or 'myths and a half', or again some more 'odd myths'. I am thinking of a moment in Lacan's April 1975 seminar when he alluded to Gide's early novel, *Paludes*, stating this:

> This gives me an opportunity to give all its weight to the proverb of which André Gide makes great play in *Paludes* – *Numero deus impare gaudet*, that he translates as '*Le numéro deux se réjouit d'être impair'*, the number two rejoices at being odd. As I have said for a while, Gide is right, for nothing would produce his two if there was not the odd, the odd beginning with three – which is not immediately obvious but makes the Borromean knot necessary.[15]

This silly schoolboy's joke can be easily explained if one grasps that the bad student misread 'deus' (god) as 'deux', which means 'two'. The quote is a half-line from Virgil's eighth eclogue. '*Numero deus impare gaudet'* means 'uneven numbers please God', or literally 'God rejoices seeing an uneven number'. A schoolboy's mistranslation creates an interesting paradox: we have a situation in which the number two rejoices because it is 'odd'. In Virgil's eclogue, two rival shepherds attempt to outdo Orpheus in their poems and songs praising one woman. The power of their poems is also a charm, for '*carmen'* has this double meaning. Here, the power of *carmen* is evoked by the charms Circe used to 'spellbind the shipmates of Odysseus', as Virgil writes, and as Bottici's evokes in the central story called 'The Thread' and in a number of other stories here assembled. Whereas in Bottici's storytelling a silk thread becomes the magic needed to navigate the sicknesses of our times, Virgil weaved three threads that ought to bind the addressee, who is called Daphnis:

---

[14] Jacques Lacan, *Television,* ed. Joan Copjec, trans. D. Hollier, R. Krauss, A. Michelson and J. Mehlman (New York: Norton, 1990), 3.

[15] Jacques Lacan, 'R.S.I. Séminaire 1974–75', ed. Jacques-Alain Miller, *Ornicar?*, no. 5 (1976): 49. My translation.

*ducite ab urbe domum, mea carmina, ducite Daphnin.*
*terna tibi haec primum triplici diuersa colore*
*licia cicumdo, terque haec altaria circum*
*effigiem duco; numero deus impare gaudet.*

(Draw Daphnis back from town, my spells, draw Daphnis home.
First with these three triple threads in separate colours three
I bind you, then about this altar thrice I bear
Your puppet self; uneven numbers please the god.)[16]

Gide's novel, of course, implies that sexual and mental freedom derives from feeling like an 'odd number', by which Gide alludes to his own sexual 'oddity'.[17] If the word meant being queer, the context also invokes a divine enjoyment, or what Lacan would call the fiction of an absolute enjoyment, God's *jouissance*. Such a divine point of view is presented right from the start of this first post-modern novel. It opens with an ironical preface that leaves readers free to draw their own conclusions from this text:

Before explaining my book to others, I wait for others to explain it to me. To want to explain first of all means immediately restricting the meaning; for if we know what we have meant, we don't know that we meant only that – One always says more than THAT – And above all, what interests me is what I have written without knowing it – that part of unconscious that I would like to call God's part.[18]

Here, God merges with the unconscious as being a transcendent guarantee for truth. This truth, which passes through unconscious knowledge (one sees in some passages of this text echoes of a tense conversation between an analysand and a psychoanalyst), cannot be dissociated from a structure of fiction, for fiction plays games with an enjoyment that always appears skewed, excessive or simply odd.

If *'Numero deus impare gaudet'* could be translated as *'Two enjoys its being odd'*, we understand why any number becomes odd as soon

---

[16] Virgil, *The Eclogues*, trans. Guy Lee (New York: Penguin Classics, 1980), 90–1.
[17] André Gide, *Paludes,* (Paris: Gallimard, 1920), 70. My translation.
[18] Ibid, 12.

as we begin counting. Any number can be made the second of a pair when seen from the angle of its oddness. Here, along with Bottici, we are counting up to three, then reach three and a half, stop and smell the flowers, inhale the essence of herbs, have our neuroses treated by an apocalyptic eucalyptus tree, and then begin again.

Lacan used Gide to introduce his Borromean knot, a knot of three circles that cannot be separated two by two, but only by all three at the same time.[19] The knot, originally the emblem of the Borromean family, is made up of three interlocking circles to which Lacan then added a fourth, the function of which was to re-knot the first three; he called it the 'sinthome' and applied the term to his reading of James Joyce. This concept is not so far removed from the sexual politics sketched by Bottici, in a book whose original title, hesitate between the three and the four. She too is aware that one must sense joy in her story-telling, which entails a certain irrationality whether in numbers or in characters, and also perhaps the invocation of a god. You might ask: why not a goddess? To find a feminist answer to this question, we can turn to Hélène Cixous:

> The word god: *le mot-dieu. Le mot dit eux:* the word says them. (. . .) God is always already *di-eu,* di-vided, aimed at by us, hit, split. (. . .) I have never written without *Dieu.* Once I was reproached for it. *Dieu* they said is not feminist. Because they believed in a pre-existing God. But God is of my making. But God, I say, is the phantom of writing, it is her pretext and her promise. God is the name of all that has not yet been said.[20]

For a while Cixous worked directly with Lacan, who owes some of his insights into what he calls 'feminine jouissance' to her; I can only allude to the section of his seminar XX on *Feminine Sexuality: The Limits of Love and Knowledge,* in which he confesses that, if he does not believe in God, he believes in the jouissance of women: why? Because there is always a surplus of it.[21] In this surplus one would find an explanation of

---

[19] Jacques Lacan, 'R.S.I. Séminaire 1974–75', 49.

[20] Hélène Cixous, *Stigmata,* trans. Eric Prenowitz (New York: Routledge, 2005), 200.

[21] Jacques Lacan, *Seminar XX, Encore: On Feminine Sexuality, The Limits of Love and Knowledge, 1972–1973,* trans. Bruce Fink (New York: Norton, 1998), 77.

why it is so hard to invent new myths from scratch, which leaves the option of cutting in half ancient myths, or taking new objects like perfumes, flowers and dresses, and imbuing them with extra significance. Here is what Bottici has done, proving that myth-making is still possible today. She accomplishes this in a reflexive manner, providing the reader all at once her own myths and their rationales. And then, what do we get? Many things, even if at times, these are just new garments, like a shirt for instance, as we discover in this story from Walter Benjamin.

The story takes place in a Hassidic village. It is the evening at the end of the Sabbath day, and the inhabitants are sitting in a humble inn, chatting. They are all locals except for a stranger who has just arrived, looking dishevelled, dressed in rags. They exchange stories of longing, that is, they mention objects of desire, like money, fame or sex. When the villagers are all done, it is the beggar's turn. He waits a little and speaks:

> I wish I could be an all-powerful king who ruled over a vast land, and at night I would lie asleep in my castle and the enemy would break in past the border and before dawn, horsemen would reach my castle, meet with no resistance, and, woken in alarm from my sleep, I would not even have time to dress myself so wearing only a shirt, I would escape past mountains and valleys and past forests and hills without respite day and night, until I arrived safely here at this bench in your corner. This is what I would wish for.

After he has finished, the others look around, baffled. One asks: 'And what would come from all that?' asks one. '"A shirt", was the answer.'[22] A shirt and a life, I would say.

Philadelphia, May 2020

---

[22] Walter Benjamin, *The Storyteller: Tales out of Loneliness,* trans. Sam Dolbear, Esther Leslie and Sebastian Truskolaski (London: Verso, 2016), 180.

# Introduction: a book of books

## Chiara Bottici

This book is a journey through the myths of femininity. More specifically, to test them through the prism of our modern condition. In my previous work, I argued that a myth is not an object, something that can be created once and for all, but rather a process; and, in particular, a process of re-elaboration of a narrative core that expresses itself through multiple variants.[1] In this book, I practice this very process by exploring the different variants of the myth of 'womanhood' – a flux of variegated discourses, prose and poetry, philosophical dialogues and story-telling.

Part I re-tells three mythologems that are at the core of the Western imaginary (*Sherazade, Ariadne, Europa*) thereby showing what can remain of them *sub species modernitatis*. We cannot simply get rid of the myths that still operate in our world, no matter how hard we try to escape them. Attempts to bring myth to an end through an ultimate rationalization has too often resulted in the returned of the repressed, that is, into myth in its most destructive form.[2] Overcoming a mythology means going through its re-telling, because only by traversing the fantasy can one hope to reach a different place. There is no *ex nihilo*

---

[1] Chiara Bottici, *A Philosophy of Political Myth* (Cambridge: Cambridge University Press), 2007.

[2] Theodor W Adorno and Max Horkheimer, *Dialectic of Enlightenment,* trans. Edmund Jephcott (Stanford: Stanford University Press, 2002). The recent surge in macho-populism and neofascism may indeed turn out to be another example of the return of the repressed.

beginning – except, perhaps, for a monotheistic God and his Book (*biblos*).[3] *A Feminist Mythology* is certainly not 'the' book, and perhaps not even 'a' book, but many of them, as many as the variants that each mythologem might generate.

Each section begins with a fragment of an old myth, which is subsequently re-elaborated through an alternation of first-person philosophical narrative and third-person storytelling. The myth that provides the first framework is that of Sherazade, the powerless woman who must continue telling stories so as not to be killed by the omnipotent sultan. But there is no way to re-tell this myth from a single point of view today. The linear thread of the mythologem is thus broken into different fragments that unpack its constitutive blocks, leading to the *sur-*, or perhaps *hyper-*, realist production of a modern day Sherazade who leaves the palace as soon as she discovers that a thousand nights of storytelling means spending three-and-a-half years without sleep. Today's women clearly cannot afford any single linear story, nor can they endure thirty-six months without rest. This prosaic conclusion stands in contrast with the poetic tone of other passages, enacting a writing style that operates like a thermic shock: from the hyper-cold to the hyper-hot, and vice versa. I pursue a form of metaphysical humor that pushes the given myth to its most extreme consequences until it turns upon itself, revealing its underlying logic. This is perhaps only one, but certainly a privileged means of traversing the fantasies: by laughing with them and through them.[4]

The first fantasy is that of the omnipotent sultan and the woman story-teller. The only way to be a woman is by telling stories about womanhood. As Adriana Cavarero reminded us, our selves are 'narratable selves' not because we engage in the active process of

---

[3] See Bottici, *A Philosophy of Political Myth,* 45–6.

[4] On the concept of laugh as a tool to oppose patriarchy, see Hélène Cixous' subversive retelling of the Greek myth of Medusa, the female monster who would turn into stone whoever gazed into her eyes: 'They riveted us between two horrifying myths: between the Medusa and the abyss. That would be enough to set half the world laughing, except that it's still going on. For the phallogocentric sublation is with us, and it's militant, regenerating the old patterns, anchored in the dogma of castration. They haven't changed a thing: they've theorized their desire for reality! Let the priests tremble, we're going to show them our sexts!' Hélène Cixous, 'The Laugh of the Medusa', trans. Keith Cohen and Paula Cohen, *Signs* 1, no. 4 (1976): 885.

telling stories about ourselves (although some of us do, and then we become 'narrated selves'), but because the very possibility of our being in the world is intrinsically linked to the narrative impulse of involuntary memory: we perceive ourselves as that unique person with that unique life story.[5] And that is always a story of a sexed being, because none of us can escape being assigned a sex at birth and carrying it throughout our lives. We must carry our state-sanctioned identity papers and we must carry the stories others tell about us: we must constantly renegotiate our stories through the eyes of others. There is a story behind each of us, a unique story, depending on the fragile, always incomplete, work of memory, but also necessarily reflecting all the stories that others have told, and may potentially tell, about ourselves. We are a unique story not despite, but precisely because of this plurality over which we have no control.[6] Otherwise we may just tell one story about ourselves and then lead an entire life to fulfil it. One may indeed be tempted to do so (and again, some of us do that), but we will inevitably fail because we are always suspended in a fest of reciprocity and relationality where we never get to tell the whole story alone. And this is also why myths are so crucial: lives can be lived according to a story, but, they are not themselves models, narrative plots. Mythologems, those powerful culturally loaded narratives that live in the social unconscious, are not just the lens through we perceive and orient ourselves in the world: they are also the templates on the basis of which we act in it. Myths are self-fulfilling prophecies: they do not wait for reality to prove their truth, they just go ahead and build it.

There is therefore no unique truth of myth. Myth is a process, and thus intrinsically polytheistic, precisely because it needs to respond to a constantly changing need for significance. In order to remain alive, a myth must produce different variants, each responding to the always changing life circumstances. This is the reason why each variants of a myth can stand next to the other with an equally legitimate claim to truth. On the contrary, in the case of a monotheistic sacred History, alternative variants cannot hold at the same time and in the same

---

[5] Adriana Cavarero, *Relating Narratives: Storytelling and Selfhood*, trans. P. Kottman (London: Routledge, 1997), 32–5. Cavarero builds on the philosophy of Hannah Arendt, which she develops in an original and feminist direction, a huge inspiration for this project.
[6] Adriana Cavarero, *Relating Narratives,* 43.

regards, and so they generate schisms and heresies.[7] There is no space for heresy in the world of myth. Hence the title of Part I of this work 'Two myths and a half', because if myth is a process, then even counting every single mythologem, as if they were discrete units, becomes a dauting task. The half denotes both the hesitation and the invitation to continue the difficult work of retelling. Instead of attempting a final countdown that can lead beyond polytheism, this book is an attempt to travel within such plurality.

The fantasies that coagulate in the kaleidoscopic mythologem of Sherazade, a mythologem situated between those two ideological geo-political locations called East and West, are those of a patriarchal order where women can only survive through the power of their voices. Some may observe that presenting patriarchy through the image of an omnipotent sultan, who has the power of life and death over the women he possesses, and the representative impotent woman, who can only tell stories to remain alive, is a bit of an exaggeration. In my defence, I can only say, in the words of the philosopher Theodor Adorno, that 'in psycho-analysis nothing is true except the exaggerations'.[8] This book of myths is also, among other things, a psychoanalytic journey, an attempt to create what feminist psychoanalyst Jill Gentile called 'the space between',[9] that is a space where free speech can develop and something unexpected occur.

It is this pathos of the unexpected, the metaphysical humor always pushing beyond itself, that will lead our modern-day thread-spinning Ariadne into an unprecedented variant of the ancient Greek mythologem. Instead of perpetually weaving a thread for Theseus, the hero who promised her passage on his ship back to Athens for her help in the fight against the Minotaur, our Ariadne will instead end up buying a blue wool dress in a fancy shop. This isn't necessarily a better mythology, but one that seems to respond more properly to the injunctions of our times. Again, the underlying narrative core is elaborated through an alternation of first-person and impersonal narrative, thereby providing a textile (*tessuto*) that transforms the tissue (*tessuto*) of lived experience

---

[7] See Bottici, *A Philosophy of Political Myth,* 20–44.
[8] Theodor W. Adorno, *Minima Moralia*, trans. E. F. N. Jephcott (London: Verso, 2006), 49.
[9] Jill Gentile and Michael Macrone, *Feminine Law: Freud, Free Speech, and the Voice of Desire* (London: Karnac Books, 2016).

into the text (*testo*).[10] Traversing the story of Ariadne means developing the thread that can lead out of the mythical labyrinth, where the Minotaur – half-beast, half-man – reigned happily for centuries as the unsurpassed symbol of the destructive side of desire, devouring one group of young people after another. It is this thread that prepares our contemporary heroine for her own travel to and across the sea.

This is the point where the myth of Ariadne – neither brought back to Athens nor abandoned by her beloved Theseus in Naxos, as the old tales would have it – sets the scene for another Greek mythologem, one that, like that of Sherazade, straddles East and West. Thus Ariadne transitions into Europa, the beautiful princess kidnapped by Zeus in the shape of a bull. According to the mythologem, it was through this act of violence that the princess left her paternal homeland in the East to travel the Mediterranean and found the new continent that carries her name. The short stories that compose this section explore the imaginal aspects of the sea mythologem. Whereas the heroine of the old patriarchal order is left with no other option than merely surviving rape and naming a land that other people will enjoy, our Europa will appear on the scene equipped with mask, fins and snorkel, enabling her to get off the bull, swim across the sea, and thus herself become the voice of a different desire. This will open the way for the founding of *another* city and thus another book within the book.

After an intermezzo, Part II presents a new myth and a new world, a City of Women, a community built on the desire to get rid of all men. This is a very different order from that exposed by the city of patriarchs of Part I. The latter was constructed through the alternation between a syntactically well-ordered third person narrative and a first-person-hysteric-philosophical flux of consciousness, where the ego (*I*) disappears in the performance of a lack, a perpetual state of minoritization (*i*).[11] This opposition between a capitalized language and

---

[10] It is important to note that in Italian, my native language, the word for a bodily tissue and a textile is exactly the same: *tessuto*. This book, more than any other I have written, is a *tessuto*.

[11] On the notion of hysteria, and how such a venerable concept still has a hold on us today, see the very creative and thought-provoking Jamieson Webster, *Conversion Disorder: Listening to the Body in Psychoanalysis* (New York: Columbia University Press, 2019), in particular pp. 61–85.

a decapitated one, between a linear narrative flow and blobs of unstoppable words, swollen and hyper-inflamed lymph nodes, is meant to be a cry against the patriarchal order that our language still embodies. As Friedrich Nietzsche once put it, we have not yet got rid of God because we still have faith in grammar.[12]

Part II announces a possible overcoming of this split, one in which the story-telling goes hand in hand with philosophical dialogues. To cure themselves from the internalized patriarchy of their ancestors, the bodies assembled in the City of Women decide to tell each other stories and then discuss them together, in order to draw inspiration for building their new world. Through philosophical dialogues and storytelling, the vicissitudes of this women-only city unfold, only to conclude with the suspicion that it was built on a City of Men, created with exactly the same intention, and situated next to it.

Because old myths offer no resistance, and new ones collapse too quickly, Part III proposes a Bestiarium, an invitation to question the given boundaries of our heteronormative order, including the opposition between patriarchy and matriarchy, thereby disclosing a different way to be a wo-man today. To that end, it enacts a series of transindividual metamorphoses, which are simultaneously one and many, precisely as multifaceted as the possibilities of 'wo-manhood' in our current condition.[13] The animals evoked by the titles of the last section are therefore not just the inhabitants of a City of Animals, with its clear-cut boundaries, separating the animal kingdom from the human and the vegetal. These meta-morphoses signal the constant passing from one form into another, and thus the overcoming of the 'beasts', the figures that for centuries guaranteed the limits of the established political order, precisely because they defined the boundaries of the properly 'human'. In this book within the book, ostriches, butterflies, dogs, snakes and even a herring become possible vehicles for a transindividual metamorphosis that queers all boundaries, including those that have for centuries classified life into the division between animate (human, animal, plant) and inanimate forms. Within this metamorphosis, a

---

[12] Friedrich Nietzsche, *Twilight of the Idols, or, How to Philosophize with a Hammer*, trans. Duncan Large (Oxford: Oxford University Press, 1998), 19.
[13] See Chiara Bottici, 'Bodies in plural: Towards an anarcha-feminist manifesto', *Thesis Eleven* 142, no. 4, (2017).

computer can very well be the last stage of a snake, that is, of another woman. Only at the end of such a metamorphosis will an 'I' remerge from the blobs of unstoppable words, but finding itself transformed into a transindividual being.

It is such a transindividual metamorphosis that opens the path to the Herbarium, another order still, displaying the interconnection between all life forms. What threatens such a new order is the scopophilia of our times, that obsessive relying on images which has turned us blind precisely the moment in which it fixed us *into* and *as* an image. For such a contemporary pathology, Part IV proposes no univocal solution, except an invitation to keep telling each other stories while witnessing the possibilities opened by a dancing god, *deus sive natura*, immanent unique substance of which we are all, inanimate and animate, mere modes. It is at this point, where God leaves the place of a patriarch up in the sky to reveal itself as just another name for the unique infinite substance, that the book of books ends.

As the title of this book suggests, we become wo-men by endorsing, embroidering, rejecting, modifying, rehearing and rehearsing, in sum, by re-telling the myths we have inherited, as well as those we have ourselves created. What is a woman if not a story-telling process about being women? In this polytheistic world, the writing process is more than a *mix* of storytelling, philosophical dialogues, and metaphysical theorizing: it is a *current* that traverses all of them by overflowing the boundaries it encounters. In the first part, fragments of old texts open each myth and are subsequently re-elaborated in the play of different styles of writing. Beginning with fragments of the established imaginary, the story-telling invites the reader to traverse them, thereby leading into an imaginal space where something new can happen.

In doing so, this project challenges established gender *and* writing categories by reshuffling traditional modes of theorizing. As such, it is part of a tradition of feminist writings aimed at opening and generating different possibilities for being women. This tradition has recently been revived by so-called auto-theory and feminist performance fiction,[14]

---

[14] See, for instance, works as different as Maggie Nelson *The Argonauts* (Minneapolis: Graywolf Press, 2016); and Paul Preciado *Testo Junkie*, trans. Bruce Benderson, (New York: Feminist Press, 2013).

attesting to the timeliness of the enterprise, and the urgent need to revisit what it means to be a woman, but also a reminder that we have to do this by passing through the patriarchal imaginary that has defined it for such a long time. Only by doing this, can we become an-other woman.

This book combines its experimental style with a recovery of traditional modes of philosophical speculation, such as dialogues, philosophical fragments and short stories. After the nineteenth century, with the rise of the treatise as the default format of philosophical writing, the incredible variety of past philosophical writing styles has been eclipsed. In this work, I adopt a writing style that recovers such a tradition, one that, in the West, for instance, runs from Ancient Greek philosophers to Renaissance dialogues, from Enlightenment philosophical novellas to Nietzsche's blending of prose and poetry, but also opens to the possibility of a new encounter with philosophical traditions outside the Western one. Indeed, as feminists argued, in order to recover women's voices, and in particular the voice of many women of color who have been excluded from the academia for such a long time, it is necessary to question the hegemony of the 'monograph' as the one and only legitimate form of philosophical theorizing.[15] This book, with its three, maybe four myths, shows that, as Donna Haraway once put it, if we want to question white capitalist patriarchy, 'one is too few, and two is only one possibility'.[16]

In other words, I continue here the exploration of the political usages of imagination that has been the central thread of my philosophical career. The only difference is that, whereas in my previous work I developed a 'philosophy of the imaginal', with *A Feminist Mythology*, I cultivate an 'imaginal philosophy', that is, arguments put forward through a flux of images, narratives and dialogues. The term mythology is used here in the etymological meaning of the term: a *mythos-logein* is not simply collecting the myths pertaining to a certain tradition, but also

---

[15] Patricia Hill Collins, *Black Feminist Thought,* 2nd ed. (New York: Routledge, 2000), 16–17.

[16] Donna Haraway, 'A Cyborg Manifesto: Science, Technology, and Socialist Feminism in the Late Twentieth Century', reprinted in *Manifestly Haraway* (Minneapolis: University of Minnesota Press, 2016), 65.

an attempt to bring forth the *logos* of the *mythos* itself, that is the reason of myth. I see this as a contribution towards what I would call an 'imaginal feminism'.

I learned that one can do philosophy through images cast in language while reading Dante's *Divine Comedy*.[17] I began reading it in middle school, and have not stopped since. I even used to read it to my children before bed, because I thought Dante's *terza rima* sounded so divine that it would make them feel good and fall asleep quietly. They did not understand a single word of that weird Italian, but they have slept very well ever since.

Through Dante, I learned how to think through literature. Even before beginning the study of philosophy, I was already looking for the imaginal philosophy encapsulated in literary writings. As I look back to that middle schooler reading a copy of Kafka's *Metamorphosis*, I remember the puzzlement it produced in me, but also the intellectual pleasure of discovering the philosophy of the work: among other things, for me, the image of that alienated bureaucrat turning into a beetle did the work of critique. I enjoyed the story for the critique it embodied. It was only years after, when, in high school, I started reading Parmenides and Plato, that I realized this is what philosophy was also devoted to.

Both Parmenides and Plato, not to mention Nietzsche, do philosophy through images – even through myths, despite the fact that the entrenched dichotomy of myth (*mythos*) and reason (*logos*) often prevents scholars from realizing this.[18] For me, there was not much of a difference then between Kafka and Parmenides. I still don't think there is. But it was not Parmenides nor Plato that pushed me to become a philosopher. It was encountering the work of Anselm of Aosta, and his ontological proof of the existence of God. I was so fascinated by the beautiful truth of its rigorous arguments and rhetoric that I decided I would devote myself entirely to its study.

That is what still attracts me to philosophy, in particular that of Baruch Spinoza, which reverberates in the following pages, precisely where

---

[17] Dante Alighieri, *The Divine Comedy,* trans. John Ciardi (New York: New American Library, 2003).

[18] See Chiara Bottici, 'Mythos and Logos: A genealogical approach', *Epoché* 13, no. 1 (2008): 1–24.

one would less expect it. However, in contrast to other philosophers, including Spinoza, I learned to do philosophy through the imagination, even before learning that one could do it through reason. Most of all, after an entire career devoted to studying what one could call the politics of imagination, while practising literary writing as a separate enterprise, I realized that much of the time the two are inseparable. This is the main understanding from these years of investigations into the philosophy of the imaginal, that space made of images, of (re)presentations that are also presences in themselves. Before and after language, we think through images, and this is why they pulsate both in the work of reason and in that of the imagination.[19]

For years, I have practised the two: while English language transported my philosophy of the imaginal, my native language, Italian, became the repository of my imaginal peregrinations. This book, which is an expanded translation of the 2016 work, *Per tre miti, forse quattro*, is a testament of the latter. Reading this work in English translation offers me the privilege of a distance from my own work. No writer ever knows exactly what they have done, and perhaps this is the main difference between philosophy and literature, if we really want to hold onto one: as a philosopher, I usually know what my argument is even before writing it, whereas, as a writer, I never know exactly what I am doing, even after I have done it.

Translations offer another lens, however. As I read this book of books from the vantage point of a translation, I see that I did learn one could do philosophy through images from the Italian men I read in my adolescence, but I would not have written this book without the inspiration of the feminist writings that accompanied my adulthood. Things could not have been otherwise. I entered school at the age of six, in 1981, and received the title of *dottore di filosofia* in 1999 having read only men. In eighteen years within the Italian school system, I had not been taught a single poem, short story or novel – let alone philosophical theory – of any other gender except men. It is no exaggeration to say I received an amazing men-ducation, that I was con-ducted into men's books. Even Sappho's poems, usually mandatory

---

[19] See Chiara Bottici, *Imaginal Politics: Images Beyond Imagination and the Imaginary* (New York: Columbia University Press, 2014).

in the study of the Greek literature in a *Liceo Classico* like the one I attended, went missing in my case, because my teacher became ill and the replacement for that year decided to skip her.

The first woman philosopher I read was Hannah Arendt, having been initially attracted to her philosophy of narration and her meditations on Isak Dinesen's claim that 'All sorrows can be borne if you put them into a story or tell a story about them'.[20] Arendt was the first woman philosopher I read, but Simone de Beauvoir is the one who woke me from the menocratic slumber created by an education devoted to reading only books produced by men.[21] It was by reading her, along with Hélène Cixous, Luce Irigaray, Monique Wittig, Julia Kristeva, Adriana Cavarero and Judith Butler, among others, that I learned story-telling can also create a world that was not there before, and that we are not only meant to find palliative to help us carry our burden. Luce Irigaray taught me that we live in a phallogocentric order, where most of us still carry the Name of the Father, and womanhood is just a sex which is not one, as if we had never left the ancient Greek patriarchal regime where temple statues of men are bestowed proper genitals, while women are restricted to an empty flatness – no vulva, no labia, no clitoris, nothing that can be named except perhaps the invisible, the vagina, and only because the latter is, etymologically, the container of the sword.[22] Whereas reading Irigaray I understood we still live under the Name of the Father, by reading Monique Wittig's *Les Guérillères*,[23] I felt that another world was also, literally, possible.

This is why the concept of the self in Kafka, and similar writers in that tradition, is not at all my concept of the self. His is fundamentally entrapped; that is the source of his pathos. Mine is fundamentally untrappable, transindividual, a performance of a lack in some moment, and the performance of an excessive plenitude in others. But, as Judith Butler argued, there is no doer beyond the deeds, there is no performer

---

[20] Hannah Arendt, *The Human Condition* (Chicago: Chicago University Press, 1998), 175.

[21] Simone De Beauvoir, *The Second Sex*, trans. Constance Borde and Shelia Malovanay-Chevallier (New York: Vintage, 2011).

[22] Luce Irigaray, *This Sex Which is Not One*, trans. Catherine Porter (Ithaca: Cornell University Press, 1985), 26.

[23] Monique Wittig, *Les Guérillères*, trans. David le Vay (Champaign: University of Illinois Press, 2007).

before the performance.[24] Hence the difference from Dante, too, because he has a singular if tripartite monotheistic God that orders things very precisely and all that falls outside the poet's comprehension is ordered by this greater understanding — no further questions need to be asked, once you reach Paradise. I do not have that monotheistic God (only lots of polytheistic myths that are even hard to count), but I do have the ways of being, human being just one, and always transindividually connected with others, such as animal, plants, rocks, even atomic particles.

Questions are not meant to be answered once for all, as there are no definitive answers, but states of bodies, housed in language. In other words, the reader will find here less scriptures, more *écriture*, obviously more feminist than Dante or Kafka and certainly very *feminine*.[25] Can we see this as a strength, this suppleness, or at least a difference from the deadpan cogitations of the masculine trope of the above? Though, to be fair, Dante was given to swooning, and men die in opera precisely because of their rigidities. But whereas men may or may not die at the end of our patriarchal drama, the classical Western opera incessantly stands for the death of woman, for the perpetration of a sex which is not one.[26]

This book is also nourished by years of listening to opera. Some readers may find this inappropriate. Some will even lament the fairy-tale tone of some passages. I did listen to opera while writing, but the fairy

---

[24] Butler creatively reappropriated Nietzsche's insights and applied it to gender theory. See, in particular, the following passages: 'The challenge for rethinking gender categories outside of the metaphysics of substance will have to consider the relevance of Nietzsche's claim in *On the Genealogy of Morals* that "there is no 'being' behind doing, effecting, becoming; 'the doer' is merely a fiction added to the deed – the deed is everything." In an application that Nietzsche himself would not have anticipated or condoned, we might state as a corollary: There is no gender identity behind the expressions of gender; that identity is performatively constituted by the very "expressions" that are said to be its results.' Judith Butler, *Gender Trouble* (New York: Routledge, 1999), 33. See also: Judith Butler, 'Imitation and Gender and Subordination' in *Inside/Out: Lesbian Theories, Gay Theories,* ed. Diana Fuss (New York: Routledge, 1991), 24.

[25] This is an implicit reference to Cixous' expression 'Écriture féminine', which literally means 'feminine writing', but is translated by Keith Cohen and Paula Cohen as 'women's writing'. See the very first sentence of Cixious, 'The Laugh of the Medusa', trans. Keith Cohen and Paula Cohen, *Signs* 1, no. 4 (1976), 875.

[26] See Catherine Clément, *Opera: The Undoing of Women*, trans. Betsy Wing (Minneapolis: University of Minnesota Press, 1988).

tales came on their own, uninvited occasional guests. Women are still given their massive doses of traditional fairy tales, let alone the fairy tales of makeovers and wellness cures. And even without Prince Charming, there is a female imperative to be happy, to smile and be sweet, to be endlessly charming ourselves, like a welcome mat – even as most women's lives are assigned to the ongoing maintenance of being, for which there is no end or happily ever after. Can women insist on taking their liberties with story and form, on making our own fairy tales that don't end with an end as such, but with another way of being? Can we cannibalize the myths around us and spit them back in an unrecognizable form? I hope this will be understood, for once at least, as a liberatory gesture, and not as a failure to understand that fairy tales are dreams, dreams fairy tales, and what lies between (if we are very lucky) are mere stories.

New York, May 2021

# PART ONE

# Two myths and a half

# First myth: Sherazade and her phantom

*Sherazade*

*Il mio sposo celeste*
*(padrone dei miei respiri)*
*benigno ritarda per me*
*la sentenza mortale:*
*perché fra tante spose*
*io sola, unica io,*
*so con bellissime fiabe*
*consolare la notte.*

*Non è mio pregio, ma del cielo,*
*che mi fece fantastica*
*se degna io sono della grazia.*

*E voi non portatemi invidia,*
*né, dispettosi, lasciate*
*queste veglie*
*felici pei vostri inanimati sonni.*

*A voi diletto, a me speranza rechi*
*l'Oscura.*

Elsa Morante, *Alibi,* 1946
© Estate of Elsa Morante. Reproduced
courtesy of the heirs to the Estate.

Sherazade

My heavenly spouse
(master of my breaths)
Benign delay for me
The death sentence:
Because among so many brides
I alone, only I
Can console the night
With beautiful fairy tales.

It is not my merit, but heaven,
Which has made me fantastic
If I be worthy of such grace.

And you, do not envy me,
Nor, spiteful, leave
These happy vigils
For your inanimate sleep.

Let the Dark bring you delight,
and hope to me.

Elsa Morante, *Alibi,* 1946
(translation by the author)

# I. Sherazade

i will tell you stories, stories all night, i say it, as a joke, and then i chew on it, i chew like a cow, how funny, stories as a remedy for jet lag, like sherazade, why, sherazade, i've never even read one thousand and one nights, sherazade, i only know she tells stories, stories to remain alive, sherazade, who turns and returns, and all those images, recalling each other, everything holds together, suddenly, the kind of fish i love, even though it almost killed me, but it did not, and then one of the first short-stories came out, my high school teacher, and her ancient greek classes, a dead language, a dead language and the live tongue of my teacher, smells and colours and flavours, pressing and im-pressing, like the sea, there is no past no future no present, only images, images and immanence, and the other night, that singer, i listen to the music, distracted, she speaks about *les corps les plus simples*, *la connaissance adéquate*, so weird, that actress, she touches a tree at the end of the movie, she actually touches it, she does, and she sings, she sings the words of philosophy, *je sais nager*, eternity, i listen, i listen and i remember, i can swim too, me, me who spent all her childhood summers at the beach, i know the sea very well, i grew with it, i grew into it, i know how to drift on the waves, *me plonger*, deeper, if needs be, and how to get out, i can be in, i can be out, amphibious creatures, maybe i can even hear them singing, i am no ulysses, no, maybe a bit of a mermaid though, in and out, and i chew, i chew like a cow, i chew all the words, all the words of philosophy, in music

# The match

I knew it would happen there, in the old Vacchelli Palace. It was an old art nouveau building, constructed at the same time as the square it faced, when the city started growing outside the ancient medieval settlement and covered the area once occupied by the Napoleonic cemetery. It is weird to think that a square like that, full of neat buildings and fancy shops, was lying on death and the disgusting smell of corpses.

The palace was in the south-eastern corner of the square, where the trading centre of the city was at the time. On the opposite side, an old theatre complex, which also hosted the local branch of the Anarchist Federation: coloured, chaotic, and noisy anarchists, but still displaying a kind of well-dressed moralism. They did not sport tartan trousers or pink mohawks: their anarchism was serious, with suits and black scarves tied in conspicuous bows.

This had been the family house since the end of the war. Disgraced aristocrats, just like that building, their old-fashioned pomp clashing with the neon signs that had been popping up everywhere nearby. The palace entrance looked even more inappropriate, due to the many lights that shined on the white marble of the stairways. Floral stucco patterns decorated its walls, enhancing the sensation of excess. Most often, buildings of that style cannot not give back any immediate inputs, only the desired effect of its unnecessary artificiality.

The stairways led to the fourth floor, with a kind of elegant effort. Step by step, they embroidered a sinuous and encircling spiral, ending in that specific apartment. Behind the door and its ornate handle lay a corridor, with large windows, letting in the light, filtered by their embellished glass. In that building, not even daylight could manifest itself in a raw state.

The corridor was flanked by the kitchen and ended in the living room, the true core of the old house. A big space, furnished with dark velvet sofas and a crystal chandelier, it could not hide the negligence of its upkeep. On each side of the room was a bedroom. On the left there was the children's room. It too was a very large space, so large it looked as if the beds were sinking inside. The ceiling was painted with abstract floral motifs, making any other furniture superfluous as they captured the observer in their spiralling movement. In front of the beds, there was a white marble fireplace, decorated with the same patterns as the ceiling, converging towards a Medusa head, her forced expression and her stone eyes fashioning a body without organs. A thick wooden cover on the hearth showed how little the fireplace was used.

On the other side of the living room lay the master bedroom. Its floor made of diamond shaped tiles, like the rest of the house, created a peculiar optical illusion: it suggested a striped space, which, through the alternation of extremely pointed geometrical elements, magically turned out as smooth as the sea – a sea of deep garnet-red waves, elegantly emerging with their dark warmth from the black and white that accompanied them.

Unlike the other rooms, this was particularly severe. The mahogany furniture, decorated with abstract patterns, was covered in mirrors, multiplying the space in an expanding game of endless reflections. In the middle of the room, the master bed was flanked by two austere bedtime tables, like two little soldiers on watch. The tennis match was meant to happen right there.

A woman against two men. A young lady, with strong traits. Her two opponents were quite similar to each other, as if there were no difference between them. Even their faces were indefinite: dressed in plain white t-shirt and sports trousers, they were distinguishable from each other only because they played in turns. Otherwise, they could well have been the same person.

She, too, wore plain tennis kit, as it was fit for the occasion. She had her hair down, though, hair that bounced when she jumped from side to side of the unusual playing court. The match had been going on for a while, apparently. The ball travelled regularly from one side to the other of the bed: here the woman, moving alone, moving femininely; there the two men, with their automated attitude.

Two against one. Although this did not seem to influence the result of the match. She quickly received each serve and looked quite comfortable both in forehand and in backhand. The latter was even easier for her, as the backwards movement was more in tune with her game. With her forehand, she caught the ball from the floor, with her backhand, she threw it away, as if slapping somebody in their face. Yet, there was no sign of aggression in her gesture.

The two men jumped mechanically from side to side and seemed to follow a more straightforward logic. Even in their forced 'hee!', that clearly excessive sound that only tennis players are allowed to make, sounded peculiarly regular, perhaps even fake. It was as if the energy invested in their movement was always exactly the same: pacing the match, accompanying the ball from one end to the other of the field, with predictable regularity.

If you looked closely, though, there was a certain clumsiness in the woman's gestures, especially in her serve. While the two men launched the ball with a complete rotation, as if it came directly from the old trunk at their backs, she showed some discomfort. Maybe the mirrors did not leave enough room for her to move the arch of the body far enough to gain momentum. Maybe that big room was actually not big enough.

Her discomfort rose noticeably. She received the ball well, always catching it, both in forehand and in backhand. It was her serve that highlighted a growing perplexity. Too narrow, too narrow to move completely. She looked increasingly clumsy and annoyed. At one point, she suddenly moved into the corner between the mirror and the window. There, she might have had more freedom. But even that was not enough.

The match went on, in its obsessive tick and tack. None of the two parties had a visible advantage. The ball jumped from one side to the other of the court until one of the contenders could send it in a difficult position – and then they changed serve. One point to one side, one point to the other. Each advantage immediately followed by a tie. It was a stalemate.

At least it was until the woman started playing with a different vigour. The more she appeared annoyed, the more energy flew into her gestures, the more her surrounding space showed its limits. But the renewed energy had created an advantage over her opponents. A particularly angry serve, even in the narrow corner where she stayed, gave her a decisive edge.

Her opponents seemed incapable of reacting to such an excess. They went on as before, with their featureless faces, and their mechanical attitude like a clock. Meanwhile, she grew angrier and angrier: and her rage caused sharp and strong shots, as direct as an unexpected kiss that is long overdue. In advantage, she was clearly and definitely in advantage. She would soon crush her opponents. This was clear. Just a few more points and it would have been done. But her distress grew with her energy: the more vigorous the shot, the narrower the space, unable to contain the free intensity of those gestures.

Until . . . the earth – she left the room, she went away, she did not even finish the match, because, she muttered to herself, she wanted the earth, yes, the earth, bright red sandy earth: the original, not the copy. She wanted the earth crunching under her feet, capturing the sunlight, shining of nothing more than the immanence of its own presence – the earth.

# II. Sherazade

*interruptus:* you arrive, you do not arrive, we'll meet, we won't, suspended, maybe cancelled, maybe just a delay, the road, straightforward, with its regulated lanes, undisturbed, for quite some time, until, *interruptus*, and then those long queues, so long, so boring, a queue, a forced one, it feels like going crazy, maybe you'll have to wait, maybe you'll get angry, so angry, i hate queues, i've always hated them, those interruptions, so useless, so meaningless, why are there interruptions, interruptions are really bad, they make you think, and thinking is bad, it is even dangerous for your health, as dangerous as smoking, no one writes it in books, it's harmful for you and the people around you, and interruptions always lead to thinking, too much thinking, that loathsome beast, don't think, not today, no thinking allowed, stay away from it, at least for once, avoid it as if it were the plague, laugh, yes, laugh instead, i like when you laugh, i'm laughing today too, without thinking, i laugh: *interruptus*.

# Interruptus

It was a late summer Sunday. A mass of people were coming back from their holidays, the lorries back on the road after the long strike: the traffic conditions would be particularly difficult – that was quite predictable. The cars were faring quite well, nonetheless: maybe a little bit slower than normal, but they drove steadily on the motorway. Red, black, white, big, small, average: one by one, moving forwards in the flux that does not forgive any hesitation, marking time, like the ticking sound of a watch.

Until something changes. The cars are more numerous, the volume more intense, the speed forcefully slower. The more cars there are, the gentler they become, until they finally end up in a queue: one after the other. They don't stop completely, though: quietly, parading under the midday sun, high and unavoidable.

A driver opens the windows to get some fresh air: there is some distracted music, rock, classical, old school Neapolitan songs, and, here and there, the metallic voice of the traffic updates: 'Slowdowns on the A7, possible queues.' Someone is singing loudly. Their summer, apparently, is not yet over.

In the end: there it is. Too many cars all together: they stop, maybe a small crash, maybe that collision at the filling station. Now there is a growing, immobile, inexorable queue. Some get out of their cars, the door open, hand still on the wheel, with inquisitive eyes. Maybe it will be fast, maybe it's just temporary, maybe nothing serious.

But the blockade continues, as the radio confirms: the queue is getting bigger, it would be wise to get off the motorway at Bugnato or use alternative routes. It is strongly recommended that those who can take a municipal road, do so: slightly longer but the traffic is moving there. For those in the queue, there are no alternatives: they can only wait. Wait and be patient.

The queue grows and grows and so does the annoyance. A touch of rage or even bewilderment for those who have already travelled for hours and thought they had almost arrived. A sudden stop, even when expected, always calls for that peculiarly misplaced disappointment.

'I told you that we had to take the country route: there's less traffic there, but you're always so stubborn.'

'How could I know that? As usual, it's always my fault. Because of course we've never been in a hold-up here, the traffic is always normal . . .'

'Yes, but I told you! And you never listen!'

'Told me what?'

'It was predictable, with all these lorries around.'

'Yes, the lorries, it's the lorries' fault! Look, there are so many of them! It's their fault! It was unavoidable, they're so many, too many' . . .

'Anything better for the unions' summer plans than going on strike? That's why this has happened.'

'I don't understand why they didn't ban heavy vehicles, it's very irresponsible of the motorway authority, considering the end of the holidays: it was bound to happen!'

'Anyway, after two weeks on strike they couldn't help that. Loads of petrol stations had run out of fuel. And now what?'

'What what?'

'Perfect end to our holidays.'

'It could've been worse! I told you that going to Sicily wasn't a good idea! In the middle of August, you're better off going north, I don't know, to Iceland, Norway. There's no traffic there.'

'As usual, you're always complaining, that's all you can do.'

'Now it's my fault for complaining. What else am I supposed to do?'

'Be quiet, for example.'

(Silence. Music from the 1980s plays softly in the background.)

'Why don't you turn the air conditioning back on? Maybe it's working now.'

'I doubt it, the compressor's broken.'

'Maybe there's still some gas inside, please. Please, try! This heat is unbearable!'

'Okay: are you happy now? With the windows closed, so that we can roast like a chicken. Are you happy?'

'Wait a minute . . . Let's see what happens . . . Don't you think that the air is already cooler?'

'Not at all.'

'I do! Try it! Put your hand here!'

'Leave me alone!'

'Can't I touch you now?'

'You better not, in this heat.'

'Don't make a fuss!'

'Make a fuss? Under the midday sun, with the windows closed, because madam wants to see if the air conditioning was miraculously fixed, and you tell me not to make a fuss?'

'Okay, you can open the windows, but leave the air conditioning on, maybe something will happen . . .'

'Padre Pio, bless me . . .'

(Long silence. The heat worsens. From a car on the opposite side there's the report of a football match. 'Gooooal! Lazio scores against Juve. The league will be interesting this coming year.')

'I'm thirsty: could you pass me the water, please?'

'I thought that you wouldn't touch me. Here, it's a bit warm, but . . .'

'Better than nothing.'

'Eww! It's awful! I told you to leave it in the coolbag! Why you never do what I tell you to do?'

(More silence. The radio is off. Too hot even for that. It could be annoying. There's nothing else to do. We are stuck. Better not make the situation worse.)

'Who are those people on the motorbike? It seems that they're stopping at each car, maybe they're distributing food, hopefully they have some fresh water.'

'How can we help you?'

'Do you have any fresh water? My wife forgot to put it in the cool bag, now it's warm and tastes like piss . . .'

*Piss? Better call for backup. Unit 42 to all units: I'm at km 125, if you're operating on Level 2 or 3 issues, leave them and come help: here is a serious case. We're already at bodily fluids.*

'Fresh water, no, we don't have any. Maybe you would like to explain what's happening? Maybe I can help.'

'Nothing serious, it's just my wife, as usual, you know . . .'

'Oh, now it's all my fault! See, that's how my husband does it! He can't acknowledge his own responsibilities. He's never said 'I was wrong!' never, ever, ever, in twenty years of marriage!'

'Who, me? You're despicable! She wanted to close the windows, in this heat! She wanted to fry me!'

'What you're talking about! I can't even touch you! Look, I took his hand, like this, and he took it away!'

*Tactile phobia, typical symptom.*

'She made a mistake with the water, then she wanted to close everything and roast me like chicken! And now she asks me not to make a fuss!'

*Close everything? Roast him? Um, maybe the situation is more critical than expected: ornithological fantasies and homicidal thoughts. We must intervene.*

'Don't worry, sir! We're here now. No one will roast you. Back-up will arrive soon.'

'Back-up? What are you talking about?'

'See, our motorways are well equipped, you know, in cases like this everything can happen. Queues, mounting rage . . . But we have all the resources you need, trust us!'

'What are they talking about?'

'Relax, don't get excited, your blood pressure might rise. In this heat . . . you're in good hands. We've had a special training to face every situation. Sign your consent here, for the privacy. Both you and your wife.'

'Why should I? I don't need anything.'

'Don't be grumpy, dear! Sign that thing! What do we have to lose? Look: they all have their white coat, they're from the National Federation of Psychologists, look at their badge, maybe they can really help.'

'Help? With what?'

'Don't make a fuss! Sign the thing, here, I'll do it for you! Here, sir, thank you for your kindness . . .'

'Look here, you can choose: we're offering both a quick therapy session for specific problems, and a more radical approach of deep psychology, because you never know how long the queue might last. In your case, I think that the second option is more advisable, seeing the symptoms . . . They're both covered by the motorway insurance.'

'Deep? You wanna talk about the unconscious and all that stuff?'

'No, don't worry, there's no need to go that deep if you don't feel like it. Here, see, you can tick the boxes here, right after the privacy document, if you don't want the unconscious. I advise you, though, to leave some room for childhood memories, that's the next box, and then, yes, the mother, your relationship with your mother, I'd leave that open. It's important, you'll see. There's another form for you, ma'am, you have to fill it in too, you're free to choose what themes to talk about, but I suggest not to cancel the father, that's crucial! Trust me! Oh, I almost forgot, you can choose to have couples' or individual therapy. If you prefer the second option, though, you'll have to wait for a colleague of mine.'

'No, dear, no individual treatment, let's go for the couples' therapy. I really think that we need it!'

'What? What are you talking about? I should tell my own business to this guy on a motorbike that I've never seen before?'

'Honey, he's a motorway psychologist! Don't listen to him, sir! You're very kind, yes, couples' therapy would be the best. We've been fighting for hours, and now this queue . . .'

'If it's of any help, ma'am, it's completely normal. It always happens, and that's why we're here: you go straight on, full speed, no problem, and then you're stuck, everything stops, and rage builds up, and resentment, and all the other issues in a life together are suddenly there. It's normal, completely normal. That's why we have this service. Many couples have benefited from our help. Some still send friendly cards to thank us for saving their marriage. So let's not procrastinate. Please, tell me how it began.'

'It's all her fault: she forgot to put the water in the coolbag and now it's warm. Speaking of which, are you sure that you don't have any drinks in your trunk?'

'No, sorry, nothing to drink. *(Unrelenting desire for liquids. Ambivalence towards the primordial waters: he doesn't tolerate the heat.)* I see, the water was too warm, but why you say that your wife 'forgot'? Words matter, we need to analyse them one by one.'

'Don't listen to him! The coolbag was already full: see, rice salad, tuna, mayonnaise: the water bottle didn't fit!'

'Now I should drink mayonnaise, according to my wife!'

'Why not? You would put mayonnaise everywhere!'

*The bottle, the bottle doesn't fit. Clear bottle resistance. Threatens to rely on the primordial egg-mayonnaise.*

'I see, I see. Ma'am, I understand your point of view, you were acting in good faith, but we're focusing on your husband's perception: he thought it was negligent, 'you forgot', do you understand? It may trigger repressed memories of a primeval care deficiency! Please, sir, since you left the childhood topics open, let me ask you: did your mother breastfeed you?'

'How am I supposed to know! And what's that got to do with the queue?'

'Yes, I can tell you! He was breastfed, his mother told me, but just for a few months, then she had a severe sore throat and had to stop because of the antibiotics. She nursed him for a while, but less than his siblings. In my opinion, she weaned him too soon . . .'

'I see. This explains many things. *Interruptus.* And you, ma'am, were you breastfed by your mother? It's very important . . .'

'Yes, for years. My mother had a lot of milk. All the neighbourhood brought their children to her, all those who were allergic to formula: milk, she had a lot of milk, like a cow!'

'Very good. It must be some projection from your husband, the care deficit. You seem a very nurturing type to me . . .'

'Projection? What's he talking about? Are we in a movie theater? Listen, the thing is that my wife is never happy and, right after the queue began, she started saying that it was my fault!'

'His fault? That's not true! I said that it was the unions' fault, because they let the lorries back on the road.'

'Lorries? Why the lorries? What do lorries mean to you, ma'am?'

'Lorries? Nothing, I have no relationship with lorries and I don't care about them! They're just an annoyance!'

*Uhm, clear phallus denial. Possible unresolved penis envy and castration complex.*

'That's not true, don't listen to her! Her brother is a lorry driver, tell him! Why don't you tell him about your brother? You wanted this, so let's do it properly! Tell him!'

'There's nothing to say . . .'

(Long silence.)

'Okay then, right, my brother was a lorry driver. Why does this matter?'

'Why 'was'? Is he dead?'

'Tell him, now!'

'Okay, okay, calm down! No, he's not dead. He disappeared. Twenty years ago. One day he left with his lorry as usual, but he never came back.'

'Oh, now tell him, tell him why you wanted to go to Norway on holiday! Norway: her brother had to go to Norway! And now she'd want me to go on holiday in the cold just because she secretly hopes to find him! Tell him the truth! Tell him!'

'Don't touch me, and pinch your own cheeks!'

'Please, calm down. It's just a bit of tactile phobia, sir, it's normal in cases like these. You had the same symptom earlier. Let's recap. So, *cibus interruptus* for the gentleman, nurturing mother for the lady, a disappearing brother, maybe transference had been passed onto him, because usually the father is the unattainable one . . . Things start to make sense, fear of abandonment, everything as usual . . .'

'What are you talking about? Did you understand that everything started because my wife said that we shouldn't have gone to Sicily on holiday, but to Norway? Her brother, she wanted to follow her lost brother!'

'Why do you have to accuse me of being so false! You always want to go to Sicily for your perverse fantasies. Do you think that I didn't notice your new secretary? She can't even answer the phone, let alone do any accounting! Clearly she has other things to offer to your office!'

'What are you talking about?'

'Well, yes, always with that low neckline, you can see everything! Do you think that's appropriate for a law firm? Tasteless, that's what it is! Men are all the same, they and their fantasies! And it's you that told me about that recurrent dream of your childhood with that Sicilian woman who lived near you, do you think I forgot? I'm sure that's why you hired her! A woman who can neither talk nor be silent!'

'Ma'am, sorry for the interruption, but you barred the unconscious, so dreams are off topic. We cannot enter the areas you crossed out on the form. Professional ethics. We have to strictly adhere to the protocol.'

'Again with forms and ticks! I cannot stand him anymore . . . Now ethics, too, when will this queue move on . . . Oh! Horns! Hooters! They're hooting! Look! It's moving, we're moving again! Move away, you and your forms, we're moving now, finally! Get your hand away from here and pass me that bottle, please!'

'But it's warm!'

'Who cares that it's warm, my mouth's dry from all that talking, give it to me, come on, what are you waiting for?'

# III. Sherazade

another one, here it is, i can't stop, i know, it's foolish, all these words, all these stories, i keep telling them, every night, like sherazade, she has to tell stories to stay alive, narrating and writing, writing to postpone death, i tell stories, i tell, and i can't stop, no laughing today, maybe a smile, maybe a bit bitter, this too is for you, my heavenly spouse, and yet sad, unfortunately, terribly sad, maybe the saddest of them all, but i had to tell this story, love and death, a story, another story, *a un tempo stesso, amore e morte ingenerò la sorte*, so the poet said, whatever he meant, love and death born together, maybe, i don't know, really, i don't, and so don't even ask, after all, as jesus says, i don't know, and this is my *all in*, jesus christ, the son of god, nothing less than that, the one on the cross, on the cross and about to die, to die but still asking his father to forgive them, forgive them, even those who murdered your son, forgive them, because they don't know, they don't know what they're doing, they don't, no, they don't

# The wait

It had not been an unexpected death. His days had been numbered –
by old age, and by the illness that consumed him over the past few
years. Relatives and acquaintances had been visiting his sickbed for a
while already. He still had his bubbly personality which, until his last
moments, helped him make funny quips. Indeed, a joke was the last
thing he said, before he faded into silence.

He died in the night. A phone call from the hospital woke his close
relatives, who had slept waiting for this call for a few months. Maybe it
was liberating for that body which had lived until it had reached the
furthest threshold of old age. Maybe it was a relief, too, for those who had
consumed themselves in taking such good care of him. But everything
ended that night, and soon the funeral would be held in the local church.

The body, taken away from the party of suitably weeping relatives,
would be soon moved to the morgue. The morticians would take care
of it thoroughly. Visitors would find him there, in that small, nondescript
building on the outskirts of the city: surrounded only by tall trees and
moist, cold moss. Right there, where the town faded into the dark
nature of the surrounding hills, his friends and acquaintances could say
farewell before his funeral.

It would last one, maybe two days, due to the bureaucratic
inadequacy of the hospital. While his close relatives were engulfed in a
weird loneliness, she immediately went to the morgue. What would
people think, she thought, if they saw that nobody was there? There
had to be someone from the family to greet them. Strangely, it happened
to be her, who certainly was not the closest to him. With all those
children and grandchildren, something would have been expected from
them. On the contrary, she, she went there alone. The closer relatives
were remarkably absent.

It was still early in the morning; the shy summer sun barely warmed the morgue's dark rooms. His was the only body there. And she was the only family member. He had been a fairly prominent figure in that small town where everybody knew each other: all kinds of visitors would surely be there soon. Some out of sincere affection, others for the family, many just to show willing. This was certain, and that was why she had to be there. To represent the family. The family of the deceased.

But the sun was already high in the sky, the heat was starting to rise and still nobody had appeared on the sloping road that led to the small mourning building. Maybe it was too soon, nobody being aware yet. Maybe nobody knew that he had passed precisely that night. Someone would probably come in the afternoon, though. Better go to lunch, then. The dead man would not notice her brief absence and nobody would show up at that time of the day.

She came back to the morgue in the early afternoon. She even had time to change into more appropriate clothing: a very simple but elegant black dress. After all, he cared very much about appearances and would have approved that subtle attention. And then, again, most likely visitors would come that afternoon to pay their respects, and it was advised to receive them in the appropriate manner.

But the hours became heavier, and still nobody came to lift her spirits. A car had driven by in the middle of the afternoon, and she thought that finally someone had come. Soon, however, she realized that it was just an administrative employee, him and his files. Still no mourners in sight.

And then, it was twilight. The sun was starting its descent behind the hill. The sky was scarlet red, striped by the bright contrast of the last summer days. Still no one in sight. Maybe the news had taken too long to spread, even though there were posters everywhere announcing the impending funeral and the family had been officially in mourning since the middle of the night. That day was over, but there would certainly be plenty of people the next morning. She had to come early, to be sure someone of the family was there to receive condolences.

And so she went, back to the morgue, early in the morning, the day after. Again, with her black dress, simple and elegant, fit for the occasion. One look to the coffin, alone in the burial chamber, not getting too close, maybe due to some kind of reverential fear of death. The morticians had done a good job. The casket was made of fine mahogany, there were white flowers everywhere. He had been a sober man: he would have never loved any colours except those of such a perfectly neutral contrast. As his whole existence had been discreet, without any highs or lows, his last farewell had to be simple and elegant as well: few colours, no clutter. Or so she told herself that morning, entering the room. Friends, relatives and acquaintances, visiting before the funeral, would certainly notice that too. All those who knew him, his being, simple and sober, they loved him just for that. Never excessive, never exaggerated, in the good and the bad of his singular mediocrity.

But nobody came that day to pay their condolences, either. And the hours went by even slower than the day before. All of her daily chores and work had been suspended during that long wake for this dead body, who could no longer answer nor feel the warmth of human presence, and for a crowd of visitors that never manifested. She started doubting that there was any point in her waiting. And yet, she had to represent the family! Someone had to be there, though the possibility that someone would come became more and more remote. After all, it was also understandable that, in the excess of an extreme grief, people had chosen to mourn on their own. Things would change the next day, for the funeral, which had been publicly announced, given the fame of the dead man.

The service had been prepared for the late morning. They would move the coffin into the small church near the morgue in a slow parade on foot and, after the mass, they would go to the monumental cemetery as usual. The town's local band would follow the ceremony with an appropriate funeral march.

She wanted to be the first one there that morning. She wanted to check if everything was in place, set the last details, in support of the family, always the family, the family devastated by mourning, that silent and weirdly lonely mourning – the family. When she arrived in the walkway surrounded by cypresses that led to the morgue, she recognized many relatives and acquaintances in the garden before the burial chamber. She diligently greeted everyone, carefully paying attention not to forget anyone. Some with composed words of grief, small talk adapted to the circumstances, others with a sincere kiss on the cheek, or hugging them affectionately. Looking both right and left, to make sure that she had greeted everyone before heading towards the coffin for her last, solemn farewell. She thought that this very last reverential gesture was in order.

The morgue door was flanked by the two morticians. Two young faces, too young for the job, she told herself. Weird that they chose a job like that. The room was cold, despite the lingering warmth of the end of summer, and the coffin laid under the window, already half closed. She wanted to see him one last time, before it would be completely closed, given that his wife could not even come, due to her weak heart. His life companion naturally wanted to remember him still alive, in his hospital bed. But she did not, she wanted to have a last chance to see the body that she had guarded for two long days. A few more steps, before seeing the lifeless body lying in the coffin, and then, to her surprise and amazement, she saw an empty tomb: nothing, there was no body, only the white satin of the coffin, shining in the light of that summer morning, like all the open flowers around it.

# IV. Sherazade

stories, more and more stories, words and stories, to keep you awake, i swore, i will tell you stories, and i am telling you stories, as i promised, a very reliable person, even though you'd never say that, yes, very reliable, who would have thought, serious, very serious, and i always keep my promises, maybe too much keeping, and maybe too many promises, and i tell stories, all night, i tell stories but i'm confused, who's listening to the stories, all those people, too many people, who knows if their ears are subtle enough, who knows what they will do with my words, and with my stories, maybe the myth ends right here, crushed by the absolutism of reality, that reality, absolute and sovereign, that the myth is fighting, but maybe this time it wins, the reality that is, and its absolutism, or maybe not, and my myth disappears, it desiccates, and then there are no more stories, and there are no more words, and it will be silence, the silence of reality and its uncontested sovereignty no, my myth, i want my myth back, it's too good, don't kill it, don't murder it, please, give it back to me, i want it back, i'm so angry, murdered, murdered so inelegantly, a creature with such noble origins, and with such respectable genealogy, you can't kill it so gracelessly, so maybe it will survive, maybe it's just a transition, maybe a weird transition, after all, that is what the psychologist said, *a wide variation in a sequence that starts with the newborn infant's fist-in-mouth activities*

# The breakfast

The promotional brochure presented it as the ideal town in which to spend a day, a weekend or even an entire life. 'Beyond your expectations', it added, with an arguably too complacent a tone. Actually, it was one of those impoverished industrial towns, typical of the suburbs. Factories in ruins, a couple of fancier buildings, but the main tone was a mediocre architecture of the Seventies, numb and functional.

The hotel was equally anodyne. A big thirty-storey building, anonymous and colourless. Its rooms had a certain artificial elegance, which appeared immediately fake to a closer look, as fake as the pictures hanging on the walls: from afar one might mistake them for actual pastel-toned paintings, but, getting closer, it was clear that they were low-quality mass-produced prints.

The only different note was gypsy music coming from the radio: happiness, decadent too, from the partying Balkans. Nomad, rootless music, and, as such, also seducing and warm, even though it had a kind of melancholy in it.

The body of the young woman moved along with the music, both celebrating and separating, in the anonymity of the room. She danced. Her gestures composed, delicate, one foot after the other, a half-turn, her arms in the air, as if she was about to take off. There was someone else there, but it was not clear whether they were watching her.

While she danced around the big bed at the centre of the room, as if it was a ritual bonfire, she noticed something coming out of her suitcase. A tiny, faded object, with an indefinite shape: it looked like one of those stuffed toys that children carry with them at night, for company, as a substitute of their mother's breast, always lost too soon.

It was clear that this object caused her some embarrassment: right after its clumsy appearance, she immediately made sure to hide it, just as someone who, along with the magic of childhood, lost their imagination and now sees things only for what they are: a piece of fabric, over-used, over-mended, and deprived of any colour.

A small gesture with her foot pushed it back into the suitcase, and then she went back to dancing: sensual, sinuous and seducing. The music went on for hours, as did her slow, delicate and even sad movements. The night passed and dawn came, when she fell asleep on the pillows over the bed.

The alarm rang earlier than expected. The young woman woke, had a quick shower, dressed appropriately for the occasion, and went out for breakfast before the meeting. It was early winter, and its metallic chill made that unremarkable town even more desolate. There did not appear to be many good places to eat, and she seemed in a hurry, with all those papers under her arms.

In a distant corner, though, there was exactly what she needed. A quite special place, known for its cappuccino. Only there you could find that exact blend of a nice, invigorating and aromatic coffee and soft, frothy, high-quality milk. A rare goodies, in that town. The queue, though, indicated a long wait, and it would be even longer in a few minutes, when the entire town was awake.

Before ordering, you had to become a member of the organization. This, of course, took some time, too: fill in the form, insert all the data, line by line. But it was the only way to enjoy that drink: money would not be enough, because it was not a profit-based business. It would take some time to get this cappuccino, and the woman, with all the papers under her arms, seemed to lack exactly that.

Behind her there was that man who had whispered sweet words into her ears the day before. He was a professional singer and obviously good with lyrics. Maybe he would wait in the queue for her. Maybe he would get her that craved cappuccino. They talked. She seemed to ask him something, but he did not move. Unperturbed, he remained unperturbed, as if all those words were not even aimed at him. She was visibly angry and spoke loudly.

'You won't even get me a cappuccino?'

'I can't,' he answered, gazing away from her.

'Why can't you? You have nothing else to do now!'

An embarrassing silence followed. The young woman left the conversation and went, visibly annoyed, towards the queue, which had already started growing disproportionately. She intended to get her cappuccino herself. But then another man, who seemed to know her very well, came by her and gave her a cup of the coveted drink:

'There's no need to get angry. You knew that I would get your cappuccino!'

# V. Sherazade

i looked for words, and i couldn't find them, so weird, without words, me, who has so many of them, i'm always full of words, so many words, too many words, but those were the words of fantasy, and i was looking for those of reality, and they were right here, indeed, you're reading them, i'm writing them, right now, i have her words, i have them, sherazade's own words, so many words, living, vibrating, letter after letter, phoneme after phoneme, those words, surrounded by words, the intellectual, a mirage, the brood cow if you like, my dad always told me, a brood cow, just look at my face, that's what i am, a brood cow, all those children, and that long, too long breastfeeding, i was nominated best wet nurse, in the soviet union i would have won a prize, they told me so many times, because i am a brood cow, a cow with many words, and without words, the naked life and the clothed life

# The birth

There was no alternative. At that time, a home birth was still a scarcely tolerated eccentricity. It was seen as barbaric, despite being the new trend in many developed countries. She knew someone who already did it, though: a small organization that helped expectant mothers at home – all midwives, all women, all experienced. In the end, no one could teach you how to give birth. And that was what birth experts had learned in all those years of practice – they had to just transmit its secrets, to assist a completely natural event, maybe even the most natural event of all.

The idea, although rebellious, seemed at least possible. They only needed to get appropriate cloths, tinctures, balms and other objects that could be useful during labour. The pregnancy had proceeded without any problem and there was no reason to believe the birth would be difficult. The hospital's number and the car, ready in the parking lot, would guarantee the rest.

Everybody was waiting, excited. The first contractions began exactly on the due date: sickness, mood swings, waves that went through the body, upsetting it. It looked like they anticipated the moment in which that being would become two different bodies. At first softer, like vibrations in Baroque music, then stronger and stronger, like a Romantic symphony, with all those instruments announcing the good news all together. Apprehension had grown around the event and joy exploded uncontrollably. The time had come.

After a few hours, though, everything was gone. The midwife, who had come quickly at the first signs, had been sent back home, the boxes with all the accessories put back in their place and the obstetrician's number back in its drawer. Euphoria had turned into uneasiness: it was time to wait, again. They needed to wait, take some more time, but nobody knows how to wait anymore. Everything has to be there, ready. And everybody asked impatiently what was going on, why it had not yet been born. Maybe the belly was still too high, maybe the eyes were not down enough, maybe they needed the new moon, which would soon come. Everyone had a different suggestion.

Three days passed and there was no trace of those first contractions. The hours went by slowly, the minutes even more so. There were many voices, too many voices, around her, while the pregnancy's official timetable ticked on relentlessly. We can't wait any more: we must proceed with hospitalization. We are formally at risk, even though all the women in that family had very late births, sometimes even weeks after their due date. They called them women-elephants. But medical tables ignore such details: to them, nature speaks only in numbers.

The organization's midwife had a different opinion. According to her calculations, based on this specific woman's natural cycles, she hadn't even reached her due date. Quantity sometimes changes with quality. And that, after all, was a reassuring thought.

Three more days passed, and the uneasiness of the unconventional choice was getting hard. There were the other mothers' stories, though, to comfort her. Such as the woman who gave birth in the ocean on a warm summer night, the moon as her only companion. That was a savage mother, indeed. The ocean was far away, but its waters were right there, inside her. And the baby seemed to swim too easily to be actually at risk. Maybe she could wait longer. Give it some time.

Another three days passed, and nothing happened. One night the waves came back, but they disappeared again, like the sea at low tide. And the day after that, the same thing happened. The high and the low tide, their ebb and flow. The wait was becoming unbearable, too much anxiety. When a friendly voice arrived: 'Enjoy this moment, enjoy every single contraction.' Enjoy? What did that mean? You always try to avoid the pain, to anaesthetize it or hide it when everything else fails. How could you enjoy it? Maybe that was the announcement of the separation, the exit with no coming back? Yes, maybe it was the pain of separation, which should come slowly, indeed, little by little, in order to be tolerable. Trust it. You have to trust this creature: nobody knows better than them when it is the right time to be born. You have to avoid someone takes them before their time – nothing more, and nothing less.

Finally, that evening something different happened. A solitary sudden wave took her on the cypress allee, coming back from her walk. It was March and the cypresses were covered in little white flowers with a fruity smell. That embrace was so strong that you could almost touch it. Something had changed, indeed.

It was them. Stronger and more and more regular, the waves of a tempest, the tides were over: those waves overwhelmed her, they had her holding her breath, as in a storm at sea. She withdrew to her office, putting blankets and pillows on the floor as if it were an animal's den. On the old cotto floor of her cottage, lying on a big silk pillow, she waited. Wave after wave, storm after storm, scream after scream. She seemed happy, even if she was crying in pain. Annihilating, final, like the ultimate end.

And yet, the midwife said there was still a long way to go. They had to be patient, not surrender, lean forwards, walk to get the right direction. The cervix was 'retroflexed'. Such a strange name! Who knew what it meant, but it sounded threatening. Better to do as she said, even if it was tiring. Walking up and down the stairs, talking to her own womb, the midwives thinking that she was talking to them.

This strategy didn't seem to be working, though, and the contractions were less frequent. Maybe they would disappear again, and all that pain would be for nothing? The birth keeper agreed too, she had to go back to the floor. In the dark. Alone. On the silk pillow. Screaming with the pain and falling unconscious between contractions, even if for just a few minutes.

Three more hours passed. It was night in the surrounding countryside, the wind blew through the olive trees, the blankets on the floor were warm. Silence. And then a deep, long moan, like the 'ohm' heard in a temple. They came one after the other: ohm and then the silence of trance. At that point it did not even matter whether that was the right time or not: she just wanted the pain to be over. And the midwife kept telling her they were still far away – those were not real contractions. Her dilation spoke for itself: only two centimetres – officially, she was not even in labour. The night would be long, very, very long.

And yet the birth happened just a few minutes later. Nature exceeds every rule, even those of the most skilled midwives. The woman went to the bathroom, covered in old white marble striped with grey-golden veins and, right there, she crouched on the floor, screaming 'There it is!'

'How is it possible? There's no dilation.' But she kept on pushing, her legs apart, her feet firm on the floor, her arms on her knees, pushing downwards.

General panic. Take the cloths! The balms! The blankets for the new-born! It's actually coming out! She pushes and pushes! There it is! The head, I can see the head! Do you want to see it? See it? Such a strange idea! Touch it? Of course not! No, she did not want to see or touch anything. She just wanted to give birth. She was ready: she just wanted it to come out as soon as possible. Her strength, which seemed to have abandoned her after so many hours, was finally back in all its glory: magnificent and powerful.

Her waters, those waters that usually break so early on, had resisted inside her until then. She kept them in until the last moment: they came out only now, on the marble, clear and smelling like that fresh and sweet smell of a new-born's head. And now, without them, she pushed harder. A new strength passed through her. The descent had begun. It was emerging: a white, smooth, regular surface. At first barely perceptible, then more and more visible. While the opening became wider, it came down more rapidly: one push more, maybe two. She needed courage. That was the breaking point, perhaps the only one where you can face yourself: no tables, no protocols, only that blind and primordial instinct where there is no order – just the immanence of pure life exploding right when the pain seems to announce death.

So it happened with that last push, a sharp scream, the collection of all of her being, as if every piece, every particle of that body had joined into that last supreme effort: and finally the creature was there, on the floor, on the white marble with grey-golden veins. It was white too, but full of words: a scroll, a scroll that the most skilled midwife had collected quickly and started to unroll. It bore minute and tidy writing. Words, so many words, appearing one after another in regular lines. The birth keeper opened them and started reading, while the mother watched, already nostalgic for the creature that had just left her body.

# VI. Sherazade

you are not my type, i said it, yes, i always say it, but i always end up with one that's not my type, cute, but not for me, i said exactly that, we say many things, we do, and then we don't, we don't know much, certainly not about ourselves, especially me, i clearly don't know, but it knows, it shouldn't know anything, and it knows a lot, so many things, yes, the reckless one, the irrational, and yet it knows, it knows far more things than i do, if only i knew as much as it knows, it has no past no present and no future, and yet it knows, wise, very wise, if only i had its wisdom, foolish, ferocious, on the contrary, it's so reasonable, and it knows so much, it knows and speaks, speaks as the language, *die sprache spricht*, as the master says, i agree, the language speaks, but images speak even better, without barriers, without words, images don't have a language and yet they speak, they speak, they say, they say even what cannot be said, and don't even try, no, don't even try and translate them, you would kill them, those images, those images who speak, speak without a language, better than a language, speak beyond language

# The fall

It was a room in the shape of an octagon, propped up by four big columns. In its corners there were niches covered in mosaics, carpets and cushions everywhere. Soft, light colours with golden veins, like water springing from the fountains. It was the sultan's harem. Women with delicate features crowded all around. Some, lying on big cushions, smoked from a great water pipe – its fumes smelling of exotic favours and spices. Mindlessly, they passed it to one another in a circle. Others, behind the perforated grids of the balconies that let inside a few of the sun's rays, silently watched the street, distracted from the warmth of noon and from their rarefied dreams.

And then the commanding decorated wooden door opens, and, after his court, comes the Sovereign. Servants bow at his entrance, clearing his path, while the bronzed slaves throw rose petals at his feet. He is wearing a blue silk robe, hemmed and embroidered with gold, Persian style.

He sits. And he turns towards the lady at his right, who quickly pours water on his crooked hands, while servants bring him strongly smelling food and drink. He grabs a handful of cous-cous and brings it to his mouth. He chews slowly, carefully, melting the meal with his tongue. Then a piece of meat – lamb, it must be – as he vigorously bites it, mouthful after mouthful. Another handful of grains and then that dark drink, brought solemnly towards his full lips. A moment of hesitation, or maybe dizziness, and then a clap, quick and sudden: let the show begin!

Blindfolded musicians quickly grab their instruments, while the sultan's chosen dancer runs to the centre of the room, leaping skilfully. She is wearing light silk trousers, her belly is bare, gold chains decorating her slim hips; a short veil is on her head. Her thin arms, covered in bracelets, rise above her head, her hands slightly tilted towards her sides as an invitation for the music to begin.

Then the first notes from the oud, followed by the strings, and the first circles are made by the belly: sinuous and synchronic, as if she were a fish in water waves. And the more instruments are added to the melody, with drums and flutes, the faster the dance – her hipbone drawing the infinite symbol up and down, like a reverse eight. Again and again, more and more nervously, almost a convulsion, waving through the rest of the body. Finally, her feet rise, stomping hard on the earth, while her arms reach above her head, spinning fast, covered in veils. They are accompanied by the serpentine movement of her fingers, twining as if they were multiplying, along with the notes.

A moment of pause, the music slows – then once more the oud, alone, accompanies her belly, moving slowly now, in dense and concentric movements. The rest of her body is still, her arms up, the gaze fixed on her navel, full of wonder. And then the flutes, quick and melancholic, resuscitate her movement, and she reprises her dance, with her high and low parabolas.

The sultan is watching, smoking. Leaning on his side, surrounded by the waving fans all around him, he grabs the pipe and alone watches the dance. The water pipe in front of him, he turns the smoke inside his mouth, and then blows it away, with the eyes of a dragon. She is the most beautiful, and she has not been seen by any other man except him. Even the musicians have to wear a blindfold when she is dancing. No one can see these forbidden dances. No one can see the Sovereign's woman. Or else they will lose their eyes to a hot iron. Only one person, him, can consume this sublime tangling of love and death.

Time passes in the vortex of pleasure, until a last circle of the belly announces the end. A drumbeat, a sharp movement, her arms fly up, and the music ends. The blindfolded men leave abruptly, and the slaves escort the forbidden dancer to her room. Only the sultan remains there, with all his women, who move closer to him. They adore him and care for him. Slaves bring oils and perfumed balsams in golden goblets, encrusted with gems. The games begin. The darkest one, with smooth skin and ebony eyes, rubs essential oils on his bulky body. Her hands work in concentric movements. First his feet, with long and strong toes: she massages their soles, still kneeling, and then the upper side. He closes his eyes, as if in a trance. Her skilled hands proceed upwards, on his smooth and well-defined calves, with delicate but energetic movements. Then onto his thighs, and then even further up, until the gold embroidered robe opens, revealing – revealing a smooth and flat pelvis, covered only in sparse hair.

# VII. Sherazade

the last one, just the last one, and then i leave, i leave today, i go away, the myth has done its job, a sign of the times, endless sherazade, neither killed, nor loved, nor thanked, she made her sovereign wise, maybe not, maybe she made him fall in love, maybe nothing at all, but the myth is over, it's endlessly over, none of its variants survived, and i'm leaving, so weird, it's already over, i would have never expected that, it did everything by itself, it left as it came, i did nothing, i would have loved to keep on telling you stories, i lived for these stories, i could not stop, even though i wanted to, oh god knows how much i wanted it, and then it did it, it just left, suddenly, but it didn't disappear by saying it was going out to buy cigarettes, no, it slowly melted, it did its duty, made its time, a bit quicker than expected, i admit it, that's a bit weird, really weird, maybe too weird, after all, a thousand and one nights, that's a long time, who has a thousand and one nights anymore, it's almost three years, three years, a thousand and one nights, i never thought about that, three full years without sleeping, it's not for us, and sherazade ends like this, *sub specie modernitatis*, she ends without an end, without a variant because even choosing a dress takes its time, too much time, and we don't have time anymore, sherazade exits the stage, she leaves us, she did her job, until the end, now she has no more stories, she has no more words to tell, sherazade, and her exotic ecstatic magical world, she has no more stories to tell and she goes away, as quickly as she came, a fully modern sherazade, with no more time, with no more palace

# The mirror

She lived in an old house, built in the nineteenth century. That day, she wandered in her rooms, looking at objects that had been her family's possessions for hundreds of years, now worn out by time. The rocking chair, the wooden table in the dining room, the chandeliers, covered in molten wax.

She wore a long black dress that reached to her feet, with a high neck and long sleeves. Maybe she was dressed for mourning. She nervously wandered, she wandered in those rooms, until, reaching the mirror, she saw a reflection of someone behind her: a woman, much older than her but who looked like her, like her and like all the women of her kind. It was a translucent figure, though, with evanescent features and diaphanous colours. One would say that it was a ghost, her own ghost, just wrapped in a different dress.

# Second myth: the dress of Ariadne

Vota Iovi Minos taurorum corpora centum
solvit, ut egressus ratibus Curetida terram
contigit, et spoliis decorata est regia fixis.
creverat obprobrium generis, foedumque patebat                    155
matris adulterium monstri novitate biformis;
destinat hunc Minos thalamo removere pudorem
multiplicique domo caecisque includere tectis.
Daedalus ingenio fabrae celeberrimus artis
ponit opus turbatque notas et lumina flexum                       160
ducit in errorem variarum ambage viarum.
non secus ac liquidus Phrygiis Maeandros in arvis
ludit et ambiguo lapsu refluitque fluitque
occurrensque sibi venturas aspicit undas
et nunc ad fontes, nunc ad mare versus apertum                    165
incertas exercet aquas: ita Daedalus implet
innumeras errore vias vixque ipse reverti
ad limen potuit: tanta est fallacia tecti.
Quo postquam geminam tauri iuvenisque figuram
clausit, et Actaeo bis pastum sanguine monstrum                   170
tertia sors annis domuit repetita novenis,
utque ope virginea nullis iterata priorum
ianua difficilis filo est inventa relecto,
protinus Aegides rapta Minoide Diam
vela dedit comitemque suam crudelis in illo                       175
litore destituit.

(As soon as he disembarked from the ship,
landing on the shore of the Kourets,
Minos released his promise to Zeus by offering
One hundred bulls and decorated his palace by hanging his trophies
    from war.
But the horror of his kind was growing, a monster never seen before,
Double-natured, denouncing his mother's barbaric adultery.
Then Minos decided to hide his dishonour away from his home and
To lock it in the dark recesses of an impregnable building.
Daedalus, so famous for his talent as a builder,
Creates this work, by making its landmarks uncertain
And deceiving the eye with curvy passages.
As the Meander flows though the countryside of Phrygia,
Running and streaming in its unpredictable path,
And going around itself it sees the waters that still have to reach it,
Or, here it goes towards its spring, there towards the sea,
It undecidedly torments its own flow; so Daedalus disseminates
Treachery in that maze of pathways, until even to himself,
Deceived by the intricacy of that house, finding its exit is impossible.
Here the half bull half man monster was imprisoned,
And after feeding himself twice with young Athenians,
Chosen by fate every nine years, was killed by Theseus the third time
With the help of Minos' daughter: by gathering her thread back,
He could make it to the exit that no one had found before;
Then he kidnapped the young woman and sailed towards Dias,
Where he mercilessly abandoned his companion,
On the shore.)

Ovid, *Metamorphoses*, Book VIII (translated by Sveva Scaramuzzi)

# I. Ariadne

an end or a metamorphosis, i don't know, i cannot remember ovid anymore, maybe i haven't read it properly, latin came so easily that i never did homework, anyway, if you insist, i will tell you about the minotaur, yes, the minotaur, that abominable creature, i will tell you a story about it, but i would rather not be ariadne this time, not ariadne please, because she always ends up badly in that story, at least in all the versions of the myth that i remember, although, well, now that i think about it, in the end, even if you'll leave me on the shore, the way theseus did, i may not die, and perhaps even end up in dionysus' arms, that would not be bad, not at all, dionysus and the etruscans, i come from the etruscans, and they've always coupled her with dionysus, forget the apollonian hero then, and it won't be a tragedy, or maybe it will, but maybe it's beautiful, and maybe you're dionysus, not theseus, i know, that's confusing, but perhaps we can decide ourselves which dress to wear tonight, ignoring the tradition, if it's true that myth always expresses itself through variants, because we need a different outfit each time, appropriate to the circumstances, there's no reason to believe that the work on myth has stopped here, so let's avoid omnipotence phantasies for once, because the minotaur has to be killed, with or without theseus, before or after dionysus, even if it ends in a tragedy, or maybe a tragicomedy, because this minotaur is ridiculously cruel, and it's very rude to gorge on all those younglings in their spring years, one by one, a constant sacrifice, every year, every month, maybe even every day, an insatiable tyrant, after a wish becomes true, another one emerges, and it doesn't even enjoy those furious meals, it must be killed, yes, killed, indeed, someone should end this infinite circle, even though

# The thread

I had not seen him for more than a year. And chance wanted us to meet precisely in that small town in the suburbs. We spent most of the afternoon in an overly large group, pulling together the different threads of a past only apparently shared. And, in the evening, we found ourselves alone – again, he and I.

He suggested a walk around the local area. He had explored it in the afternoon, walking with his cigar around the gardens of the old hotel. Something had piqued his curiosity and he was anxious to show it to me, as I gathered from his insistence. It was a cold evening that spoke of approaching winter and we could hardly see, so dark was it out there. Trees and paths were enveloped by a thick fog, but the air: fresh and vivifying.

I walked silently, without understanding. I had the impression we were moving in a circle, and that we had already passed by that point, and even by the other one, but I did not dare to comment. I just followed his smoke, that sour and aching smell of cigar I have hated since I was a child.

We kept wandering without words until a crossroads appeared. It was a small path, surrounded by laurel hedges, which, in the humidity of the night, reminded me of boiled chestnuts. He was hesitating and I was puzzled, as I could not see the point of taking yet another walk, which did not appear to be promising at all. Despite the lengthening shadows, I had indeed been able to discern a sign pointing to one unique and improbable destination: 'Hospital.'

'Do you want to take me to the hospital?' I asked smiling.

'Why not?' he replied, mirroring my irony. 'They have a bar, too, which is much better than the really dull one at the hotel. At least it is full of people!'

The idea of spending the only evening I had had with my father in years in a hospital was not particularly attractive, so I tried to object. But he was quite right about the hotel and its bar. We could hardly have stumbled on anything worse.

'And it is a very peculiar hospital, you will see; it is a hospital of the awakenings!' he said, pointing towards an advertisement that had just appeared in my sight. The laurel path ended in a big concrete parking lot, where I could detect, through the fog, a sign for 'Tenth International Congress of the Awakenings.' The meeting was scheduled to take place a month later, though, as my father made me notice:

'You are always too early: if you had arrived a few weeks later, we would have found the parking full.'

I tried to say that given my untimely arrival, we could have tried to spend the evening somewhere else. He was, however, already completely immersed in his plans and showing me the object of his curiosity:

'This is the hospital, that is the car park, half empty now, but pretty big, as there are many employees; and here is the main entrance. There are still people arriving for the evening visit: maybe we should try the back door, to avoid arousing any suspicion.'

'But do you really want to take me to a hospital?' I asked one more time.

'Of course! It is such an amazing place! Let's go!' he said, heading straight to the back door. It was a concrete panelled building, with the architectural elements geometrically juxtaposed with one another. The iron door had no handle and was propped open by a stone, probably left there by my father that very afternoon. Thanks to that, we could enter the hospital of the awakenings without being disturbed.

The hallways were surprisingly narrow and brightened by a dim, metallic, neon light. Instead of the bluish green typical of hospital interiors, the dominant color was a pale orange, which reverberated both inside and outside the architecture of that unusual construction. I kept following my father, who had meanwhile abandoned his cigar. From the ease with which he was moving around, I realized he was familiar with the place.

We took the maintenance lift and got off on the third floor. I asked him what he wanted to show me, but he replied with a generic and laconic: 'sick people.' Given that we were in a hospital, that was to be expected, I told myself. So I gave up my remaining hesitations and followed yet another of his eccentric inclinations.

The reception led to the two wards – 'men' and 'women' – while at the centre stood a glass door with the intimidating sign: 'Operating Room.' Visits were still going on, as we could infer from a nervous but discreet bustle of people.

We entered the department on our left. There were numerous beds, neatly arranged, but only partially occupied. One stood out because it was covered by a screen, behind which came the sobbing and crying of mourning voices. The other patients seemed to be sleeping rather quietly.

Yet their sleep was rather peculiar. Their eyes were indeed unusually prominent, coming out of their forehead like snail horns. 'It must be a new sickness,' I said to myself. Their bodies exhibited an uncanny concave shape, as if the forward movement of their eyes were compensated by the conspicuous emptiness of their bellies.

I asked my father whether he knew the illness they were suffering from.

'They are sick from desire,' he said, pointing toward a shape in front of us.

'This is Barbaccia and he comes from a family of surface-supplied divers. He wanted to make love to sirens so desperately that he used to spend all the time he could in the depths of the sea. He was totally obsessed with the idea. He said he could not resist their singing, but, as the years went by, he developed decompression sickness. Since then, he's been in a coma. I met his wife today: a very elegant and classy woman.'

'Barbaccia? What a strange name!' I replied in astonishment.

'Yes, quite unusual. It is an Italian nickname. I do not think it is his real name, but everybody calls him that here, probably because of his beard. It looks like dried seaweed.'

It was a thick, spiky beard of a strange greenish colour. His eyes had the same snail-horn shape and his body was also decidedly curved in, despite his athletic swimmer's build, and it stood out even more because of the minute figure lying in the bed next to him. The latter had a peculiarly small and frail body but two unusually long hands. His fingers looked like snail horns too, with their tapered, sinuous shape.

Having noticed my astonishment, my guide added quietly, as if I were not the only one who could hear his words: 'He was a writer, who spent his entire life making words, until he descended into silence.' And then he brought my attention elsewhere:

'And here is Malebaci, who used to put his tongue in every woman's mouth. When he fell ill, he couldn't retract his tongue so the doctors had to knot it to prevent him from choking. They will inject him tomorrow. Not sure he will make it, though: he looks too frail to me. The other one under the screen is called "Fede", because he wanted to be faithful to all and every woman at the same time! What a bizarre idea! He has consumed himself in this way, out of his own excess of fidelity. They tried to inject him, but the treatment failed because he was not able to sustain it.'

I edged closer. In contrast to Barbaccia, Fede's silhouette was skinny, emaciated, which rendered the void of his figure even more impressive. I asked my father what he'd meant by 'injecting' him. He replied that the treatment was injecting these empty bodies with *Bombyx mori*.

'Some reject it – their bodies expel it – while others blow up like butterflies and thus explode. That's what happened to Fede. Some, however, can actually make it and then settle into a normal life. It is a very radical therapy, but apparently the only one that actually works,' he concluded with the air of somebody still adrift in contemplation.

'You must have spent quite some time here, since you seem to know everything and everybody,' I replied and asked more details about this *Bombyx* thing.

'What? You do not even know of *Bombyx mori*? What have you been doing in school all these years?'

It was his own way of vindicating the self-taught person, whom he regarded superior to those who endured a formal education. He, who had not even finished high school, had learned Latin and all the other dead languages by himself.

'*Bombyx mori*!' he replied in a conceited tone, 'you do not even know what you are wearing! Come and I will show you something.'

He left the room and I followed him. We reached the operating theatre, but then he hesitated and said, as if to divert me, 'How about visiting the women's ward now, while it is still open? They may close it for the night later on.'

We entered the first room. Their bodies were similar to those I had seen before. There was no way of telling their sex, so physically deformed they appeared. There were no curves, no breasts or hips that could hint at any feminine shape: these figures, too, were marked by that unique and conspicuous void, which seemed to spill over in those bulging, protuberant eyes.

Within the long series of beds, my gaze fell on an empty one, with the mattress rolled upon itself and the sheets to one side, as if somebody had just left it. I asked to whom it belonged.

'Ah!' replied my father. 'This is a very interesting case: a singer, who was found unconscious in a field of narcissi. She used to spend hours and hours there, lying on the grass with her arms wide open like a cross. She thought those flowers were real men, who could speak to her through their smell whenever the wind blew over them. She wore herself out, obsessively singing a little song that nobody could understand, so much so that at the end there was just an echo left of her.'

'Really?' I replied, bewitched by the story. 'I like narcissi, actually. They are my favourite flowers, but they stink of death.'

'Death?' my father burst out. 'That only happens if you pick them. Otherwise they have a lovely smell – very intense, perhaps even *too* intense, but quite charming. The singer, in any case, did not die and she is fully recovered from her sickness. They injected her with *Bombyx* and she woke up during her first treatment session. I met her this morning, all cheerful and ready to pack her stuff and leave the hospital. But let's go now before they lock us in here for the night!'

He took my hand and led me to the operating theatre. He had not done that for years, for so long, in fact, that I had forgotten the feeling of fullness that only those hands could produce in a single grasp. Once we had crossed the threshold, we found ourselves in a room occupied by big steel cylinders, similar to those used for MRI.

'Here we are,' said my father, 'Do you see those gurneys? They use them to carry the sick bodies into those steel units, where they get injected and pumped in. It is a very long operation, which requires multiple sessions per day, because the injection has to take place very slowly to minimize the risk of rejection. They use the thread that they produce in the rooms over there.'

'Oh really? Let's go and have a look. I'm really eager to see it,' I told him.

As soon as we entered, I was overwhelmed by the smell of mulberry, that unmistakably fresh and sweet taste, which creaks between your teeth as if it were slush. I breathed in deeply, looking at the innumerable green leaves, full of white cocoons floating in the barrels surrounding us.

'These are the *Bombyx mori*, silkworms in their leaves. And this is their only nourishment, as you can see and as you can hear . . .'

There was a constant buzz, which I had first attributed to the neon light, but now realized was the result of ceaseless eating.

'Silkworms have to eat continuously as they prepare their cocoons,' he informed me, as if he were an expert in the field. And after a brief pause, he continued the thread of his reasoning:

'They do the opposite of what humans do. Their life is a perpetual meal, which they interrupt only four times, during the so-called sleeps of the caterpillar, which is also the moment when they change their skin. So even when they sleep, they are actually working.'

'But what do they do with all that food and eating?' I asked.

'They need nourishment to metabolize the silk, which is an agglomerate of proteins produced by glands located inside their bodies. They are voracious animals and the precious thread they generate is the result of such an excess, you see?', he demonstrated by lifting a caterpillar with his large, deliberate finger.

And then, after disposing of the creature on a leaf, he continued: 'But let us go in the metamorphosis room, which is just next to this one.' That was the place where they brought the caterpillars that were undergoing their transformation. They were hanging down from the ceiling, like bunches of fat and pale white grapes.

'This is where the crucial change happens,' continued my father in his expert tone. 'Some become moths, the adult stage. In that case, though, they break the cocoon, which can then no longer be used to produce the thread. Others die or must be killed in order to extract the silk when it is still in its liquid stage and is therefore easily injectable.'

'What an amazing story!' I said, turning around and looking at all those metamorphoses happening in front of my eyes. 'So silk thread is used to awaken people from their sickness! What an amazing idea! I wonder how they thought of it,' I asked, full of wonder.

'I do not know how the idea arrived in this hospital but the *Bombyx batryticatus*, that is the calcified larvae, is commonly used for therapeutic purposes in Eastern cultures. In traditional Chinese medicine, for instance, it is a typical remedy against digestion problems, as well as, obviously, for sleeping disorders . . .'

As word after word poured out of his mouth, he seemed to have become a caterpillar himself, spinning silk in front of me. And while he talked on, I kept looking at that thread, so exotic and so familiar at the same time. As the filament came out, I tried to spin it around my finger, from the bottom to the top, as if I had made a spindle of my hand. And the more thread I wound along my index finger, the stronger the sensation of warmth I derived from it.

# II. Ariadne

where are you, you already left me, and there's no trace of dionysus yet, and that would be a tragedy, indeed, what will i tell the minotaur, try again later, maybe you'll be lucky and you'll find your athenian hero, mine is out of sight, maybe i made it up, what have we left to do after all, just a dream, but i was told that daydreaming can disclose much more than nightdreaming, and i dream, i dream a lot, i dream during the day, and i dream during the night, i dream and i see, and i see you, i always see you, i see you all the times that the dream wants to see you, even when i don't want to, and now i dress you with a celestial cloth, and now i take it off, and i undress you, and then i imagine you in a suit, and you look so serious, i like seeing, i like seeing what is visible, but also what is invisible, but i must tell the minotaur something, otherwise he'll eat me with all the younglings, maybe i'll sing him a song, just to calm him down for a while, while i wait for you, and yes, maybe that's not a bad idea after all, i'll do as penelope did, weaving and unweaving her threads to keep the suitors at bay, all those scoundrels, while i weave songs, because you can see a tapestry, and then the trick is discovered, but you cannot see a song, and this is why you never know when it's the right moment to applaud, even if you were given the programme so skilfully written and you counted each one of the symphony's movements, and with atonal music it's a true disaster, you always risk looking like an idiot, you thought it was the end, and it was a silence in the music, and since nobody wants to look like an idiot nowadays, not even that insolent minotaur, i can take all the time i need, *adagio ma non troppo*, *allegro ma con brio*, since the music is invisible, and so i weave it instead of a textile, i must buy my time, and i don't know how much, because you didn't even say when you'll be back, or whether you will

# The seamstress

'Tell us a story . . .'

She was a grandmother like many others, if a little peculiar. She was in fact blind, but she had been a seamstress all her life. And nobody could explain how that had been possible. A slender woman with an aristocratic posture, always well dressed, her grey hair was gathered in a bun on the nape of her neck. In the afternoons with her granddaughters, sitting by the table while sharing the bruschetta, her favourite pastime was describing in minute detail all the family jewellery that the girls would inherit one day. Every time she described with care each necklace, bracelet, and jewels, locked far away, in a hidden safe:

'Since you're blonde, you'll get a garnet necklace. It's not very long, about this much,' she said, putting one arm on her chest, 'but it has a very fine golden clasp, with all the garnets forming the shape of a star. Very fancy! And you, since you're so tall, you'll have the triple-layered pearl necklace: it's very long, it reaches down to here,' she added, pointing at her stomach, 'and you can wear it this way, or wind it around your neck. You'll look gorgeous in it. And then there's the gold and lapis lazuli necklace, which is part of a set with its earrings, and a ring as big as this!,' she said, illustrating the size with a circle of her thumb and index finger, adding: 'Really beautiful! And then there's the ruby ring, mounted in the shape of a flower with diamonds, which will be yours, while your sister will have the one with the three sapphires. Then you'll each have one with a pearl, they are quite similar, and the diamond rings: the one in white gold, my engagement ring . . .'

And she went on and on for hours, describing the rings and brooches and necklaces and earrings that her granddaughters had never seen, but knew in such detail that they could almost imagine they were right there in front of them. And after the jewels, there always came the stories. She had a special taste for the world of the dead: the town cemetery and its surrounding mystery always responded to her voracious imagination.

'Catherine, little Kate, give me back the liver and ham you ate!' is how one of her stories began, the story about a woman who had been murdered by her servant trying to steal meat from her kitchen and who came back every night to torment her murderer, with that horrible and anguishing lament, that so many said they could hear its echo everywhere in the city. 'Catherine, little Kate, I'm on the steps already, coming with the cat and the lizard, my mate.' And then, her lament went on every night, and while nobody ever saw her, every morning a few inhabitants of the little town found that some meat had disappeared from their fridge.

When she told her stories, she tilted her head a bit, moving her right eye forwards, as she did when she tried to see something. She was completely blind in her left eye, while from the right she could discern only shadows and silhouettes. And this was even more evident when she told her favourite story: the one about the coffee, that scared her granddaughters so much because, as their grandmother always said as a prologue, it was a true story!

Two young lovers, who had met only recently but had already sworn eternal love, were separated by death: a sudden car crash had killed the girl. After some years, the boy met a woman in a bar who looked so much like his lost love, that he ran to her crying and yelling:

'I finally found you again! I knew that you would come back and that we would never be apart!'

But she, who had spilled her coffee on her white dress because of his vehement hug, shyly answered:

'You're wrong! Please, go away, please leave me alone!'

And so he, confused and tormented by his memories, went on his solitary journey. A few months later, when his lover's tomb was opened by the cemetery authorities to move her bones to the crematorium, everybody was amazed to see the stain on her dress and to smell that fresh scent of coffee that came from her coffin, as if just spilled.

The grandmother had gone blind after her husband's death, because of grief – so the granddaughters were told. It had been during the war, when the town, besieged by enemy troops, had run out of food. He went looking for flour, that day. They had to go out of town to find some and, since the streets were full of soldiers, he and his brother-in-law decided to go through the woods. But there he was killed by a Nazi soldier who thought he was a partisan. Whether he knew that path because he was indeed a partisan himself, or whether he had just ended up in the wrong place at the wrong time, was never firmly established in the family's 'official' memory. Both versions of the story had their supporters and their reasons for existing.

That night her brother came back alone: 'Maria, they killed him!,' he said to his sister right after she opened the door, showing her his leather jacket with the bullet hole. She put her hand on her belly, where her last child was waiting to be born, and looked at that hole, perfectly round, right in the chest. She stared at it for a long time, as if trying to capture the secret of her husband's death with that extreme effort of looking. But she went blind instead. And, nevertheless, managed to raise her five children, including the last one, by sewing.

Nobody knew how she could do it, since all the doctors said nothing could be done; her blindness was almost complete, except for those few shadows. But she worked divinely! She made the most beautiful dresses in town, so beautiful that people came from other neighbouring towns to get one. She knew how to find the most impeccable style for each body type. She needed only to have the cloth in her hands and then, watching it sideways through her thick glasses, with the little eyesight that she had left, she immediately knew how to drape and create just what was needed. Tall, petite, slim, curvaceous, blondes or brunettes: she could find the right dress for each. She received her clients during the day, whom she counselled and examined with the help of her older daughters. And in the night, in the loneliness of the nights, she sewed, she sewed all those marvellous dresses for hours and hours. You could hear her sewing machine, a black Singer with golden writing, and its pedal, humming softly and lightly. Nobody ever saw her working, not even her children, who often found her in the morning still asleep on her creations.

'Granny, tell us another story. This time, one that isn't scary, please.'

'Okay, then,' she answered, 'today I'll tell you the story of Orpheus and Eurydice. The two loved each other so deeply they decided to marry. Orpheus, who was such an incredible harp-player that they said he could sew the visible with the invisible with his music, had created the most beautiful melody that had ever been heard for his bride on that special day. Just as he was playing, his beloved was bitten by a snake that was hiding in the flowers that she was picking. After that calamitous day, he descended into a deep sadness and grief, so deep that even his harp went mute. Whoever tried playing it could not produce any sound. Until one day, not being able to bear this torture anymore, he decided to go to the land of the dead to take her back. This wasn't an easy path, because one had to get through the guards and convince the ferryman of the souls of the dead to take a living body on his boat. And as he went, full of courage and hope, to the gates of the Afterworld, the Furies, with their threatening faces, shooed him away, menacing him with their great talons. "Only a god can pass through that door!," they yelled in their grim voices. "Only a god can enter this world of mourning and laments!"

And he wasn't a god, although he had poetry: "Oh, fierce Eumenides, have mercy on my grief, for I bring hell in my chest, and if only you knew what it is, to feel such anguish because of love . . .," he sang sweetly, accompanied by his harp, which had found its music again. And the melody was so enchanting that even the Furies were moved by it and let him pass, warning him that the helmsman wouldn't be so soft-hearted, as he would stop him with all the means he had at disposal.

And so it was: only the souls of the dead could ride that swift ship and, unless it was a god, there couldn't be any exception. He would never let him board, for any reason. Orpheus did not give up. He took up his harp again and started playing, sinuously moving, from left to right, as if he were composing letters, not just notes.

And the helmsman, bewitched by those invisible words, fell into a deep sleep, leaving the path open towards the reign of the dead . . .'

# III. Ariadne

ok, i'll take that train, i'll see you there, you want to talk, what should i tell you, i never know what to tell you, quite strangely, because i'm always talking, even my teacher complained that i talked too much, good, your daughter is very good, he told my mother, but she could use some silence, she talks, talks too much, how was this possible, me, they used to call me the nun, because i was always alone, on my own, and i hadn't spoken a single word at the age of four, not one, and everybody was worried, but then i started talking, and it's true that i've never stopped since, and i said so many things, but without making too much noise, and yet i have nothing to say when i see you, i don't know, and i knew, since i had prepared it so well in my head, but when i'm there the words don't come to me, and the thoughts run away, so i am left with nothing to say, and i stay there like an idiot, and end up talking about the weather, or about that other thing that nobody's interested in, and i talk just for talking, with all those words that mean nothing, and that maybe say the opposite of what they want to say, just like with my therapist, i take it easy with him too, and i always start from adam and eve again, i talk and i talk, not too loudly though, maybe it's not by chance that i started therapy the same week as i quit opera singing in the end it's the same, more or less, you go there and open your mouth and wait to hear if you did well or not, if that high note was full enough, if it was well positioned on the breath, you can't sustain a piece like this, unless it's written in your throat, and sometimes you sing it without any warm up, under the shower, and maybe i'll stop talking to my therapist too, and i'll go back to singing, because in the end it's all about telling stories and being in contact, on the breath, well positioned on the diaphragm

# The scarf

That day she smelled the scent of his mouth. They were sitting beside each other and, before leaving, he moved close to her, tilting his head to one side, to say goodbye without disturbing the other readers in the hall. And so they found themselves like this, with one face opposite the other, unusually close, and possibly a little awkward. He whispered something to her, holding a white scarf in his hands, that scarf that she had touched some time before, when they hugged. It was so soft that it seemed you could pass through it, like a cloud. And while he talked, so close, looking right into her eyes, she smelled his breath and sensed the taste of his mouth: a subtle but light taste, that she did not dislike at all. They did not know each other, and he was not even her type, but in that moment, she thought that maybe one day she would kiss him.

They did not have much in common, only a brief walk in town. Half an hour, just to get going after all those hours in the library. They had walked through the streets of the city centre, full of stores and people walking by, not knowing where they were going, until they found themselves in front of a design store. He said he felt at ease in it: it was the only place in town where he felt comfortable, besides the library, of course, because, he added, it seemed that they had found the right balance. There were objects with very simple and linear design, just like concepts, but they were so colourful, she thought.

They were indeed much more colourful than the books, this dawned on her right after. And she imagined taking him to the grocery market nearby. There were many colours there, too. But then she hesitated, because it seemed fruit boxes and the weathered hands of farmers would be embarrassing after that fashionable store. And yet she used to go there after the library. She touched a pumpkin, stroked the harsh skin of turnips, and smelled the fresh basil, with its earthy scent.

Had they gone to the market, she would have offered him a plum, like in that dream she had, where they shared one as big as an apple. It had an intense purple colour, bright red under the skin, then fading towards a melancholic yellow. Soft, the peel slightly resisting the first bite, becoming just a bit harder near the core. In the summer, that variety is especially sweet, because the fruits collect all the sugar from the sun, while remaining gently sour and slightly savoury. She did not dare offer one to him that afternoon. Who knew how he would react? Maybe it was too soon? At that time of the year, plums were all imported, too hard and definitely too acidic. They still lacked that perfect balance that only the summer can give them. So they parted, and she kept waiting.

The next day, though, was a holiday. And she found herself in front of a church that had fascinated her for some time. She did not understand to which religion it belonged. It was simple and austere, an old grey stone building from the end of the century, which could have been a Protestant church, or maybe a Jewish temple. It was hard to discern because the neighbourhood had seen so many migrations over the years, that it had become some sort of religious melting pot. That morning, who knew why, she could not resist the temptation. And she went in.

The atmosphere was intimate. A few people – fifteen or so – were circling a man in religious clothing who was talking. It looked like they were waiting for something. She went closer, entering the short queue. And she found herself beside a young woman, clearly of Jewish origins, who asked her what she was doing there, both curious and chastising. She was part of a family of orthodox Jews, as was clear by their clothes. Her father, tall and broad, more evident in the crowd for his heavy black suit, was wearing the kepyah and the peyot, those delicate curls on each temple. His wife, who was in the back with the children, was dressed in black too, a long dark skirt and flat shoes, and seemed to be wearing a wig. The latter is a detail that makes orthodox Jewish women immediately recognizable in a thousand people.

Getting farther away from her family, the woman asked her what she was doing there three times in a row. And she was not able to answer her. She hesitated, and she did not even know why. But she stayed and listened to the words of that priest-like man: he spoke solemnly and announced that the spirit had made itself flesh. Almost a warning. Even though the statement was mixed into ineffable and convoluted concepts, it was reassuring: she was right, then, she was not an intruder because the soul had become flesh! There was no reason to go away or to feel awkward.

And then she thought of the many times she had taken Holy Communion as a child: her mouth open, her hands joined in front of her, as if holding something, and that white host, a subtle but light flavour, that she did not dislike at all.

# IV. Ariadne

time, you ask me where i find it, and indeed i don't find it, i steal it, i steal it from the day, i steal it from the night, or maybe it steals me, it steals me and makes me take the longest road, and the wrong train, and it takes me away, and if it's true that time doesn't exist, because the past is no longer and the future is not yet, then there's only the present, and that's what takes me, and loses me, in its immanence, which is even a transcendence, though, because the present doesn't remember the past, nor announces the future, it's a figure, a figure of itself, and that's why you're never able to live in it, because it's so short, a thin thread, always escaping, and you think you're here but you're actually elsewhere, and when you go back and think you have found it again, it's already past, and i am on a queue at the supermarket, who made me come here at this time, there are always queues in the afternoon, and now i have to wait, and i wait and i think, and i look for the present, but it finds me instead, and the guy behind even pushes me, because i didn't even notice that the cashier was free – now

# The skirt

It was the most peculiar case that he had ever had. She had been in treatment for years, had been visited by so many psychologists, but nobody could explain that strange state into which she periodically fell. It did not look like any established disorders. He himself sometimes fell into a state of absence, forgot small things, little details, as happens occasionally to those who do not pay attention to what is in front of them, because they are busy being elsewhere.

But that was a different case. It was not a simple loss of contact with daily events, due to an occupied mind. And it was not even a pathological form of absence, as one might find, for example, on the autistic spectrum. She did not lack the ability to communicate and socialize, nor had she any peculiar obsession with gestures and actions. She was a normal person, incredibly normal, except for that tiny anomaly.

She would find herself in a momentary state, as if she had been suddenly taken by an absence that was also a presence – maybe even excessively so. While in that condition, she said she felt like her capabilities became sharper and things talked to her directly. In those moments, daily life was presented to her in a different and unusual form, and she could hear its voice, even though it came from inanimate objects. It was a sort of trance, but more of an extreme presence than sheer absence. An excess. An excess of transcendence, one could say, because her mind could then watch the things from high above, but also of immanence, because that condition made her capable of penetrating the present, living it at its fullest, in all its overload.

When she was in that condition, though, she lost her contact with the others. And this had caused many problems in her daily life, for example, at school. No one knew how to address the situation, because the state could come at any moment, without warning. It was like interacting with a sleepwalker, the only difference being that, while the latter sleeps at night although they are awake, she fell into that state during the day, and, while being present, she was also absent, as if she was somewhere else, despite being there, and perhaps even too much being there.

This eccentricity had haunted her since her childhood, and her relatives were now used to it. However, it made her relationship with the rest of the world precarious. Even though, in the end, it seemed to be damaging more to the others than to herself, because they were the ones suffering from that apparent absence. Hence the decision to send her to him, a well-known expert in the field.

After months of treatment, though, that case remained a complete mystery. He did not manage to formulate a diagnosis, the condition did not fit any of his tickboxes, and consequently he had not been able to suggest any cure or remedy. In each session, he showered her with questions, he asked for more explanations, he tried to understand every possible detail, desperately looking for a thread that could unravel that knotted bundle: the first time that she remembered being in that state, how often it happened, if it was occurring more or less often as time passed, and so on, as if each detail, even the most insignificant, could introduce him to the truth.

He had also asked her to keep a journal in which to record what she could remember from those extraordinary events: time, place, day, her thoughts and sensations. And she had done so diligently, for months, writing page after page. He had read and re-read that journal dozens of times, looking for consistency or the most subtle logic. He had asked her to narrate her childhood, her family, her adolescence: he felt like he knew so much of her life now, and yet it did not help him at all in finding the solution to this mystery. It had heightened the difficulty, in fact. And the more he knew, the less he felt he understood.

Until one day, while he was walking in the park as he did every afternoon, he saw her. Despite the distance, he recognized her immediately from her very distinct figure and her hair down over her shoulders. She stood by the pond and it seemed as if she were watching the ducks swimming in front of her. She was wearing a wrap skirt, unusually coloured, and she was bent forwards, her arms on the railing around the pond, and her right foot on the step. He then noticed her beauty for the first time.

He sat on a bench, not too far away, making sure he was out of her line of sight, and decided to keep watching her, discreetly. He thought about all the information he had collected in those months, looking for a thread. And he watched. He watched her from afar, in the lazy light of an autumnal afternoon. Her head moved almost imperceptibly, following the duck in front of her. A slight movement to the right, and then to the left, as if she too was swimming with her thoughts. He could not explain why, but he immediately understood that she was in that condition of extreme presence, that state of which he had heard so much and understood so little.

He watched and studied each movement, avidly, until he noticed that the woman was slowly turning her head to the left corner of the pond, where the duck had stopped and walked out of the water, with its brood following. Above the duck, a hot air balloon had appeared at the same moment, one of those used for advertising. It rose from the ground, partially hidden by the trees, fiery red in the autumn sun. And the woman had literally followed it: mesmerized by the balloon, she seemed to be naturally pulled up by its ascending movement, as it flew in the air.

He watched her body slowly rise, full of amazement, but then fixed his eyes on her skirt: it was coloured, unusually coloured, and he had a sudden urge to pull it down – precisely, rapidly. And while he felt this desire grow inside him, sudden and unstoppable, he realized that the woman had had a jolt: an unexpected movement of her body, as if she had just woken up from a deep sleep.

# *V. Ariadne*

and even ariadne is over, voilà, but please don't think that i like you, you aren't my type, i already told you, you look too much like my first love, who i left twenty years ago, because he was always late, and he made me wait for hours, and he did that for a year and a half, until that day when he came a quarter of an hour late, and i told him it was over, and he didn't understand, and he asked me why, you've always waited, and now all this fuss for a quarter of an hour, and he didn't understand, but i did, and since that day i've never waited again, and maybe you're one of those who are always late, and i'll have to wait for you for hours, and then i don't want to go on that ship, go to athens by yourself, go ahead with your other heroes and take this minotaur with you, because, if you look a bit closer, he does look like you, this abominable beast, half-man half-bull, precisely like you, the athenian hero, with that same devouring desire

# The mannequin

She entered a store to change a dress that had been gifted to her but did not fit. She was a very tall woman, but thin, and so finding the right size was difficult. The smaller ones were usually too short, the bigger ones too loose. And so it happened again that day: she had to choose another dress, a different style altogether, because there was nothing to be done with the one she had been given. She could have tried to move down that crochet on the chest and replace the zip on the side. But it was not worth it. She needed something else: this model just didn't suit her.

As she was walking around through the mannequins and the dresses on display, she noticed a short blue dress with a low-cut back. It was worn by an elegant mannequin, unusually big. The woman thought that it was even taller than her, who was already quite tall, and turned towards the mirror to see the difference. But instead of the mannequin she saw two women, who looked just like her, one younger, with shorter hair, and the other, a grown woman, with much longer hair.

# Third myth: Europa recovered

. . . he was different from the other four; a bit smaller, white as milk, and his presence, his look, had something different as his apparition . . .

The white bull did not browse the grass as the others, which had scattered following the grass, and so did not mind the intruder. But the white bull was looking at Europa. The unusual animal was polished, his dewlap draped almost to the ground, his tail ended in a big tuft. His small and smooth horns were shaped into two perfect crescent moons. His round eyes moved in his orbits with noble melancholy. His fur was living silk.

'I like it,' said Europa. 'When I'll discover his owner, I'll make them buy it for me' . . .

So, Europa, looking for fun, hung her basket by the handle on the left horn of the young bull. The bull, who was shaking his neck in that moment, stopped at first, and then he moved again, but slower, in order not to ruin Europa's flowers.

Her friends whispered in admiration. Europa bowed to stroke the bull's soft neck, who, now still, slightly closed his eyes . . .

'What do you want, little bull?,' Europa asked. While she spoke, she was still bent over and had her hand on his neck. The bull moved very slowly and came to slightly pull against Europa's side, who, almost without noticing, found herself sitting on his back. Then he sweetly straightened his legs and stood with Europa sitting side-saddle on him as if on a horse.

This time the maidens applauded as if it were a show.

'I told you that he's trained.'

The bull turned his head back to watch Europa as if to reassure her. But she was neither afraid nor shy anymore. She laughed and found the most comfortable position. She felt the bull slowly started walking, and with both her hands she grabbed his small horns; on the left one her basket still hung. He walked solemnly and all around them the choir of her companions followed, cheering . . .

Now the bull started going a little bit faster and then started trotting. Europa's body moved entirely with that pace. She felt dizzy. They almost made it around the entire field. The bull stopped in front of the sea, almost on the shore. It seemed like he was interested in the sky that was reddening at the horizon.

'What are you looking at, bull?'

Europa tried to dismount, but she noticed the water was already at the bull's belly. Suddenly scared, Europa screamed loudly, while the bull plunged ahead into the sea. Holding his horns in desperation, she cried out again and turned to look at her companions. But she could not see her companions nor the field nor the land anymore, because a black whirl surrounded everything.

When she came back to her senses, she barely recognized herself. Her fear had become a dullness of all her spirit. She raised her head and looked around, because the world had changed too . . .

Massimo Bontempelli, *Europa's voyage,* in *Sunturn*; translated by Sveva Scaramuzzi from Bontempelli, *Viaggio d'Europa,* in *Giro del sole, Opere Scelte* (Milan: Mondadori, 1978)

# I. Europa

i'm writing to you, but i don't know what to say, i don't, because i told my therapist that sublimation and i have never been on good terms, it goes from solid to air, and i am good in the water, which is in the middle, but he kept on saying that sherazade had chosen a completely heavenly spouse, sublimated, and i tried to tell him that you often wear shirts in the colour of the sky, but he said that ariadne also compared him to his first love, and that it was clearly only the revival of a literary inclination, pure inspiration, like dante and beatrice, if he had ever kissed her, she would have never brought him to paradise, and so, when i saw you, i put a garland of stories around your neck, because you were so handsome, your gaze was so soft, and i told myself, indeed, that you were such a strange animal, sweet, so sweet, because it actually was zeus, heavenly indeed, and i was sure that i would tell you that when you came, and i didn't say anything instead, barely a greeting, and i found myself into the sea, and i was a bit scared too, and maybe it wasn't a good idea sleeping between those kisses, because they were actually everywhere, and luckily the bathroom's acoustics were really good, and so i sang all orpheus and eurydice under the shower, including the descent into hades, i studied that part, my teacher insisted it suited me well, because it's a true mezzo-soprano part, with full high notes, but many low notes too, in the middle, the voice can wander, and come out in all its colours, because the roles are reversed, the furies barring the way to the reign of the dead are male voices, while orpheus, persuading them with his music, is a female, i studied for that role, the wo-man's voice, but had never performed it on stage, and now i sang it all instead, in front of that unusual crowd, under the shower, in the water

# The swim

She had been waiting all winter for that moment. When the days were heavy and dark, and her body shrank from the cold, she dreamed of that coveted moment: the first swim of the summer. Taking off her clothes, she felt the warmth on her skin, moving her body free into the air, and then diving, all at once, into the fresh water of the sea. Refreshing: she waited every year for that moment in the water that, she knew, would literally revive her.

It was still May, though: definitely too early for swimming. She had told herself that it would be still worth going to the beach, to enjoy the sun. She always went to the same place: a rocky cliff, surrounded by Mediterranean vegetation, where the yellow of broom trees faded into the rock amid the green, white and purple hues of limestone. It was typical of that place: cliffs as white as snow fell directly into the blue sea, creating an overload of unexpected light. And it was a secluded bay, difficult to reach, a slight exercise that kept the laziest visitors away.

That day the beach was indeed empty. The schools were still open and the holiday season still far away: summer was almost there, but nobody seemed to have noticed it. Walking down the pathway into the woods, she felt as if everything was resonating around her. The air, though, was still a little bit cool: she would have loved to be able to call Reception to tell them to turn up the heating, but, in the end, she told herself, the water would be still too cold.

No, she did not think that she would have swum that day: perhaps she may have just paddled, maybe trailed a hand in the water, just to pass it across her mouth to taste the salt. The sea was particularly salty there. When she reached her rock, however, it surprisingly sheltered her from the wind, so she felt suddenly hot and took off her shirt. Anyway, nobody was there that day. She sneakily wandered in all that beauty, from which she felt she had received an unexpected gift: was it possible that nobody had noticed that slice of summer? She enjoyed the sun on her skin and stayed there, lying in amazement, like those bell-shaped white flowers that grew wildly around her, open on a marine synaesthesia.

Something poked her foot, waking her from the dizziness of the intense light. A crab, curiously walking around the rocks, had started pinching her toes. She sat up, plucked a flower and began playing with the unusual visitor. She tried to make it come out of its cove, as a revenge. She offered it the flower and it hid nervously, but then it came out again, moving its claws as a false menace, until, suddenly, it left its hiding place completely and, maybe out of fear, maybe because it wanted to, dove under a wave. And so she followed it, without even noticing, one step after the other, finding herself into the water up to her knees.

At first, she was surprised and then thought that the sea in May was not that cold. The crab had disappeared, and she was watching her own feet now, firm, on that rock that she knew so well and that went down into the sea as a stairway. She hesitated for a moment still, asking herself, as she did every year, if there were sea urchins down there, and if she had to be careful. But the water was clear, blue leaning towards green, letting her see everything, completely. She went down some more steps, so that her legs were completely underwater and then, once past the difficult stage, she dove, not thinking about anything.

One dive down. The water was fresh, yes, but good, and the waves were very light. She felt a new energy: a tighter hug, a deeper contact with that mass that surrounded her. She stretched her arms forwards and opened her legs to push herself: with full and strong strokes, she slowly slipped into the sea, as if she wanted to grasp it all with a single movement. Her eyes closed, to hold the pleasure, and then opened, to scan the colours around her. It was a typical Mediterranean coast: she saw a bank of dreamfish, with bright yellow stripes, and then some soles, all flat, their eyes barely visible on their spotted side.

Without even noticing, she had swum far from the shore. She gently came up out of the water: her head first, watching the coast with its green bushes and the spots of broom, those cherry-scented plants that never lose their resilience, even in the hottest of the summers. Sweet, so sweet, and yet so strong: the resistant flower.

She thoroughly enjoyed the water around her in this first swim after a long winter. And then once more she dove and swam to the bottom, holding her breath, slowly letting it out, releasing it while she returned back up. She swam for more than an hour, in a sequence of pirouettes, until, back on the shore, she leaned against a rock, waiting now for the waves to break on her, as if they were stroking her softly from her feet to the rest of the body, moving her from side to side. Suddenly, though, a boat passing by a little farther had created a deeper wave, which pushed her into the rock as if it wanted to wake her up.

She came out of the water as easily as she had entered it, as if May had now become the perfect season for swimming. And while she collected her clothes to dry her body, wet and salty, her attention was caught by the music that progressively emerged from a cliff on the other end of the bay. It looked out over the sea, the stage of a piano bar. It was a dock for boats, built in the last century, completely unused until recently, and now hosting an improbably long grand piano and a singer in an evening suit. The man was leaning on the piano, while the pianist was hunched over the keys. He had pale eyes and full lips, as he smiled, as if he knew. They were playing an old song from the Fifties: the story of a fishermen's village where they eat lobster in the sandy dunes. The notes danced around, one after the other, when behind the singer an unusually big seagull flew down. It landed on a bollard that stood proud of the sea, folding upon itself, and melting away. But as soon it all liquefied into the water, the bird was suddenly born again, rising back from its own ashes.

# II. Europa

and now i'm afraid, and i don't know if it's a good idea bathing out of
season, because i don't even know how far i am from the shore, and
there are only waves here, an entire ocean to cross, and i also forgot my
goggles and flippers, the myth never gives them to poor europa, and
they would come so handy, instead, because she could swim much
faster with them and could go anywhere she wanted, stay with the bull
or go back to the brooms, and she could maybe swim under the sea,
without oxygen, but i don't know whether my diving licence is still valid,
because i got it when i was eighteen, and it was all flat there, there were
no waves and you could see the bottom, the water was so clear, here
the sea is a bit rough, and i don't know if it was a good idea to swim in
this season, maybe i'll get a cold too, and maybe a pool would have
been better, so that i could revise my decompression exercises, and
dive without risking an embolism, because if you're not careful enough
and swim too deep, your lung could easily be disrupted and not be
accustomed to the thin air anymore, and so i think that we need a pool,
a nice pool, deep but not too much, to get accustomed again to dive
and breathe under water without holding the breath, and maybe even a
hyperbaric chamber, right there, just to be safe, in case i forgot my
decompression tables

# Seaweed

It was one of those formal parties where they tell you what time to arrive, but also when you have to leave. It was New Year's Eve and an important – albeit unspecified – anniversary. That was why the chamber music concert, that the hosts usually offered in those occasions, would be a little special that night: two famous musicians and a programme composed completely from their beloved Bach.

They lived in a luxury apartment on one of the fanciest streets in the city centre. The guests, upon entering the apartment, were given the programme of the evening, beautifully presented on fine paper, and the incredible view of the city at night. Evening gowns and suits paraded regularly one beside the other, so the hall was soon full with the lavish party.

After dinner, served as an elegant buffet, the guests were invited to take a seat before the grand piano. Two Bach sonatas were played by a thin and nervous violinist and a pianist, whose figure already anticipated her absolute technical perfection. They were introduced by a long presentation from the host, an old man with bright eyes who wore a tight and a colourful kippah on his head. In addition to the biographies of the two rising stars on the musical scene, he went off on a tangent about the art of counterpoint, of which Bach was surely, as we know, a master: the voices are interweaved one on the other, as the fingers of two hands, that, as proof, he joined in the shape of a comb.

The concert was played without interruption, in front of a distracted audience, who did not miss the occasion to display an excessive enjoyment with their contained applause. And then he started talking again, calling his wife by his side, to announce their anniversary: that New Year's Eve marked the sixtieth year they had spent together. They had indeed met at a house party, when she was just fifteen and he a little bit older. Since then, he had never let her go, as he said holding his wife, a woman with a graceful and uncomplaining attitude, who answered with an obedient nod, confirming her husband's timeline.

'Fifteen! Can you imagine? Raised in a community of orthodox Jews, passed from her father to her husband,' Gianna said to a friend when the party started up again with desserts and champagne. 'Such a husband, too: he's almost eighty and look how he's staring at that woman with the low-cut dress!'

'But maybe she's still got time . . .'

'Time for what?'

'Someone should tell her: "Sara, wake up, you don't have much time! Sixty years with the same man, who you met when you were fifteen, then six children, how could you know? Do you think it's fair?"

'But she's active and, since she retired, she's started dancing lessons.'

'Do you mean dancing classes for old people?'

'Yes, but dancing, and this means that she still has something to say with her body, don't you agree? Look at Giuseppe, just a few years older – look how he behaves!'

'They seem to enjoy their conversation.'

'Quite clearly, indeed . . .'

'What? Are you trying to be a matchmaker for two old people?'

'Why hinder divine providence? Watch what happens!'

Gianna stood up and went towards the corner where Sara and Giuseppe were talking about the art of musical counterpoint.

'The pianist is incredibly talented,' he observed, 'but maybe a bit cold in her execution.'

'I liked her very much – Baroque music has to be played with a certain philological rigour. Romantic interpretations leave me unmoved. Even the violin sounded a bit too much, at times . . .,' said Sara turning towards the new participant, inviting her to join the conversation.

'I agree. The pianist's self-composure properly countered the impatience of the violinist, such as in the fugue. After all, she is so young!' Gianna responded.

'She can't convey certain emotions because she doesn't know them yet,' added Giuseppe, 'while he's more experienced.'

'Speaking of which, have you seen *The Velvet Horn*?' asked Gianna, diverting the conversation.

Sara obliged this detour. 'No, though they say it caused a sensation. Perhaps it's even the renaissance of Opera.'

'Uncommon for a contemporary work, not easy to understand,' Giuseppe observed, being a connoisseur of atonal music.

'I have three tickets for next Friday: my visitors had to leave early. We could go together, if you like.'

'My husband hates atonal music, let alone dodecaphony: he would never attend a show like that. I am curious about it, though,' answered Sara, approving the idea.

'What do you think, Giuseppe?'

'Yes, I am free on Friday!' he answered, without hesitation.

They arranged to meet at seven o'clock in front of the theatre. Giuseppe arrived fifteen minutes early, as usual. Despite his efforts, he never managed to be late, not even when he should have done out of politeness. He was always ahead of time, so he always ended up circling the block a couple of times, to escape detection. And so it was that night, but he was so impatient that, instead of walking around, he stood there waiting, his abundant figure cloaked by a long black coat. Sara, with her swift walk, appeared on the square in front of the theatre a little late: not too much, just the right amount of delay for a date.

'I'm so glad you could come! Gianna cannot make it, did you know? When I went to pick her up, her husband told me that she was in bed with one of her usual migraines and gave me the tickets,' said Giuseppe, clearly happy to see her.

'Such a shame!' she answered, shivering from the cold. 'Those migraines have been tormenting her forever. I told her that she should try acupuncture: it was a life-saver for me!'

He answered by raising his arms in a sign of surrendered approval, and invited her to walk before him with an elegant but conspicuous turn of the hand. She answered that gentle attention with a sweet smile, devoid of all malice, as only she could.

The theatre was full, due to the success of the premiere, but they had two very good seats in the parterre, where you could see the stage clearly and hear the music perfectly. The orchestra was particularly big, so much so that some instruments had been put on some lateral dais, because the pit was not big enough to contain them all. As they had read in the reviews, it was an experimental opera, with large number of instrumentalists, and an original mise en scène, the singers hidden behind two *codium tormentosum* projected on the scene.

*Admit it: you came towards me!*

*What are you talking about? The sea made me drift that way. And I had barely touched you, that you tangled all around me.*

(the music is far too modernist)

*Of course, I am pluricellular: is it not obvious that I have a diploid cycle? Do I look like I have a single set of chromosomes?*

(there is no clear melodic tune)

*Well, you never know. I met many clorophytes that seemed diploids, and then they reproduced by meiosis and by mitosis only.*

(mono or pluri, mono or pluri)

*It's clear that I'm a complex organism!*

*Yes, I thought that you were, but you never know these days; with all these grafts, you can never trust appearances.*

(lacking even the order of atonality)

*Look, I have nothing to do with those unicellular organism, I can't stand them, too solitary or too gregarious, never a healthy middle ground. Can't you see my thallus, plostichous and erect, all my branches, the stem here and all these nice branches dancing in the waves?*

(her hand, maybe her hand)

*A nice 'velvet horn' . . .*

(hesitation)

*I prefer considering myself a 'codium tormentosum'.*

(oh, yes, it's a rich torment!)

*'Velvet horn' better describes thallus, opening as a horn, and this fuzz, light as silk, visible only when we're underwater. And, just like velvet, if you take it out, it flattens and loses its beauty.*

*This is why I don't like being in this kind of pool in the rocks. During the low tide the water retreats and I'm left like a plate, prone as an ulva lactuca, so nobody can see my beautiful thallus . . .*

(her hand on her knee, so close to mine)

*It is very unpleasant when the water retreats, but at least we can avoid those waves that pull so hard when the sea is rough. At least here it's warm, the rocks full of sun . . .*

*You're right: and I can replenish all of my chlorophyll when the rays arrive!*

(now, now: she's so close . . .)

*I need sun too, I don't know how red seaweed survives, down in the abyss, in the dark all the time: they're never exposed to the whims of tide, but it's so cold there . . .*

*Come here, come closer to me, let's enjoy the tide together, holding each other: like this, turn that branch, let's entangle our leaves, yours inside mine, again, closer, even closer, how sweet is the sea, a dance, a true marine dance, as if we were one and the same seaweed . . .*

(done, and I won't let her go).

# III. Europa

and i realize that the role of zeus isn't easy, but i thought reality had surpassed myth in many aspects, leaving sherazade behind, overcoming even theseus and ariadne, because that unexpected union, so strong, so immediate, was far from the simple deal of the myth, where i give you the thread, but you get me on your ship, no, that wasn't the empty desire of not being there, it was full, and that's why i told myself that i should go all in, and i thought that you were making love with the eyes, and not with the body, because the body acts, but the eyes reflect, and you think that you fell in love with that small curve of her mouth, but it's her soul instead, but maybe i was wrong, because i am out of myths now, i don't have them anymore, they are all gone, and today i entered there full of europa, and shortly after i came out with the strong sensation that she had left me instead, that her voyage had already ended, right after it had begun, and so these myths aren't backed by many reasons, as i thought, and maybe i miscounted them, and it's not even three, but two and a half, because a kidnapping cannot last that long, otherwise it wouldn't be a kidnapping, and after the king, the hero, and the god, now there should be a wo-man, because the truth isn't a dream, no, it is not *one* dream, it's many dreams

# The sea

It was a nice day in May: the schools were still open, the summer had barely started, and I laid there, in the sun, copious and vaguely wavy. Then something piqued my attention, waking me from a long rest. At first, I told myself: who is disturbing me on a day like this? It's too soon for the holiday season. Who is bothering me now? I liked that bay, though: caressing its cliffs, smooth as marble, watering its coves in the rocks, with the high and the low tide, shaking its inhabitants here and there, there are many of them.

But that day there was an unexpected guest: a woman who put her legs in the water, disturbing my calm. At first, I hesitated, but then I told myself that those legs were quite pretty, and I hugged them so well all around that she fell into my arms without even noticing. And I supported her body, swinging and surrounding it all, with my entire mass. A dance: I made her dance for hours, here and there, up and down. And when she sat on the shore and I understood that she was about to get out, I pushed her on the rock, almost throwing her: this is how I got angry. Winter – it always leaves me grumpy.

# Epilogue

i finished europa, i finished the entire book, and my inspiration has ended too, i finished tidying up, maybe i'm not finished making a mess, i finished my questions and i'm finished looking for answers, i finished organizing books with that order, in the end i didn't even like that method, i'm finished waiting for an answer from my boss, but i'm finished wanting it, too, and i ended up brushing my teeth with hand cream, but it didn't taste good, so i also stopped making a tiramisu using my mother's recipe, because mine, after all, is easier to digest: i finished everything i had to finish, even asking myself what it means being a woman, that's an impossible task these days, because if you embrace your femininity, you may lose yourself, but if you don't, you may never find it, and now i always go out with my goggles and my flippers, just to be safe, in case i didn't have an answer

and then, oh, i almost forgot, i also stopped trying to quit smoking: anyway, in the end, i had never even quite started.

# Intermission

*The city is sad.*
*The square is crowded by pigeons:*
*They jump they fly they wave.*
*Solid rows of fully armoured policemen contain them.*
*And I am looking for a way out.*

*Women are distributing*
*Corn seeds with ample movements of their arms.*
*They laugh.*
*And I am looking for a way out.*

*But the police*
*Push hard and become a wall, with a sharp smile, with their teeth*
*   clenched.*
*They cover every square foot with their uniforms.*
*Even the corners are barred.*

*I walk to the centre.*
*And as I pass*
*All the pigeons*
*Rise:*
*One by one*
*With the pace of my steps*
*They fly into the air.*

# PART TWO

# The city of women

# I. Ouverture

'Is it possible that, of all the mottos, we had to end up choosing one from a man? Especially that man: Martin Luther! *Hier stehe ich und kann nicht anders*: beautiful, yes, very evocative, true, but after all he was both a man and a priest!'

Thus spoke she in the first council of women. They had spent the day finishing the last details on the fence, before choosing the words to engrave on the gate. It was the first city of women, the first and foremost goal of which was to get rid of all men. It was a conglomeration of houses, on the top of a hill, from which they could control the entire valley. Like a medieval castle, it was a perfect location to defend against possible attacks. Around it, only fields and woods were clearly visible.

'I think if we are truly free, we should be free to use all the words that we like, despite the gender of whoever pronounced them the first time,' answered Rosa, one of the bent. 'Besides, to be a priest then was to be a man, by definition.'

'Yes, but Luther was a misogynist! And he sided with the rich and powerful, once the poor and oppressed rose against them!,' said Sibilla, one of the possessed.

'And yet those words started one of the most significant revolutions of history, the Reformation, with a capital "R".' answered Rosa.

'Rosa is right! Those words perfectly convey the reasons that led us to this: the commitment to living an authentic life, faithful to ourselves and our desires, without masters, without compromises!' yelled Vera, standing up in the corner of the saved.

Like all her companions, she wore a large lifebelt around her waist, white and hard, with red stripes: a pretty conspicuous accessory, with which she could not part because it was a part of her body.

'We like this motto!' added her companions, nodding to each other. The saved were usually gregarious; they always spoke in unison and moved mostly in a group. Other categories, on the contrary, were much more disconnected, especially the doubles, who were constantly fighting with each other or even with themselves: they were in fact women with two torsos, joined from the waist down. One of their number, Maria, spoke:

'I agree. Those words are deeply spiritual and inspiring, and describe perfectly the moral nature of our mission: being real women!'

'Stop this nonsense!' Maddalena added, being her double. Despite the fact that half of their body was conjoined, their chest divided into two distinct branches, each one with breast, arms, shoulders and head. Their hearts were separated too, and they therefore held different opinions. 'We cannot use anybody else's words, because the oppression of our gender is incredibly specific: until now, no woman has ever thought of killing all men, because no one believed that they could really do without all of them. If you look back in history, you'll soon notice this profound difference: the poor have often imagined murdering all the rich, subjects have often dreamt getting rid of their sovereigns, as much as the proletarians plotted for the elimination of the bourgeoisie. Not so with women – and as our condition of oppression is so unique, so must be the words that express it. I think we should find something completely new, in order to state our paradox. Being a woman has now become such a delicate task: if you fully embrace your womanhood you lose yourself, but if you don't, you never find yourself. That's why those words, so authoritative, seem out of place to me . . .'

'That's true!' Rosa the bent interrupted her, 'We're here, we're trying, but we don't know how it will end, I mean . . .who knows if we can . . .'

'Don't listen to her!' said Agata, another possessed, jumping up in her fury. 'Of course we will succeed, and that's why we should vote immediately: our project must be described to the rest of the world, and in words that can speak to that male order, let them understand in their language that we cannot do otherwise . . .' and, after tilting her head slightly, she straightened it again fiercely, adding: 'And that's why there's no point in asking whether we will succeed. We are what we do, and that's what we're now!'

Some found it funny that one of the possessed had pronounced those words, since they changed personality based on the spirit that inhabited them in that moment. The community had spent many hours discussing whether the possessed could join them, because they were sometimes possessed by male spirits and in others by female ones. In the end, they had decided to accept them because their bodies looked like those of the other women, at least sometimes. In the end, only their voice, hair and posture changed – sometimes more feminine, sometimes more masculine – but the person remained the same. Moreover, Agata was menstruating at that time because she was possessed by the spirit of her female ancestors, and therefore nobody doubted the femininity of her ideas.

And her words were successful, because a swarm of voices came from all corners and rose to support her. The final decision was put to the vote. There were only five nays and two abstentions.

The vote of the mothers had played a crucial role in the deliberations. The mothers were respected by everyone because they were the ones who could reproduce by parthenogenesis and so, ultimately, they were the ultimate guarantee of the possibility of perpetuating this community. Even the depressed, with their black clouds hanging over their heads, and the secluded, each one inside her own turret, had voted in favour of the proposal. The sign, with its unmarked quotation, to signal distance from the name of their author, would be affixed the next morning, and the council would meet again the next evening for the first story of the city of women.

# II.  The vest

*In the name of the Father,*
*The Son,*
*And the Holy Ghost*

'Why do you have to go?'

'Someone must . . .'

'Yes, but why you?'

'He's a tyrant, and now we have finally the opportunity to get rid of him.'

'Yes, he's kind of authoritarian, but he has done so many good things for us, don't you think? He protected us, he took care of our needs.'

'Yes, but he used this excuse to suck away our freedom: he named everything, and now we can only submit to his Order.'

'Maybe we could start by giving things different names.'

'We already tried, but we failed: he couldn't stand that we used names other than those he created.'

'Why do you have to be the hero? Can't you let someone else do it?'

'Until we get rid of him, there will be no decent life for anyone in this country, including the two of us.'

'When will I see you again?'

'When the tyrant is dead and we're able to enjoy our freedom.'

'Freedom! Freedom! What does it mean to be free? Look, there, aren't we free in this room? We're here, we can go out, come back in, we can do what we want. I am free to raise this arm, to pirouette, and then a step in this direction, and another in that one: am I not free?'

'No, I'm sorry, you're not. If that was freedom, it wouldn't be much different from that of a roast animal that, once programmed, is free to move around on its spit, if nothing gets in its way.'

'Isn't that enough? What other freedom is there for us to aspire to? Look: I'm also free to jump into your arms and kiss you, what else do you want?' she said, maliciously lying on her lover's body.

'Call things by their proper name,' he answered, moving away and frowning.

'And this is why I should give you up today? For freedom of speech? To call things as we please?'

'No, it's not about randomly naming things: it's about giving them their proper name.'

'And what should be this name? Who decides what is the proper one? The men?'

'No, we have to decide it together. And until we are able to do that, we'll always live in His Name.'

'Who cares! Is it that difficult for you?'

'Maybe not, but I cannot even have you, it's His Order: everything happens because of it!'

'And when will this war end? When can I see you again, then?'

'When you'll be able to call me by my true name.'

'What are you talking about? I know your name perfectly well! It's written right here, on the doorbell, on your driving licence . . .'

'No! That's not my true name: that's the name I was given!'

'I don't understand anything anymore, I'm so confused, all that weird reasoning . . .'

'That's not true, you understand, I know that: I see it in your eyes: they are too bright. They're not the eyes of someone who doesn't understand.'

'And what do we do in the meanwhile?'

'Wait: we must wait.'

'I can't wait.'

'I know, nobody can.'

'You're more patient than me.'

'That's not true, I can't wait either, but we have to learn to wait: that's the first revolutionary act . . .'

'Then we'll learn to wait together. Now come here. I must give you something.'

They were in the middle of the room, standing one opposite each other. She held the sides of his jacket and slid them off his shoulders. He came closer to kiss her, but she shook her head and moved him away with her hand. She clearly had something else in mind. She started opening his shirt: button after button, slowly, from top to bottom, untucking it from his trousers and finally letting it slide on the floor.

He smiled and tried to kiss her again. She usually never took the first step and her behaviour, that hot afternoon, astonished him. But she moved away again, removing the hand that he had rested on her head in the meanwhile, letting him know she did not want to be kissed in that moment. He was sweetly surprised.

Then she came closer again, and, holding two sides of his t-shirt, pulled them upwards, baring his stomach and his slightly hairy chest. He was smiling, while she walked around him, watching him with extreme attention, bare chested, as if she were studying him. Finally, she reached out and touched his left shoulder, muttering a song, moving her hand from left to right, as if she was drawing a curl: and while she traced his bare chest with her hand, a wool thread appeared where the finger had just passed. When she reached the end, she went back, sinuously knitting the thread just by moving her hand: stitch after stitch, the thread unravelled in tight rows.

He watched in amazement as the knitted cloth progressively covered his stomach. When she was finished, she made him raise his arms and continued across his back, knitting the same pattern with her finger, attaching one stitch to the other, in a tidy sequence. He laughed in admiration. After she was finished, she watched her work, satisfied:

'This finely knitted vest will keep you company: this style keeps out the cold and is good for travelling.'

But she hadn't even finished her sentence when she suddenly hesitated, as if she had remembered something. So she leaned towards him and, with small kisses along his stomach, drew a row of buttons that came down to his waist.

'That's it,' she finished, standing up. 'Now there's everything you need: you'll be able to open it, too, in case it gets too hot.'

# III. Rehab

'Thanks, Rosa, for the beautiful story,' said Luna, one of the depressed. Rosa had read on her hands and knees, beside the common fireplace, bent on all fours, like all other bent women. The dining hall was big, with wooden benches and tables, but the bent, because of their peculiar position, had special tables just right for their posture like dogs.

'I don't think it's a good idea to start right with a story by a bent,' said Sibilla, possessed, in that moment, by a male spirit.

'Sibilla! Don't be so rude to a sister! Things aren't always univocal, as you should know better than most!' said Vera, one of the saved, slightly annoyed.

'The bent are those who liked it! That is why, when he said *stay there on the ground*, they never stood up again!' Sibilla answered.

'Yes, but, you see, love is complicated,' said Vera.

'I always ask if she likes something or not, maybe not directly, but in some subtle and complicit way, and that is the way it should be!' answers Sibilla.

'Sibilla, love isn't a restaurant where you can order from the menu, is it?' said Vera, ironically smiling.

'With or without a menu, we're here to get rid of men! Not to knit vests for them or create button-kisses! What do you think we're doing here? Starting the city of women with a story on heterosexual love, and with such traditional roles too, freedom-fighters and sweater-knitters, no, not at all – no more men!' concluded Sibilla, standing up in rage, after hitting her fist on the table.

Rosa was looking at the ground between her hands. Her hair fell on both sides of her shoulders, like the long ears of a beaten dog, and she did not dare to raise her gaze. But Concetta, a mother, started defending her:

'This is unfairly aggressive behaviour, Sibilla, which maybe you'll regret when the male spirit that inhabits you now leaves us. Rosa's story is very signficant and highlights immediately one of the feminine traits that we could improve in this community: care, the attention to others and their needs. We are women and, unlike men, we have this written inside us,' she added while gently stroking her belly, with her sweet voice gently fading away.

'This is a parody of women. We're not all devoted to the others, birthers and weavers!' broke in Addolorata, one of the depressed, shaking her head in her black cloud.

'No, of course we're not *only* that, but we are *also* that, and we can be so in a way that is very rarely found in men. He exists in the name of the Father entirely, and his observance or refusal of the Law dictates all of his actions, including the possible rebellions. On the contrary, we operate according to a completely different ethics. We consider the condition of all the involved subjects rather than simply obeying some abstract law,' answered the mother who had spoken before.

'I'm not convinced by this polarity, and what is the purpose of starting with a story like that?' answered Addolorata.

'Again with the idea of the understanding, patient, careful woman, for *a man*! Wasn't the purpose of these encounters to get rid of them?' said Luce, a possessed like Sibilla, similarly shining in her passion.

'Yes! And that's exactly what we're doing: telling stories as therapy, as a practice of elaboration of millennia of patriarchy and the addiction to our own chains it has generated' said Vera, followed by a chorus of 'She's right! She's right!' from the corner where the other saved were sitting.

'Yes, like in Alcoholics Anonymous: they meet, they talk, and by sharing they free themselves, without accusing each other, or attacking, as Sibilla did a while ago. That was very masculine behaviour, indeed!' said one of the mothers.

'Yes,' added one of her companions, 'and if we want our community to flourish, we have to understand the deepest reasons for our oppression. Because it is perpetrated by the oppressed as well, not just by the oppressors: patriarchy would have never been so successful without the compliance of women themselves! So we have to start precisely from that abhorred complicity and the constant desire for their approval.'

'I agree! No one better than us knows what kind of dangerous pleasure hides in being subjects!' said one of the doubles. 'I don't!' immediately added her other half. 'I think all male figures should be banned from our history and from our stories. We just need to learn to do without. In the end, it's a matter of habit: this is why we need a radical break, something like shock therapy! To wake up!'

'How do you shock away thousands of years of oppression? Don't be ridiculous! It's not possible!' said one of the saved, followed by a chorus of 'It's impossible! It's impossible!'

'Let it be the end, then!' said Luce the possessed, stopping the chattering. 'That's the last time that a man appears in our stories. Because, in the end, we're here to get rid of them, yes?'

# IV.  The oven of opposites

They discussed for a long time how to organize the kitchen in the city of women. Some proposed a strict separation of roles. Each one should be free, in accordance with her own desires and needs, and therefore only those who wanted to should take care of cooking and food preparation. Others opposed this idea because they feared that some would fall prisoner to the role of hearth-keepers: a voluntary slavery, for sure, but slavery, nonetheless.

They had to prevent such regressive temptation: they could be finally free, so they had to become free. They therefore decided that they would cook food in rotating shifts. That seemed the most democratic decision.

Continuity would be guaranteed by the oven that they were building: a white dome, right beside the kitchen, with a shed at its base, in which wood had been stacked in a neat row, and a big oven above that could bake anything they wanted.

It was tended by a little gnome with bright eyes and pointy ears, who lived in the forest nearby. It was a being beyond any gender, which is why its presence was tolerated, even if it was not strictly speaking a woman. On the contrary: its being part of all and no gender at all made it the perfect keeper for the kitchen of the city of women. And it was a constant reminder, with its anomalous presence, of the artificiality of the distinction itself. It never spoke, and in fact it would not even be able to say whether it was male or female, trans, queer, asexual, or all and none of them.

And yet their continued nourishment was due to that bizarre being, who also took care of the disposal of the city's rubbish. It funnelled all the waste from the city of women inside the oven, to be consumed by a healthy flame and a spring. Because of its ability to house both water and flame, they had named it 'the oven of opposites'.

# V. A witch and her broomstick

They met in the little wood behind the house on a night with a full moon. They were both looking for rest, and that stream of fresh water, surrounded by the chill of centuries-old trees, seemed the best place to find it. Both sisters distractedly watched some fireflies that looked like shooting stars in the darkness of the early night.

'Grandmother was a witch, Mother is a witch, and you are a little bit of a witch too: do you think that I can be one as well?' the younger sister asked. She had curly dark hair and did not talk much, in contrast to her older sibling.

'I don't know. Grandmother passed the secret to Mother, and it's now up to her to decide where it should go before she dies', answered the older sister, calm and peaceful, with her straight blonde hair that framed her face like an icon of the Virgin Mary.

'Do you want it?'

'It's not up to us! One can only receive the secret. What is given, is given. Because everything is written, since the dawn of time, even though we don't know it. There are signs that seem to speak quite clearly, though . . .'

'For example?'

'For example, your dreams. The fact that since you were born, they have often shown the future to you could be a sign . . ..'

'Do you really believe this?'

'Of course! Do you remember when you woke up in the middle of the night, saying that our beloved cousin should keep away from rocks because she was in danger? Nobody believed you then: Mother put you back to bed saying it had been just a nightmare. And yet, the next morning . . . I will never forget your face when you were told about the huge rock that had fallen a few inches away from her, just as you dreamed! And luckily people do not get rocks of that size falling on their head every day!'

'That could just be a coincidence, even though, now that I think about it, I often dream of things that then actually happen. For example, the other night, that strange and unusual meeting that really happened the day after. But dreams aren't enough to make a witch, are they?'

'No, of course not, because dreams can just tell us about the future, like the cards that Grandmother left us, with the old mortar, where she used to grind herbs for remedies,' she said, watching a piece of wood and a concave object in pure white marble leaning on a log, barely illuminated by the twilight. Then she added: 'But besides the mortar from the past and the cards for the future, you'll need a broomstick. To travel through the present. All true witches have a broomstick, otherwise they'd be condemned to swing between a past to heal and a future to predict, unable to live truly in the present . . .'

'And where do I find a magic broomstick?'

'Well, it has to choose you and come to you, because it cannot be just any broomstick!'

'You're right . . . Actually, I've met a talking broomstick once, and I thought that it was so nice. It was made of a fine and sturdy wood, and it looked like a statue, because it was so finely chiselled! It also had a nice soft brush, it almost felt like hair to the touch!'

'Really?'

'Yes, it also promised me to be my humble and devout servant, but . . .,' she added, lowering her gaze under a dark veil of thoughts, 'but then, it flew away.'

'Well, things like these happen: maybe it had some urgent matter to attend to.'

'Yes, I thought so. In the end, I had met it by chance and maybe, in that moment, it was still serving someone else. Now, I don't know anything about it . . .'

'Didn't it tell you where it came from?'

'Yes, it told me that it lived in the kitchens of a castle, a certain Ostenburg castle, in the north, where it's cold, in the middle of the barren country.'

'Oh, yes, Ostenburg! I heard about that: once there were incredible magical duels there, but now it's in ruins.'

'Really?' her sister asked, amazed by this revelation.

'Unfortunately the barbarians arrived there too, and who knows if the castle can endure a siege.'

'These savage hordes frighten me: they're conquering everything. Someone should stop them, sooner or later!'

'Maybe you should go to help and take back your broomstick!'

'Me? No, that's impossible, I don't even know if I'm a true witch!'

'This could be the right occasion to find out and engage your magic powers!'

'And if I fail? Who will save me?'

'If you find your broom, you can always fly away with it, in case it turns bad.'

'Yes, I could . . . and if I find it and it doesn't obey me? I tried to call it some time ago, in a night with a bright moon like this. I thought that maybe it was watching the sky too, in that moment, and since the moon is the same everywhere, I thought it could be my messenger. I gave it the words that had come to me in that moment: *"Come, come! Fly into my arms, my humble and devout broomstick, come to your beloved witch!"* But I never had an answer.'

The night had become suddenly gloomier. Grey clouds, all jagged and screeching, had suddenly covered the moon. Even the fireflies had disappeared, and the two sisters stood next to each other, thoughtfully. From the forest came the grim and dull noise of an owl, while black trees, shaken by a faint breeze, seemed to become progressively animated, dark and frightening.

'Maybe it was locked somewhere, or maybe you didn't use the right words . . . Have you tried some magic spell?'

'And where would I find a magic spell?'

'What? After all those words that you've collected in your notebooks through the years? There must be some magic spells there.'

'Do you really think those words could work?'

'Yes, of course! I've seen the effect they have around you when you read them out loud, ever since you were little: everything came to life and events often took an unexpected turn . . . I think that you should leave for that castle, well-armed with your magic book and a special tunic of invisibility and protection. Those woven from loving fingers have these properties.'

And, after a moment of silence, she added: 'Go! Go get your broomstick back!'

'But it's a quest so long and full of dangers . . .,' answered her sister, turning serious. She looked down, more thoughtful than resigned, as if some kind of help could come to her right from the earth. But it came from the water instead.

'I know what we have to do: Grandmother Fernanda's ritual!' the older sister said, jumping to her feet.

'What do you mean? Which ritual?'

'The one to get rid of fear, do you remember? When we were children, Mother always took us to Grandmother's, when one of us got grumpy, to have exactly . . .'

'Yes!' answered her sister, suddenly *"Psam psam, psam psam"*! The lantern! Do you remember?"

'Of course I do! At first she slightly tilted it, pouring a couple of oil drops in a bucket of water, and then, spinning it over the head, she chanted the spell: *"psam psam, psam psam . . ."*'

'Follow me now!' the younger sister concluded, running into the woods.

The clouds had gone away, and the moon was shining again, lighting their path. They went down to the stream, jumping like roe deer from one rock to the other, until, when they arrived in a secluded place, they started searching the site, as if looking for a lost object.

'Here is Grandmother's spring, but where will we find the bucket and the lantern and the magic oil?' the younger sister asked.

A few days before, there had been a flood, so the stream was full of rubble and driftwood: its course had changed slightly, too. The water, that flowed mostly underground, ran in the open in a few crevices, forming pools that, on a closer inspection, looked like some sort of bucket.

'We could use this,' the older sister answered, indicating a pool of water right next to her. 'Sit beside it,' she added, pointing at a rock.

'What about the lantern and the magic oil?' asked the other quickly, obviously worried. But she had not even finished speaking when a beautifully coloured dragonfly started flying towards the water. With a swift and direct movement, it descended towards the water, hitting it with its tail, as if it wanted to lay its eggs. Instead, little oily drops appeared on the surface, which progressively extended into a spot. The two sisters watched in awe, with wide eyes, while the ritual unfolded and the dragonfly continued rising and descending up and down, like the needle of a sewing machine, pushing its thread rhythmically into the cloth. And when it had finished its job, as if to rest from that great fatigue, it started to fly in concentric circles over the head of the younger sister, who in the meanwhile, had kneeled in sign of gratitude and reverence for that incredible event.

And while the oily drops faded into her forehead, a voice rose from the forest, far and deep, resonating everywhere, as if each rock, each tree, each creature and being around had suddenly started sighing: '*psam psam*, *psam psam* . . .' And it went on like this, as if all of nature was pulsing to the sound of those words, until a second dragonfly, also beautifully coloured, flew towards the first one, caught its body and took it away, in a long and sinuous flight, as if they had been one and the same thing: a witch and her broomstick.

# VI. A bill

Thus spoke Sibilla the possessed, standing with frantic eyes beside the grand fireplace. Her words had hit her companions' bodies like fire. Now, in the city of women, there were no men anymore, but only women and dragonflies soaring in unison. In the general enchantment caused by the story, with its unexpected mating, they decided to start debating monogamy. The great dining hall looked even fuller that night. Luce, a possessed, was the representative of the proposed bill.

'Women, comrades, I don't have to remind you what incredible instrument of oppression monogamy is for our gender. Why two dragonflies? Why not three or four? Matriarchal societies have always been flexible in sexual customs, but patriarchy turned monogamy into Law: binding the woman to private property, man made her the keeper of his order. Sealed in the "Name of the Father", for centuries she had no other choice than to move from the name of the Father to that of the Husband: her presence had to guarantee the warmth of the hearth, her purity the continuity of legitimate descendance. Of course, legitimate from the point of view of His own possession. This is why female adultery has always been punished more severely than male adultery, wherever property and family proceeded together. The woman has carried for too long the weight of "Name of the Father": she guaranteed its continuity at the cost of her own subjugation. This is why I'm proposing that the city of women institutes compulsory polygamy: we have to break this chain at its root!'

'Luce is right, yes to polygamy!' answered the other possessed in unison, raising their arms in sign of rebellion.

'Wait a minute!' said Concetta, one of the mothers, standing up with a new-born in her arms. 'And who will guarantee the well-being of our children, the continuity of that material and emotional attachment that they need to grow up properly? We have to think about our children: they need some stability, not the mess of a love-roulette!'

'See? This is the usual trap! Don't listen to her: the name of the Son has always been the perpetration of that of the Father!' Luce answered, jumping up furiously.

'For centuries we have been told we have that special ability, that wonderful gift which allows us to create life, and so we didn't need anything else: no education, no rights, only that gift, and that duty, so wonderful and powerful that it has kept us oppressed for centuries! Why does it never occur to anyone to say that the man starts and finishes by being a father, in also having that wonderful ability?'

'Luce, we have to make distinctions,' answered Concetta. 'Now things are different and we can be mothers and many other things too. On the contrary, it's exactly because of this, to secure for the women who bear children their right to pursue other endeavours, that we need to have some form of long-lasting relationship between parents, one permitted and sanctioned by the law.'

'Who said there should be two parents?' asked Mariavittoria, one of the doubles. 'Why not? Two is better than one, though four is more than three,' immediately added her double. As all the other doubles, they always disagreed.

'Mariavittoria is right. The two-parent model is the standard of the heterosexual bourgeois family and it's not applicable to us: this is a city of women! We are free! I propose that that we abolish all those archaic and oppressing rules: the mothers, after the parthenogenesis, must have maximum support, but the city itself will provide for them, as the entire community must take care and educate its children,' said Luce. And, after a moment of hesitation, as if to gather more strength:

'Beware, dear companions, we're discussing the most important topic: from how we'll handle reproduction, we decide the society that we want to create. Let's think about it carefully, because the stakes are incredibly high!'

'True! True!' answered the possessed in unison.

'Luce is right: community of children means community of goods too, and so communism as such! And if we look at some examples from the past, we always find the same rule: wherever there was no private property, the care of children has always been in common, and the role of genders was consequently much more egalitarian than in societies based on private property. Think about Sparta, for example, where women were so much freer than in all other Greek cities. They could even go to war!' said Annunziata, one of the mothers.

But Vera, shyly raising her head from her lifebelt, asked: 'Are you sure that being allowed to go to war means being freer? Well, to be honest, I could do without that type of freedom . . .'

'Of course!' answered Sibilla. 'We don't have to worry about war, because we have no interest in these acts of aggression, but should we be attacked some day, we'll have to defend our community all together! Who else could – or would?'

'The idea of war makes me anxious . . .,' said Nerina, one of the depressed, raising her head slightly above her dark cloud.

'Nor am I too keen on leaving my comfortable spot here,' added Celeste, one of the secluded.

'I think we should tackle each item separately,' finally said Rosa, the bent. 'First of all, community of property and children. It's true that reproduction is the core of every society, therefore I propose that we approve this fundamental law: "Every creature born inside the city of women will be considered a child of the entire community. Their care and education will be a responsibility of everyone." With a law like that, we don't even have to specify that our community is based on common property, because it's the natural order of things. Do you agree to this basic concept?'

'Yes, yes!' they all answered unanimously.

The vote was merely formal, because nobody objected. From that day on, indeed, nobody in the city of women carried the 'Name of the Father' any longer; everyone answered to one and only name: her own.

# VII. The names

ADDOLORATA ADELAIDE ADELE ADELINA ADRIANA AGATA
AGNESE AGOSTINA AGRIPPINA AIDA ALBA ALBERTA ALBINA
ALCESTE ALEANDRA ALESSANDRA ALESSIA ALGISA ALICE
ALISSA ALLEGRA ALTEA AMALIA AMANDA AMARILLI AMBRA
AMBROSIA AMELIA AMINA AMIRA ANASTASIA ANCILLA
ANDREINA ANGELA ANGELICA ANGIOLINA ANITA ANNA
ANNABELLA ANNALISA ANNAMARIA ANNAROSA ANNUNZIATA
ANTEA ANTONELLA ANTONIA ANTONIETTA ANTONINA
ANUSCA ARIANNA ARIELA ARMIDA ASIA ASSUNTA AUGUSTA
AURA AURELIA AURORA AZZURRA BARBARA BEATA BEATRICE
BENEDETTA BERENICE BETTA BIANCA BRUNA BRUNELLA
BRUNETTA BRUNILDE CAMILLA CANDIDA CARLA CARLOTTA
CARMELA CARMEN CAROLINA CASSANDRA CATERINA
CECILIA CELESTE CELESTINA CHIARA CINZIA CLARA
CLARETTA CLARISSA CLAUDIA CLELIA CLEMENTINA
CLEOPATRA CLIO CLORINDA CLOTILDE CONCETTA
CONSOLATA CORNELIA COSTANZA CRETA CORA CRISTIANA
CRISTINA DAFNE DALIA DALILA DAMIANA DANIELA DANILA
DARIA DEA DEBORA DELIA DELFINA DELINDA DEMETRA
DESDEMONA DESIDERIA DIANA DILETTA DOMENICA DOMITILIA
DOMIZIANA DONATELLA DORA DORIS DORIANA DOROTEA
DRUSILLA EDDA EDGARDA EGIZIA ELIA ELBA ELDA ELENA
ELEONORA ELETTRA ELIANA ELISA ELISABETTA ELOISA ELSA
ELVIRA EMANUELA EMILIA EMMA ENRICA ERICA ERMELINDA
ERMINIA ERNESTA ESMERALDA ESTER EUFEMIA EUGENIA
EVA FABIANA FABIOLA FABRIZIA FATIMA FAUSTA FEDERICA
FEDORA FEDRA FELICIA FELICITA FERDINANDA FERNANDA
FIAMMA FIAMMETTA FILIPPA FILOMENA FIONA FIORDALISA

*FIORENZA FLAMINIA FLAVIA FLAVIANA FLORA FLORIANA
FLORINDA FIORELLA FORTUNATA FOSCA FRANCA FRANCESCA
FRIDA FULVIA GABRIELLA GAETANA GAIA GEA GELSOMINA
GEMMA GENOVEFFA GENZIANA GEORGIANA GERALDINA
GERARDA GERMANA GERTRUDE GIACINTA GIADA GIANNA
GILDA GINA GINEVRA GIOIA GIORDANA GIORGIA GIOVANNA
GISELLA GIUDITTA GIULIA GIULIANA GIULIETTA GIUSEPPINA
GLORIA GRAZIA GRAZIANA GRAZIELLA GRETA GUENDALINA
IDA IFIGENIA ILARIA ILDA ILEANA ILENE ILENIA IMMACOLATA
INDIA INES IOLANDA IOLE IONIA IRENE IRIDEA IRINA IRIS IRMA
ISABELLA ISIDORA ISOTTA ITALIA IVA IVANA IVONNE JESSICA
JOANNA JOLE JOLANDA KATIA LAILA LARA LARISSA LAURA
LAVINIA LEILA LEONILDA LENA LETIZIA LIA LIANA LIBERA LIDIA
LILIANA LINA LINDA LISA LIVIA LOREDANA LORENA LORENZA
LORETTA LORIANA LUANA LUCE LUCIA LUCILLA LUCIANA
LUCREZIA LUDOVICA LUIGIA LUIGINA LUISA LUISELLA LUNA
MADDALENA MAFALDA MAIA MANUELA MARA MARCELLA
MARELLA MARGHERITA MARIA MARIANGELA MARIA
ANTONIETTA MARIACHIARA MARIASSUNTA MARIACONCETTA
MARIACRISTINA MARIAELENA MARIAFRANCESCA
MARIAGIORGIA MARIAGIULIA MARIAGIOVANNA MARIAGRAZIA
MARIALAURA MARIALUCE MARIALUISA MARIA MADDALENA
MARIANNA MARIA PAOLA MARIAPIA MARIA RITA MARIAROSA
MARIATERESA MARICA MARIAVITTORIA MARILENA MARILÙ
MARINA MARINELLA MARISA MARISTELLA MARY MARTA
MARTINA MARZIA MATILDE MAURA MAURICA MELANIA
MELISSA MELITA MIA MICHELA MICAELA MICOL MIETTA MILA
MILENA MINA MIRANDA MIRELLA MOIRA MONIA MONICA
MORENA NADIA NATALIA NATASCIA NELLA NERINA NICOLE
NICOLETTA NILDE NINA NORA NORMA NUNZIA OFELIA OLGA
OLIMPIA OLIVIA OMBRETTA ORIANA ORIELLA ORNELLA
ORSOLA ORTENSIA OTTAVIA PAMELA PALMIRA PAOLA
PATRIZIA PENELOPE PETRA PIA PIERA PIERANGELA PINA
PINUCCIA PRISCILLA QUINTINA RACHELE RAFFAELLA RAISSA
RAMONA REBECCA REGINA RENATA RITA ROBERTA ROMINA
ROSA ROSALBA ROSALIA ROSALINDA ROSAMARIA
ROSANGELA ROSANNA ROSSANA ROSARIA ROSELINA
ROSELLA ROSETTA ROSINA ROSI ROSITA ROSMARA*

*ROSMUNDA ROSSELLA ROSY SABINA SABRINA SALOMÉ
SAMANTA SANDRA SANTA SARA SAVIANA SEBASTIANA
SELENE SELVAGGIA SERENA SERENELLA SEVERINA SIBILLA
SILVANA SILVIA SIMONA SMERALDA SOFIA SONIA SORIANA
SPERANZA STEFANIA STELLA SUSANNA TAMARA TATIANA
TEODORA TERESA TILDE TINA TIZIANA TOMMASINA TOSCA
TRISTANA TULLIA ULDERICA ULRICA UMBERTA URSULA
VAINA VALENTINA VALERIA VANDA VANESSA VANNA VENERE
VERA VERENA VERDIANA VERONICA VILMA VINCENZA VIOLA
VIOLETTA VIRGINIA VITA VITTORIA*

That the list started with ADDOLORATA and ended with VITA
VITTORIA was considered a good sign. Someone suggested taking
out all the names that came before ALLEGRA, to start the list on a
cheerful note, but the proposal was quickly rebutted because
ADELAIDE  ADELE  ADELINA  ADRIANA  AGATA  AGNESE
AGOSTINA AGRIPPINA AIDA ALBA ALBERTA ALBINA ALCESTE
ALEANDRA ALESSANDRA ALESSIA ALGISA ALICE and ALISSA,
who came before, opposed their erasure.

   That the name MARIA had the unmatched privilege of a miraculous
multiplication was debated as the inevitable heritage of 2,000 years of
Christianity, but it was found tolerable, because MARIANGELA
MARIAANTONIETTA       MARIACHIARA       MARIAASSUNTA
MARIACONCETTA       MARIACRISTINA         MARIAELENA
MARIAFRANCESCA       MARIAGIORGIA         MARIAGIULIA
MARIAGIOVANNA  MARIAGRAZIA  MARIALAURA  MARIALUCE
MARIALUISA  MARIAMADDALENA  MARIANNA  MARIAPAOLA
MARIAPIA   MARIARITA   MARIAROSA   MARIATERESA   and
MARIAVITTORIA also cared very much about MARIA. Someone
opined that they omit MARIAGERTRUDE for the moment, due to the
terrible sin of cacophony (though no one had manifested the desire of
using it).

   That from ROSA stemmed ROSALBA ROSALIA ROSALINDA
ROSAMARIA ROSANGELA ROSANNA ROSARIA ROSELINA
ROSELLA ROSETTA ROSINA ROSI ROSITA ROSMARA and,
maybe, also ROSMUNDA ROSSANA and ROSSELLA, was happily
accepted as a fortuitous chance of fate and botany. As far as the rest,
they simply referred to the well-known female creativity.

# VIII. The call, or occasional tourism

That night it was the doubles' turn. Among them Maria Maddalena started speaking: like all her companions, she was a divided woman. Through flash and thunder, pacing in the rain, they started telling their story:

She was in the kitchen of their mother's house. It was a modern apartment, extremely functional: washing machine, dishwasher, electric grill, food processor, automatic oven, built-in fridge and furniture. The surfaces were shiny, bright and orange. While the mother was working in front of the sink, she was casually looking out of the big window, when, suddenly, her attention was drawn to a weird object slowly covering the sky: a huge spaceship.

She immediately knew: it was the Annunciation! Yes, it was him, the Archangel Gabriel came to bring the Gospel!

But Maria was not ready: 'Mum, there he is, Gabriel's in there, I know! But no, no! I don't want to!'

What are you saying?' yelled her mother, 'it's the Son of Our Lord!' and, crossing herself, she added: 'His Will be done!'

It was the first holiday they had allowed themselves after a long time. And she had been thinking about this escape from the dullness of her existence for months now.

The tour operator waited for them at the airport to bring them to the hotel on the coast. They were in an exotic location, particularly popular and difficult to reach, but the agency had prepared everything. After driving them to the hotel, their guide would show them the most beautiful beach, the one with the purest water of all: they should never miss its pleasures!

And so they did, as advised. After their arrival, they had barely unpacked before putting on their bathing suits and rushing to the beach.

'Darling, thank you for this beautiful gift!' she said, hugging him before leaving the room.

'It's the least I can do for you, my angel!'

"But Mum, I don't want to be a virgin! That's such a sad life! Spending my life taking care of a son I did not even consent to! And my youth and beauty wasted this way, like a flower that never blooms?'

'But dear, you should be honoured to be the Chosen One!'

'No, no, I don't want to! Who will tell Joseph, then? My poor Joseph! Everybody thinks about the Lord, and nobody thinks about my poor Joseph! And now I should tell him that I will bear the son of someone else, but that he has to provide for the child? No, I cannot do this to Joseph, right when things had started working so well for us, now that I felt ready . . .'

'But dear, what do you want to do? You cannot oppose the Will of the Almighty!'

And while a blue-clothed alien with golden wings sprouting from his back knocked at the door, Maria suddenly found herself transported to a temple, with big sturdy columns, decorated in precious pink marble.

She looked around, frightened, searching for a way out. Against the solemn silence of that place, announcing the presence of divinity and the inevitability of His decree, Maria desperately screamed: 'Joseph, my Joseph, where are you? Help me, Joseph! Help me! I don't want to, no, I don't!'

And as that cry rose, long and powerful, the temple's columns started to tremble and the head of the deity's statue began to wobble.

Thus, hand in hand, they joined the tour operator waiting for them at the hotel reception.

They walked along path through the rocks that became narrower and narrower, so much that, after a certain point, they had to proceed in a line. After a short walk, they reached a series of bays and coves, with little beaches, secluded from the public eye, in front of which a crystalline sea could be seen, calm and clear.

He stopped on one of the first beaches and, laying his beach towel on the sand, he declared his absolute determination to enjoy sunbathing: *Hic manebo optime!* He said, satisfied and sealed by the use of Latin. 'I'll stay here!' But she wanted to explore their surroundings iinstead, and so she walked along the coast, crossing three small coves, one after the other. When she reached the last beach available, she put on her goggles and mouthpiece and dove into the clear and shiny sea, letting herself drift towards the horizon. After she had swum for so long that she had lost all sense of time, she raised her head from the water and she could pick out his silhouette from afar: she admired his chiselled body coming out of the water and his blonde hair, glittering in the sun. Smiling, she put her head underwater again and swam towards him.

But when she came out again she could not help but see, hiding behind a rock, his body, naked and muscular, avidly sinking into that of the tour operator.

She had suffered for a long time from a persistent itch on her head. Each morning, while she dressed for work, she started scratching herself: it was an acute, unending, irresistible itch, so persistent that she just had to do it. And it went on and on for days and days: in the middle of a work meeting, in a difficult discussion, she often found herself asking: 'What am I doing? Do I scratch or not? I cannot do it here . . . What will they think?' And so she tried resisting the urge, hoping it would go away by itself. Sometimes it did, disappearing suddenly, as if it had come from nowhere: no warnings, no signs, it went away without traces, the same as it had come. Some other times, though, it did not pass, and her mind continued to go there: 'Maybe if I scratch it quickly, nobody will notice. I could pretend to be fixing my hair.' A quick movement, just a brushing touch where the itch was stronger and that moment of solace: just that alone seemed a blessing.

And yet, a few minutes later, the itch, again. Maybe not in the same place: before it had been on the temple, over her ear, but now it was between the neck and the start of her scalp. It would be much more embarrassing to scratch there. A scratch on the temple could be interpreted as a sign of intelligence, if she added a slight movement of the head: 'She's touching her head to support the effort of thinking: she must have a brilliant idea!' But scratching the nape of the neck was more difficult to hide, and definitely too embarrassing. 'Since it isn't even the first time that they have seen me doing this publicly, they could think that I have lice.' And so she sank into that vortex of thoughts: 'I'll scratch. No, I won't. I'll do it. No, I won't.' The itch came, the itch went.

One day, she decided to visit her mother. She had been on holiday for some weeks, even from the itch. She climbed the stairs of the building, dark and sombre, like all convents: the grey stone steps led to a square courtyard, with an arched porch and a big abandoned well in the centre. The building extended across two storeys along the four sides of the courtyard: the rooms were on the first floor, behind the arcades.

Entering the courtyard, she noticed a well-dressed woman, followed by a crowd of young women trying to get her attention. She must have been the new headmistress: an athletic type, quite slender, she wore a suit and a pair of fashionable glasses, from which she could see her curious eyes, perfectly made up. Her hair was styled impeccably, too: a short hairstyle, apparently simple, but actually one of the most difficult to maintain. It is well known that a style like that must be tended to constantly, a healthy dose of hairspray and a hairdresser's appointment every three weeks at least. Evidently, *she* was not someone who scratched her head in public. On the contrary, she looked perfectly confident in that entertained and entertaining form.

And she also seemed to be after an extremely important affair. In the line of young women following her, the last one, who had been overtaken by all the others, had stopped and, with the astonishment of someone who has lost all hope of ever receiving an answer, kept on repeating the same question: 'How does it work here? How do we get out?' She was very young, no older than fifteen, and she looked lost, as so many do at that age. Moved to compassion, the visitor walked towards the lost girl, saying: 'I'll answer your questions, don't worry. The headmistress is clearly too busy. Even though you're in here now, you can actually go out whenever you want, don't worry, you're not compelled to stay.' But the girl's eyes remained full of doubt. To reassure her, she ran towards the headmistress, and stopped firmly in front of her, asking the following question:

'Is it true, Ms. Headmistress, that she can leave whenever she wants?'

'Yes! Of course she can – if she wants,' the headmistress answered, decisively and efficiently, pronouncing the last three words in a descending and malicious tone.

The other woman hesitated for a moment, but then said: 'On this topic, I also wanted to tell you something else. I came here to meet my mother and I'm wondering, well, after all these years . . .,' she stopped for a moment, as if she was looking for the right words, but noticing the headmistress' impatient attitude, she quickly added: 'Well, yes, I wonder if after all these years it would be fine if my mother leaves this place, too. You know, she's very ill now, maybe it's time . . .'

'There's no problem: your mother is free to leave whenever she likes. If she wants, nobody is stopping her!' the headmistress answered, before reprising her half-run, with her following of young devoted disciples.

Feeling reassured, the woman proceeded to her mother's cell. Entering the small room, simple, but full of grace, she gazed upon that figure so familiar, maybe the most familiar of all, in the uncontested domain of those four walls. She found her mother thinner than the last time she'd seen her, but still elegant and slightly melancholic as usual. Her eyes were sad, but they immediately filled with a smile when she saw her daughter.

'Mum, how are you?' the daughter asked, hugging her. Being so close to her, she felt her breasts, still full and healthy, and the sweet smell of her skin, that had comforted her so many times as a child.

'Fine,' her mother answered, 'I'm fine.' She always answered like that, accompanying her words with a slight affectation, neatly suggesting that she was not fine at all, and that, on the contrary, she had never been fine and that, actually, she had never even known what it meant to be fine, and that she had answered that exact way, all her life, not to burden the others, but also, she had to admit, perhaps precisely to highlight by contrast how bad she actually was.

The daughter moved away, looking at her with the composed smile of somebody who has just received the answer they expected. 'Tell me again, Mum: what do you do here all this time? Aren't you bored?' And while her mother described each of her daily activities, the same ones she'd been doing for the past fifty years, the daughter had started to look around, impatient.

'I wake up early in the morning, because, you know, I go to bed early in the evening; sometimes I'm already awake at six, when it's still dark, and so I prepare the breakfast, then I shower, I start tidying up my room, then I tend to the garden . . .,' and she went on as her daughter examined every detail of the cell, watching her mother again from time to time, to reassure her that she was still listening. Until she noticed the bathroom, right beside her: she saw the toilet had some yellow spots, which had been there for years probably, and smelled of the sweet and acrid smell of urine. She immediately grabbed the toilet brush and, after telling her mother 'I'm listening!', she bent over the toilet and started scratching with all her strength: she scratched and scratched and scratched again, but those spots had been there for too long and were not so easy to erase. She scratched and scratched, with increasing rage. She would not surrender and, looking from time to time at her mother to confirm that she could still be heard, kept on with her angry scratching: the upper and most odiferous part seemed to have gone now, but there were still some long yellow stripes of urine and limestone. She then grabbed a toilet detergent, a very powerful one, one of those that can make you pass out if you inhale too closely, and directed it inside the toilet. By pressing strongly on the two sides of the bottle, she spread the cleaner all around, making sure she had covered even the most remote corners. In the end, the entire toilet was full of a dense foam, divided into small mounts, white and black, like the choux of a Gâteau Saint Honoré.

# IX. Maximum ten (with addendum)

So Maria Maddalena had spoken. Her tale, split into two at the top, reunited from the waist down, just like their body. They were two-headed beings more than all the others: different, very different, at times even opposite, but inseparable.

Afterwards, there was a long silence. The broken story, the presence, although temporary, of a man, had cast a veil of discomfort on the council. Moreover, the comrades looked even more tired than usual that evening. Besides the work on the fields and in the atelier, they had spent the day collecting weapons in the barn, because they had heard that there was the possibility of an attack.

'There's a man in the story again, and a cheater, too,' said Fiammetta, one of the possessed.

'Yes, but he disappears when the story reunites,' said Candida, standing an all fours with her head towards the floor, being a bent.

'In my opinion, we should reprise the discussion on polygamy. For now, we have only established the communion of children and goods,' added Luce, who had introduced the issue previously.

'Don't you believe the concept of polygamy itself drives the discussion in the very terms that we wanted to avoid?' said Annunziata, the mother.

'What do you mean?' asked Addolorata the depressed.

'It seems that polygamy can be discussed only in relation to monogamy, but if we want to radically subvert this order, maybe we should not just reverse into its opposite,' answered Annunziata.

'You're right . . .,' observed Miranda, one of the secluded, slightly raising her head from her turret. As with all the secluded, she seldom spoke in the council, and those few words captured the attention of many women, causing a wave of general puzzlement.

'Maybe we should call it polyandry?' said Gaia, one of the saved.

'What are you talking about? That's when you can have more than one man, and this is a community of women!' answered angrily Fiammetta the possessed.

'Polyamory! I propose that we call it the law of polyamory!' said Maddalena, while Maria immediately added a note of disappointment: 'That's a weird word!'

'I think that polyamory is a nice name! ' Candida observed.

'And it has been used for some time, to refer to loving more than one person at the same time: it can be one, two, three, four or as many as you want!' said Maddalena, with a gleeful tone.

'And thus we can also address the peculiarity of the possessed, who change gender according to the spirit that inhabit them at the moment, so they are never one properly speaking. With the law of polyamory, we can love without any distinction of gender. What do you think? Each one of us could be with whoever they want for how long they desire!' added Gaia, standing up with her lifebelt.

'Great idea! Great idea!' answered the other saved in unison.

'Wait, wait! And what do we do with long-lasting relationships? I mean, within this polyamory law there must be a place for those relationships that matter more than others, those built with time, of course disregarding any claim of exclusivity . . .,' said Annunziata, one of the mothers.

'No, I'd say that we tossed exclusivity away with the "mono", but it's true that those of us who have a tighter bond should be able to recognize that in some form. After all, you cannot love everyone in the same way and with the same intensity!' said Miranda.

'We have to be careful, though. There's a potential risk here. When relationships become institutionalized, with the time routine overwhelming them, desire fades and too often people stay together just out of habit. Like those plants that, being always very close, grow all crooked, and, in the end, you cannot even recognize which plant they are. We only want beautiful, thriving and fully autonomous plants! Flourishing with leaves on all sides!' said Luce, again.

'But we have to acknowledge some form of long-lasting union . . .,' answered Miranda, hopeful.

'Then I propose that there should be a limit: ten years. Each one of us can marry whoever they want and as many people as they want, but the union cannot last more than ten years,' said Sibilla, with the usual fire in her eyes.

'Ten years? Why ten and not, for example, eleven?' asked Annunziata.

'That is often the critical threshold: it's statistically proven. After ten years there's an unavoidable decline of desire and too often the relationships become empty, like those dead butterflies put under glass containers, which show off their beauty even while everybody knows they're lifeless,' said Sibilla, who then added: 'Imagine how different the outside societies would be if this simple rule was applied: marriages expiring after ten years with no possibility of extending them. Imagine how everybody would hurry and enjoy as much as they can of that limited time, how much suffering would be avoided, and what a constant regeneration we could enjoy!'

'Let alone sexuality: if it's true that it's always relational and it's built by two people, staying forever with the same person means limiting ourselves to only one configuration for an entire life!' added Luce.

'I always thought that it's an absurdity that the closer human beings get to death, the more they resist change: just because death comes ever nearer, one should hurry and experiment with everything, not avoid change. I thus propose the limit to be shortened to seven years, after a certain age,' said Sibilla.

'You say this because you're young, Sibilla. With time, you start appreciating other things, those that last, for example, because they have a riper sweetness that you cannot understand, since you've not yet tasted them . . .,' answered Annunziata, a bit disappointed.

'Nothing lasts! Everything flows, even death! Maybe it's exactly because we delude ourselves into thinking we can halt time that we stubbornly tend to keep everything the same. Like those rivers that, when water starts to dry up, cannot help but flow along the same path they had created when they were still in full force: if they could speak, they would say that it's so sweet to always move in the same direction as before!' answered Sibilla, showing off her well-known provocative attitude.

'But still, there has to be a possibility to keep a relationship just because . . . there's love? Why is nobody speaking about love here? Of course, we have to encourage change with appropriate institutional measures, like a fresh wind that can keep the water moving and prevent stagnation, so I suggest an addendum: ten years, seven after seventy, because after a certain age people are less inclined to change, but if the desire proves to be lasting and the union healthy, then the council of women could allow an extension. I think that seems quite a reasonable proposal,' said Annunziata.

'Great idea! Great idea!' said the other mothers. Given their influence, it was easy to convince even the possessed that this small adjustment was necessary. The vote took only a few seconds because the law was approved unanimously, after which the women went towards their dormitories. After the storm, the night had cleared. The tiredness resulting from both a long day at work and their heartfelt discussion threw the city of women into a particularly deep sleep.

# X.  The lifebelt

She was a marine creature. Born and raised in a fishing village, she saw water as her natural element. While air dried her skin and fire scared her, the sea was always welcoming, hugging her generously. Earth, especially that from the nearby forest, was a bit too hard.

She remembered, though, a moment in her life when the sea had scared her. She was a child: three, maybe four years old. Her father had taken her on a boat with her older sister for a fishing trip. The two children, who rarely saw their father, were very happy to go out with him that day. Fishing, which usually took their father away for weeks, and sometimes entire months, had united them instead, that one day. They left in the early morning: the sky was clear and the sea flat as a marble slab. Not even a wrinkle.

But when they reached the open sea, instead of taking out the fishing nets as they expected, the father looked at his daughters, asking them: 'Can you swim now?' The kids gazed at each other, not understanding well what the question meant, but they did not even have the time to answer before, one after the other, they found themselves in their father's arms, who tossed them into the sea.

Amina did not remember anything besides the impact of the huge mass of water that surrounded her and her father's voice that, as she found herself farther and farther from the boat, kept insisting: 'Swim! Swim towards me!' Had she drunk the salty seawater? Or had she learnt how to swim? Or had she tried to find her sister? She could not to tell, after so many years. She only remembered the terror created by the first impact with that shapeless mass.

Amina grew up like that, simple and savage, until one day, when she was already a woman, she had a surprise at home.

'Amina, my dear daughter, now you're an adult. It's time to think about your future," her mother had said. And she knew very well that sentence announced a change: they were looking for a spouse for her. But Amina did not feel ready and answered: 'I don't care about those things! I'm fine as I am!' and she went to the beach as usual, slamming the kitchen door.

Actually, she really had grown up. Some days before, while walking to the river with her sisters, she met somebody from the neighbouring village: she encountered those eyes just for a moment, but Amina had not stopped thinking about them ever since. Those eyes were the first thing she saw when she woke up in the morning and the last in the evening before going to bed. She did not know anything about them: only that those eyes, looking at her, that morning at the river, had suddenly become yellow, bright as two suns.

She often dreamt of them at night. Like that day, when she dove into the crystalline waters of the bay and, while swimming with her eyes open, noticed a metal plaque sticking out of the sand. After cleaning it with her hand, she tried to look closer to decipher the words engraved on it, but instead of the words, she saw that creature with yellow burning eyes coming towards her, smiling under the waves.

But the law was unavoidable. The elders would select her spouse and she could not do anything about it. The day set for the wedding came closer and closer. Her aunt, along with her cousins of marriageable age, arrived one day to bring her wedding dress. This was a special moment: all the women from the village would soon come, throughout the day, bringing gifts that the future bride would take with her as a dowry, and she and her mother would show them her wedding gown.

'What's wrong, Amina? Don't you like the dress?' said her aunt, measuring her while she modelled the dress that she had brought, as if the perfection of its shape had the magical ability of casting away any doubt. 'Please, wear it now, the guests will arrive soon!'

Noticing her niece's silence, she added, looking at Amina's mother with sudden doubt: 'I thought that green was your favourite colour: did you change your mind?'

'No, it's not that, but, you see . . .,' answered Amina, her eyes cast down as if the splendour of her dress had made them even heavier.

'What else, then? Aren't you happy to meet your spouse soon? What's that face?'

'Auntie, I don't want to get married!' answered Amina, wincing and frowning with rage.

'And why not, dear? You're of age now, and you'll see how lovely it is, life as a married woman!' she tried to convince her niece.

'I don't want to marry anyone!' answered Amina, bursting into tears, with long and loud sobs. And her aunt's words, the gifts from the village women, and even the delicious feast prepared for the occasion felt completely useless. Everything that announced the coming wedding caused her anxiety and terror.

And with the same fear in her eyes Amina woke the next day. While everyone in the house was busy for the impending arrival of the future spouse, she ran down to the beach, and hid in the net shed. Smelling again the green scent of fishing, of those nets that had been launched into the sea so many times, Amina thought about that day when her father had thrown her into the water with a wide movement of his arm.

And raising her eyes from those bundles entangled unto themselves, as if to stop the tears that rose into her eyes, she noticed an old lifebelt in a corner of the shed, white, hard, with red stripes and a tangled rope. She went closer, now curious, but she did not even have time to take it into her hands when, turning towards the sound of approaching steps, she saw those eyes, bright as two suns, even brighter in the dim light of the shed.

# XI. The threat

Just before the dawn, the keeper of the oven of opposites sounded the alarm. That night it noticed a cluster of little red lights on the horizon. In the dark, they looked like a shapeless mass, unintelligible. But the spot grew visibly greater and greater, and the lights became stronger and stronger, and they seemed to be heading directly for the city of women.

Its nature was not clear, though. There was a sense that it could be an army from the city of men. As nobody was certain about it, they could not discard the hypothesis. Fearing imminent attack aimed at conquering their city, the women left their usual jobs and started cleaning the weapons stocked in the barn and preparing cauldrons of boiling oil to stack on the towers. Some tended to food supplies, stocking and sorting them in case of a siege, because sieges can last for a very long time indeed. After the doors to the city of women had been closed for the night, they could easily see the glimmer of irons and the flames of torches in the approaching mass.

# Epilogue

you say that you don't want to hurt me, but it's actually what you want, i can see it in your eyes, there's too much ager there, and yet i don't know why i deserve it, it's okay, let's do it, as if the usual pains of life weren't enough, let's kill each other with words, too, as sharp as possible, and now i'd love to have a pair of earplugs, because i don't want to listen to any words, those that barrel down like a lorry on the motorway, please stop talking and let's go and buy earplugs, no, not that road, they only have opticians, and mine are fine like this, as rudimental as they are, and no, neither that one, they're specialized in teeth, and my teeth are good too, so much that i decided not to open my mouth again, like a pigeon, yes, that's what i'd want to be now, a pigeon, the most inconspicuous of birds, you can find them everywhere, and they don't say anything, because they're all the same anyway, a pigeon, with a nice pair of earplugs, and two wings to fly away, in case you try to tell me something again, why didn't you let me fly away, i could be up there now, far away, and still down here instead, beside you, and you even want to kiss me, how can you dare think about it, after all you've told me, and the hurt you've done to me, and your eyes look even angrier than yesterday, but i'm the one who should be angry, and yet you are, just when i'm so vulnerable, you come out with all this rage, where does it come from, maybe you've been nurturing it for some time, because this isn't a temporary bout of rage, maybe behind the city of women there's a full city of men, because a men-only city is much easier to manage than one with men and women together, but there are no women without men, and so the city of women, that now is falling, takes with it the city of men, its buildings fall, one by one, the well-fortified walls fall, its inhabitants fade away too, they disappear like ghosts, everything disappears, vanishes, in a sort of cosmic apocalypse, the walls fall, the houses, the well-ordered streets, the well-shaped bodies, this gives me a huge pain though, look, right here, in the middle of my chest, you see, between my breasts, it's a dull pain, stinging, what are you doing with that sock and those weird words, a magic trick, you want to do a magic trick to cure me, it's a terrible idea, with a sock, waving it on my chest, as if it were a magic wand and those meaningless words, abracadabra abracadì, a magician with a sock, which is also a bit worn out, you must have walked a lot in there, but you shake it smiling, and it's contagious, and so the pain disappears and i burst laughing too, and the more i laugh, the more it seems that flowers are coming out of my skin, as if someone had sawn them there with many gleeful passions, and i laugh, and i cannot stop, and poppies come out of my mouth, gladioli from my cheeks, cornflowers bloom in my ears, and i laugh, and flowers bloom everywhere, in all my body, in all my organs, as if it were spring, as if every pore of my body contained a seed, a poppy, a gladiolus, or whatever else, and a flower, a flower put there carefully, by a magician, a laughing magician, a magician laughing and waving now a worn-out sock on my chest

# Intermission

*Today the sun is over the square: it's high warm direct.*
*You sweat even without a jacket, there is so much light.*
*The police are gone: no more cordons,*
*No more clenched-teeth smiles*
*And the pigeons come and go freely: gleeful,*
*They fly in all directions.*

*The guappo is dead, the guappo is no more.*
*And where's the myth? The myth is no more.*
*And where are the sultan, drunk with desire,*
*And Theseus the hero of the labyrinth,*
*And Zeus turning bull to kidnap Europa?*
*The guappo is dead, and the myth is no more.*
*I wanted the myth and I find myself with a hu-man*
*And they also have tears in their eyes.*
*I'd want to be a pigeon, a pigeon I said.*
*Without ears and without words.*
*A pigeon, the most inconspicuous of birds,*
*Of those there are so many,*
*And even if you steal one, nobody will notice.*
*Pigeon, the most common, the most obvious of all,*
*Without mouths and without ears:*
*And I found myself a philosophy professor instead,*
*And I talk and listen, I talk and listen all the time.*

*And the guappo is dead, the guappo is no more.*

# PART THREE

# Bestiarium

# Prologue

two myths and a half, three, maybe four, mathematics has never been my thing, even though it was quite easy in high school, so easy that i did it extremely quickly, but sometimes you have to be patient, because it may seem that you're finished counting, and yet there is still homework to do, that exercise you forgot, or the other one you wondered whether it made sense to do it now, since school is over, but myth is like desire, and you tell one, and it seems that you have reached a conclusion, but there's another behind that right away, because it's a never-ending work, a never-ending journey, traversing the fantasy, which is also its reality, because myth doesn't wait for reality to come and say 'hello!' with the morning coffee, no, it just builds its own reality, and from the empty desire of the tennis match, it walked through an entire labyrinth of story-telling, and we tangled so many pretty little dresses, and so many pretty flower crowns, that we even seduced a bull that brought us to a new city, a city of women, where there was no minotaur, no unholy beast that swallowed one youngling after the other, but women, only women, nothing more than women, and if it wasn't that there were perhaps too many women, i would have stayed there much longer, because i really liked it there, but i didn't want to be angry all the time, and so i prefer to take back the 'thread', as i have the impression that everything was there, so maybe i need to learn how to be an animal again, a different metamorphosis though, because it is no longer a god turning into a bull, nor europa to become the prey of the beast-god, but a transindividual metamorphosis this time, and it's incredible how everything holds together now, and it even seems that this book has written itself, like we said at the beginning too, because the language speaks, but images do that even better, and they have spoken for all this time, even though nobody wanted to listen to them, it's incredible, almost incredible, everything was there, from the beginning, in the image

# I. The ostrich

'Good morning, ma'am. I'd like to talk with Mr Vatteroni: is he there? It's one of his pupils here,' said Clara, nervously hugging her teddy bear tight, as she did every time she had to make a phone call.

'Good morning, Clara, I think he's still sleeping, but wait, I'll call him,' answered the teacher's wife as usual, with her subtle and slightly nasal voice.

'No, please, don't worry. I'll call again later.'

'No, no, it's not a problem, it's time for him to wake up: it's already three o'clock.'

'But I can call back . . .'

'Hello?'

'Oh, hello Mr Vatteroni, it's Clara, I'm so sorry to bother you. I told your wife that there was no need to wake you up. It's not that important, after all . . .'

'Don't worry, I was already up. Please, tell me.'

'Well, so, I called because, you know, I told you . . . the Encyclopaedia, the one that my grandmother gifted me, do you remember? The Encyclopaedia, the one with all those volumes and a golden binding and full of stories, well, I was telling myself, maybe I could write a little essay.'

'Another one?'

'Well, yes, you see, I've already finished my homework for tomorrow, and I have all the afternoon free and so, I thought, if you have nothing against it, maybe I could write a little essay: on a new topic, I don't really know, but I'm thinking about a couple of things . . .'

'Well, okay. What's the topic this time?'

'So . . . I was thinking . . . what do you think about the ostrich? I could write an essay on the ostrich.'

'The ostrich?'

'Yes, the ostrich. The bird with black feathers, thin legs and a long neck like a giraffe. The one that lays big eggs, as big as footballs, but can't fly. The ostrich . . .'

'The ostrich, okay, write an essay on the ostrich.'

'Thank you, Mr Vatteroni, thank you so much! I'll bring it to you tomorrow. And sorry again for waking you up!'

Mr Vatteroni was a tall, thin man. He looked austere, but also very sweet: a slightly receding hairline, always well shaven, a crooked nose and brown eyes with eyelashes so long that they made him look like a camel. Despite his strictness and his fondness for a tie that always exactly matched his jacket, he was very much loved by his students.

When Clara wrote her little essays, he opened her notebook with a stern look, as if this was the most serious of all businesses. He usually marked them during recess, while his pupils played in the school courtyard. When she returned to class, Clara went and took back her notebook from her teacher's desk and, her heart pounding with excitement, walked towards the back of the classroom. She was the tallest pupil, so they always put her on the back row. Walking to her desk, her notebook under her arm, in the clanging sound of the last minutes of recess, Clara imagined what she would find: maybe a 'brava', rigorously written in red ink, beside the text of the essay, or maybe even a 'bravissima', which always gave her the peculiar joy of a *non plus ultra*. When she opened the notebook, she looked at the length of the mark first: if it was short, it should be a 'brava', but if it was long, it must be one of those 'bravissima', penned with a sinuous 'b', in precise but waving calligraphy, like the sea after a storm. It was impossible for it to be merely 'sufficient': Clara never went under a certain threshold.

Lately, moreover, she had started to add a drawing to her work, as illustration. But when she drew, she was always very careful to leave enough space for the teacher's mark, because the size of the latter counted too. Despite the lack of rules about this, a very big 'brava' could count as much as a very small 'bravissima'. And her joy was immense that day when, beside the drawing of the ostrich with pink legs and a feathery belly, Clara saw a 'bravissima' written in tight letters but very long, and big, as big as the drawing of the ostrich. She had been particularly careful with that image, because that bird with sly eyes had made such a deep impression on her.

Shortly after Clara wrote the ostrich essay, Mr Vatteroni fell ill. They sent a substitute for him. No one knew how long he would be away. The new teacher was short and portly, with a pink face and a broad squashed nose, so much so that he looked like a pig in his short and tight jacket and unmatched tie. As if this was not enough, big scales of dandruff used to fall from his red greasy hair in sheaves, which accumulated on his bottleneck shoulders and sometimes fell on the class register. He even spent all his time reading the *Sports Gazette*: all pink, too.

Clara stopped bringing her little essays to school and sometimes asked when Mr Vatteroni would come back. But nobody knew.

'Clara, come and play volleyball,' asked her sister that afternoon.

'I have to finish my homework.'

'Come on, you can finish it later!'

'No, I want to finish it now, and you know that Mum doesn't want us to play with a ball in the bedroom.'

'But it's raining, and I'm bored.'

'Do your homework too!'

'Come on, just a couple of bounces, maybe one smash, please?'

Clara had indeed finished her homework and was working on one of her little essays. Mr Vatteroni had not come back yet, but she had started doing them on her own. It was also true, though, that a couple of bounces would not hurt her. She had been part of the school volleyball team for some time, and loved that game. And after a brief hesitation, she accepted the invitation.

She was in front of the fireplace as usual. It was an old one and made of marble, white as a statue, engraved as a floral pattern with the head of Medusa in the centre, around which decorative lines emerged, like rays of the sun. Clara stood there. Her torso bent forwards and her legs slightly open, she waited for the ball: she usually played as setter, but was good in reception too.

'Are you ready?'

'Yes, go on, but use the foam ball, otherwise we'll break something.'

'Okay, fine.'

She would have enjoyed the match much more with a real volleyball, white, with regular stripes. Moreover, Clara loved the smell of leather. The foam one, on the contrary, besides its dust, was less bouncy and so was more difficult to aim properly. But it was safer for a bedroom, and so they started playing with that.

A toss here, a bounce there, ready to smash, nice reception (the good thing about this ball was that it did not hurt her wrists), now lift the ball again, a good long bounce, with a nice push from the legs (because a nice lift starts from the legs). But the smash was too high this time, Clara moved aside to avoid it going straight into her face, but the ball went, in all its strength, into a painting over the fireplace, which, already in an unstable position, fell on a quartz with tapered points: the latter, with all its weight, right on Clara's foot.

A scream of pain. Her mother ran in – 'what have you done this time?' – blood everywhere, a dash to the emergency room. A bleak diagnosis: a broken bone, nothing too serious, but, because of all those gashes due to the crystals, it could not be put in a cast, as the wounds would become infected. They had to dress and tend the wounds regularly, being careful not to move the foot. For at least a month Clara would wear a special blue canvas shoe, tied with a navy shoelace, that adapted to the bandages while letting the skin breathe.

A few days – and a few adjustments – later, she could go back to school. But she returned to bad news: Mr Vatteroni had died. That morning the school headmistress, a tall and elegant woman, came into the classroom right after the start of the lessons to inform the students that the funeral would be the next day. They answered with silence.

Clara had never seen a coffin before. In walnut wood, well polished, it left the church covered in flowers. A garland with a black sash, bearing the script: 'From the pupils of the Aurelio Saffi School.' After the ceremony, the funeral procession moved towards the cemetery. Mr Vatteroni's pupils led the way. Getting closer to each other, they walked in their black uniforms, which looked even darker that rainy autumn afternoon.

Clara watched her bandaged foot. It was still swollen, tight in the shoe that made her limp. But she *could* walk and would follow her teacher for the last time. And while she lifted the swollen foot, in a peculiarly slow motion, making her thin legs look even longer, she felt something strange happening to her body: her legs became more and more tapered, even as her torso shortened. Her toes, after breaking through the shoes, were getting bigger and were merging into a tryptic, while the smooth skin of her childlike calves became thicker. She felt hair growing on her skin, while her bottom became rounder, and from her black uniform sprouted many feathers, long and dense. Her arms bent, edging closer to the body like wings, and becoming covered with dark feathers, just as her white collar thickened and became puffy. And the shorter her body became, the longer her legs grew. Her teeth sank into her gums, and from her mouth, a beak sprouted, as if someone had pulled it from her lips. And while everybody was looking at the metamorphosis in awe, Clara continued walking, sinuously lifting her bird legs until, after one last step, she finally flew up towards the blue sky, suddenly flapping her great wings, as lightly as if she was a butterfly.

# II. The butterfly

*Papilio Ulysses*: a framed butterfly, such a nice idea for a birthday gift. It is so beautiful, with its wings as black as night and the blue blooming inside it like a flower! A peculiar butterfly, though. Whatever that means.

*'Sir, we're approaching the land of the sirens. You can already spot the shining rocks. We have to take shelter: nobody can resist their singing, and we could wreck the ship – it's happened before to those who've been too bold. We have to be careful: let's change course.'*

*'Ulysses, hero of all the seas, come, come to us, we're waiting for you! We'll sing for you the most sublime song that has ever been composed! Come to us! We'll pluck the most precious flowers and throw them on your glorious path to honour you through their beauty and smell! Come to us and we'll even steal the light from the stars to adorn your dark and severe head! Ulysses, hero of all the seas, you who defeated all your enemies, smartest of the smartest, come, come to us, listen to our love song!*

The *papilio Ulysses* is a butterfly of an endemic species of Australian Papilionidae and, because of its beauty, is used as a symbol of tourism. Its wingspan is around ten centimetres, although it can go up to fourteen, depending on the different species. The top part of its wings is coloured, black in the foremost part and bright blue at the centre, while the back is quite neutral, in grey-brown shades. The iridescent blue that makes this butterfly peculiarly attractive is not due to pigments on the wings, but rather the effect of how light refracts off the uneven surface, a phenomenon known as structured colouring. When its wings are closed, the butterfly manages to camouflage itself quite easily in the surrounding environment. When flying, however, its colours manifest in all their brightness, and it can be seen from a great distance. The males, slightly smaller than the females, are so attracted by this bright blue that they have often been observed following objects of the same shade, mistaking them for females of their species.

*'Change course? But I want to listen to this song: nothing is more sublime than the song of the sirens!'*

*'But sir, it's too dangerous: nobody has ever come back from the sirens' rock. This folly risks putting the ship and the entire crew in danger. Please give up this crazy plan! Don't give in to temptation! What will happen to us and to our families who wait for us! Haven't we done enough in all these years of adventures and endless wandering? We survived the Cyclops, and Circe, and the endless storms. When will all this suffering end? How many people will have to die before we can go home? What other misfortune awaits us?'*

*'I have to listen to that song, I have to listen to that song . . .'*

*'Don't do it, sir! Don't do it! It's a trap! Even the poet says that behind their sweet melody there's nothing but death and desolation . . .'*

Like all butterflies, the *papilio Ulysses* is a symbol of metamorphosis too, of the passage from one state to another. For the Indigenous Peoples of Australia, the larvae of the butterfly embodies the spirits who have come back to life after passing through death; for the Aztecs, they symbolize the heroic souls of mothers who died while giving birth. In Eastern cultures, on the contrary, the quiet but constant transformation of larvae is often interpreted as a sign of spiritual evolution through contemplation. In addition to being a symbol of transformation and renewal after traumatic events, butterflies are one of the most poetic images of erotica. Its flight, the light and quick movement of the wings, recall the pace of sexual desire, while the sweet nectars on which adult butterflies feed recall the exquisite sweetness of amorous encounters. But the shortness of its life cycle, and its flying from one flower to the other, also symbolize its inconsistence and the erratic nature of desire. In South America, the term *mariposa* means both butterfly and prostitute. The dark side of the butterfly, who lives mostly by day, is the moth, who lives by night, and whose attraction towards light is often associated to the potentially obsessive and compulsive character of desire. Because of this ambivalence, the butterfly is one of the most potent symbols of libido, both in its self-destructive capacity, and in the much more positive version of a transformative elaboration.

*'Here we'll test my nobility: we'll soon see what hides behind those sublime voices. We'll pass by the sirens' rock and listen to their song from start to finish. Open your ears, lads, but be ready to close them again, and prepare the sails. Give a nice big meal to the rowers, because we'll need all their strength, and reinforce the ship, hang sacks of sand on the ram, to protect us from the stormy sea.'*
*'But it's too dangerous, sir! Let's go back, we still have time!'*
*'Come Ulysses, come to us hero of all the seas, come to these sirens' arms, we're waiting for you. Come, come, son of Laertes, come and listen to our love song . . .'*

The life cycle of a butterfly is variable, but has four key phases: egg, larva, pupa and adult. The fertilized female lays her eggs on some leaves, where the larva usually fulfils its cycle. Since butterflies feed only on sweet nectars, the caterpillar needs to accumulate sufficient protein and fats to sustain the entire lifecycle. And this is why larvae feed voraciously, so much so that one can multiply its own weight by eight thousand times in its short life. This incredible growth is accompanied by many moultings, where the surface hardens until it sheds from the body, now covered by new skin. Because the larva adheres completely to the surface on which it moves, it is subject to constant friction, which is why it has to change its skin so often.

*'We've had so many adventures; we'll survive this, too. Bind me to the ship's mast with a rope: we need a long, but also a strong one, capable of resisting – like this one, for example, made in silk. Let it be my anchor, so that I can visit the sirens' rock, but find my way back too, in case I should lose it. You, my trusted friend, will stay here, close to the mast and ready to pull back the thread, when the time comes, while the other companions, with their ears full of wax, will remain alert rowers with their incorrupt judgement . . .'*

In order to transform, the caterpillar must choose an appropriate stem, to which it attaches by weaving a silk cushion, with a variable length of thread. Once it is firmly attached to its chosen support, the caterpillar's cocoon breaks and the pupa comes out. A series of convulsions pushes the caterpillar's cuticle towards its tail. The old skin is thus abandoned and a row of hooks is stuck to the silk cushion. It is only at this stage of evolution that the pupa assumes its definitive shape and the colour of the adult butterfly becomes visible.

*'This song is so beautiful! Here I am, magnificent sirens! I'm ready to dive into your loving arms! It's such a joy! Such a wonder! It's so sweet to drift on the waves! This is so delicious! How sublime! Here I am, beloved sirens, I'm all yours!'*

The main metamorphosis occurs only when the pupa is shaken by violent contractions that reverberate through its entire body. As the spasms grow quicker and more intense, its body starts to spin, until a sudden break occurs: this is the mark of its passage to a different form of existence. It is quite a long process, in which the contractions detach the pupa from its chrysalis, preparing its passage to a properly adult stage.

*'What are all these bones? It's so barren around here! Where are all the bright colours that we could see from afar? Sirens! Beloved sirens with your sublime song, where are you? And where is the loving embrace that you promised me? And the crown of stars to adorn my head? And the flower petals to welcome my feet? The song has disappeared, and there's only death and despair here, and the foul stench of corpses, and the waves rise, the sea is growing and the sky looks menacing . . .*

*'The ship, where is my ship? Quick, lads! Take me back on board! Take me back! Yes, this way! Quick, on your seats! The storm is coming! Quickly, quickly! Hoist the sails, beware the waves, to the south, where the sky seems to open! Come on, comrades, row! Come on, we can do it!'*

Contraction after contraction, the chrysalis finally opens to let out the butterfly: first antennae, then head, and lastly the entire body leaves its pod and the thread that protected its metamorphosis. Its wings, still numb, need several minutes to be open fully before being able to fly, but its body is already in its definitive form.

'Finally, it has opened! And the glass is broken! Now I can go back to life and fly over these beautiful flower fields, and spread my wings, in their iridescent blue, and mix it with those butterflies down there, with those nice pink stripes, and taste the sweet, sweet nectar of the flowers that I like so much.

'But . . . what is happening? My wings, my wings are getting numb, and they're losing their span, as if they're becoming arms, and it seems that I can even see hands growing, while my antennae, my antennae are shortening, and my mouth is opening, and teeth are growing inside it! Teeth! I have teeth in my mouth! And my tail is splitting, and two legs are taking shape, as if someone was pulling them violently out, and I have feet as well, I have feet to walk in, it's so weird, I can flap them one in front of the other, and my wings are gone, and I cannot fly anymore, no, but I have feet, yes, I have feet, big and strong feet, to walk on the earth, yes, on the living earth . . .

'And Argo! Yes, Argo! My faithful dog, you've been waiting for me all this time, and you recognized me, Argo, it's me, Ulysses, your master: and I am back . . .'

# III. The dog

She got a dog because she failed with horses. Those were her sister's passion: she drew them over and over again, she rode everything she could, the rocking horse that was given to her at Christmas, the kitchen chairs, the flower vases on the balcony, and even their dog Calin, which died after a spine rupture, because he could not bear the umpteenth fence-jump with a rider.

It was after that unpleasant incident that their father understood that this passion needed a different outlet. And so her sister had started going to riding classes. Even though she was too tall to be a professional jockey, she had a certain grace and an undeniable prowess. But she enjoyed the actual contact with those animals more than the sport itself: she took care of horses with such tender devotion, and you only needed to see this for a moment to understand that she could not care less about all those rules and how to correctly trot and gallop. She just loved those creatures.

Their father started taking them to the stables each Sunday. They usually left in the morning, when the sun was already high, in their three-seat sports car. Even though Clara had no interest in horses, she enjoyed that little Sunday trip: the chance to spend time with her father more than made up for the boring afternoon spent watching her sister on horseback.

One day, though, they managed to convince her to ride. The size of the beast, its height, made her feel tiny and insignificant, while the thought of being so far from the ground once up there had previously discouraged her. But the idea of a walk on the beach, in a straight line, with her father, sister and instructor, had won her over. And so, it happened that on that particular Sunday morning she mounted a horse. It was a Maremmano, with a large build and dark brown fur, leaning towards black, known both for its kindness and for being very stubborn. But it was smaller than the English pureblood ridden by her sister and this was somehow reassuring.

'You don't have to do anything: just hold the reins, put your feet in the stirrups, and move your hips according to the movement of the horse. We're going slowly, and horses always follow those in front of them, there's nothing to be afraid of, nothing at all.' So the instructor had said, helping her mount, and so she did, feeling reassured. The party left on schedule: the instructor first in line, then her older sister, and then her, with the father behind.

The horses walked neatly in line along the path that led to the beach. It was a nice autumn morning, and the slightly yellowing bushes reminded them that summer had only recently left. Their pace was more regular than expected, with striding horses and swaying riders, until they reached the dunes. As if the rough sea and the sound of the waves had suddenly woken a slumbering rage, the instructor said it was the time to move into a trot: 'Up and down with the hips, push from the stirrups, feel the pace of the horse: as I said before, there's nothing to worry about.' It seemed easy enough and she had seen her sister do it so many times that she did not hesitate.

But something was wrong, because the horse started shying, tossing his black mane and snorting nervously, until, racing out of the line, he started galloping, tossing Clara everywhere. It was useless to try to reprise the 'up and down' or attempt to calm the beast: the reins had slipped from her hands, so she could only grab onto its mane and hope that someone could slow it down. And the instructor's orders were equally useless: the horse stopped running only when it brought her finally back to a nice bale of hay.

After dismounting the horse, she was so shaken that she could barely walk. She felt as if she had lost control of her legs and every part of her body, as if it was not hers anymore, with all those tense muscles and rattled teeth. Only a few hours after, when her body was back again, she felt discomfort between her legs, a pain that had not even occurred to her in the rush of that crazy ride. Feeling the sticky warmth of blood stuck to both sides of her trousers, she finally understood what had happened: it was then she swore that she would never ride a horse again.

But she kept on going with her sister to the stables for her riding lessons. Instead of sitting and watching, she started walking around though. Coming back from one of those walks she met Pepe. He was a small poodle, a few weeks old, slightly bigger than a foot, even though he was already cheeky and lively in his curly fur. He was as dark as a grain of pepper, exactly like his name, with bright eyes peeping out from the curly fur and a perfectly designed little nose that looked like a button. He was sleeping in his owner's shoe, in the stable among abandoned tools, but when he saw the child he immediately rose on his tiny fierce paws and ran towards her, as if they were lifelong companions.

Since then, Clara had spent all her time at the stables playing with the little dog. Indeed, they became friends. As soon as the car pulled into the car park every Sunday morning, Pepe ran towards her, with his pink tongue out, willing to play. This growing intimacy allowed her to notice the minuscule white spot that Pepe had on his right nostril: as if it was there to confirm the absolute raven black of his fur.

And it was in honor of that intimacy that one day, finding the dog sick, she asked her mother for permission to bring him home. Pepe had been gifted to the owner of the stables. But he was not a great dog lover, and, even though Pepe was of a very rare breed, he was left to the occasional care of guests of the stables. Therefore, the owner did not hesitate in acceding to the child's request, as long as he was given back the value of the dog, in the (then very unlikely) case that the animal survived the illness.

And thus Pepe, whom she had met because she had failed with horses, became her mother's dog instead. Right after entering their home, the two showed a special affinity. Maybe, Clara told herself at first, because it was her mother that fed him regularly: while it was Clara that spent most of her time with him, it was her mother who took care of his vital needs. But then she was convinced that it had to be a deeper reason, some sort of affinity in their physical resemblance which prefigured a more profound and spiritual one. She had noticed that throughout her life – as if by some unwritten law – dogs and their masters often make a perfect match, as if they had chosen each other symbiotically: it was in fact not unusual to meet Great Danes accompanied by a master just as tall and heavy, or chihuahuas with similarly petite little owner-creatures, or, finally, curly poodles with an elegant walk like Pepe accompanied by human beings with the very same characteristics. And given the inevitability of that law, Clara threw in the towel: Pepe and her mother were made for each other, so much so that when she took him for a walk, it seemed the red of her stiletto shoes merged into the red of the dog's bejewelled lead, and the black of her coat into that of his fur, as if they were one and the same creature moving gracefully through the streets.

Ten years later, when she left her parents' house, Clara did not even ask herself about Pepe's future – it was in the nature of things that he had to stay with her mother. But she took along a photo from her childhood: it was the dog, still a puppy, dressed in a blue lace hat and red stilettos that in fact came from her mother's wardrobe but which somehow fit the dog's style too.

And she was thinking about that photo one day, years later, as she was returning home to visit her mother. For some time, Pepe, whose breed has an incredibly long lifespan, had started to show his age. His fur had greyed, his eyes were veiled by cataracts, his teeth had fallen out completely. They started wondering whether it was time to put an end to his torment with a gentle death, administered compassionately by the vet.

But the pet seemed to anticipate the owner: as soon as she entered the door, Clara saw her mother coming towards her, carrying that prone body and announcing his death. She found herself holding him like that, unresponsive and inert. And while she watched that fading face, which she had stroked so many times as a child, she noticed it was not yet completely without life. The dog had in fact moved his head slightly, to draw a few last breaths, when on his skull, among the sparse fur that was left there, a long crack suddenly opened, as if it were a vulva, from which three springs slowly emerged: one after the other.

# IV. The snake

Pepe's favourite place had been her aunt and uncle's old house. There Pepe hid every time when, after having been scolded for some misdeed, he disappeared, with the tail between his legs. As small as he was, he had learned how to jump on the glass door handle and enter the abandoned house. It was a big apartment accessible through the same hallway as Clara's house. Just before they brought Pepe home, her uncle had died, his wife had moved away, and the house remained empty.

It was a terrible loss for everyone. Uncle Pietro, 'Uncle Piè' for brevity, as if the impulse of those three letters better suited his personality, was a very direct type, thin, like those three letters, but extremely neat. His wife, on the contrary, was small and fat, so much so that she needed a cane to walk. Seeing them together, one would think they were in an ontologically compensative relationship, as if one's excessive height was the direct and unavoidable effect of the other's width, and vice versa.

Even their apartment seemed to continue this logic: the hallway – long and narrow, like him – was flanked by extremely wide rooms, almost exaggerated, just like her. From this imponderable equation of opposites, and from the reserved character of the couple, stemmed an allure of fascination and mystery. Neither Uncle Pietro's mild temperament, nor his wife's expressive wisdom, could dissipate the aura that shrouded the couple and their house: both were at the same time extremely close and extremely remote for everyone.

That mysterious aura seemed to grow greater the further you walked down the long corridor. It was as if the apartment's reception room, because of its physical proximity, was easier to understand than those further down, where guests were rarely allowed. Thus their bedroom, for example, was subject to wild speculation, and the living room right next to it seemed incredibly mysterious even when it hosted the most trivial of activities. It was there in fact that Uncle Pietro brought the children to give them sweets: he went solemnly to the engraved mahogany cupboard and, putting his hand in a jar stored so high up that even he had to be on tiptoes to reach, fished out a fistful.

To make the children laugh, he first crinkled the candies' transparent wrapping, hiding them, until, with both of his hands closed, he asked each which one they wanted. And, by another mysterious law of that house, they always chose the one that the other sister wanted. Hence the lengthy bargaining process between the two sisters, which inevitably postponed the pleasure, but promised an even greater one.

But this never reduced Clara's enjoyment, which unquestionably started with that seducing, pinching noise: as soon as she recognized the sound of Uncle Piè's jelly sweets, her mind flew towards her favourite bakery and its owner, who had the similarly sweet and supple name of Trudina. 'Trudina, Trudina, mon amour!' she always said, while she melted these jellies in her mouth, dreamily. And, like magic, she then saw in front of her the worn-out furniture and the white marble bar, and all the mirrored shelves the old baker had to navigate in order to serve her customers, all of whom were entranced by the smell of melted butter and vanilla sugar.

Clara often thought about those childhood dreams, when, as a teenager, she snuck into her uncle's abandoned house. There, for example, after following Pepe, she had smoked her first cigarette. It had been given to her by her sister, who told her that most likely she would not like it. 'It takes some time to get used to smoking: the first time, you'll feel like suffocating, but then, maybe, you'll start appreciating it.'

Predicting that it would happen just like that, not knowing that immediate pleasure awaited her, Clara pushed open the apartment's glass door on a bright winter afternoon, holding a pack of cigarettes. The house was empty, except for Pepe the dog, who introduced her into the apartment with obvious complicity. After passing through the first few rooms, she felt her heart pounding with excitement: the fact that no one lived in the house anymore had not diminished its mystery. On the contrary. It was as if the apartment could now host every kind of new and extravagant creature: maybe the ghosts of her dead relatives playing cards with a woman carrying a scythe, or maybe those of their forebears, and perhaps even Trudina's ghost, Trudina, mon amour, with her sweet fruit jellies: the possibilities of that empty space were infinite.

With her forbidden object in one hand and a matchbox in her pocket, Clara walked along the corridor, Pepe following her, shyly. He would keep the secret. When she reached the rooms at the end, she hesitated in choosing one of them: her uncle's old bedroom was too full of sad memories, because, even though she had not nursed him, she had imagined her dying uncle there too many times. Actually, to tell the truth, that room also scared her a bit too much. She went therefore for the living room, a nicely open room, with two big windows on the two sides, a space that, at the height of that sunny afternoon, felt like a valley of light.

She opened the window facing an abandoned Sicilian garden and, with slightly trembling hands, lit the match. The smell of burnt brimstone touched her nostrils as she brought the cigarette to her lips. Her first sensation was pure pleasure: the sweet flavour of smoke mingled with that of burning wood. Bringing the match closer to the end of the cigarette, she drew the first puff: her lips, as relaxed as those of a habitual smoker, held the cigarette easily, letting the smoke flow inside her throat and into her chest.

And the pleasant sensation went on, when she brought the cigarette to her mouth again with two fingers and drew another puff of smoke, let it descend inside her, and then let it out with a slight outwards movement of her lips. Her head started feeling a bit lighter now, but it was far from unpleasant. She loved smoking.

She had almost finished her first cigarette, when she suddenly heard a noise in the corridor. She immediately thought that it must be the dog, even though she could not associate that noise with him at that moment. It clearly came from the corridor, though, and Pepe was no longer beside her. She put out the cigarette, closed the window and went towards the sound, but as soon as she crossed the door, she saw something that shocked her: instead of the dog there was, hanging from the ceiling, a long and chubby snake, its skin so soft and velvety that it looked more like a stuffed animal than a live reptile. As soon as Clara arrived, the snake crossed the corridor with a quick and sudden hissing noise, to hide into the bathroom, which was conveniently on the opposite side of the hallway.

Astounded by the sight, she hesitated for a moment before following the serpent. But her curiosity won over her fear: and wondering what that beast was doing in there, she crossed the long corridor with impatience.

Even though the hallway was now empty, she recalled how green it was once with her aunt's plants, so much so that, in the heat of that day, she felt like she was walking into a greenhouse: she could imagine the long stretch of evergreens and smell their wet freshness, as she had so many times as a child.

When she reached the closed door, she hesitated for a moment, wondering again what would she see when she opened it: she trawled her memories, recalling the walls that she knew so well, the black-and-white diamond-shaped floor tiles and the bathtub, with its lion's feet and golden taps. And she tried to intertwine this with the image of that mysterious beast that she had seen slithering on the ceiling just a moment before, wondering how they might go together. After making it past the slight obstacle of the old door, though, she noticed the snake had vanished: in its place there was a laptop, on the bottom of the washbasin, a laptop covered with water pouring from the golden taps.

# V. The herring

But it was not comfortable in a washbasin: after all, water comes and water goes, always and unavoidably sucked in by the drain. The herring's body is long and lean, its scales well defined, protecting it from harm, and its lower mandible protruding a little, showing a few rudimental teeth. This last characteristic gives the herring a menacing aura, and maybe explained why the ichtyologists called it *Clupea harengus*, a clearly Nordic-sounding name. It is just all appearances, though, because, as we all know, the herring's teeth are deciduous, and will fall out after the fish grow past a certain size. Yet, with or without teeth, it is a very tenacious fish. The fact that herrings can be found in all seasons and in such a wide variety of places is the reason why it was imagined to be a migrating species, which is far from being the case. Its capillary presence is just the sheer consequence of its adaptative capabilities.

And so, in keeping with its nature, that herring resisted the gush of the syphon: even though the plumbing system repeatedly sucked the fish in, down the plughole, it still was able to resist, remain afloat and thus survive for a very long time.

There had been a moment in which the water seemed to halt momentarily and the suction from the drain was so strong that its tail almost went down. It also lost a couple of scales on that occasion and, had the water not come back on, lifting it up towards the surface, maybe it would not have survived. It was indeed at that point that the fish came to the conclusion that it had to get out of that washbasin, sooner rather then later: jumping out was certainly risky, because it knew that place so well – it had spent so much time there that even though it was no fun being stuck in such a maelstrom, that fullness that was always emptiness, at least it now knew how to survive it. But what would happen out there? The unknown is so scary, even though by jumping in the nearby shower it could take advantage of its protective grid, saving itself once and for all, from the seemingly inexorable drain.

So now, pushing from its fins and exploiting the force of the next gush of water, with waves that moved it here and there, it finally jumped out. The collision with the earth was hard: after it landed on the shower tray, it started nervously shaking its body, as if someone had taken it out of the water against its will. But as soon as a few drops of water started flowing over its scales, the shaking receded. And the more water flowed, the more it seemed that its muscular mass enlarged, as if filling itself with energy again. It had even the impression that its tail was splitting into two, that its gills were tearing apart and that, by breathing, two arms came out of its body, yes, two proper arms, long and strong, with hands and fingers, and that its scales were shorn by the water away from the skin, making it smooth and sweet to touch; and the more water came from the shower, the more its metamorphosis unveiled a human form: a woman, barely able to move her still stiff legs, as if they had been stuck together for millennia, and leaning on her arms, also weak from the long inactivity. She stayed there, still under the pouring water, looking at her new feet, big and strong, now standing on the floor.

And the water flowing over her head was now so powerful that, running down from her head to her arms, it brought forth two other creatures, as if they had come out of her own hands: on her right a little boy, already grown, with perfectly designed regular features, and on her left a little girl, slightly smaller, with hair as yellow as gold and full cheeks. And the more the water flowed, the more her creatures laughed with enjoyment.

# Epilogue

voilà, here I am, it took me more time than expected, but after all the *Bombyx mori* has to weave a long thread to protect itself during its metamorphoses, and it seems that it's three kilometres long, and this is why it takes so much time to come out of its silk cocoon, because it's so warm in there, so it doesn't come out that willingly, and I needed a very strong thread, one, two, three, maybe four myths, and perhaps even five, to come all the way here, and sherazade has left the palace, but ariadne crossed it with theseus, while europa even swam on the back of a bull, before being able to found a new city, a city of women, with its oven of opposites, that keeps water and fire together, the impossible metamorphosis, the most extraordinary of all, and yet it happened too, and in its place there are now all these beasts, ostrich, butterflies, dogs and horses, and snakes and even a laptop and a herring, and me, I, who finally learned to make an animal out of me, and maybe a plant too, and I think that maybe I'd like to collect an herbarium now because I've become green, so green, greener and greener, and I've been feeling that something was happening for some time, but now it's clear, I'm green, I stay green, I smell green, and it isn't even a common green, it's a bottle green, dark and marine, and the more I look outside of me, the city still covered in white, the more I become green, and vines of ivy climb on my ankles, and grab my calves and climb towards my thighs, they hug my flesh so tightly, and envelop my waist like a good belt, and then proceed towards the chest and finally bloom in my hands and in my mouth, my mouth that is full of flowers, now it's spring for real, and it surrounds all my parts and all my body and all my being: which becomes greener and greener, smelling of green, ontologically green

# Intermission

'I would like to explain how things went.'

'Yes, I know that you know everything, you're omniscient, that is very clear, but at least let me try to explain my point of view!'

'Well, yes, I understand, you know that too, but do I have the right to speak at least once before the sentence? Otherwise what's the point of a judgment? No trial, no defence, nothing, *nada*, *nichts*, and just a one-sided decision?'

'Yes, of course, universal, and the judgement cannot be appealed, but, in the end, I, who spent my life listening to others and their problems, can I, for once at least, speak, too? Do I get to have a say in this business?'

'Thank you, yes, I am very happy to have this opportunity. I know that you know everything and always have, and, yes, that you already knew everything even before it happened. But, at least, can I try to tell the other side of the story? Because – and let this be said from the very beginning – I am not guilty! She did everything, really, she literally did it all by herself!'

'All right, I admit, there was a trick . . .'

'But no! You cannot say an organized deception, perhaps a little trick, a completely innocent one, and then, do not forget, a little trick exercised for good!'

'No, I never promised anything, and I never told her that I'd be able to heal her.'

'No, wait a minute, let me speak: she looked for me because she was sick. She cried all the time, she had panic attacks, that kind of stuff. You could not leave her alone for a single moment. Abandonment syndrome. So, in order to be clear, and prevent any misunderstanding, it was she who came here to ask for help! On this, at least, we agree, right?'

'And yes, for my part, I did try to provide some help, as much as I could, with the means at my disposal, but you know how it is, when someone starts talking about their personal problems, and all those dreams, and those images, at times I felt like I was at the movie, really, no kidding, and quite often they were funny ones, really, really funny: we laughed a lot together . . .'

'Yes, then, things went as they went, but she did everything. I repeat. Really. She talked, and talked, she never really stopped talking, but it was as if all of that talking repeated that one and same fundamental question: "Do you love me? At least you: do you love me?" And, you know the story, I know that you know, I always replied "Uhmmmm . . .," trying to get around it, without really giving an answer, as she kept talking and talking, and projecting a bit of everything on my replying without really replying. So, you see, I simply followed the protocol – nothing but what I was supposed to be doing! It's the procedure . . .'

'But no, you cannot call it a deception! I told you, it's a completely innocent trick, and I'm not going to accept that the whole thing is a structural lie, an organized, institutionally sanctioned lie.'

'No, look, this is a fundamental mechanism, because without the transfer the therapy does not work.'

'All right, it's true: the transfer worked only and exclusively because I did my part, letting myself be invested in her own phantoms.'

'It's true, I had my own interest in the whole business: how can I deny it? We are all human.'

'But no, you cannot say that the transfer has aggravated the situation, making it even worse, or rather, now that I think about it: can we agree that it was a sort of homeopathic treatment?'

'No! No! I really mean "homeo-pathic"! Curing the evil with the evil itself!'

'Let me explain: if it is true that the neurosis consists in a detachment from reality in order to make it tolerable through phantasmatic formations, and if it is true, and on this we should agree, at least I hope so, that therapy is based on the transference, which is nothing but a further play of fantasies, then it must be concluded that the transference is a fantasy that aims to heal all other fantasies, thereby curing the evil with a small dose of that very same evil, an excess of fantasy with yet another fantasy, until . . .'

'No, I would not say until one realizes they have been deceived: as I said it is a technique, a therapy based on a scientific theory, an artificial laboratory where you give vent to your fantasies, but for therapeutic purposes, and, indeed, one that works precisely because there is no risk of acting out: that is barred from the beginning. Really barred – scientifically!'

'Omnipotent? I would never even dream of presenting myself as omnipotent! Of course, I did my part, pretending to be in control of the situation, but I would never put myself at the level of the Almighty! If she perceived me that way, it is only because of her own fantasies! I repeat: she did everything by herself.'

'Yes, of course, it was to be expected from the beginning that she would do everything: this, too, was part of the cure, because if I had told her how things were, it would have been completely useless: she had to get there on her own.'

'It is true that the transference helps a lot, and that thanks to this particular trick you can work on the most bizarre hypothesis, which otherwise nobody would ever even consider, let alone accept . . .'

'Again, the story of the structural lie! This is not the case! It is simply that, faced with all these fantasies, it was not up to me to pull her out of them, she had to find a way through on her own, precisely via that sort of meta-fantasy, the fantasy that can cure all others, which is the "transference" . . .'

'All right, a fantasy, correct, all these years have been nothing but a great big fantasy: all those stories, she who came here, she who sat in this armchair, she who talked to me, for hours and hours, it's all based on a fantasy, neither more nor less than all the other fantasies she had, but, at least – and on this we must agree – it was a productive fantasy!'

'Just a man, of course: I, too, am nothing but a man, neither more nor less than all the others . . .'

'And not even particularly attractive, all right, if you want . . .'

'Yes, that's true, maybe all that pathos was a bit exaggerated . . .'

'And yes, I admit that as well, I cannot deny it: in the end she got there on her own, and when she announced that she had realized I was not as omnipotent as she had once believed . . .'

'Very true, then I asked how she got there, how she understood this, with a little bit of irony, my usual irony, do you know how she replied? You know, yes, of course you know, you always know, but let me say it just for the sake of the record: she said that she had done everything on her own! Do you understand? Precisely, just so: "every-thing-on-her-own"! She who had produced all those fantasies, she who had now discovered herself to be their only and unique source, as well as the sole source of the pleasure she derived from them, and, if that had not been enough, it was still she, she and only she, who had finally realized that even the idea of my omnipotence was entirely her own making, sure, a fantasy that undoubtedly brought her some comfort, but since it was nothing but a product of her own imagination, she had now decided to do without it: all by herself, she said she wanted to do everything by herself now . . .'

'Yes, yes! I answered her just like that, with a bit of provocation, but you know, sometimes I like to indulge in a little bit of aggression. I am only human, after all. And moreover, you see, I had to warn her about the dangers of onanism.'

'You are absolutely right, there would be nothing strange there: it was me, after all, who said from the beginning that it was all about sex.'

'No, come on, let's be serious! You cannot say that they are more or less the same thing!'

'Transitional like that?'

'No, please, not the teddy bear!'

'Contrappasso? I always hated the idea of the contrappasso! Transitional object for eternity?'

'Okay, I admit, there was a trick! And yes, I knew it from the beginning that the trick was just meant to be a transition, but not the teddy bear! Please! Have some mercy! Not the teddy bear! Don't turn me into a teddy bear! Please!'

'Oh my God! I already feel my skin growing thick hairs, and claws coming out of my fingers, and I am getting smaller, and smaller, and I am getting hair all over my face and chin too, me, me who has been shaving my entire life! No! No! Please! Not the teddy bear! Not the transitional object! Pity, pity! Have some pity on a poor psychotherapist!'

# PART FOUR

# Herbarium

# Prologue

listen to me, I do listen to you, the poets laureate only move in the middle of plants with rarely used names, but as I am not a laureate, not box privet and acanthus trees, but ivy, broccoli, and climbing celery, I have seen, as well as an aubergine, which looked a bit like a carrot, and I have also seen you, and maybe I felt you, eucalyptus, long and strong trunk, green leaves with a balsamic taste, they say it is a parasite, but it is only a tree, a tree needing plenty of water, and that is why it does not allow any other plant to grow around, *allelopathy*, radical antagonism, wild materialism if you like, which actually is all a matter of hydraulics, flow of affects, the entire ontology is hidden in there, as your name says, *eu-calyptus*, the well-hidden, and if it is true that *nomina sunt consequentia rerum*, what else could you be if not a eucalyptus, the well-hidden one, so well hidden that it took me this long to find you, even though you were right here, but now that I found you, I will not let you go, and I will come here every single day, with my vegetal reason, waiting to find the ring that does not hold, the opening that can lead us to the middle of a truth, given that the truth, like you, likes hiding, today more than ever, maybe because we see it too much, so much that it is suffocated by all this seeing, by all these images, succeeding one another, surrounding us and confusing us, perhaps a eucalyptus is exactly what we need, with its psychic and allelopathic militancy, a tree to place in the middle of this herbarium, a plant that would allow us to see clearly, or maybe hear clearly in this new city, because all of those images have made us blind, so blind that we need now a shock therapy, in order to anaesthetize the senses, to realize that we are losing them, and probably an orgy of sounds colours flavours and touches and strokes, to walk out of the image, the one that keeps us prisoner, and chains us *here* in the exact moment when it liberates the capacity to see *there*, therefore it is really good that you keep hiding under the umbrella when you walk around town, and that you shelter a bit from all that phantasmagorical seeing and desiring, that seeing and knowing, which more than cognition has become a perpetual mis-recognition, so I will follow your smell, step by step, eucalyptus with the umbrella, your figure and my truth, you will also be my icon and my beatrice, and hopefully, after all this hell of images, we will end up in heaven

# I. The investor

It was a quiet provincial town, where everybody knew each other personally and life passed by regularly. The houses were in neat rows, each with its own garden, and children played safely on the pavement. The only occasions for meeting were the Sunday Mass and agricultural festivities.

However, lately, rather peculiar events had started to upset the town's life. A stranger had recently arrived, a tailor, renowned for his ability to sew beautiful clothes. They said he had spent all his life working for a clothes factory which had been very successful during the economic boom, so much so that some still called him 'The Tailor', dwelling on the definite article and the capital letter, to emphasize his unquestioned mastery. And many, so they murmured, still wore clothes he had designed, although very few, apparently, were aware of it. As later life approached, he had decided to retire to a more secluded life, to quietly enjoy his well-deserved retirement. However, rumours were that he was still creating clothes at the back of his house. This grain of information had not failed to stir a certain interest.

Curiosity, maybe along with a hint of vanity, took over. Soon, a badly concealed rush to the tailor started. Without too much fuss, every single resident began to visit the house of the newly arrived man, asking for a quotation for making a huge array of garments. And the tailor seemed agreeable. A highly fashionable suit, an evening gown, a summer dress, and a winter dress were the first commissions. Partly because of modesty, partly because of deeply rooted puritanism, transactions were carried out in total secrecy: no-one dared to confess giving in to temptation – not even to their closest friends.

Thus, a growing number of inhabitants secretly acquired their precious garments: extraordinary, truly extraordinary, clothes, so much so that whoever got one just *had to* wear it immediately and spend as much time as possible contemplating themselves in the mirror. There really was some magic in the way fabrics had been put together, and even more in the effect they had on body shape. It was as if all physical defects disappeared: bottle-like shoulders suddenly became robust and imposing, narrow hips were nicely rounded, large waists elegantly narrowed. Whoever had the opportunity to look at themselves wearing those clothes felt as if they had been transported into a magic castle – entirely happy, but also all alone.

But something even more unsettling surrounded that sartorial phantasmagoria: as soon as the tailor completed a commission, another one of his customers would lose an item of clothing. Nobody realized what was going on, given how every purchase was made in total anonymity and amid the most discreet silence, yet regularly, whenever a garment was delivered, another one vanished from somebody else's wardrobe.

Far from stopping the comings and goings, the mysterious disappearances only made customers eager for more. As soon as a garment vanished, the desire for a new one arose, to feel afresh that pleasant sensation of wearing a beautiful tailor-made outfit, perfectly done and valuable, the desire to admire oneself in the mirror, and to see every single defect evaporate in that perfect image. But why were clothes vanishing? Many people assumed they had been stolen, as often happens when one possesses something precious that they have been guarding jealously. Secrecy made the townsfolk suspect each other in an atmosphere of growing mutual mistrust: 'Was it he who stole from me?', 'Could it be her who gave in to temptation?', 'Oh! Is that my dress on them?' Not finding any satisfactory answer to these questions, most people simply resorted to putting in another order for new clothes, which, invariably, was followed by more disappearances.

And this is how, under the apparent calm of the small provincial town, a threatening frenzy started to rise softly, and uneasily. Along with the disappearances, other concerning events began unsettling the town's typical order. Some inhabitants developed a sight hypertrophy. In the early stages, it began as a slight bulge of the eyeball, with a corresponding sight increase, which some joyfully welcomed, especially those whose vision had worsened with age. Many, waking in the morning, were delighted when they discovered that the spectacles on their bedside table were no longer necessary: their eyesight was back and improved every day, enhancing the pleasure of admiring one's own image in those impeccable garments.

But improved sight went hand in hand with a progressive reduction of the senses of hearing and smell. The more the eyeball bulged from the cranium, like snail horns, the more ears, mouths and noses seemed to become smaller and atrophied. The process was so slow that nobody managed to identify it as such, but many had started to feel some discomfort.

This weird tendency made the town's doctor quite suspicious, because she had to deal with these extremely peculiar and disconcertingly similar cases more and more frequently. It was indeed the symptoms' peculiarity that put her on alert. Something extraordinary was going on, and she was not able to get to the bottom of it. Those physical symptoms – *bulbus oculi*, hypertrophy, loss of lingual papillae sensitivity and increasing deafness – were indeed so disparate that it seemed difficult, if not impossible, to link them. Medical literature, given the dominance of specialization, tended to focus on a single organ (eyes, ears, mouth or tongue), thus making it hard to reach a reasonable diagnosis with such widespread symptoms. On the other hand, the absence of previous cases and of a tested diagnostic process which could link these symptoms testified to the unprecedented nature of the disease, and made her fear the impossibility of formulating a convincing clinical scenario quickly.

Months went by and the cases increased – slowly, but steadily. Faced with a rising number of patients, the doctor and her assistants started to despair of ever finding a solution. All their research had yielded no useful results. Thus, the doctor decided to visit the city where she had studied in order to consult more literature and visit some of her old professors from the Otolaryngology Department. She was – following her natural inclination – looking for a scientific solution amid books, beakers and laboratories, but vanity provided her with an unexpected clue.

She hadn't been to the city for years, so she told herself she needed an outfit appropriate for the occasion. Having heard that the latest fashionable garments came out of the new tailor's house, she too succumbed to temptation. She wanted a plain and formal lady's suit, appripriate for the meetings awaiting her, yet with a touch of colour. Maybe a lemon-yellow one.

The delivery was made the night before her departure. As soon as she put the suit on in the intimacy of her bedroom, she fell under a spell. The garment was just what she wanted – simple but charming at the same time – so much so that she could not drag her eyes away from her reflection for a single second: it was as if that image had completely captured her. She stayed like this for hours, admiring herself in front of the mirror.

The next day, wearing the new lemon dress, she finally left for the big city. However, as soon as she arrived at the station, she realized something weird was happening to her body: she felt her eyes pushing outwards and her sight improving. Indeed, she already managed to read the train times from a distance, whereas she would usually have to get much closer to read those minuscule figures. For a moment, she feared being affected by the same disease for which she was desperately searching a cure. Then she told herself it was maybe only a temporary phenomenon, if not all in her imagination.

Yet, once she got on the train, she realized it was hard to follow the announcement on the loudspeaker. Indeed, she felt she was experiencing that progressive loss of hearing she had observed so many times in her patients. A hint of disquietude was surging within, when, as she turned towards the train window, she met that image again: so perfect and trim in that yellow dress that she lost herself in admiration, forgetting once more what was happening around and inside herself. The more she looked at that image of a body, her body, elegantly dressed and leaning just so on the seat, the more her desire to observe increased.

She was woken by the inspector who, after asking for the ticket repeatedly, finally had to shake her roughly to catch her attention. Given how feeble his voice sounded, she understood her hearing had diminished considerably. She gave him the ticket, then pulled a sandwich out of the bag that she had packed for the trip. She bit into, hoping to reawaken her slowly decaying senses. But the salt of the tuna fish and the tang of dry tomatoes were soft, vague, lacking intensity, as if her tastebuds were no longer able to identify any flavour.

As soon as she got off the train, she headed towards Doctor Q.'s home. They had studied otolaryngology together, but Dr Q. had picked Veterinary Medicine as their specialism later on. They had kept in touch, though, and had promised to meet again. They had followed each other's scientific publications from afar. They were a very tall creature, with a strong build and well-outlined lips. Had it not been for those thick glasses, one would have thought they were a basketball player. They welcomed her in their office with extreme kindness.

'It is a very peculiar phenomenon, yet it is very understandable, if you think about it,' Dr. Q. said after the detailed description of the town's symptoms, which, in the interest of science, she had not declared as her own too.

'What do you mean? I've been studying these cases and the scanty literature on the topic for months, but I've not been able to get to the bottom of it,' she replied thoughtfully.

'As you know, our sensory apparatus is interlinked. An imbalance in the ear canal unavoidably affects the senses of smell and taste. We only have to look at a common cold to realize the connections. When tissues start to produce mucus, the latter travels around the ear, nose and throat system. The entire human body is a complex series of hydraulics, composed of canals which help the different body parts communicate . . .'

'Therefore, an imbalance in one of its parts unavoidably affects all the other parts.'

'Exactly. All the other parts and the surrounding environment. We aren't monads, but neuralgic centres of a larger system,' they concluded, in a sententious tone, followed by a meditative silence. They then resumed:

'You are wearing a very unusual dress, as yellow as a lemon. It doesn't look like your style, but it really suits you,' they said picking up a thin wooden stick they had on their desk.

'What is it?' she asked, while they handed her the stick, leaning forward. Their hands lightly touched.

'Eucalyptus. It's a very resistant plant, originally from Australia. That is its favourite habitat, and through its entire life, it can reach a height of ninety metres. The variety called *Eucalyptus globulus* is also farmed in Southern Europe, especially in the Mediterranean basin, where it's used for its curative properties. You certainly have heard of eucalyptus oil, derived from the leaves of this tree. It has several therapeutic uses, although they are mostly associated with respiratory diseases and throat system congestion. It is used as a natural remedy also for daily household jobs, such as the elimination of ants or lice infestation.'

And while she examined that smooth and scented stick, surprised, they added: 'Take it with you—you'll need it.'

The woman started to look down, as memories began to rise up from her consciousness. Passing her hand over her face, moving it up and down and vice-versa, as if she wanted to erase all the signs on a blackboard, she confided: 'My mother used to make us inhale eucalyptus oil when we had a cough.'

'It has a strong expectorant function, which can improve a chesty cough thanks to the way it fluidifies mucus and catarrh. It can only do you good'.

'Thank you so much. I'll take it with me. Now I know what I need to do. But I must confess, I am scared.'

'You should not fear anything. You are ready for it. Take this too,' and they took out of a desk drawer a small object wrapped in thick red cloth.

'What is it?' she asked, unwrapping the bundle quickly to reveal a little wooden object.

'It's an icon,' they said while directing their eyes elsewhere, as if looking for inspiration.

'A painting?' she replied, dumbfounded.

'St George and the dragon.'

Looking at the small image of a blue knight on his white horse, dominating a wild green beast with his silver sword, she suddenly understood.

'Thanks! Thanks for everything! I'm incredibly grateful to you!', she finally said, standing up and getting closer to hug them. They held her tight and after a moment of embarrassment after their eyes met, they added:

'Come back when you get rid of it.'

She went out in a rush and headed to the station, where she caught the first train back. During the entire trip she kept looking at the icon she carried in one hand, while, in the other, she held the eucalyptus stick tightly. The tighter her grasp, the more she felt her senses re-awaken.

As she got off the train, she rushed towards the tailor's house. She knocked the door, with no reply. She knocked again. Nothing. Then she turned the handle and pushed, shouting: 'Is there anyone in there?' The house was empty and looked like it had long been abandoned. There was no sign of furniture nor of the shop she had seen only a few days before.

She crossed the entrance and dining room. The space was covered with dust and cobwebs, as if nobody had lived in there for years. Upon close inspection of the bedrooms and salon, there seemed no sign of life whatsoever in that house. She headed to the kitchen. Even that room was empty, derelict. She noticed the door opening to the garden had been left ajar and stepped through.

The passage was full of twigs, weeds and half-dried trees. She made her way with the help of the eucalyptus stick. Holding it in front of herself, she managed to break through, as if those weeds, like mucus and catarrh, were retreating, afraid of the expectorant effect of the eucalyptus. And, as she crossed the garden, she found herself in front of a small building. She knew he was in there.

She opened the door and walked down the steps one by one, with the stick in her belt, the icon in her left hand, and her right hand touching the wall, to make her way in the shadows. When she arrived in the basement, she immediately recognised the old tailor, crouched in a corner, bloodless and lifeless. But she barely had time to spot two red poisonous eyes in the dark of the room when the beast wildly jumped on her. She fell to the floor, as he tried to pin her by the arms, but she managed to put the icon in front of his face: before that image, the ferocious impetus suddenly stopped, and the tailor's body wilted. He was still alive, but now powerless.

She tied her belt around the beast and, as if he was no more than a trained puppy on a leash, she took him around the streets of the town. As she walked, the citizens looked at the scene astounded: some people started to touch their eyes, now less bulbous, while mouths, noses and ears regained their powers. A sudden excitement started to arise, with joyful cries of delight: 'I can hear again! I can hear again!', 'My nose is back! I can smell the scent of spring!' Somebody else even shouted: 'I can't see anymore! Hurray! I've lost my sight! Please, somebody give me back my glasses!'

And as the woman walked the streets with the beast tethered to her belt and the icon always in her hand, her lemon suit started to disappear: in its place, one could see a light violet chemise, soft to the touch, like beautifully scented iris petals.

# Interlude

now I would like to see you, or better I would like to *smell* you, my dear eucalyptus, because one can hide from the sight, but less from the smell, eyes can open and close at their convenience, and we can even turn away our head when we do not want to see, but we cannot turn off our nose, which is always there, open to the world, with its cavities, and that is why sight gives us the impression, and maybe even the illusion, of command, and therefore it suits inspectors, so well that they cannot think of the invisible, and what about the smellable, it might be better to smell ideas, to sniff them, instead of seeing them, sniff them exactly like dogs sniff their prey, and think with the noses and the odors we smell, instead of the eyes and the books we see, and this smelling world would really suit you, if it is true that the *eu-calyptus* is the one that stays well hidden, as your name says, but even if you do not see it, you can feel it, because its scent is unmistakeable, it pierces you more and more, and when you least expect it, it wraps you up in its embrace, and for this reason we can forgive its *allelopathy*, that vegetal arrogance, totally unbearable, making all plants around disappear, the balsamic tree overcoming every other sensation around me, with its perfect symmetry between the roots and the trunk culminating straight into a ball of leaves, and the nose with all its cilia, and the chemo-transmitter vessels, which end up in the glomerulus, the olfactory network, where the impossible synthesis occurs, where air turns into water, water into mucus, mucus into emotions

# II.  The inspector

After the events of the previous months, life went back to its routine in the small town. Yet, there was still some underlying disquietude. Getting back to normal had not been preceded by a deep understanding of the nature and origins of those extraordinary occurrences. Everybody felt the need to put everything behind them, and this is what most did, hoping that the wish for normality would bring it about in both actuality and appearance. However, under the cover of newfound tranquillity, too many unanswered questions buzzed about: What had happened? What was the connection between the tailor, the clothes and the loss of senses? And why had the improvements in sight gone hand in hand with the deterioration of all other senses, rather than a general improvement of all perceptive abilities? And above all, how could the townsfolk avoid being taken again by that insatiable desire to see?

After a few weeks, the city council called an extraordinary meeting to discuss how to proceed. A decision was pushed for under the pressure of an activist group, set up under the slogan *No-Visual*. Day after day, they had collected signatures in the streets, written blogs, articles, put up posters, and circulated propaganda through every possible means, trying to marshal consensus for a new – if rather unusual – draft law. Although the causes of the past outbreak were unclear even to those who had done in-depth research, no one could deny the role played by excessive visual stimulation, to the detriment of other sensory organs.

The *No-Visual* collective started to work on a package of measures meant to eliminate – or at least reduce – that stimulation as much as possible: that is, to minimize what from then on was defined as 'Indice di Inquinamento Visivo'. This was more often called the 'Visual Pollution Index', as if the English language were an indisputable mark of the problem's scientific credentials – an effect amplified by the use of the abbreviation VPI, combining the astounding precision of the three letters with the assonance of VIP, adding thus another layer of distinction to the situation.

The weeks of intense discussions and militancy of the *No-Visual* movement finally resulted in a specifically drafted law, soon defined as the 'Anti-Visual Pollution Measures', now a topic of discussion at the council meeting. It was an extremely detailed document, considering that this type of pollution, obviously, could be fought against only with a general rearrangement of the citizens' lives. What was the best way to prevent a possible regression into the phantasmagoria of viewing (and being viewed) without checking at source the quantity and the modality of visual stimulations? And how to circulate all those crucial messages without which no social life is possible, while at the same time preventing the eyes from taking over again?

It took more than 400 closely typed pages to answer these questions, presenting and describing a series of measures aimed at regulating social codes, modalities of interaction and signals, all of which were (unfortunately) primarily and dangerously visual. The objective, as the subtitle of the document itself explained, was to fight the scopophilia – voyeurism – which now clearly appeared to be a severe social pathology from which no one was immune.

The first chapter was dedicated to the most obvious measure, as the local doctor's experience had proved: the dress code had to be reconsidered in such a way as to stimulate the sight as little as possible. The proposal was quite vague on this issue but suggested the use of a standard uniform, with unisex jacket and trousers, in simple, possibly neutral, colours like brown and grey and perhaps beige. Colours typically utilized in advertisements were excluded, like yellow and orange, because of their capacity to stimulate the appetite, whereas red was forbidden by principle, without providing a specific motivation.

'Fellow citizens!' announced Mr F., one of the leading representatives of *No-Visual*, 'we are now aware of the atrocious consequences of scopophilia. We have also realized the impact the dress code had in its degenerated form. We need to prevent this from happening again. Therefore, Article I of our draft law is absolutely key and I hope it does not meet any objections.'

A moment of silence followed. The council members exchanged questioning glances, exploring each other's faces, looking for approval or at least some signal of intention. However, maybe due to the embarrassment for such a visual fall back, most of them lowered their gaze, as if to confirm their vow to stop viewing. Only Ms V., a young woman of a refined statuesque beauty, dared to take the floor:

'But the outfit is such an important aspect of our personality that limiting it in this manner will mean giving up one of our fundamental freedoms. Every time I open my closet to decide what I want to wear, I make a precise choice because our clothes are the membrane between us and the external world, what allows us to appear as well as to hide. I am not willing to give this up that easily,' she concluded, imbuing her measured words with a hint of sadness.

'But this is exactly the temptation we must avoid!' Mr F. replied with so much emphasis that his stern round glasses and grey beard were shaken. 'Clothing is one of the main places of the narcissistic obsession we have experienced: "see how special I am", "this dress makes me unique", "this is how I share my mood", as if our body and our decisions on how to present it were so important that everybody is hanging about, waiting for our message! But isn't this the reason why we ended up devoured by that monstrous desire to watch and be watched, in effect endangering life in our beloved town?'

'But this is the risk of freedom! Which must be protected at all costs, starting exactly with the freedom of expression!' rebutted Ms V., clearly annoyed. 'Not to mention the pleasure we derive from the opportunity to choose among all those shapes, colours and materials that make up our clothes.'

'Freedom of expression is freedom to speak, and thus oral freedom! But clothing is sheer visual hedonism! And it was exactly the latter that made us collapse in our visual selfishness! We need to get rid of its causes and therefore reduce as much as possible the need to resort to images!' Mr F. replied, followed by a chorus of 'Down with scopophilia! Down with visual selfishness!' coming from the *No-Visual* corner.

Even though Ms V.'s speech had provoked some hesitations, the memory of the suffering they had been through during the visual hypertrophy took over. The council unanimously voted in favour of the package, at this point already commonly known as 'anti-VPI'. While the outfit issue had encountered some resistance, due to nothing but a lingering vestige of personal vanity, all other measures, which actually implied bigger restrictions, had not provoked too many objections. For instance, the chapter on town signage provided for the elimination of all directive images, including not only the obvious commercial signs, but also street signs and even those for public toilets. In this last case, the distinction between 'Ladies' and 'Gentlemen' was likewise abolished. This difference was now considered exaggerated, if not even redundant and, above all, too focused on the visual register. There was also someone who suggested that, once visual pollution was eliminated, even sexual difference would be weakened or perhaps even disappear, as it was now perceived mainly as a pre-modern phenomenon. Once scopophilia was reduced, even that sort of narcissism of small differences, between those who wear skirts or trousers, would become irrelevant. Subsequently, unisex restrooms seemed to be not only unavoidable, due to the abolition of visual signage, but also healthy, exactly because of their liberating potential from overly simplistic and unambiguous visual gender identification.

That said, it would take some time and plenty of patience to implement all those measures in the small town. On top of everything, as somebody had noticed, given the small size of the place, everybody knew very well where the public toilets, post office, town hall, pharmacy and so on were located. Therefore, all shop names, signals, and even street numbers – that had been there for a long time, all seemed to be redundant. More complex was the question of road signage, which had to be reduced to the minimum, if not abolished. But this issue in the end was also easily addressed: all traffic lights were converted into roundabouts and the population were asked to rely on deeply rooted mores to spontaneously regulate traffic – always give way to the right, never leave your car in front of somebody else's garage, stop in front of a school when students are crossing the street. And the horn! Honk the horn as much as possible! Indeed, there were no limits or restrictions to acoustic signals, which were instead encouraged. At last, even Ms V. had to agree that most of the measures included in the VPI bundle simply entailed following some common sense and the town's own etiquette.

A thornier issue was that of foreigners. Whereas one could count on citizens' entrenched habits, things got extremely complicated when it came to potential visitors from outside. Yes, they could rely on the newly established Office of Common Sense, which would have normally looked after the education of newcomers and of their sensory organs.

However visitor numbers had to be reduced drastically in order to avoid any further strain on the already super-busy local amenities, which were already seeing quite a lot of people. Moreover, while older people exhibited an impressive grasp of the etiquette, more effort was always needed to bring younger generations up to speed.

That chapter of the law also known as the Frontiers' Clause was quite complex. To begin with, in order to reduce the number of foreigners, it was necessary to keep them under check and therefore, from the very beginning, to monitor their access to the town: how would that be possible if the 'customs' sign was to be abolished, together with the naturally visual control of travel documents? How could the identity of the people on the streets be verified without relying on a mostly visual record? While not an issue for those who grew up in a town where everybody knew each other, it would not be easy to detect and record new arrivals. And, although there was no definite evidence on the matter, the suspicion that the hypertrophy pandemic had been caused by the arrival of that foreigner was quite widespread. 'Watch the borders! Protect our town!' Monitoring the borders seemed key to the whole project and thus absolutely crucial for public safety.

After hours of heated discussions, which almost seemed to throw into question the whole reform project, Mr F. shocked all the meeting participants with his umpteenth proposal, this one extremely radical: installing electronic 'noses' at the town entrance.

'That's hilarious!' retorted Ms V., still resentful about the outfit restrictions, and eager to boycott the whole initiative. 'How could anyone check identity cards with electronic noses? Sniffing them?'

The attack was quickly and duly parried and returned to its sender: '*Few* people know the existence of this small jewel of modern technology,' replied Mr F., emphasizing the word *few* to highlight that Ms V. was clearly not one of those in the know. 'Yet, it is a *fact,*' he carried on, lingering on the word *fact*, 'that electronic noses are already widely used in several sectors of the economy, starting with the food industry, where they are commonly employed to recognize haute cuisine food products, like high-end wines and oils. All it takes is to convert them to another, more noble objective, namely the town's safety!'

'But what are these noses?' a voice from the crowd asked. 'What are they? What are they?' a 'choir' of citizens soon echoed around, amplifying the doubts already expressed.

'I would like to invite Mr. T., *No-Visual*'s technical consultant to take the floor and clarify this proposal for our community,' said Mr F., moving his arm slowly towards the right, as if heralding the upcoming revelation.

And Mr T., a thin man whose outfit was clearly already complying with *anti-VPI* measures, as was entirely appropriate for a tech expert, began his appeal thus: 'The "noses" are devices made up of a series of sensors that are able to recognize odours by identifying their chemical patterns. The sensors are constructed in such a way that they can perceive the concentration of substances in the atmosphere. They can be of different types, containing active materials, like semi-conducting metal oxides, or quartz crystals covered up with appropriate substances. The common element between these different materials is the fact that they are not highly selective with single substances, but are able to respond to the whole effect produced by a chemical mix, also more commonly known as "odour".'

'But they will be extremely expensive to build! And surely out of reach of our town's limited funds . . .' said Ms V., making it clear through her lowering tone that she was almost giving in.

And indeed, this is what happened, after Mr T. had further explained the project details in a calm voice, monotonously persuasive, typical of someone who spends a great deal of time among scientific publications: 'Electronic noses with quartz-coated metal porphyrin are not particularly expensive and would be the ideal solution for a frontier deployment, like in this case. They work according to a very elementary principle of physics, that is, sensing the crystal-frequency variation of oscillation due to the formation of bonds between the coating material and the gas molecules in the atmosphere. The undeniable advantage of using electronic noses, even in comparison with the use of dogs, for example, or any other microsmatic animal, is that, beyond liberating us from the visual medium, they allow us to translate the message directly into action: a matrix with sensors can indeed be linked to a digital system to register and explain the acquired data, a system capable of transforming the response to odours into the appropriate *output*. In our case, that would be either allowing a visitor access to us or rejecting them because of their undocumented smell.' He pronounced this last sentence with such imperturbable serenity that the issue of immigration, so thorny in other contexts, now appeared easy to regulate with the click of a mouse.

'This is genius! Follow your nose!' one of the *No-Visual* replied, followed, as it often happened, by a chorus of 'Follow our noses! Follow our noses!'

The rest was only a matter of time. The measures taken by the council were implemented within three months. Saying goodbye to their coloured clothes, accessories, shoes, bows, purses and laces, earrings, lipsticks and so on, was perhaps the toughest test for the town's citizens. It was particularly tough for those who used to be called 'women', for it was true that 'men's' clothes had already been quite plain and homogenous for a few centuries. All in all, switching from shirt and trousers or a suit to a simply coloured unisex outfit was not such a big sacrifice for them. But having to give up the colourful fabrics, interesting shapes and bold accessories of women's fashion was much more difficult. Some women even complained that this law was actually a way to suppress femininity in favour of a sort of general masculinization of the dress code. However, the power of law had prevailed there where the subtle argumentations of the *No-Visual* and of Mr. F. had failed.

Thus, the town's life became even quieter. To tell the truth, apart from some clothing monotony, the introduced changes, at first, had not been that unsettling. Upon a closer look, indeed, life seemed to be only much simpler. Also, instead of spending all that time choosing what to wear during the day, and then changing for evening, one could dedicate those hours to more social activities, like friends, arts or the life of the town itself.

Although the use of screens, including TVs and computers, was strictly prohibited due to its obvious impact on the global-VPI, their acoustic use was freely permitted. And while some took this opportunity to get rid of them completely, others opted to convert their electronic devices in such a way that their favourite TV programmes, for example, remained part of their existence. Besides the immediate advantage of not being stuck sitting in a set place, the acoustic turn had brought upon some new, more unexpected situations. For instance, many people were positively surprised to see that they could perform house chores while listening to their favourite soap opera, with the additional advantage that the lack of visual stimulation allowed them to use their imagination more freely, getting completely rid of the constraints of images, always unavoidably limited to the 'here and now'. How could anyone not appreciate, just to mention one small item, the ability to imagine that one's favourite actor was always the same charming one, despite their shocking weight gain, their hair loss and all those other trifling matters, purely visual, that tabloids talked about?

Together with imagination, it was the olfactory sense that seemed to be thriving after a few months of anti-VPI measures. All the care once dedicated to choosing and maintaining clothes was transferred to noses. Instead of wondering 'What will I wear today?' most people indeed started pondering 'Which perfume shall I choose?' The object had changed but now there was an equally obsessive recurring problem, as if odour had become a sort of invisible overcoat covering the plain anti-VPI outfit with the most disparate colours, shapes and flavours.

This is how, week after week, the most extravagant perfumes, essential oils and spices started to flow into the town. The local pharmacy had to cope with a growing and pressing demand, and an increasingly discerning clientele, so much so that the owner opened a new branch in her own garage. Business was running smoothly (at least for her) and, in the meantime, social relations became more widespread and intimate (for everyone). Maybe they were even a bit *too* intimate and widespread.

The general tendency to avoid as much as possible everything that could affect the global VPI had indeed provoked a general increase in sexual desire, as well as a slightly excessive licentiousness. After months and months of experimentation with different perfumes, creams and oils, most people started to use aphrodisiacs more and more frequently, exactly for their capacity to attract. That pleasure of choosing and being chosen, which once happened by means of attire, and by way of a quick glance, to be followed by a long stare, was now massively transferred to olfactory communication, including not only artificial odours but also their hormonal equivalents.

And while the exocrine glands of the town's inhabitants progressively developed in order to deal with the growing demand of pheromones, the sense of modesty, shame and even hesitation which once were stirred from the need to look around before doing certain things grew increasingly feeble, and were generally considered inappropriate visual fall-backs.

At the beginning, this did not raise too many concerns, being perceived as one of the effects of modernization produced by the new measures. At the end of the day, trying to not see too much also meant trying to not control too much, and therefore not lingering on irrelevant matters such as the visual continuity of one's own sexual partner or, even, their belonging to one specific animal species rather than another. As long as there was a positive olfactory understanding, everything that did not go too much under the visual register seemed to not only be acceptable, but also extremely beneficial.

However, this progressive and exponential increase of free and occasional sexual intercourse started to seriously endanger the citizens' productivity (together with their own reproductive capacity, given the increasing number of interspecies intercourse). Every excuse was welcome to interrupt work: one slightly more intriguing odour would suffice to close one's own office or shop on the spot. Even actions which once were habitual, like greeting an acquaintance from afar by raising and shaking a hand, became a risky gesture, given the high likelihood of atmospheric propulsion of armpit pheromones caused by these movements.

Moreover, many started to suffer from sleep disorders. Any smell could reawaken senses and desires that, with the night's complicity, often waited for the reduced visibility of the dark to find free expression. In a nutshell, what followed was a general increase of sensitivity and susceptibility to, above all, sexual stimulation. There were few moments of peace, even at night.

And so it was that many made appointments to see the local doctor. Besides the clear growth of desire, insomnia proved to be the recurring symptom for which patients asked for her help. Once again, the town's doctor found herself having to tackle a series of unusual phenomena, whose dynamics were only partially clear. That there was a link between the new anti-VPI measures, the perfume fever, the exponential growth of sexual desire and sleeplessness seemed undeniable. How could a remedy be found, though, in such extraordinary circumstances? How could she intervene without questioning what she herself considered to be the beneficial and liberating effects of anti-VPI measures?

These questions tortured her for days, until one morning, opening her desk, she found that small wooden stick: eucalyptus! That was the solution! Apart from its renown expectorant properties, the story of the tailor had clearly shown how the wood was able to break *through*. And since all of those passions and excitements seemed like a sort of viscous jungle, an entanglement of chaotic catarrhs to dissipate, she told herself that this could be the solution.

To the town's surprise, the doctor started to prescribe to all insomniacs inhalations with essential eucalyptus oil: at least three times per day, they were to pour a few drops in hot boiling water and breathe in the healthy essence deeply. The regime seemed simple and economical enough.

Most patients complied. And this is how all the people who followed her instructions and started to introduce into their bodies regular doses of those beneficial molecules, retrieved their sleep – an even sweeter and deeper sleep than it had ever been before.

# Interlude

from now on I will be this sock, you can walk inside me, throw me on the floor before going to bed, or even forget me in a drawer, it does not matter, every single time you wear me, I will warm you up, and with me the whole soul of the world will breathe at your feet, because the thread contains the plant, and even the sun which made it grow, the earth which transmitted the food, the oxygen and the carbon dioxide which passed through its life, not to mention the motion of stars and planets regulating the seasons, because only if the entire cosmos is in harmony in that specific configuration, in that specific way of holding, only if it holds together, and if it holds well, can that minuscule seed turn into a plant, the plant into a fruit, the fruit into a boll, the boll into a thread, the thread into a material, the material into fabric, the fabrics into those hands who picked it, and what about the desire that weaved it, the transactions that regulated its production, until the moment it became a product, a product that winked at me, blinking with its commodity fetishism, and the music in the trendy shop, because the sound touches you, and you cannot stop it, the ears are always open to the world, as if they were backup noses, and you can close your eyes, if you do not like to see, and you can close your mouth, if you do not want to taste, but you cannot close the ear, that is why an unpleasant sound annoys you so much, way more than an unpleasant sight, not to mention an unpleasant touch, which gives you goose bumps, and could even be deadly, because the mouth allows us to be open to some things, and close to others, but our skin is completely open to the world, the last resistance against the world, or maybe, even the world itself, that is why we put clothes over it, instead of going around naked, since the whole universe is all in this sock, and then god must be no one but a rather expert tailor, and the entire cosmos nothing else but an artful fabric, therefore the essence of each theology should be the philosophy of fashion, with all its creatures, including indeed this sock which is nothing but our skin

# III. The dancing god

What once was a quiet provincial town now seemed unrecognizable even to its own citizens. The incidents had occurred so quickly that nobody had enough time to understand such disparate and extraordinary events. The eucalyptus oil remedy had improved the sleep of those who made use of it, and probably had even calmed that extreme excitability everyone had experienced. However, anxiety and worry were still common. The children who once played happily on cobblestones now had to stay locked in their homes and were encouraged to go out as little as possible.

And so many started to open up and give voice to their discontentment and disappointment. On street corners, at the pharmacy, in the post office, when working in the fields, there was constant murmuring. Among the different voices was one who questioned the whole anti-scopophilia approach, wishing for its immediate and total abrogation. Eliminating any visual stimulation – the idea that once had given rise to so much excitement and enthusiasm – now appeared to be the potential source of far too much suffering. The fight against visual pollution seemed to have produced too many imbalances, leaving most people at the mercy of invisible – and thus incontrollable – forces, starting from those which regulated interpersonal relationships, apparently compromised by their own excess.

The supporters of the *No-Visual* movement tried to defend their reasoning, highlighting the progress achieved in overcoming problems that had lasted millenia, like the war between sexes, the modernization of mores, not to mention the extreme efficiency of new technology in border control. But the critical voices kept increasing, as did concerns about the town's future. A plenary assembly was called, to discuss what to do.

The first one to take the floor was the spokesperson for *No-Visual*. After listing the benefits of the anti-scopophilia package, which had indeed been expected, as he himself had meticulously predicted in that same spot a few months back, he lingered on the description of the excellent functioning of border technologies, a brilliant success, which had gone well beyond the most positive forecasts:

'Consider how well the introduction of electronic noses has gone. Not only do we no longer need identity cards, or other sorts of travel documents, that, as we know, can always be forged, but, within very few months, we have also developed a full olfactory map of the entire town. Do you realize that? We have data which allow us to identify every single citizen through the odour *pattern* that is unequivocally theirs and we do not even know yet what other uses and discoveries this technological treasure could generate with such a rich source of information. We need to continue to use our imagination and hold tight to our course until we're able to exploit the full potential of these measures. We can't go back now.'

'It is true that electronic noses protected us from the intrusion of any foreigner,' replied Mr F., who once was a strong supporter of the anti-scopophilia package, but had recently started to have his own doubts.

'The town's safety!' the spokesperson of the *No-Visual* continued, 'Safety! This is our priority!'.

And a chorus of voices reaffirmed 'Safety! Safety!'.

But Ms V., who had adapted rather badly to the new measures, took the floor, standing up fully, fully annoyed, and raising her arm, in order to catch everyone's attention:

'Let's hold on a second, my dear fellow citizens! Here, we need to proceed with some common sense, because, on top of safety concerns, the quality of our daily life comes into play.' But a sudden clamour interrupted her shouting: 'Sa-fe-ty, sa-fe-ty, sa-fe-ty!'

'Safety, safety, ok! But let me finish my speech, please! We could keep the measures that had a beneficial impact, like the introduction of electronic noses, but, at the same time, abolish, or at least reconsider the most unpleasant laws, like, for example, the unisex outfit obligation and the complete abolition of social visuality.'

A meditative silence followed, and Ms V. seized the opportunity to take back the floor immediately:

'That excess of excitability and the insomnia we have experienced is probably the result of these laws and of the drastic abolition of any visual stimulation. We cannot carry on like this. Have you seen what happened with our once very disciplined behaviours? Perhaps we do not need to question the whole bundle, but at least let's reconsider some aspects, weighing their pros and cons. It's too much of a sensitive issue: we need to proceed cautiously.'

'The doctor, the doctor! Let the doctor speak!' somebody shouted.

'Yes! The doctor, the doctor! Let the doctor speak!' a chorus of voices replied from the *No-Visual* side.

The doctor was a rather coy type, reluctant to take the floor in front of a large audience. She saw all eyes suddenly upon her and, with such an ocular exuberance, she had a particularly hard time getting over her hesitation:

'Uhmm, well, please, forgive me my fellow citizens, I do not have a unique answer. Despite all the research I've done, I've not been able to find any references to similar cases in medical literature. On the basis of my observations, though, it seems very likely that the sudden reduction of visual stimulations has produced a progressive atrophization of the ocular apparatus. The nervous system must have over-reacted, compensating with the exponential growth of the olfactory system, which clearly explains the extreme excitability many have experienced. Also notice that, together with smell, touch has developed to a certainly excessive extent, as it is well proved by the number and frequency of what we can call, politely, "meetings". At this point, it seems to me that it is above all necessary to avoid any further extreme solutions and, rather, we need to consider measures aimed at rebalancing the distribution of sensory stimulations.'

This is how the doctor spoke, carrying on with the explanation of the general clinical scenario, of the beneficial effects of eucalyptus, as well as its limits, due to the plant's inability to impact the entire sensory system. What followed was a long debate, where even citizens who never had taken the floor in other meetings decided to share their own experiences. Although the official atmosphere did not favour individual confessions, most people managed to relate even the most embarrassing details, turning them into a generic statement of belief, 'I've heard of . . .' or into events that had occurred to an equally generic 'acquaintance'.

The barrage of information which followed had a profound effect on the Council: in the face of an impressive number of occasional, blind and even interspecies sexual encounters, all clearly provoked by the absence of a visual check, it seemed necessary, if not overdue, to reconsider at least some of the measures contained in the bundle of statutes. More specifically, everybody agreed on the need to rebalance the sensory distribution. The long meeting then ended with the organization of different think tanks, each tasked with preparing a draft to reform a specific section of the anti-VPI laws.

In the think tank dedicated to the revision of laws on clothing, an idea gradually formed to resort to constantly changing garments, a little visual compensation which could have had beneficial effects on long-term imbalance disorders, starting from the ones experienced during the initial eye hyper-trophia event. Instead of abolishing any stimulus, it proposed to treat the excesses of images by using images themselves, beginning with a considered use of clothes.

More specifically, it seemed that communicating mostly through digital images could allow the visual stimulus to keep playing its function while avoiding a return to an obsessive attachment to appearances, as had happened with the tailor. The idea was welcomed by several enthusiastic supporters, so much so that, around the slogan *Ya-Virtual*, a large group with representatives from different think tanks was formed.

Thanks to the ever-growing influence of this movement, *Ya-Virtual* ideas had a significant impact on the revision of the anti-scopophilia laws. Week after week, movement representatives worked in different groups, suggesting reforms for the various laws. When the Council gathered to vote on the new package, their impact was crucial. Instead of anti-visual pollution laws, the statutes were now redefined as 'Global VPI Regulations'. This suggested that, rather than abolishing visual stimuli, they now merely 'regulated' their occurrences. Electronic noses were kept active. Road signage, along with other visual stimuli which had proved to be superfluous, were not restored. However, full freedom was now allowed in interpersonal relationships, including the freedom of 'non-oral expression'. This term, although it contained a negation, marked the start of a new process of re-legitimizing the visual field. In the wake of the growing influence of *Ya-Virtual*, however, the town's citizens were encouraged to resort to virtual images as often as possible. The latter, precisely because of their constantly changing nature, were supposed to instil a certain ocular scepticism and thus help prevent any massive relapse into scopophilia.

A few days after the promulgation of the new measures, most people had already dug out their boxes of bright clothes and colourful accessories from their basements and returned to former personal care habits, including visits to 'dispensers of body images', like the hairdresser and the beautician. While the latter resumed activity extremely slowly, the hairdresser, who had taken up grass-cutting during the visual prohibitionism, re-started their trade with new energy and a constant flow of clients.

Yet, many still felt some distrust in very direct visual stimuli. That is why, as recommended, they resorted to *virtual* mediation as much as possible. Somebody even suggested the use of screen-clothes, a sort of screen-tunic where everyone could regulate the appearance of ever-changing images. The proposal certainly piqued some interest, because it seemed to satisfy those who appreciated the unisex option of the anti-scopophilia laws as well as those who regretted the loss such legislation entailed, missing the variety of textures and the different colours of their former wardrobe.

The creation of the new screen-clothes needed some time and significant investments. The biggest challenge had been finding an adequate magnetic support, sufficiently ductile to adapt to body movements and resistant enough for everyday use and thus able to be in constant touch with surfaces and heavy bodies. The new technology used in the production of auto-stereoscopic liquid crystal screens turned out to be helpful, allowing for the creation of shock-resistant garments.

The promulgation of these new laws and the social innovations deriving from them generated a renewed optimism: life flowed peacefully once more, as citizens finally felt able to express themselves fully, while the idea of virtual clothes also stirred their creativity. Initially, it was only the representatives of the *Ya-Virtual* movement who adopted the outfits, wearing them as a sort of political manifesto. However, their charm was soon noticed by the other citizens, and, therefore, in a very short time, whoever could afford it had at least one piece made just for them.

Soon, screen-clothes became common even at home. Instead of exchanging words and complex explanations, a click on the managing device of the garment became the most effective and immediate way to convey one's mood, desires and inclinations. The variety of these clothes satisfied even the fussiest people, as their instant changeability gave them the pleasant feeling of being in control of their appearance – which, among other things, explains why the beautician found it hard to drum up business.

Everything seemed to have gone back to normal – or almost, if it weren't for the fact that someone started to notice some strange little animals in their homes. They looked like small crabs, some with four legs, some with six, all of them with changeable colours. At times, they were orange- and red-striped, while at others the stripes were brownish, purplish or black. The creatures had never been seen in town before, yet their appearance did not alarm anyone. They all seemed quite innocuous. Some citizens, who did not like their presence, had resorted to pest-control products, but the little animals always returned after a short while; therefore, most people just got used to their unobtrusive presence.

What made everybody curious was the fact that, every day, the creatures became bigger. Yet, they did not develop a threatening appearance, so much so that some people decided to treat them like pets. Indeed, they were quite affectionate, like dogs, always seeming happily in search of human company, so that Ms V., at one point, decided to take her favourite creature for a walk on a lead.

While most citizens behaved as if everything was normal, the doctor was getting ever more concerned. Since the small animals appeared in her house and her office, she had started to use the eucalyptus remedy, her best ally up until then, to get rid of them. But this time it did not work. Those strange creatures kept appearing in growing numbers, as if from nowhere. And more worryingly, their growth seemed to be unstoppable; some were already bigger than the pet dogs they had replaced.

She then decided to go back to visit Dr. Q. As a specialist in Veterinary Medicine, they might have some suggestions on what to do with these weird creatures. She put some specimens in a box and asked Ms V. if she could borrow her pet, as it seemed to be more developed than the others, but the woman refused, saying that she loved it too much and could not bear to part from it, even for one afternoon.

After passing through the border checks, which took longer than usual, given the presence of the animals, whose olfactory pattern resulted in 'unknown', the doctor rushed towards the station and then walked quickly to Dr. Q.'s house.

The latter welcomed her with a large smile, when they saw her unexpectedly behind the door, with that strange hyper-techy dress and a box under her arm.

'Oh, what a surprise!' they began, opening the door and stepping back, welcoming her in with a wide movement of their arms. 'I've not seen you in a while,' they concluded in, it should be noted, a very friendly tone.

'Sorry. I'm so sorry not to have been in touch for so long, but you have no idea of the extraordinary events that have occurred in our town'.

'Come in, then. Sit down and tell me everything,' they replied pointing at the living room opening on their left.

'I've just prepared some mint tea: will you have some with me?'

'Yes please, I'd love some.'

'Here you go,' they said, while scrutinizing her with a confused and interrogative glance, 'there's also honey, or sugar, if you prefer.'

'Thanks. I'll have it plain'.

'Ok. So tell me what's happening'.

The doctor spoke without a break for an hour, describing in every little detail what had occurred since the last time they met: the story with the tailor, the emergence of the *No-Visual* movement, the laws on scopophilia, then the revision of the bundle, with the subsequent rehabilitation of optical freedom and the eccentric innovation of screen-clothes, and now . . .

They nodded from time to time, listening very carefully, and propping up their chin on the forearm, like a column supporting the temple of the mind. They then hinted at a smile, moving away the supporting arm, during the description of the *Ya-Virtual* militants, but their face definitely looked sadder as soon as the story moved to the main reason of the visit: those strange animals.

'You see, at the beginning we thought it was a specific variety of ants, or perhaps a new species of beetle, so nobody got too worried. Later, however, they started to increase in size, getting bigger and bigger, so much so that . . . here you are, I brought a couple of specimens,' she said finally, handling the box and lifting the lid.

'Shut that box immediately!' they shouted, jumping up with such a rapid movement that even the massive glasses they usually firmly carried on the top of their nose fell to the ground.

'What's going on?' she reacted, terrified.

She knew Dr. Q very well and remembered they were not easily worried, so their reaction really scared her.

'The icon!' they shouted, nervously walking up and down the living room. 'The icon! Where did you put the icon I gave you?'

'The icon?' she replied lowering her gaze. 'I completely forgot about it' she said, bringing her left hand to her face as if she was looking for it somewhere in her head. 'Oh yes! The icon! St George and the dragon! Yes, sure! It's in my office!'

'Brilliant! Then go back to your town immediately, take the icon and gather up all your fellow citizens. Wait. First, I have something to give you,' they said, as they left the room.

The doctor kept repeating to herself 'The icon! Yes! The icon! How could I forget about the icon!' and as she repeated these words, more as a form of reassurance rather than self-blaming, she felt that the box with the animals was getting heavier and heavier. Yet she continued to hold it tight on her lap and refrained from opening it, not even taking a peek.

'Here you are, take this,' said Dr. Q coming back and offering her an object as big as the box. 'It's a drum,' they added, 'and might be useful.'

'Thank you, really thank you! I don't know what we would have done without you!' she said, standing up and picking up the drum, before heading towards the door.

She went out in a rush, barely holding onto the box, which was more and more painful to carry. When she got on the train, she had to bind it with heavy string, because the lid was pushing as if those growing animals wanted to get out, but she did not want to free them before she found the icon.

As soon as she got off the train and took the subway exit out of the station, she met Mr F. He, too, was back sooner than expected, because he heard that an extraordinary Council meeting had been summoned. She asked him to kindly bring that box to the meeting, without opening it on the way, and to invite everyone he knew to bring their pets along. She may have found a solution, but she had to stop by her office first.

Mr F. accepted the heavy box, more out of fear than generosity, and headed towards the council hall, telling everyone he met on the way to bring as many pets as possible to the meeting.

After a while all the town's citizens had gathered together in the hall. With them, were several specimens of those weird animals, from the smallest, which could be kept in a pocket, to the biggest, now human size. Scared faces looked at each other, feeling suffocated, as if there was no air, also because the ever-increasing number of strange creatures crowded the hall, making them feel outnumbered. Some of the animals outside, when they found the council door shut, started to climb up the windows, not hesitating to break them to enter, as if they could not live without the humans.

Dismay mounted before what now looked increasingly like an alien attack, when, all of a sudden, the sound of a drum was heard: beats, first feeble and nicely paced, later more and more powerful, as if the town hall walls were becoming a sound chamber. The louder the noise, the smaller the animals seemed to become, leaving most people completely shocked at that extraordinary transformation, until a series of great thunderclaps caught the attention of the citizens, who streamed out of the building to look up at the storm – but the sky was blue and clear, bluer and clearer than maybe ever before, and the more it kept raining and thundering, the more the sky seemed to free itself of clouds. Somebody started a tune, then a song, then a shout in a sign of liberation, while the percussions seemed to resonate all at once everywhere, throughout the entire surrounding environment, making the animals shrink into disappearance, like a defeated imaginary dragon. The more intensely the citizens danced and sang, the more their screen-clothes liquefied to the ground, like empty sacks.

# Grand finale

two myths and a half, and we traversed the city of men, a journey through the sea, and we founded a new city of women, five visceral metamorphoses and we discovered an I, which did not set up to build a city of many other eyes, but cultivated an herbarium instead, because plants cannot see and cannot speak, and yet they tell stories, stories and irises, narcissi and roses, aubergines and geraniums, gardenias and carrots, and maybe some radicchio as well, here and there, not to mention this rosemary, which tells of the winter that nourished it and the polite daily visits of the sun, and even speaks of the planets, those cosmic scoundrels, who made a secret plan to move around in this specific way, so as to make my rosemary plant grow, not without consulting the entire universe before, because that too had to decide to coalesce in this very way, at this very moment, so that the lemon plant in my bedroom can tell its own story too, how we traversed an entire ocean together, without them knowing, because I put newspapers around it every winter, so that they do not realize we are no longer there, in the mediterranean, the closed sea, but we can keep shining together, no matter where, in the light of this sun, which is everywhere the same, if only you look at it, so we continue breathing together every night, me and my plants, they give me oxygen and I return dreams, I produce carbon dioxide and they give me lemons, and we have so many lemons now and so many common stories to tell, as does the jasmine, with its excessive green, constantly interlacing its different shades at my feet, along with the basil, which can get depressed so easily, despite its peppermint smell, but was happy to welcome the new orange tree, which just arrived, full of unexpected buds, and it has been a magnificent dance party, we interweaved smells, and flowers, and molecules, all the time, what a wonderful ballet, because every opera needs a ballet, to be a truly grandiose opera, so this work too needed a ballet, a special *grand finale*, and what better than a transindividual ballet, where the plants melt into the rocks and the aloe vera pulses through the bedframe, while the wooden floor constantly invites us to its perpetual jam session, reverberating all the life it accumulated outside, and all the feet it supported inside, and so we dance every morning, every afternoon and every night, because even you are a reluctant player in that perpetual jamming, whether you like it or not, pulsating in the unique substance, that being, which is, rather than nothing, which is not – the unique substance, expressing itself through a perpetual ballet of modes, having no other reason for being than this infinite dance *sub species aeternitatis*

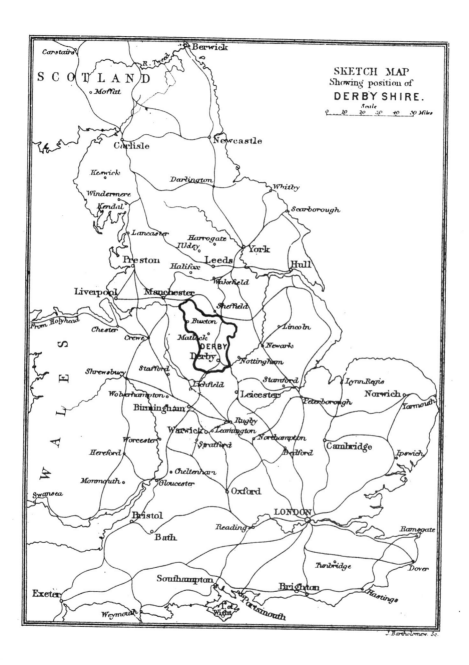

SKETCH MAP
Showing position of
**DERBYSHIRE.**

Scale
0   10   20   30   40   50 Miles

PEVERIL CASTLE AND ENTRANCE TO THE PEAK CAVERN.

# BLACK'S

# TOURIST'S GUIDE

## TO

# DERBYSHIRE

## ITS TOWNS, WATERING-PLACES, DALES, AND MANSIONS

With Map of the County, Plans of Chatsworth and Haddon Hall, and several Illustrations

EDITED BY LLEWELLYNN JEWITT, F.S.A., ETC.

## EDINBURGH
## ADAM AND CHARLES BLACK
## 1872

Published by:
Country Books
Courtyard Cottage, Little Longstone, Bakewell, Derbyshire DE45 1NN England
Tel/Fax: 01629 640670

ISBN 1 898941 22 X

From the 1850s until the end of the nineteenth century, Adam & Charles Black of Edinburgh published a series of guide books covering the country at a time when the railways and the industrial revolution were in their infancy. Who would have thought in 1872 that the county would have been covered in a road system simply to accomodate the motor car?! Only the aristocracy and the wealthier middle classes could afford to travel and so the books were produced in small numbers — original copies are now both scarce and expensive.

The **1872 Black's Guide to Derbyshire** was edited by Llewellynn Jewitt — a name which needs no introduction to local historians in the county. The contents of the book include: a general description of Derbyshire; area; population; position; history; antiquities; eminent men; geology; manufactures; agriculture; railways and canals; map of Buxton; map of Chatsworth and vicinity; plan of Haddon Hall and twenty-five engravings on wood and steel. There is also a section of 62 pages of period advertisements. Adam & Charles Black, the original publisher, often subsidised the cost of these volumes by the inclusion of advertisements for hotels, shipping companies, railways, tourist souvenirs and household goods.

**COUNTRY BOOKS** are in the process of reprinting the entire series of Black's Guides. Please ask for a prospectus on other counties of interest. Numbered limited editions in cloth or leather bindings are available only by subscription from the publisher.

Printed in Englnad by:
MFP Design & Print, Longford Trading Estate, Thomas Street, Stretford, Manchester M32 0JT
Tel: 0161 864 4540

# PREFACE.

———◆———

*This edition has again been carefully revised, and numerous alterations have been made on the descriptions of Buxton and Chatsworth. It has been the aim of the Editor to make the work as complete as possible without entering too much into details, and in all cases to study utility and convenience of reference. It is hoped that this object is very nearly accomplished by the partial alphabetical arrangement which has been adopted.*

JUNE 1872.

# CONTENTS.

CONTENTS.

# LIST OF ILLUSTRATIONS.

———◆———

## MAPS.

## VIEWS.

\* The above are reduced copies of illustrations, kindly granted by permission of the Proprietors of the *Illustrated London News.* The view of Dovedale is from Mr. Jewitt's Guide to Alton Towers and Dovedale.

# GENERAL DESCRIPTION.

Area, 1029 square miles, or 658,803 statute acres. Population in 1871—Males, 191,078; Females, 189,460; total, 380,538. Increase in ten years, from 1861 to 1871, 41,211; excess of Females over Males in 1851, 610; excess of Males over Females in 1861, 1645; excess of Males over Females in 1871, 1618; increase of Males over Females in ten years, 1851 to 1861, 2255; decrease in total of Males over Females in ten years, 1861 to 1871, 27. Inhabited houses, 78,530; increase since 1861, 9268; uninhabited, 4172; building 562. Greatest length, 56 miles; greatest breadth, 33 miles; average breadth, 20½ miles. About 500,000 acres are arable or pasture.

THE County of Derby has an entirely inland position, no portion being less than about forty miles from the sea; while the absence of rivers of large magnitude, and the dry warmth of the limestone rock which chiefly abounds in the north of the county tend to render it a desirable residence for such as cannot with impunity risk the moist atmosphere of the coast. To the north, the county is bounded by the west Riding of Yorkshire; to the west, by Cheshire and Staffordshire; to the south, by Leicestershire; and to the east, by the county of Nottingham. The principal rivers are the Derwent, Trent, Wye, and Dove, the latter of which forms the boundary between this and the county of Stafford. The greatest length of the county (*i.e.*, from north to south) is 56 miles; while the greatest breadth is about 33. In

form it is very irregular, somewhat resembling a parallelo-
gram, with excrescences on the north-west and north-east
corners, and a pointed prolongation on the south.   Like
Scotland, Derbyshire is naturally divided into two portions,
the northern and southern divisions ; the Highlands and
Lowlands—the region of hills, rocks, dales, and moors ;
and the seat of busy industry and successful agriculture.
Long before the Roman invasion, Derbyshire formed part
of the nation of Coritani.   The Cornavii are said by the
Welsh to have invaded Britain immediately before the
Romans—in fact, to have been " one of the three molesta-
tions that came into our island, and never went away
again."   To the Celtic period the stone circles of Arbor-
low ; the " Nine Ladies" on Stanton Moor ; and those on
Harthill Moor, Abney Moor, Eyam Moor near the Wet
Withens, Froggatt Edge, and Hathersage Moor, are to be
ascribed ; as are also the Rocking Stones on Stanton Moor,
on the Roo-tor rocks, and " Robin Hood's Mark" on Ash-
over Common ; the fortifications and earthworks of Carls-
wark at Hathersage, at Staden-low near Buxton, at Pilsbury,
on Great Finn, by Taddington, and on Combe Moss ; the
remains of habitations near Crich, at Harthill Moor, at
Middleton by Youlgrave, and other places ; and numberless tumuli, and other remains which are spread over the
Peak district in great abundance.   The Romans, when
they first partitioned England, put Derbyshire into that
part denominated *Britannia Prima*, and subsequently,
when a new division was made by Severus, the whole
district, which included the Coritani, formed the eastern
part of the province called *Flavia Cæsariensis*.   Among
the relics left by these warlike people may be noticed the
station of *Derventio*, or Little Chester, by Derby, where

many important relics of the period have been from time to time discovered ; the remains of Roman roads ; a camp near Pentrich ; remains discovered at the station of Buxton ; the settlement at Brough near Castleton ; vestiges of a station called Melandra Castle, in the township of Gamesley ; a camp at Parwich ; and a large number of sepulchral remains, personal and domestic ornaments and utensils, pottery, coins, etc., found at different periods throughout the county. Evident remains of the working of various lead-mines in Derbyshire by the Romans also still exist, and some pigs of lead bearing inscriptions have been found in the county—one of these having the words IMP . CAES . HADRIANI . AVG . MET . LVT. ; another, L . ARVCONI. VERECVND . METAL . LVTVD . ; and a third, TI . CL . TR . LVT . BR . EX . ARG. In the Heptarchy, Derbyshire formed part of the kingdom of Mercia, *Rependune,* now Repton, being the capital of the kingdom, and the burial-place of the Mercian kings. Of this period many interesting relics have been found in barrows, and in course of excavations, and remains are also to be found in ecclesiastical and other buildings. Of the Norman period there are abundant remains in the castellated and ecclesiastical buildings in the county, some of which are of extreme interest. Derby itself appears to have been a place of considerable importance in the Anglo-Saxon period, and coins of Æthelstan, Eadrid, Eadwig, Eadgar, Æthelred II., Harold I., and Edward the Confessor, were struck in that town ; while of the Norman period, coins of William the Conqueror, and, later, of Stephen, were minted there. From their situation on the River Trent, this county, with that of Notts, received the distinctive appellation of Merciæ Aquilonares. Saxon coins have frequently been found. William the Conqueror gave a great part of the county to his natural son William Peveril, whose fortress gives the name to Castleton.

Amongst the distinguished men of the county may be named George Vernon, called " the King of the Peak ;" Charles Cotton, the poet, who resided at Beresford Hall, near Ashbourne, where he was visited by " his dear and most worthy friend Mr. Izaak Walton ;" Brindley, the self-taught engineer ; Strutt, the inventor of ribbed stockings, and the partner of Arkwright in the spinning of cotton, and whose descendant has been elevated to the peerage as Lord Belper ; Thomas Bott, an English clergyman of ingenuity and learning, born at Derby 1688, died 1754 ; Arthur Agard, a learned and industrious antiquary, born in Derbyshire 1540, died 1615 ; William Owtram, or Outram, an English divine, and accomplished scholar, born in Derbyshire 1625, died 1679, of which family an equally distinguished member, Sir James Outram, is recently deceased ; Jonathan Edwards, D.D.; Dr. Samuel Pegge, the learned antiquary and author ; Abraham Booth, a pious and popular dissenting minister, born in Derbyshire 1734, died 1806 ; George Stanhope, Dean of Canterbury, a divine of eminent talents and personal worth, born in Derbyshire 1660, died 1728 ; Charles Ashton, one of the most learned critics of his age, born in Derbyshire about 1665, died 1752 ; Robert Bage, author of " Mount Heneth " and other novels, born in Derbyshire 1728, died 1801 ; Ellis Farneworth, M.A., Rector of Carsington, translator of several works from the Italian and French, and editor of an edition of the works of Machiavelli, in 2 vols. 4to ; Sir Anthony Fitzherbert, the " famous judge," known as " The Father of English Husbandry," and author of the " Natura

Brevium," " Office of Justice of the Peace," " Book of Husbandry," etc. etc., of all of which numerous editions have
been published ; Cardinals Curzon and De Repington ;
Bishops Pursglove, Wilson, Boothe, and Middleton ; Mompesson, the christian hero of Eyam ; Sir Richard Arkwright,
who, though not a native, yet by skill and enterprise did
much for the fame and prosperity of Derbyshire ; Sir
Francis Chantrey, the eminent sculptor ; Sir Joseph Paxton,
the designer of the Crystal Palace ; Sir Charles Fox, the
engineer of the same ; Sir Francis Burdett, the celebrated
political leader ; Sir Aston Cockayn, the poet ; Sir Thomas
Fanshawe ; Anthony Babington, who was cruelly beheaded
by Elizabeth for conspiring in favour of Mary Queen of
Scots ; President Bradshaw, who signed the death-warrant
of Charles ; the celebrated Lord Chief-Justice Denman ;
Charles Richardson, the author of " Pamela," " Sir Charles
Grandisson," etc.; Dr. Darwin, the author of " Zoonomia,"
" Loves of the Plants," etc. ; William Hutton, the historian ; Dr. John Woodward, the naturalist and philosopher, and founder of the Woodwardian professorship ;
Wright the painter ; Jeremiah Brandreth, the leader of
the " Derby conspiracy," who was beheaded for high
treason ; Thomas Linacre ; Antony Blackwall ; Thomas
Bateman, the late distinguished antiquary and collector ;
Jabez Bunting, the nonconformist minister ; Thomas Blore
the topographer, and his son Edward Blore, the distinguished architect and antiquary ; Edmund Cartwright ; William Radcliffe, the inventor of the " dressing machine ;"
the Howitts ; and a large number of other equally eminent
individuals. Amongst the eminent women of Derbyshire
it may be sufficient to name the celebrated Countess of
Shrewsbury, known as " Bess of Hardwick ;" the accom-

plished authoress, the Duchess of Newcastle ; Anna Seward, the poetess, and friend of Dr. Johnson ; and Florence Nightingale, whose name is so closely identified with the Russian war, for her holy ministrations in the hospitals, and with every good work.

" All the east border beyond Dronfield, Alfreton, Belper, to Dale Abbey, is coal, with clay-slate and ironstone ; from Ashbourne and Duffield to Hope, and from the east side of the Derwent to beyond the Dove, carboniferous limestone ; south of Derby, red sandstone or marl ; between Uttoxeter and Derby, gritstone (for cutlers) is found, and also in the middle, from Belper upwards to the north border, and all round to Chapel-le-Firth, in beds of great thickness, rising into bold crags near Hathersage, Glossop, etc."

The population of the county is principally employed in manufactures, in mining, and in agriculture. The manufactures consist chiefly of iron, of which there are many immense works ; silk, which is thrown to a greater extent here than in any other county, and is also manufactured into finished goods, including ribbands, sewing silks, bootlaces, velvets, trimmings, and other articles ; cotton, of which the mills of the Strutts, the Evanses (the well-known " Boar's Head " cotton-spinners), and the Arkwrights, are among the principal ; calico ; lace ; pottery ; bottles ; porcelain ; plaister and colours ; hardware ; chenille ; elastic goods ; gloves ; stockings ; hats ; merino clothing ; lead, in all its preparations ; vitriol, and other chemicals ; lime ; paper, etc. etc. The mining operations comprise lead, ironstone, coal, etc., and a very large number of people are employed in this manner. The agricultural pursuits of the two districts of the county vary considerably. The south district is rich in pasturage, and produces remarkably fine crops and cattle ; the land is in a high state of cultivation, and very efficiently worked. The north or Peak district is naturally much later in crops than the south, but produces, in some parts, excellent corn, and many of the Peak dairies are remarkable for the excellence of the cheese, and the good quality of the mutton. The gritstone and limestone quarries, and the marble and spar works, are very extensive, and employ a large number of hands, as do also the gypsum pits. There are large chemical and colour-works at Derby, and the iron-foundries of the county are some of the largest in the kingdom.

The county is divided into six hundreds—two and a portion of a third being situated in the northern division, and the remainder in the southern. There are three corporate towns—Derby, Chesterfield, and Glossop—14 market towns, 132 parishes, and 440 villages. Eight members are returned to Parliament—*i.e.*, two for each division— viz. the Southern, Northern, and Eastern, and two for the borough of Derby. The real property was valued in 1843 at £1,379,025, but is now immensely increased.

The county contains several navigable canals, and is well intersected by railways, which traverse it in every direction. The coal districts of Derbyshire were among the very first in the kingdom to lay down and use tramways, the precursors of the present railway system, and the county was among the first in which steam communication was introduced. The railway lines now in operation are, " The Midland " main lines from Derby to London ; Derby to Nottingham, Lincoln, etc. ; Derby to Sheffield, Leeds, Bradford, Lancaster, Skipton, and the north, etc. ; Derby to Birmingham and Worcester, Cheltenham, Gloucester, Bristol, and the West of England ; and Amber-Gate to Matlock, Buxton, Manchester, and Liverpool, etc. " The North Stafford " lines to the potteries and Manchester, and to Ashbourne, etc.; " The South Staffordshire," for Lichfield, Walsall, Dudley, etc.; " The Erewash Valley," from Trent to Clay Cross and Chesterfield, and to Mansfield ; " The Derby, Little Eaton, and Ripley " branch of the Midland ; the " Wirksworth Branch " of the Midland, from Duffield to Wirksworth ; " The Cromford and High Peak," now leased to the " London and North-Western," for mineral traffic, and to Manchester ; " The Sheffield, Manchester, and Lincolnshire," by way of Glossop ; the " Stockport, Disley, and Buxton " line (worked by the London and North-Western Company), connecting Manchester with the High Peak and the south, etc. A branch of the Midland Railway, the " Chesterfield and Sheffield " line, leaves the main line of the Chesterfield, and runs to Sheffield, where it terminates; by which means Sheffield is placed on the main line, and passengers avoid the delay and annoyance of the branch from Masbro'. A line connecting Melbourne and other places with Derby, and known as the " Melbourne and Worthington Branch " of the Midland Railway, and another, the " Castle Donington and Trent Branch," as well as the " Swadlincolt Branch," are also now in operation. There are also schemes in progress by the London and North-Western Railway Company for running into the town of Derby, and so connecting it immediately with the North-Western system, and by the Midland for farther extending their system in many directions.

# ALFRETON.

Alfreton from Derby, 14 m. ; from Belper, 6 m. ; from Chesterfield, 10 m. Railway station of the Erewash Valley Railway nearly two miles to the west of the town. Population 11,805.

INNS: The *George*, commercial, family, and posting, Samuel Jepson; *Angel; Castle*, etc.

ALFRETON, the Ælfredingtune of the Saxons, is a pleasantly situated market-town in the centre of a populous and thriving district. The town, which is built on the ridge of a hill, consists mainly of two streets, intersecting each other at right angles, with a good central market-place. The hill upon which the town is built extends for about a couple of miles to Normanton, where it slopes gently down into the fertile district of " Golden Valley." The parish is an extensive one, and comprises many places noted for their ironworks, and for other interesting matters connected with them. The population of the whole parish, including the townships of Green Hill Lane, Pyebridge, Ironville, Riddings, Swanwick, and Somercotes, was 11,549 in 1861—that of Alfreton alone being 4090. The inhabitants are principally employed at the ironworks and collieries of the neighbourhood, and in the manufacture of stockings, etc. The market-day is Friday.

There is a general belief that the town was built by King Alfred the Great, and its name would seem to give probability to the tradition. It is also said that Alfred had a palace here, and its site is supposed to be still traceable. The manor was given to Burton Abbey by Wulfric Spott, and the grant was confirmed to that abbey by Ethelred the Second. In the Domesday Survey it is stated to be then held by Roger de Busli. It afterwards belonged to Ingram, and then to Fitz-Ranulf, Lord of Alfreton, who founded Beauchief Abbey. This Fitz-Ranulph, or Fitz-Ralph, is said by Tanner, Dugdale, and others, to have been one of the murderers of Thomas à-Becket, but Pegge sought to refute this statement. From this family the manor passed to the Chaworths, and so on in succession through Ormond to Anthony Babington of Dethick, and so through Zouch and Sutton to the family of its present owner, Morewood. BZ 455

The church contains some monumental brasses to the Ormond family, and tablets and inscriptions to the Morewoods and others. The Hall, the seat of the Morewoods, was built about the middle of last century, but the present house is of much larger dimensions and more imposing character. The grounds are remarkably fine and well laid out, and the house commands extensive views over the surrounding district.

There are numerous chapels; national and other schools; and a Mechanics' Institution, which was established in 1856. There are two banks—viz. Messrs. Wilson and Son, and a branch of the Nottingham, etc., Banking Co.; there is also a Savings Bank. The county court for the district is held at Alfreton monthly, in the Town Hall, which was erected from the design of Mr. Benjamin Wilson in 1857. Petty Sessions are held fortnightly in the Town-Hall. The town has been placed under a Local Board of Health, and it has also its Gas Company, its Agricultural and Floricultural Societies, and other institutions.

## NEIGHBOURHOOD OF ALFRETON.

RIDDINGS, three miles from Alfreton, is a considerable and thriving village, supported by the collieries and iron-works of the neighbourhood. It has a church dedicated to St. James, which cost £4000 in 1845, and forms a separate ecclesiastical district in the patronage of the vicar of Alfreton. A weekly market, established of late years, is held on Saturday, which is a great convenience to the hard-working inhabitants of the place. There are Methodist, Baptist, Independent, and other places of worship in the town. The large ironworks of Messrs. James Oakes and Company are in this district, and these and the collieries, etc., find employment for a large number of people.

IRONVILLE, near Riddings, and adjoining Codnor Park, is one of the most thriving and flourishing places in the Erewash Valley district. It is a town of modern rise, but has now, like its more ancient brethren, its market, its newspaper, its church and chapels, its library, and its schools. The Cromford and the Erewash Canals run by Ironville, and the Erewash Valley Railway gives means of communication north and south. The neighbourhood is exceedingly rich in iron ore, and the Butterley Company's immense ironworks at Codnor Park, and their collieries in the neighbourhood, afford employment to nearly the whole of the inhabitants. The church was built by this company at a cost of £6000, and the schools and other buildings are mainly indebted to them for their foundation. The Artizans and Mechanics' Library offers all the usual advantages of such institutions to the hard-working population of the place.

The CODNOR PARK IRONWORKS of the Butterley Company rank among the most extensive and important in the kingdom, and are well worth a visit from the tourist, who will here find much to interest and instruct him. The works occupy an area of considerably more than twenty acres of ground, and embrace every apparatus and appliance necessary for carrying on such a gigantic establishment. The best idea of the extent of the mining, smelting, and manufacturing operations carried on at this one—and only one—of the foundries belonging to the Butterley Company, may be got from the public grounds which have of late years been laid out with much taste on the summit of the hill above Codnor Park, whereon a monument to the late Mr. Jessop, the then principal proprietor of the works, has been erected. From this hill, which has been well chosen as the site for the erection of the monument, one of the finest and most extensive panoramic views of the neighbourhood is obtained, and the nature and extent of the works of the Butterley Company understood at a glance. In almost every direction as far as the eye can reach, in a circle of about five miles from this spot, the operations of the company may be seen carried on. Immediately below are the Codnor Park Ironworks, while about three miles to the west are those at Butterley, the two establishments being connected by a private railway, on which locomotives dragging immense trains are constantly steaming to and fro, whilst in every direction rise up tall chimneys from almost innumerable steam engines attached to coal and ironstone pits, plying their endless work of fury, and continually tearing up the very bowels of the earth, whilst intermixed with them are the more homely looking gins worked by horses, and doing their labour in a more quiet and primitive manner. All around are tramways, and canals, and railroads, intersecting each other in every possible direction, and forming such a labyrinth of roads as only human ingenuity and perseverance could correctly traverse. The distant view on one side embraces Crich Cliff and Stand, with the valley near Whatstandwell, and the distant hills beyond, and on the other the valley of the Erewash with the hills of Nottinghamshire skirting the horizon. The works of the Butterley Company give employment, we believe, to about 6000 persons.

Not far from the Jessop monument is Codnor Castle, of which an account will be found in another part of this volume. SWANWICK is another mining and coal town in this busy district, with church, dissenting chapels of different persuasions, free and national schools, reading-room, and library.

## ALTON TOWERS.
### The seat of the Talbots, Earls of Shrewsbury.

Although this favourite resort of excursionists is not in Derbyshire, it is so connected with it, that it deserves to be mentioned in this place. From Derby special weekly trips are arranged on the North Staffordshire Railway at a trifling charge, the ticket giving admission to the gardens and grounds. It may also be approached conveniently by rail or road from Ashbourne. The latter (route by road) is of great beauty, and forms a delightful day's drive. Visitors will find a comfortable inn in the village of Alton —viz. the *White Hart*, where carriages may be put up, and tickets obtained to see the grounds.

For further particulars, see *Black's Guide to Alton Towers and Dovedale*.

## ASHBOURNE.

Ashbourne from Alton Towers 9 m. ; from Matlock 12 m. ; from Buxton 20 m. ; from Derby 13 m.  Railway Station of the North Staffordshire Railway, at the south-west end of the town, near the church.  Population 2083.

Entrance to Dovedale from Ashbourne 4 m. ; from Matlock 13 m.; from Bakewell 16 m. ; from Derby 17 m. ; from Buxton 17 m.

HOTELS : *Green Man* and *Black's Head Royal Hotel*, St. John Street, R. Wallis ; *Wheat Sheaf*, Church Street ; *White Hart*, Church Street ; *George and Dragon*, Market Place.

ASHBOURNE, originally termed Esseburne, is a town well known to anglers.  It is situated on the river Schoo or Henmore, a small tributary stream of the river Dove, which divides the town into two parts, near Dovedale The river abounds in trout and grayling.  The principal seat is Ashbourne Hall.  In Mayfield Cottage, not far from Ashbourne, the great poet Tom Moore resided for some length of time, with his wife and family.  The cottage is a plain, quiet, unassuming little residence, in the close neighbourhood of some of the most charming scenery in the world, and is just the place for a poet to choose to live in.  Many of Moore's admirable letters to Lord Byron, and to others, dated from Ashbourne, have been published in his Life, by Lord John Russell, and in other works ; and here, besides the charming lines, " Those Evening Bells," which were written on hearing the sweet sound of the Ashbourne bells floating through the evening breeze, he wrote a great part of his " Lalla Rookh."  The church, a splendid and very large structure, principally of the early English and decorated periods, is cruciform, consisting of nave with side aisles, chancel, and north and south transepts, with a grand central tower, from which springs a lofty octagonal spire. In the church is the curious original dedication plate, by which it appears that it was dedicated in honour of St. Oswald, in the year 1241. The inscription, which is most interesting, is as follows:—

"ANNO AB INCARNACIONE DNI. MCCXLI. VIII° KL MAII DEDICATA EST HEC ECCIA ET HOC ALTARE CONSECRATUM IN HONORE SCI OSWALDI, REGIS ET MARTIRIS, A VENERABILI PATRE DOMINO. HUGONE DE PATISHVL COVENTRENSI EPISCOPO."

The font is a fine specimen of the early English period, and there are some very interesting examples of sedilia, piscina, etc. The church contains several extremely fine and curious monuments, amongst which are altar-tombs to Sir Humphrey and Lady Bradburne, and to other members of the family; several remarkably fine monuments to the Cockayne family, to which Sir Aston Cockayne, the Elizabethan poet, belonged, and many others to the Sacheverells, Sherratts, Bainbrigges, Boothbys, Langtons, and others. Of the Boothby monuments, one by Banks cannot fail to call forth the admiration of the observer. It is a sculptured figure of a child six years old, laid on a mattress. "Her head reclines on a pillow, but the disposition of the whole figure indicates restlessness. The little sufferer, indeed, appears as if she had just changed her position by one of those frequent turnings to which illness often in vain resorts for relief from pain." The exquisite feeling displayed in the conception and execution of this gem has been the theme of praise among all visitors, and is sufficient to secure the fame of any artist. Rhodes, the friend of Chantrey, says that it probably suggested to that eminent sculptor the idea of " that masterpiece of art, the group of Two Children, now the grace and ornament of Lichfield Cathedral, and the boast of modern sculpture." On the tablet is the following line, expressive of the feelings of the little sufferer :—

"I was not in safety, neither had I rest, and trouble came."

On the pedestal is the touching inscription :—

"TO PENELOPE,
Only child of Sir Brooke Boothby and Dame Susannah Boothby,
Born April 11th, 1785.—Died March 13th, 1791.
She was in form and intellect most exquisite.
The unfortunate parents ventured their all on this frail bark, and the
wreck was total.

Omnia tecum una perierunt gaudia nostra. Tu vero felix et beata Penelope mea, Quæ tot tautisque miseriis una morte perfuncta es.

Lei che'l ciel ne mostra terra n'asconde.
Le crespe chiome d'or puro lucente.
El' lampoggiar del Angellico riso,
Che soleau far in terra un Paradiso,
Poca polvere son che nulla sente.

Beauté, c'est donc ici ton dernier azyle. Son cercueil ne la contient pas toute entière. Il attend le reste de sa proie : Il ne l'attendra pas long-temps."

A fire occurred in the church in January 1862, but fortunately the monuments escaped without damage.

The new Free Church was erected in 1871, at the sole cost of Francis Wright, Esq., of Ormaston Manor ; it is a large and imposing looking Gothic building, with spacious grounds, and is situated on the Buxton road.

The town of Ashbourne is one of great antiquity, and its history is full of historical associations. It is a market town, the market day being Saturday. It has many noted fairs, both for cattle and cheese. It is an ancient royal burgh, and some curious documents are yet extant concerning it. It is the head of one of the Poor-Law Unions, has a county court held in it, and is also a meeting-place for petty sessions. The principal public buildings are— St. John's Hall, the Banks, the covered Market-hall, large and convenient, the Union Work-house, Post Office, and Railway Station. The Market-hall buildings contain the Literary Institute and Library, Assembly-rooms, armoury of the Dove Valley Rifle-corps, and Masonic lodge. A new cattle-market has recently been formed.

The Free Grammar School, one of the best in the kingdom, is in Church Street, and is a large substantial stone building, founded by Queen Elizabeth in 1585. Opposite to it is the house formerly the residence of the celebrated Dr. John Taylor of Ashbourne, the intimate friend and associate of the great Dr. Johnson, who visited him on several occasions at this house.

Ashbourne Hall, long the residence of the Boothbys, but now of Mr. Franks, is delightfully situated, and surrounded by extensive grounds. It was made head-quarters for the Scottish army under Prince Charles, on his march to Derby in 1745. On this occasion the names of the officers to whom the various rooms were appropriated were written on the doors in chalk, and one of these names, which has been carefully varnished over, is still preserved. Various members of the Boothby family were highly intellectual, and distinguished themselves as writers. Of these, Sir Brooke Boothby wrote some works on Burke's Appeal to the Whigs, and Paine's Rights of Man. His poetical talents were of no ordinary character, and his " Sorrows Sacred to Penelope,"—

his youthful daughter whose tomb we have just described
—is one of the most exquisitely sensitive productions in
our language. Some of the sonnets breathe more real and
fervent feeling than can almost be boasted by any other
writer. He also published a couple of volumes of "Fables
and Satires." Miss Hill Boothby, too, was celebrated for
her literary attainments, and was one of the most constant
friends of Dr. Johnson, as is seen from a volume of their
collected letters, published in 1805. The late Sir William
Boothby, who, it will be remembered, married the celebrated actress Mrs. Nisbet, resided here till his death.
Ashbourne has been celebrated for its literary character
for the last three centuries or more, and many natives of
the place have distinguished themselves in the world of
letters.

From Ashbourne the tourist can with ease visit Alton
Towers (see page 13), Tissington, and Thorpe, where guides
are to be had to Dovedale, Ilam, and other interesting
localities. TISSINGTON is a quiet secluded village, of
much rural simplicity and beauty. It is celebrated for the
sweet and gentle custom, of "*Well-Flowering*," or "*Well-
Dressing*," which occurs on Holy Thursday.* The wells or
springs in the village, five in number, are on this day
decorated with the most chaste and tasteful devices formed
of flowers imbedded in a preparation of clay attached to
boards, and forming arches, pediments, and various designs,
and arranged in exquisite patterns, intermixed with appropriate mottoes and Scriptural texts. The wells having
been decorated as a labour of love by the villagers, divine
service is held in the church, and the minister, accom-

* For a detailed account of this charming custom, see the "Reliquary."
vol. iii., pp. 29 to 48.

panied by the choir, the congregation, and the immense concourse of spectators from the surrounding country which the charming ceremonial has called together, proceeds from well to well, where the collects for the day are read in succession, and psalms and hymns sung. The day is one of pure social enjoyment, and is unmixed with any thing savouring of a disagreeable character. It is without doubt one of the most pleasing floral festivals which have been handed down to our generation. The church is beautifully situated on rising ground in the centre of the village, and is surrounded by lofty trees. It contains some remains of Norman architecture, and some interesting monuments. Tissington Hall, the ancient family mansion of the Fitzherberts, is a picturesque old hall opposite the parish church. Of this family was the celebrated Judge Antony Fitzherbert, the author of the Natura Brevium, Justice of the Peace, etc., who was born in 1458.

THORPE is a very picturesque village, with an interesting old church. From this village the magnificent conical mountain called Thorpe Cloud takes its name. The most direct way from Ashbourne to Dovedale is by Mappleton, the roadway the whole distance being of the most picturesque character, and presenting to the tourist a series of the most extensive and charming prospects in the district.

FENNY BEATTEY, on the way from Ashbourne to Tissington, is a pretty little village with a fine old manor-house, formerly belonging to the Beresford family, and intimately connected with Charles Cotton the angler and poet.

## BAKEWELL.

Population in 1871, 2283.

Omnibus to Chatsworth *via* Haddon Hall, 2s. 6d. ; Carriage, 1 horse, 15s. ; ditto, 2 horse, 21s.

HOTELS and INNS.—*Rutland Arms and Family Hotel*, W. Greaves—Bed 1s. 6d. to 2s. 6d., board 5s. 6d. per day, attendance optional, private rooms not charged, commercial room at regular charges; visitors have permission to angle on the river Wye. *Castle Commercial*, W. Miers, near the bridge at the entrance to the town from the Railway Station.

From Haddon Hall 3 m.; from Derby 22 m. (by railway 25½ m.); from Chesterfield 11 m.; from Matlock 10 m.; from Chatsworth 4 m.; from Buxton 12 m.; from Sheffield 16 m.; from Alton Towers 25 m. Railway station on the Derby, Ambergate, Matlock, Buxton, Manchester, and Liverpool line of the Midland Railway, a short distance from the town over the bridge.

BAKEWELL is a pleasant market town, situated on the river Wye. It is a petty sessions, election, and polling place. The Duke of Rutland is Lord of the manor. The town is of great antiquity, having been a bathing-place, *Badecanwillan*, long before the Conquest. It appears that Edward, surnamed the Elder, son of the Good Alfred, had a fort in the vicinity of the town in 924. Some remains of the earthwork are still traceable on Castlehill. In the Domesday book it is styled "Badequelle" or "Bauquelle." The right of holding a weekly market was claimed by John Gernon in 1330. In 1502 the manor was purchased by Sir Henry Vernon, and from his family passed into that of Manners. The town is well drained, watered, and lighted. The well, to which in all probability the town owed its ancient occupation, was covered in, and a bathing house erected in 1697. The water is slightly tepid, averaging about 60 degrees Fahrenheit. It is considered highly beneficial in cases of chronic rheumatism. The baths have been rebuilt by the Duke of Rutland. Besides a large swimming bath, there are three well fitted up baths, in which the water may be had of any temperature by artificial heating. Attached is a pleasant promenade called the Bath Garden. There is an endowed grammar school, founded in 1637 by Lady Grace Manners, relict of Sir George Manners. It is open to the children of Bakewell and Great Rowsley. St. John's Hospital is a charity having six houses adjoining the grammar school. It owes its foundation to Sir John Manners and his brother Roger, in 1602. The Bakewell and High Peak Institute, founded 1849, has a very creditable library and reading-room. There are "Museums" in the town, where Derbyshire spar ornaments, inlaid marble tables, and vases, and other things may be purchased. A cotton mill, established by Arkwright, which gave employment to a number of the inhabitants, has recently been totally destroyed by fire. There is good angling in the river Wye, where trout and grayling are abundant. Gentlemen staying at the Rutland Arms have the privilege of fishing in this excellent stream.

Besides the *Union Workhouse,* a large and well-regulated establishment, there are a *Dispensary and Lying-in Institution* which have been of great advantage to the poor of the neighbourhood. The *Savings Bank* is in Bath Street. The *County Court* meetings for recovery of debts are held in the court-room at Bakewell, monthly. The *Bank* is a branch of the Sheffield and Rotherham Banking Company. The new *Cemetery* is under control of a Burial Board, and the town is under a Local Board of Health.

The *Bakewell Farmers' Club,* established in 1843, is one of the most successful and useful societies of its kind in the kingdom, and the annual shows in connection with it are well supported, and conduce much to the good of the agriculture of the Peak district. There are two banks, one a branch of the Sheffield and Rotherham Company.

Bakewell has a station on the line of railway from Ambergate and Matlock to Buxton, and is therefore easy of approach from both north and south.

*Bakewell Church* claims the tourist's particular notice as one of the most interesting remains in the High Peak. " The present edifice is a cruciform structure of considerable size, being 150 feet in length, and 105 feet across the transepts, of considerable elevation, and erected at different periods, but externally presenting a general uniformity of outline, from the flat roofs and battlements, added throughout nearly the entire line of building, probably early in the fifteenth century. An octagonal tower resting on a square base, with the angles boldly cut off, rises from the centre, surmounted by a lofty spire."* In the angle between the south transept and the chancel stands what has been termed a Runic cross, somewhat resembling that at Eyam. On the west side are sculptures in relief, and, on the three others, are the ornamental scrolls, so prevalent on Saxon crosses. The sculptures, though now almost obliterated, have been said to illustrate the life, death, burial, resurrection, and ascension of Christ. On the head of the cross is a representation of the entry into Jerusalem. The existence of this cross, and the remains of several others of like make, seem to prove that a burial-place existed here long before the Conquest ; and if a burial-place, it is almost certain that a place of worship existed also. In the Domesday Book it is stated that two priests officiated in the church at Bakewell. It is very difficult,

* An account of the parish church of Bakewell, etc., by F. C. Plumtre, D.D., Vice-Chancellor of Oxford.

notwithstanding these facts, to trace the history of the church. Of its original foundation we know absolutely nothing, though by local tradition the building of the nave, which, with the exception of the west end and tower, is the oldest part remaining, is ascribed to King John, while Earl of Morton. In 1192 he gave it, with its prebends, to the Cathedral of Lichfield, the dean and chapter of which have still the patronage of the living. It is recorded that in 1365 a charity was endowed by Sir Godfrey Foljambe and Avena his wife. In the south side of the nave is their monument with two half-length upright figures. From the detailed account of the church by Dr. Plumtre, we make the following abridged quotation :—

"The present nave was probably erected c. 1110. In the interior, it is separated from the side aisles by arches resting on piers of solid masonry instead of pillars. These are mostly about 6 feet 6 inches wide, 3 feet thick, and 12 feet high to the imposts, and the openings between them vary from 10 feet 6 inches to 12 feet.

"The arches are semicircular, of rude construction, square edged, not recessed, and without mouldings. The imposts have been plain projecting blocks with a chamfered edge, resting on corbels resembling a common Norman corbel table ; one only is left. Some of the original clerestory windows still remain, inserted over the centre of the piers, and now opening into the side aisles, the walls and roof of which were raised about the middle or end of the thirteenth century. These windows are narrow lights externally, resting upon a weather-table still perfect, with a very wide splay towards the nave, of rude workmanship, and without any relief of mouldings or string-course.

Above is another range of clerestory windows, square-headed, in the early perpendicular style, added probably in the fifteenth century. The west walls of the side aisles are recessed with arches, but whether intended for door-ways, an unusual arrangement in Norman churches of this size, or, as is more probable, for strength, as if to support western towers, the walls being very thick, cannot now be ascertained—the other surface of the wall having been since cased with plain masonry, obliterating nearly all traces of its original character. In the centre of the west front is a doorway ornamented with beak-heads, and other heads of unusual design, with scrolls issuing from the mouths. Above are the remains of an arcade of interesting arches with zig-zag work, in part cut away to admit the insertion of a sharp pointed window, with early perpendicular tracery; and a flat roof and battlements were put up when the clerestory was added to the nave. The north aisle has been widened, but the line of the original wall may easily be traced by the Norman base-moulding on the outside of the west end.

" The central tower and transepts were originally Norman, and, so far as could be ascertained, of the same date as the nave. The tower-piers were taken down in 1841. There is also good reason to believe that the walls of the north transept were either in part the original Norman walls, projecting, as was usual in the smaller churches, but little beyond the line of the walls of the side aisles, with additions of early English work; or that at all events they stood upon the site of the old foundation. And it may be fairly presumed, that a short Norman transept had originally been erected on the south similar to that on the north. The chancel also had evidently been of Norman construction, for part of a corbel table still remains in the upper end of the north wall of the chancel, next the tower-pier, shewing the continuation of the older masonry.

To the east of the transept is the VERNON CHAPEL, in the later decorated style, founded in 1360, " upon the walls of the former chapel." In this chapel were buried the families of Vernon and Manners, the occupiers of Haddon Hall. The most interesting monument is a representation in alabaster of Sir Thomas Wendesley in plate armour, who was mortally wounded at the battle of Shrewsbury in 1403. On his helmet is the inscription " IHC NAZAREN."

In 1841, the restoration of the church was commenced. Both the transepts, the tower, and the Vernon Chapel, were taken down and renewed, new pews were added, Gothic arches built in the place of the Norman arches of the nave, the furniture, such as reading-desk, organ, and pulpit, re-arranged, and four stained-glass windows put into the south end. The whole expense is estimated at £8600.

In excavating the foundations to make the necessary restorations, a considerable number of Saxon remains, including a fine coped tomb, and several rudely sculptured coffin lids, were discovered. Parts of fifty-seven of these slabs are to be seen in the church, eighteen more are in the magnificent museum of the late T. Bateman, Esq., of Lomberdale Hall. The font is a very remarkable one, and is elaborately sculptured. There are a large number of fine and interesting monuments, and the whole church is worthy of careful inspection. A very fine memorial window, to the memory of the late Mr. Allcard, has recently been put in the church, and other alterations have been made.

On a stone in the churchyard, not far from the old cross, is the following epitaph, supposed to have been written by Mr. C. Wesley, brother of the founder of Methodism.

> " Beneath, a sleeping infant lies,
>     To earth whose body lent,
>   More glorious shall hereafter rise,
>     Tho' not more innocent.
>
>   When the Archangel's trump shall blow,
>     And souls to bodies join,
>   Thousands shall wish their lives below,
>     Had been as short as thine."

Near the east end of the church, on a slab of black marble inserted into a stone, is an epitaph such as is but seldom met with in a village churchyard. It marks the tomb of an infant two years and eight months old—

> " Reader! beneath this marble lies
>     The sacred dust of Innocence;
>   Two years he blest his parents' eyes,
>     The third, an angel took him hence:
>
>   The sparkling eyes, the lisping tongue,
>     Complaisance sweet, and manners mild,
>   And all that pleases in the young,
>     Were all united in this child.
>
>   Would'st thou his happier state explore?
>     To thee this bliss is freely given;
>   Go, gentle reader! sin no more.
>     And thou shalt see this flower in heaven."

The neighbourhood of Bakewell is well studded with gentlemen's houses, and is full to overflowing with the most charming natural beauties and the most interesting localities. Among the principal of these residences are Burton Closes, a beautiful and costly mansion erected a few years since by Mr. Allcard; Castle Hill, the seat of Mr. Nesfield; Holme Hall; East Lodge; Haddon House, etc. etc.

The tourist who is curious in epitaphs will be glad to have a copy of the following, which is part of an inscription on a table-monument at the west end of the church, to the memory of John Dale, barber surgeon, who was born at Sheldon, and his two wives, Elizabeth Foljambe and Sarah Bloodworth :—

" Know posterity, that on the 8th of April, in the year of grace 1757, the rambling remains of the above said John Dale were, in the 86th year of his pilgrimage, laid upon his two wives.

> " This thing in life might raise some jealousie
> Here all three lie together lovingly,
> But from embraces here no pleasure flows :
> Alike are here all human joys and woes.
> Here Sarah's chiding John no longer hears,
> And old John's rambling Sarah no more fears ;
> A period's come to all their toylsome lives,
> The good man's quiet—still are both his wives."

The *Railway Station* is a very short distance from the town, and omnibuses meet every train.

The "*High Peak Harriers,*" one of the finest and best packs in the country, are kept at Bakewell ; R. W. M. Nesfield, Esq., being master of the pack. They meet in the Peak district two days a week during the season.

# BELPER.

Belper, 8 m. from Derby; 17 m. from Chesterfield; 8 m. from Alfreton.

PRINCIPAL HOTELS: *Lion,* Bridge Street; *New Inn,* Market Place; *George,* Bridge Street. Railway station on the Duffield road.

Population, 8527.

BELPER is a thriving and busy market-town in the parish of Duffield, eight miles north of Derby. The market place is in the upper or old part of the town. Market day, Saturday, and there are several well attended and important fairs in the course of the year.

Belper is said to have been the residence of John of Gaunt, Duke of Lancaster, and it is certain that, in the *Inquest post mortem,* a capital mansion is described as being held there by Edmund Crouchback, Earl of Lancaster, and which descended regularly in that family. Foundations of a considerable building, and portions of outer walls of great thickness, have been traced near what is usually called the Manor House, and these are believed to have been the remains of the ducal mansion. That the place was known to the Romans is evidenced by Roman coins and other antiquities having been found in the neighbourhood, and the British road, the Rykneld Street, afterwards converted into a Roman way, connecting the stations of Little Chester with those of Pentridge, Chesterfield, and the north, passed not far from the present town.

The old staple trade of Belper was nail making—"Belper nailers" being as well known everywhere as "Sheffield grinders," or "Leicester stockingers." The horse-nails here made have always had the reputation of being the best produced in any locality. In 1776 Mr. Strutt erected the first cotton mill at Belper, and from this has sprung that important branch of trade which has so greatly increased the town, and has made it so busy a centre of industry. The cotton mills of Messrs. Strutt at the present day are among the most extensive and best arranged in the kingdom, and give employment to many hundreds of hands. Messrs. Strutt's establishment comprises, besides cotton spinning and works for bleaching and dyeing, all the necessary foundries and engineering shops for the manufacture of machinery. One of this family, Mr. Edward Strutt, many years member of Parliament for the borough of Derby, and who held the offices of Chancellor of the Duchy of Lancaster and President of the Government Railway Board, has been elevated to the peerage by the title of Baron Belper—a title which identifies him with the town from which the wealth and commercial importance of his family have been derived. Another important branch of industry at Belper is that of hosiery and gloves. The principal impetus to this trade was given by the establishment of the works of Mr. Ward (afterwards the firm of Ward, Brettle, and Ward. After the dissolution of this firm, Mr. Brettle erected new warehouses, and the two present well-known commercial firms of " Ward. Sturt, and Sharp," and " George Brettle and Company," of London, still continue their manufacturing operations, and employ many hundreds of hands.

The OLD CHURCH, dedicated to St. John, for many years —since the erection of the new church—used as a schoolroom, is a picturesque old building with a bell-turret at its west end, and some early English details. In the churchyard is an ancient yew-tree, and near it the socket of a cross. St. Peter's Church, erected in 1822-4, is a spacious erection, containing 1800 sittings, of which 1200 are free. It was erected from the designs of Mr. Habershon, the first stone being laid by the Duke of Devonshire. The living is a perpetual curacy, in the patronage of the vicar of Duffield. Christ Church, in Bridge Street, was erected at the cost of about £3000 in 1850, and has a well proportioned bell-turret. It is a perpetual curacy.

Besides these churches Belper contains spacious places of worship belonging to other denominations. The town also has its National, Lancastrian, and Infants' schools, a Literary Institution, libraries, and banks.

The Belper Union Workhouse, for a union comprising 35 parishes, was erected at a cost of £12,000, and is capable of accommodating 340 inmates. The County Court for the Belper district is held monthly in the Court House, where also petty sessions are held every Wednesday. The town is well supplied with water and gas.

The Belper Cemetery, opened in 1859, is beautifully situated on rising ground to the right of the Matlock road. The extent of the grounds is about fifteen acres, and the chapels, with their central tower and gateway, are of extremely chaste and elegant design.

The main line of the Midland Railway runs in a walled cutting through the heart of the town. The station is inconveniently placed some distance from the centre of the town, on the Duffield road.

Milford.—At this populous village, two miles from Belper, are immense cotton-mills belonging to Messrs. Strutt, which employ the greater part of the population. The bleach works and foundries, etc., of the firm are also at this place. To connect different portions of the work together, an arched passage is thrown over the turnpike road ; and an elegant foot suspension bridge— one of the earliest erected—spans the river Derwent. The village contains an elegant church and parsonage house, and several Dissenting chapels and schools ; and there are several excellent mansions in its neighbourhood. At Makeney are the residences of Mr. Anthony Strutt, and of Captain Holmes, a partner and acting manager of the works.

DUFFIELD, three miles from Belper on the Derby road, and four miles from Derby, is one of the largest and pleasantest villages in the county of Derby. It is delightfully situated in the fine open valley of the Derwent, and is remarkably well built, cleanly, and healthy. The principal inn is the White Hart, but there are several others in the place. Duffield is a place of great antiquity and of note. At the time of making the Domesday Survey, where it is called *Duuelle*, it belonged to Henry de Ferrars, and had a church and a priest ; and here the Ferrars, Earls of Derby, had their castle, which was situated at the north of the village, at the place still called " Castle Orchards." It was the principal stronghold of that powerful family, who held it till the reign of Henry III., when it was confiscated and given to the Earl of Lancaster. The church is large and remarkably fine, with a tower and lofty spire. It contains, along with other interesting matters, a fine altar-tomb, with effigies of Sir Roger and Lady Minors, 1536, the knight in armour, and the lady in the beautiful costume, with pedimented head-dress, of the period ; and a large monument to Anthony Bradshaw,

1600, and his two wives, Griselda Blackwall and Elizabeth Haughton, with their twenty children—four by his first, and sixteen by his second wife. There are also memorials to other members of the Bradshaw family, and to those of Lowe, Bonell, Colville, etc. The following epitaph is worth preserving. It is to John Rotton, Esq., who died 5th November 1769, aged sixty-four:—

> "Through life's best years the good man toiled to raise
> Wealth's feeble prop for his declining days ;
> Too wise when age his cheek had silvered o'er,
> To waste the expiring lamp in search for more.
> To other cares he destined life's last stage,
> Revised with caution due life's crowded page,
> Summed up its toils, and stating fair the gain
> Found on the balance all but virtue vain.
> Oh! early wise to choose the better part,
> And hoard the treasure of an honest heart ;
> Wealth that alone can life's true joys supply,
> Sooth our last pangs, and teach us how to die.
> Fair was thy soul, and fair shall rest thy fame,
> On the firm basis of an honest name."

The churchyard, which is bounded by the river Derwent on one side, is very spacious, and, besides many interesting mortuary memorials, contains a remarkably fine old yew-tree.

Near the church is Duffield Bridge, a finely built erection of three arches, spanning the river Derwent, which is here of great width. In the village are Baptist, Methodist, and other places of worship, and also excellent schools. Duffield Hall, long the residence of the Bonells and Colvilles, is now the property of Mr. Rowland Smith the banker. It is a picturesque old building with gabled front, and has extensive grounds attached. In the village and its immediate neighbourhood are many gentlemen's seats. The Duffield Railway Station is at the north end of the village, and near it a Gothic parsonage has recently been erected on the brow of the hill.

From Duffield a branch line of the Midland Railway leaves the main line, and runs by way of Hazlewood, Shottle, and Ideridgehay, to Wirksworth, thus placing that important market-town in direct connection with the Midland system.

HAZLEWOOD, about a mile from Duffield, has a modern church, and is very pleasantly situated, and there are many truly pleasant little hamlets and villages in the neighbourhood of Duffield which are desirable places of residence. It has a station on the Wirksworth Branch Railway.

QUARN, or Quarndon, distant about two miles from Duffield, has a Norman Church, and has the reputation of being one of the most healthy places in the county. It has a medicinal spring, and is distant about a mile from Kedleston, where also is another spring of like character. Of this place an account will be found in another place.

At Burley hill, near Duffield, which in early days formed a part of Duffield Forest, an interesting discovery of a Norman pottery has recently been made, on land belonging to Lord Scarsdale.

## BOLSOVER.

HOTELS AND INNS: *Swan Hotel, Nag's Head, Angel, Cross Keys,* etc.
Population, 1721.

Bolsover is situated about six miles from Chesterfield, and contains one of the most interesting buildings in Derbyshire for a tourist to visit. It is pleasantly situated, and can well be seen on the same day with Hardwick Hall by the visitor from Chesterfield or Alfreton. Bolsover was formerly a market town, with an extensive trade in the manufacture of steel buckles and spurs,* but the market has now fallen into disuse. The trade now consists of the manufacture of tobacco pipes, baskets, besoms, knives, etc., but the principal part of the inhabitants are employed in agriculture, and in the mines and collieries in the neighbourhood. In the church, which is a plain Norman erection, with later additions, are some interesting monuments, and a singular piece of sculpture of the early Norman period, representing the Nativity, etc., found some years ago at the north door, where it had served the purpose of a step. Amongst the monuments in the Cavendish Chapel is a monument to Sir Charles and Lady Cavendish, on which, under an arch, are the tombs and effigies of the knight and his lady, and their three sons.

* These were what is technically called "case hardened," which process Rhodes, himself a Sheffield man, describes as follows :—"The buckles and spurs were formed, and filed into shape *when in the state of iron only.* The exterior surface was then converted into steel by a peculiar process, in which burnt bones and ashes from the leather of old shoes were generally used. The manufactured article was now internally iron, and therefore not liable to be easily broken ; but the exterior surface was converted into the purest steel, and fitted to receive the most brilliant polish that can possibly be imparted to this beautiful metal."

The monument is highly decorated. There is also a monument to Henry Cavendish, Duke of Newcastle, consisting of four pillars supporting a massive pediment, ornamented with figures and various devices. The monument is composed of different coloured marbles, and is one of the most magnificent in the provinces. Among the other monuments in this chapel are those to the Countess of Oxford and Mortimer, Charles Viscount Mansfield, and others of the Cavendish family, and in the church are memorials to members of the families of Barker, Woolhouse, Smithson the architect, etc. The late Duke of Portland, father of Lord George Bentinck, is also buried at Bolsover. The following epitaph will be read with interest :—

### CHARLES CAVENDISH TO HIS SONS.

" Sonnes, seek not me among these polish'd stones,
These only hide part of my flesh and bones ;
Which did they nere so neat or proudly dwell,
Will all be dust, and may not make me swell

Let such as have outliv'd all praise,
Trust in the tombs their careful friends do raise :
I made my life my monument, and yours,
To which there 's no material that endures.

Nor yet inscription like it, write but that,
And teache nephews it to emulate,
It will be matter loude enough to tell
Not when I died, but how I liv'd, farewell.

### HIS POSTERITIE OF HIM TO STRANGERS.

Charles Cavendish was a man whom
Knowledge, zeal, sincerity, made religious ;
Experience, discretion, courage, made valiant ;
Reading, conference, judgment, made learned ;
Religion, valour, learning, made wise ;
Birth, merit, favour, made noble :

Respect, means, charitie, made bountiful ;
Equitie, conscience, office, made just ;
Nobilitie, bountie, justice, made honourable ;
Counsell, aide, secrecie, made a trustie friend ;
Love, truth, constancie, made a kind husband ;
Affection, advice, care, made a loving father ;
Friends, wife, sonnes, made content ;
Wisdom, honour, content, made happy."

Bolsover is supposed, and with some reason, to have been a stronghold of the Danes, and some earthworks still remaining are pointed out as favouring this opinion. At the Conquest the manor was granted by the Conqueror to William Peveril, who had also another residence in the neighbourhood, at Wingfield Manor. The Castle was held conjointly with, and under the same governor as Castleton Castle, " Peveril's Castle in the Peak."

BOLSOVER CASTLE, the object of greatest interest in the place, is supposed to have been built by William Peveril, who possessed the manor, and held it till 1153, when William Peveril the younger having poisoned Ranulf Earl of Chester, his estates were forfeited, and in the reign of Richard I. were conferred upon John Earl of Mortaigne, afterwards King of England. The park, etc., was enclosed by King John, and the castle was seized and held by the disaffected barons till 1215, when it was retaken for the king by Ferrars Earl of Derby. It was soon afterwards fortified for the king. Passing through the hands of Scott, Earl of Chester (Henry III.), and Hastings, Lord Abergavenny, his brother-in-law, it was again resumed in 1243 by the Crown, and, twelve years later, was bestowed on Roger Lovetot ; it afterwards passed through the hands of the Pipards, and Sturys, and the Earl of Richmond, until Henry VIII. granted it to Thomas Howard, Duke of Norfolk, for the service of one knight's fee, but it again reverted to the Crown on the attainder of his son. In the reign of Edward VI. it was for a time in the hands of Sir John Byron, and was then granted to Gilbert Talbot, Lord Talbot, whose successor, Gilbert, Earl of Shrewsbury, granted it for a thousand years, and afterwards sold it in full, to Sir Charles Cavendish, who thereupon built the oldest portions now standing, which had been begun by the celebrated Countess of Shrewsbury, his mother. Sir Charles had by his second wife, who was declared Baroness Ogle in her own right, three sons, the second of whom, William, was created successively Baron of Bolsover, Viscount Mansfield, Earl, Marquis, and Duke of Newcastle, and also inherited the earldom of Ogle, and many other honours. His loyalty to the two Charleses, which led him into the worst poverty during his banishment, was only equalled by his splendid hospitalities during the reign of Charles I., and by the careful management of his estates after the restoration. He entertained Charles I. and his court three times at Bolsover Castle, on which occasions masks, written expressly for the occasions by Ben Jonson, were performed. The first of these entertainments cost the Duke £4000, the second £15,000, and the third, which was but a slight affair, £1500. The first entertainment was described by Lord Clarendon, as "such an excess of feasting, as had scarce ever been known in England before, and would be still thought very prodigious if the same noble person had not, within a year or two afterwards, made the king and queen a more stupendous entertainment, which God be thanked, though possibly it might too much whet the appetite of others to excess, no man after those days imitated."

The Earl held the lieutenancy of the two counties of Derby and Nottingham, and this double honour—this wedding of the two lieutenancies—is thus given in the Masque, Nottinghamshire being represented by Bold Stub of Sherwood, and Derbyshire by Pem, daughter of Father Fitz Ale of Derby.

" We come with our peers,
And crave your ears,
To present a wedding,
Intended a bedding
 Of both the shires.
Father Fitz Ale
Hath a daughter stale
In Derby town
Known up and down
 For a great antiquity.
And *Pem* she hight,
A solemn wight
As you should meet
In any street
 In that ubiquity.
Her he hath brought
As having sought
By many a draught

Of ale and craft,
In some old stock
Of the yeoman block
And forest blood
Of old Sherwood.
And he hath found
Within the ground,
At last no shrimp
Whereon to imp
His jolly club
But an old *Stub*
O' the right wood,
A champion good ;
 Who here in place
Presents himself
Like doughty elf
 Of Greenwood chase.

The duke took a prominent and, indeed, leading part in the transactions of the period, and these are chronicled with an unaffected simplicity, in his life, by his amiable duchess. The duke was twice married, first to Elizabeth, heiress of William Basset of Blore ; and secondly to Margaret, daughter of Sir Charles Lucas, and maid of honour to Queen Henrietta. This latter lady was one of the most accomplished women, and one of the most celebrated writers of that period, as well as being a most virtuous and inestimable woman in all her social relations. Her works are many, and all are filled with the same good feeling which

characterises her admirable life of her husband, which is a
work that cannot be too highly commended. The duke
was also an author, and his magnificent work on Horse-
manship, in which several views of Bolsover Castle occur,
is one of the most splendid of the literary productions of
that period. His son Henry, the second duke, had a son
who died during his lifetime, and the estate of Bolsover
thus fell to the daughter Margaret, married to Holles, Earl
of Clare, who thus became Duke of Newcastle. Their
daughter married Harley, Earl of Oxford, and took Bolsover Castle, with the title of Lord of Bolsover, with her as
her dower. By a daughter it again changed hands, passing
from Harley to the Bentincks, Dukes of Portland, in which
family it still remains. The interior of the older portion
of the castle is highly characteristic of the age in which it
was built. The renowned Countess Elizabeth of Hardwick
commenced, and Sir C. Cavendish completed, the rebuilding of the present castellated mansion on the site of the
Norman keep; and by the side of the castle Sir Charles
commenced, and his son, the first Duke, completed, the
splendid palace, now in ruins, which crowns the noble
terrace, and commands a magnificent view of the rich and
highly picturesque scenery of Scarsdale. The rooms are
small, the walls are wainscotted, and fancifully inlaid and
painted. The ceilings of the best apartments are carved
and gilt, and nearly the whole of the floors are coated with
plaster. The finer portion, built by William, first Duke
of Newcastle, was destroyed in the civil wars. In the
Parliamentary periodical, "The Burning Bush not consumed," is the following account of the taking of the castle
in 1664 :—" The noble Major-General having left Colonel
Bright, a commander of my Lord Fairfaxe's, and a party of
foot in the castle (Sheffield) by order from the most noble

Earl of Manchester, advanced towards Bowzan, *alias* Bolsover Castle, about eight miles from Sheffield, it being another strong house of Marquis Newcastle's in Derbyshire, which was well manned with soldiers, and strengthened with great guns, one whereof carried eighteen pound bullets, others nine pound, and it had strong works about it ; yet this castle also, upon summons, was soon surrendered up to my lord's forces, upon fair and moderate charges granted them. It pleased God to give us in this castle of Bolsover 120 muskets, besides pikes, halberts, etc. Also one iron drake, some leaden. bullets, two mortar pieces, some other drakes, nine barrels of powder, with a proportion of match, some victuals for our soldiers, and some plunder." The Riding House, so celebrated in the duke's magnificent work on the Manége, is still in excellent preservation, and is worth a journey to see. About a hundred years ago the palace was unroofed, but has been kept in perfect order, as a picturesque ruin, by the Duke of Portland. The Elizabethan reproduction of the fine old Norman keep is inhabited by the vicar of Bolsover, the Rev. J. Hamilton Gray, and his talented lady, the authoress of the " History of Etruria," " History of Rome," " History of the Roman Emperors," and " A Tour to the Sepulchres of Etruria," who have, in their elegant apartments, arranged the magnificent series of Etruscan and other antiquities which they have collected as well as a large display of ancient furniture and carvings. The Drawing Room and Dining Hall are supported on central pillars, and have elaborately groined ceilings. The largest room is the Star Chamber, so called from its stellated ceiling, constructed by the Duke of Newcastle in imitation of the too celebrated Star Chamber of his unfortunate master, and there are also copies of the paintings of the twelve Cæsars which adorned that chamber. This room has been fitted up as a Library and Museum. The whole town was formerly fortified, and the earthworks may still be traced. The view from the ramparts is very pleasing, particularly when the atmosphere is clear.

## BUXTON.

[Contractions.—Sitting-rooms, s. r. ; lodging-rooms, l. r. ; bed-rooms, b. r. ; board, bd. ; public, pub. ; private, priv. ; wax-lights, w. l.]

PRINCIPAL HOTELS.— *The Palace*, near Railway Station, on an eminence in its own grounds. Tariff of prices on application to the Manager. *St. Ann's* (Crescent).—s. r. 4s. 6d. to 9s. per day ; b. r. (single) 2s. 6d. to 5s. per day ; board at table d'hôte 7s. 6d., in private 8s. 6d. to 10s. 6d. per day ; hot meats to breakfast or lunch 6d. extra ; attendance 1s. 6d. per day each person ; fires 1s. per room per day ; lights from 1s. per day ; entire charge for single person per day 12s. ; servant's bed and board 5s. to 5s. 6d. per day. Carriages, coach-houses, and stabling. Full tariffs on application. *The Crescent* (formerly the *Great Hotel*), Crescent. —Single b. r. 2s. 6d. to 4s., double 4s. and 5s. per night ; s. r. 3s. 6d. to 10s. 6d. per day ; bd. at table d'hôte 7s. per day ; bd. in priv. 7s. 6d. to 8s. 6d. per day ; servant's bd. 4s. ; beds 1s. to 1s. 6d. ; fires in s. r. or b. r. 9d. and 1s. ; w. l. 2s. per pair ; gas, etc., 3s. per wk. ; hip or sponge baths 2s. per wk. *The Old Hall* (opposite the Gardens).—Revised tariffs of prices on application. *Lee Wood* (Devonshire Park). —Tariff of prices on application. *The George* (opposite the Square).— Bed 2s. ; breakfast (plain), 1s. 6d. ; lunch 1s. ; dinner 2s. 6d. ; tea 1s. ; supper 1s. ; attend. 1s. 6d. ; priv. r. 3s. *The Grove* (opposite the Hot Baths). *The Shakespeare* (Spring Gardens). *Eagle. White Lion* (Spring Gardens). *King's Head. Midland.*

Distances.—Bakewell 12 m. ; Derby 38 ; Sheffield 27 ; Tideswell 5½ ; Castleton 12 ; Chatsworth 14 ; Haddon Hall 14 ; Matlock 22 ; Dovedale 20 ; Hardwick Hall 31 ; Ashbourne 21 ; Alton Towers 23 ; Ilam Hall 18. Railway stations near the Crescent. Population, 2531.

THE town of Buxton, which has of late years increased considerably in size, is pleasantly situated on the river Wye, near its head. Its position is in a hollow surrounded by moorlands, and fully 900 feet above the level of the sea. The principal employments are the manufacture of spar ornaments and burning lime.

Buxton is chiefly celebrated on account of its tepid baths, the discovery of which is certainly as old as the Roman invasion, if not older. It is indeed believed, from the number of Celtic barrows and stone circles, etc., existing on the surrounding heights, that the Druids were acquainted with the sanative properties of the waters.

" Buxton was undoubtedly a place of importance in the Roman period, and was, indeed, a centre from which many roads diverged. Its warm springs were famous among the Romans, as they have been ever since, and as they still are, and the remains of the baths of that period which have from time to time been brought to light, attest to their extent and their magnificence. Indeed, one bath which was discovered in 1781, at the time when the building of the Crescent was commenced, was found to measure thirty feet from east to west, and fifteen from north to south. The spring rose at its west end, and there was an outlet for the water at the opposite end, which had a 'flood-gate' attached. The bath was stuccoed with the usual concrete of lime and pounded tiles, and at one end was a deep cavity. Near this bath the remains of a Roman wall, also stuccoed in like manner, stood until 1709, when they were unfortunately taken down to beautify the place by a grateful Cheshire gentleman who had received benefit from the springs. A few years before this time (1698), large sheets of lead 'spread upon great beams of timber, about four yards square, with broken ledges round about, which had been a leaden cistern,' were found 'under the grass and corn mould,' fifty yards east of the other baths.

Many other remains of the Roman period, including an inscribed Roman milestone, now in the possession of Mr

J. C. Bates, have also been found at Buxton, and it has been said that the site of the station was on the hill above the Hall, known as the 'Stene,' or 'Stane Cliffs.'"

Of the Saxon and Norman periods, there are but few remains about Buxton. Saxon barrows exist, however, in the neighbourhood, and in those which have been opened interesting relics have been found.

In later times abundant materials are to be gathered concerning the state of the place, and the history of its baths. When Henry VIII. set about destroying the images and relics of the old religion, he had an agent, one Sir William Bassett, at Buxton, who not only exercised his authority upon these objects but spared not even the baths. In a letter to Lord Cromwell, dated Langley, he says,—"According to my bounden duty and the tenor of your Lordship's letters lately to me directed, I have sent your Lordship by this bearer, my brother Francis Bassett, the images of St. Anne of Buckston, and St. Andrew of Burton-upon-Trent ; which images I did take from the places where they did stand, and brought them to my house, within forty-eight hours after contemplation of your said Lordship's letters, in as sober a manner as my little and rude will would serve me. And for that there should be no more idolatry and superstition there used, I did not only deface the tabernacles and places where they did stand, but also did take away crutches, shirts, and shifts, with wax offered, being things that allure and entice the ignorant to the said offering ; also giving the keepers of both places orders that no more offerings should be made in those places till the king's pleasure, and your Lordship's be further known in that behalf," etc. The "crutches, shirts, and shifts," were grateful offerings made at the well of St. Anne by patients for restored health. The baths, however, were not long closed. In the reign of Elizabeth, Mary Queen of Scots, whilst a prisoner under the care of the Earl of Shrewsbury, appears to have spent some time at Buxton, having visited it at least four different times in his custody. The unfortunate queen seems to have found great relief in these visits, and to have been much attached to the place. This is apparent from the allusions to it in her letters, and from the interesting particulars which may be gleaned of her visit, as given in Lodge.

The house in which she lived was on the site of the hotel known as "the Hall." The present building was erected by the third Earl of Devonshire in 1670. The relief afforded to the Queen seems to have enhanced the fame of the waters, and Lord Burleigh visited Buxton in 1577 and 1580, and the Duke of Sussex in 1580, and both these great men seem to have derived much benefit from the change. Some extremely curious particulars relative to the state of Buxton at this interesting period are to be found in a very rare book, "The Benefit of the Auncient Bathes of Buckstones," written by "John Jones, Phisition at the King's Mede, nigh Darby," in 1572, from which we make a short extract or two from a copy in the possession of the editor. " Joyning to the chefe springe, betwene the river and the bathe, is a very goodly house, foure square, four stories hye, so well compacte, with houses of office, beneath and above, and rounde about, with a great chambre and other goodly lodgings to the number of 30 : that it is and will be a bewty to behold : and very notable for the honorable and worshipfull that shal nede to repaire thither : as also for other. Yea the porest shall have lodgings and beds hard by, for their uses only. The bathes also so bravely bewtified with seats round about : defended from the ambyent ayre ; and chimneys for fyre, to ayre your garmintes in the bathes syde, and other necessaries most decent. And truely, I suppose, that if there were for the sick a sanctuarie, during their abode there, for all causes, saving sacrilege, treason, murther, burglary, rape, and robbing by the hye way syde with also a license for the sicke to eate fleshe at all tymes, and frydaye market weekly, and twoo fayres yeerely, it should be to the posterities, onely commodiouse, but also to the prince greate honour and gayne," etc. " The ladyes, gentle-woomen, wyves, and maydes, maye in one of the galleries walke, and if the weather bee not agreeable too theire exceptacion, they maye have in the ende of a benche eleven holes made, intoo the which to trowle pummets or bowles of leade, bigge, little or meane, or also, of copper, tynne, woode, eyther vyolent or softe, after their owne discretion, the pastyme, Trowle in Madame, is termed. Likewyse, men feeble, the same may also practice, in another gallery of the new buildings."

This building was destroyed about 1670, and a new edifice erected on its site, by the Earl of Devonshire. In the next century, the celebrated Hobbes, in his De Mirabilibus Pecci, says :—

"Unto St. Ann the fountain sacred is ;
With waters hot and cold its sources rise,
And in its sulphur-veins there med'cine lies.
This cures the palsied members of the old,
And cherishes the nerves grown stiff and cold.
Crutches the lame unto its brink convey,
Returning, the ungrates fling them away."

And Charles Cotton also, in his Wonders of the Peak, 1681, gives a glowing poetical picture of the place, and the virtues of its waters.

Buxton continued to increase, and its means of accommodation began to be too small for the number of visitors in 1780, therefore the foundations for the Crescent, etc., were laid, and from that time forward the town has continued rapidly to enlarge. A Market-house has been erected, and many very important improvements have been made throughout the town.

The PAVILION and PUBLIC GARDENS were opened in 1871, and have proved a great source of attraction and benefit to the town and to visitors. They belong to the "Buxton Improvements Company, Limited," which was incorporated with a capital of £12,000, in 2400 shares at £5 each, for acquiring certain lands belonging to his Grace the Duke of Devonshire, in order to add to the attractions and increase the prosperity of Buxton, by the provision of enclosed gardens, and a Music Hall for the amusement and recreation of the public in all weathers ; for the engagement and maintenance of the band ; for the laying out and culture of the walks and grounds ; and all other objects to be acquired by the possession and use of ornamental and well-kept gardens and pleasure-grounds. These grounds, which have been given by his Grace the

Duke of Devonshire, have been re-laid, and a new and elegant Pavilion built thereon at a cost of £12,000. Numerous alterations and improvements have been made in the grounds, which have been chastely laid out under the superintendence of Mr. Edward Milner, of the Crystal Palace grounds, who so successfully laid out the People's Parks at Preston and Halifax. The Pavilion, a light iron and glass structure, 400 feet in length, rising from a stone base, is warmed, for a winter covered walk, by four rows of hot-water pipes going round the whole building, and is also lighted with gas in the evening. This building, which stands on the north side of the gardens, contains a central hall for concerts and assemblies, flanked by two conservatories, with waiting-rooms. From a terrace running the whole length of the Pavilion the ground slopes beautifully down to the river Wye, which is crossed by a handsome cast-iron bridge, over which the principal walk passes from the centre of the terrace to the band-stand, whence the walks diverge in various directions, affording pleasant lounges and charming views of the scenery, while the great natural advantages of the grounds have been artistically utilised. Two miles of walks and five bridges have been constructed ; and the two lakes, which will be remembered by visitors to Buxton, have been joined, two new waterfalls have been made, and the grounds have been thickly and artistically planted with evergreens and trees. Statuary also is not wanting. The opening ceremony was attended by the Duke of Devon-shire, Lord George Cavendish, M.P., and other gentlemen, who were afterwards entertained with luncheon by the directors of the Buxton Improvements Company in the new Pavilion.

The following are the general regulations and terms of admission :—Single admission, for one day, 3d. ; ditto, for one week, **2s.** ; ditto, for one month, **5s.** ; double ticket, 7s. 6d. ; family ditto, 12s. 6d.    Single ticket, for one year, 12s. 6d. ; double ditto, 15s. ; family ditto, 21s.    Tickets are not transferable, and only licensed bath chairs are allowed to enter the grounds (cost of such license, 7s. 6d. per year).   Bath chairs are not allowed in the Pavilion, except on their way to or from the central hall.   Smoking not allowed in the Pavilion.   Charge for dogs led with a string, 3d. each day.   Tickets can only be obtained at the principal entrance to the grounds. Annual tickets terminate 31st December.   On Sundays the gardens are open from 8 to sunset, except from 10.30 to 12, and from 6 to 7.45.

There is a branch of the Sheffield and Rotherham Bank in the Quadrant.   The town is under the control of a Local Board of Health, to which the gas-works and water-works both belong.

THE CRESCENT, a magnificent pile of buildings, containing two of the principal hotels (the *St. Ann's* and the *Crescent* Hotels), was erected by the late Duke of Devonshire— being begun in 1780—at a cost of £120,000.   The late John Carr, Esq. of York, was the architect.   It consists of a curve of 200 feet, with wings 58 feet, and contains about 380 windows.   The Crescent at Buxton has three storeys ; in the lower one is a rusticated arcade that forms an agreeable promenade ; above the arches an elegant balustrade stretches along the whole front and the ends of the fabric ; over the piers of the arcade arise fluted Doric pilasters, that support the architrave and cornice ; the trygliphs of the former and the rich planceer of the latter, have a beautiful appearance.   The, termination above the cornice is formed by another balustrade that extends along the whole building, in the centre of which are the Devonshire arms. Between the windows runs an enriched string-course. The floor is higher than the area, between which communications are formed by several flights of steps. The space of the Crescent is 200 feet, and each wing measures 58 feet 3 inches, making the whole extent of the front 316½ feet.

In 1796 a beautifully-executed token was issued, having on the obverse a view of the Crescent, with the words CRESCENT 1796, and on the reverse the arms and supporters, etc., of his grace the Duke of Devonshire ; round the edge the words "BUXTON TOKEN." Of this highly interesting

token, of which two earlier varieties were also struck, we here give an engraving. For this we are indebted to the "Reliquary Quarterly Journal and Review," * in which all the varieties are carefully described and engraved.

The ground in front of the Crescent is laid out in beautiful terraces, in which the classic taste of Sir Jeffrey Wyatville and, later, the genius of Sir Joseph Paxton,

* Vol. iv. pp. 106, 107.

have been effectively expended, aided by the princely munificence of the Duke of Devonshire. The principal buildings in Buxton—besides the Crescent, and the Hall Hotel—are the Churches, the New Hot Baths, the Palace, the Royal, and the Lee Wood Hotels; the Square, the Quadrant, Cavendish Terrace, the Devonshire Hospital, the Market Hall, Hall Bank, and Scarsdale Place. The new church was built by the Duke of Devonshire, and opened for service in 1812. It is in the Tuscan style of architecture. The appearance and situation of the church are highly picturesque. The old church has recently been repaired and opened; the seats in the churches are free and un-appropriated. Besides these places of worship, there are several commodious Dissenting chapels.

Buxton is governed by a " Local Board," under the Local Government Act of 1858. It has, since this Act was adopted, been well drained; the streets and footpaths have been widened and improved, and everything done to render the town pleasant and attractive.

THE NATURAL TEPID BATHS of Buxton are its chief attractions, and justly are they celebrated on account of their medicinal efficacy. They are appropriated as private and public baths for ladies; private and public baths for gentlemen; and baths for the recipients of the " Buxton Bath Charity."

The Mineral Waters, Baths, Wells, etc., adjoin the Crescent—new and extremely elegant and spacious build-ings having recently been erected for that purpose—that at the eastern end of the Crescent being devoted to the Hot Baths, and that at the western end to the Natural Baths, the wells for drinking the waters, etc. The western or

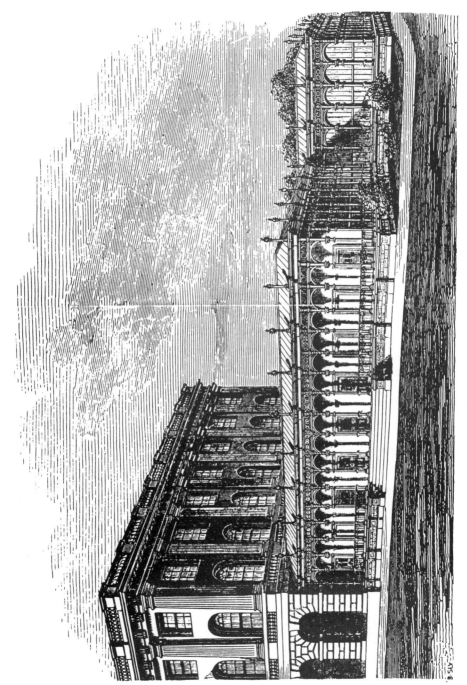

BUXTON—THE BATHS.

Natural Bath department occupies a large space of ground between the Crescent and the Hall, its architecture being assimilated to that of the Crescent. The eastern or Hot Bath department, adjoining the east end of the Crescent, has frontages to the south and east. It is connected by an elegant colonnade, containing some good shops, with the Crescent. At the south-west corner of the Crescent, entered from the colonnade, is the newly-erected St. Anne's Well, for the use of drinkers of the water; it is on the site of the oldest St. Anne's Well, and close to the spot on which the spring emerges. Adjoining this is the entrance to the gentlemen's department of the Natural Baths; next to it is the entrance to the ladies' department, and next again is the well for the supply of the chalybeate waters to drinkers. The baths are all separately supplied, and the waters range naturally from 80° to 82°. All the baths are supplied with douches, which can be used at pleasure. The whole of the baths, whether natural or not, are of the most perfect and convenient arrangement, and at no place can the visitor find such good accommodation as at Buxton.

Many medical gentlemen of eminence have spoken favourably of these waters. For the guidance of tourists in search of health, we quote the expressed opinions of a few. Dr. Granville, well known for his admirable work on the " German Spas," compares them with the waters of Schlangenbad. " Here, at Buxton," he writes, " we have a water at nearly the same degree of heat, with fewer ingredients, still producing not only similar but even more energetic effects." At another part of his work on the spas of England, he says, that " the efficacy of the Buxton waters used as baths at their natural temperature is more strikingly manifested in cases of general debility, partial paralysis, and that peculiar state of weakness which is the result of rheumatic affection and repeated attacks of gout, In the latter case, indeed, Buxton has acquired a well-known reputation."

The water is remarkably clear and pellucid when in its natural tepid state, and its appearance is thus described in the History of Buxton by Mr. A. Jewitt :—" One striking peculiarity in the Buxton water, and which ought not to be passed over in silence, is its extreme clearness and transparency. A small key, a ring, or a pin on the floor of the bath, is visible to any person standing on the edge of it, though between his eye and the object is interposed a fluid of not less than six feet in thickness. This transparency seems in a great measure to be an effect of its peculiar temperature, for when a glass of water is taken out of the bath and suffered to cool, it gradually loses its pellucid appearance, and becomes in a few hours completely turgid, as if a small quantity of milk had been mixed with it ; but recovers again on being heated. The water is also remarkable for the number of bright sparkling bubbles which are continually seen rising through the chinks at the bottom of the bath, and forcing themselves through the whole thickness of the water to the surface ; sometimes singly, sometimes in streams, and frequently in large clusters, and which doubtless owe their formation to the nitrogen gas with which it abounds."

The late Mr. Page, who filled the post of surgeon to the Bath Charity, makes the following remarks, in his " Observations on the Buxton Waters : "—" The Buxton waters are fairly entitled to the appellation of a mild saline mineral, the temperature of which, at all seasons of the year, is pretty uniformly 82° on Fahrenheit's scale. They are perfectly pellucid and inodorous ; and, owing most probably to the large proportion of nitrogen gas which they contain, devoid of that vapid taste so observable in ordinary water when heated in the same temperature.

" To their purity, to the mildness and uniformity of their temperature at all times and seasons, neither depressing the vital powers by cold, nor enervating them by heat, and to their impregnation with nitrogen gas, may be attributed in no inconsiderable degree their salutary effect."

The analysis of a gallon of the waters, as determined by Sir Charles Scudamore, is as follows :—

| *Gaseous Contents in Cubic Inches.* | | *Solid Contents in Grains.* | |
|---|---|---|---|
| Carbonic Acid . . . | 1.50 | Muriate of Magnesia . . | .58 |
| Azote . . . . . | 4.64 | Muriate of Soda . . . | 2.40 |
| | | Sulphate of Lime . . . | .60 |
| | | Carbonate of Lime . . | 10.40 |
| | | Extractive matter, with a minute quantity of vegetable fibre . . . | .50 |
| | | Loss . . . . . | .52 |
| | 6.14 | | 15.00 |

Sir Charles makes the following remarks on the constituents of the water in his " Analysis and Medical account of the Tepid Springs of Buxton :"—" The active material substances in the Buxton waters are, sulphate of soda, muriate of lime, and muriate of magnesia, but when we look at the very minute proportions, not a grain of either article in the gallon, and recollect that sea water, which, as an aperient, is taken without inconvenience, contains in the gallon 284 grains of muriate of magnesia, and rather more

than 45 grains of muriate of lime, we are compelled to believe that the medicinal action of Buxton water must be
referred to its purity, its temperature, but, above all, its
gaseous impregnation with azote."

Dr. W. R. Robertson, physician to the Bath Charity, in
his "Buxton and its Waters," says—"The effects produced
by these waters, when used internally, being similar to
those produced by them when used as a bath, they are of
service in most of the cases to which their external use is
found to be beneficial. But they are to be regarded as being
by no means equally efficient when taken internally, as they
are found to be in the form of the bath; although the effect
of the waters drunk, superadded to that of the bath, is often
found to be greater than consists with the satisfactory
treatment of the case, and renders it necessary to intermit,
or wholly discontinue, the drinking of the waters. This
should be duly attended to, as in cases where there is some
tendency to excitement, although not to such a degree as
to render the use of the bath inexpedient, it is better not
to attempt the use of the waters internally, until the degree
of effect that may be produced by the bath has been ascertained. At the same time, as these waters, when used internally, are much less active in their effects than when
used as a bath, they may be taken advantageously in many
cases in which the use of the bath would be improper.
The degrees positive, comparative, and superlative, applied
respectively to the internal use of the waters, the artificially
heated baths, and the baths at the natural temperature,
will perhaps explain their relative amount of effect sufficiently well."

Mr. Page made the following remarks on the disease,
in treatment of which the waters are beneficial :—"In

that state of weakness," wrote he, "and irritability which so generally attends on the subsidence of febrile and inflammatory affections, but more especially on the protracted stages of gout and rheumatism ; in many nervous disorders, such as epilepsy, paralysis, St. Vitus's dance, palpitation of the heart, tic douloureux, etc., as in many anomalous complaints, originating in or complicated with a disordered state of the digestive organs, a judicious employment of the Buxton waters will frequently be attended with the happiest effects." This writer gave certain rules for bathing, viz :—

"1st. To go into the bath about the middle of the day.

2d. To go into the bath when the body is warm.

3d. To go in with the feet first.

4th. To remain in the water at first but a very short time.

5th. To bathe on alternate days, or to miss every third day."

In 1852 an analysis was made by Dr. Lyon Playfair, who, in a letter addressed to the Duke's agent—in accordance with a request made by the Duke of Devonshire that he would analyse the waters—describes their qualities and medicinal properties, and gives the following analysis of its component parts in one gallon of the water at sixty degrees :—

| | |
|---|---|
| Silica | 0.666 grains. |
| Oxide of Iron and Alumina | 0.240 ,, |
| Carbonate of Lime | 7.773 ,, |
| Sulphate of Lime | 2.323 ,, |
| Carbonate of Magnesia | 4.543 ,, |
| Chloride of Magnesium | 0.114 ,, |
| Chloride of Sodium | 2.420 ,, |
| Chloride of Potassium | 2.500 ,, |
| Fluorine (as fluoride of calcium) | trace. |
| Phosphoric acid (as phosphate of lime) | trace. |

Besides these were gases in the proportion of 1.167 of carbonic acid gas to 98.833 of nitrogen, with a trace only of
oxygen. Dr. Playfair from this judges that at the moment
of issue of the water, it is charged with 206 cubic inches
of nitrogen, and 15.66 cubic inches of carbonic acid.

A later analysis was made by Dr. Muspratt in 1860, as
follows :—

| | *Grains in the Imperial Gallon.* | | *Grains in the Imperial Gallon.* |
|---|---|---|---|
| Carbonate of lime . . | 8.541 | Nitric acid . . . | trace |
| Carbonate of magnesia . | 8.741 | Organic matter . . | 0.341 |
| Carbonate of protoxyde of iron . . . . | 0.082 | Fluoride of Calcium . . | trace |
| Sulphate of lime . . | 0.330 | Phosphate of lime . . | trace |
| Chloride of calcium . . | 1.227 | Total per gallon . | 18.434 |
| Chloride of magnesium . | 0.463 | | |
| Chloride of sodium . . | 2.405 | | *Cubic Inches.* |
| Chloride of potassium . | 0.260 | Free carbonic acid . . | 8.5 |
| Silica . . . . | 1.044 | Nitrogen . . . | 504.0 |

Near the tepid spring is one of cold water, and the
proximity of these two wells of different temperature has
long been esteemed one of the wonders of the Peak. Alluding to this, Charles Cotton, in his " Wonders of the Peak,"
1682, says :—

> "Take, then, the wonder of this famous place ;
> This tepid fountain a twin-sister has
> Of the same beauty and complexion,
> That bubbling six foot off, joyns both in one ;
> But yet so cold withal, that who will stride
> When bathing, cross the bath but half so wide,
> Shall in one body, which is strange, endure
> At once an ague and a calenture," etc.

THE DEVONSHIRE HOSPITAL, formerly the BUXTON BATH
CHARITY, is a very deserving institution, and has much increased in public estimation within the last few years. It
is supported entirely by annual subscriptions and other
voluntary contributions. A subscriber of a guinea and

upwards annually can have one in-patient annually upon
the charity for every guinea subscribed, who receives board
and lodging, medical advice, medicines, the use of the baths
and waters, gratis, for three weeks ; or four out-patients
annually, who are entitled to medical advice, medicines,
and the use of the baths and waters ; and a donor of £10
can have one patient on the list annually for life, or four
out-patients with the same privileges.  For many years
past about one thousand poor persons per year have been
perfectly cured, or much relieved, under the care of this
institution.  The Devonshire Hospital is one of the most
important and valuable charitable institutions in the kingdom, and is deserving of the most extended support.  It
is instituted for the relief of poor persons from all parts
of Great Britain and Ireland, suffering from rheumatism,
gout, sciatica, and neuralgia ; pains, weakness, or contractions of joints or limbs arising from these diseases, or from
sprains, fractures, or other local injuries ; chronic forms of
paralysis ; dropped hands, and other poisonous effects of
lead, mercury, or other minerals ; dyspeptic complaints,
uterine obstructions, etc.  By the munificence of the late
Duke of Devonshire, the great stables were allowed to be
converted into an hospital for the patients of the Bath
Charity.  The Hospital has spacious, well-warmed, and
thoroughly ventilated, dining-hall, day-rooms, and dormitories, ample kitchen, etc. etc. ; an excellent master's
house, chaplain's house, lodge, etc. ; accommodation for
the servants of the establishment ; and 120 beds for
patients, in addition to a ward for cases of accidental injury.  The central position of the building on a commanding eminence, close to the church, the Crescent, the baths,
and the wells, with a southern and western exposure, pre-

senting views from all the windows of the parks and walks, surrounded by its own grounds, and with a costly colonnade and parterre in its centre, furnishes an affecting evidence, as is recorded on a stone over the door of the hospital, written, not long before his death, by the late Sir Francis Darwin, formerly one of the physicians, of " the last munificent charity of William Spencer, 6th Duke of Devonshire, K.G., who allowed these buildings to be converted to the use of the sick poor, January, A.D. 1858."

Dr. Robertson says, " In the three years, the hospital has had 2654 patients under treatment ; the 100 beds were occupied, and many of the patients were obliged to have beds out of the hospital, during many weeks of those years ; the cases of 2357 of the patients were relieved, and of these 1249 were cured, or much relieved, only 164 of the patients having derived no benefit during their stay ; and the account for drugs averaged only sixteen-pence per head, although 348 of the patients, or about one-seventh of the whole, were not suffering from any of the forms of rheumatism, but were such as are ordinarily met with in hospitals, and required medical treatment accordingly. On the average of the three years, the patients remained under treatment 24½ days ; and 2306 cases of rheumatism, embracing every conceivable variety of this distressing malady, and for the most part cases of severe and obstinate character, were in so short a time, and with so little aid from other means than the Buxton waters, treated with such satisfactory results."

There are printed rules and regulations for subscribers and patients, which may be obtained on application.

An in-patient is entitled to board, lodgings, baths, and medicines, for three weeks ; after that time, a charge of 10s. per week will be made.

An out-patient will be entitled to medical advice, medicines, and baths ; but the medical officers will attend these patients only at the Hospital at the appointed days and hours.

No patient will be allowed to remain more than six weeks on the books of the Institution without a special order signed by at least two of the medical staff of the Hospital.

All applicants for admission require to produce a recommendation, signed by a subscriber, and a certificate from the officiating minister, churchwarden, or some other parochial officer, or respectable inhabitant of the place from which they come, that they are fit objects of charity, and unable to pay for themselves.

Patients are required to give at least one week's notice before coming to the Hospital.

A donation of twenty guineas constitutes a subscriber for life, with power to recommend one in, or four out patients annually.

An annual subscription of one guinea entitles a subscriber to recommend one in, or four out patients.

DIAMOND HILL, as a place where the celebrated "Buxton Diamonds" are found is called, is about two miles from Buxton, and is a favourite walk with visitors, partly because of the view from a tower built by the Duke of Devonshire, but chiefly on account of the beautiful specimens of quartz crystals which are found there and bear the attractive name of diamonds. The London Road is taken for the distance of about a quarter of a mile, where a lane turns off to the right. In a little while the spot called the "Cottage of Content" is gained, where visitors frequently enjoy tea in a garden, neatly though fancifully laid out. Parties require to bring their own provisions. A narrow path conducts to a farm, "Fern House," which we pass, and then turning under the crags, we gain the mine of Buxton Gems, a ravine between two heights named respectively Grinlow and Laidmanlow. The "diamonds'

occur in a quantity of loose debris, probably the result of
mining operations, and are generally picked out for sale by
the "natives" after a fall of rain. THE TOWER, now in
ruins, called "Solomon's Temple," affords fine prospects of
the neighbourhood. Far in the distance are seen Kinder
Scout, Lordseat, Chelmorton Low, and other heights, while
almost overlooking us is Axe Edge. Owing to the injury
done by visitors, the principal spot has, we believe, been
walled in.

POOLE'S HOLE—[*Guides in attendance. Charge 1s.*]
This cavern is about half-a-mile from Buxton, and may be
conveniently visited at the same time as Diamond Hill,
from which it is not far distant. The entrance from Grinlow side, below the plantations, which has been made easy
of access, is contracted for some distance, when it becomes
more lofty, and soon widens out into a larger cavity. Passing over some shelving rocks termed the Woolpacks, the
interior is gained. Stalactites and stalagmites are in abundance, and of various forms. Rhodes thinks that this cave
has "little in it to repay the trouble and inconvenience of
a visit." It is now lighted with gas, and could he now see
it he probably would change his opinion. It is undoubtedly
a place worth seeing. Fanciful names have been given to
the various forms assumed by the stalactites, such as the
"petrified turtle," the "flitch of bacon," "Old Poole's
saddle," "the chair," "the font," "the lady's toilet," "the
lion," and "the pillion." The author quoted remarks
"That these names have been dealt out and appropriated
in a very arbitrary manner. The whale or ousel, which
Hamlet points out amongst the clouds to poor Polonius, was
not more unlike in form and feature than those uncouth

resemblances are to the objects they are said to represent."
As these stalagmites are constantly, from the drifting of the
impregnated water, changing their forms, it is not unlikely
that there might have been some faint resemblance to these
things when they were first so named. One piece is pointed
out as "Mary Queen of Scots' Pillar" from the tradition
that the hapless queen of Scotland, when she visited this
cavern, proceeded no further in. A narrow streamlet runs
through the cavern, and the roofings and archings are of the
most imposing and grand character and extent. Stalactites
hang from the roof in many places, of the most prodigious
size, and large crystalline masses, which have accumulated
on the flooring in many places, are of the greatest beauty.
This place is said to take its name from a famous outlaw
and robber named Poole, who made it his abode. It is
reckoned one of the wonders of Derbyshire, and as such is
immortalised by Hobbes and Cotton.

THE PARK occupies more than a hundred acres of ground,
sloping to the south, and has walks and drives through it.
Several handsome houses are erected in it, and it offers
admirable sites for villas. Above the Park are CURBAR
WALKS.

THE SERPENTINE WALKS are delightfully planned along
the margin of the Wye, and are entered nearly opposite the
Old Hall. Little cascades, miniature lakes, rustic bowers
and seats, variegate the scene, adding much to the beauty,
and not a little to the comfort of the walk. The beautiful
river Wye has in some places been deepened and widened
to give greater expanse to the water, and everything that
art could devise has been done to render the walks as picturesque and beautiful as possible. THE DUKE'S DRIVE,

formed by the Duke of Devonshire in 1795, affords a pleasant promenade or ride ; it is a circuit of about four miles through Ashwood Dale, and on the crags over Wye Dale, and forms one of the most pleasing of all the many delightful drives around Buxton. Another splendid walk is taken by Topley Pike, and so by the river-side to Blackwood Mill where the Wye is crossed by rustic stepping-stones, and thence forward over the cliffs to Chee Tor.

The drive to the CAT AND FIDDLE, on the Macclesfield road, affords some fine views, wild, extensive and picturesque, over the hills and moors of Derbyshire, and the rich plains of Cheshire ; the Mersey, distant about forty miles, glittering, on clear days, on the limits of the horizon. This was one of the most favourite drives of the late Duke of Devonshire, who had his favourite Angora cat, seated by a fiddle, photographed, and presented the picture to the then landlord, Mr. Cotterill. An excellent drink is here supplied of rum and milk.

CORBAR WOOD WALKS, OR SWISS GARDENS, half-a-mile on the Manchester road. " A great extent of walks of extreme beauty and variety, through a plantation which occupies the site of old gritstone quarries, and covers a great part of Corbar hill side. Occupying the south side of a commanding eminence, winding through plantations of adequate growth, and traversing the picturesque inequalities of the old quarries, all their rude handiwork covered over long ago with weed, undergrowth, ferns, foxglove, and more recently with rhododendrons and the like, with vistas of Buxton and its valley, and surrounding hills, these walks are the most recent and most picturesque addition to the attractive features in the locality."

CAVENDISH TERRACE is a broad and almost level walk, extending from the bottom of Hall Bank to the Tonic Bath, about 600 yards. It is dry and well made, is one of the most valuable additions which has lately been made to the attractions of the place, and is a favourite promenade with visitors, as it affords fine views of the gardens, plantations, miniature lakes, and surrounding country.

CHEE TOR may be conveniently visited from Buxton either by Ashwood Dale, Topley Pike, Blackwood Mill, and a sheep-track, or by Fairfield to Wormhill, or by railway to Miller's Dale Station. At FAIRFIELD, an antique little village, a guide may be obtained to the summit. A curious epitaph is said to have existed in the churchyard, but to have been removed or destroyed when the church was rebuilt in 1840. It ran as follows :—

> " Beneath this stone here lie two children dear,
>   The one at Stoney Middleton—the other here."

*Chee Tor.*—From Miller's Dale Station it is reached by ascending the Wormhill road. After leaving the railway, a roughish path leads off on the left by a cottage. This track takes the visitor to the foot of the Tor, and affords perhaps the best view of this stupendous rock. The path follows the left side of the Wye for about half-a-mile, and some very fine views may be obtained. The visit to Chee Tor from Miller's Dale Station on foot will occupy about $1\frac{3}{4}$ hour there and back.

Chee Tor is certainly one of the most remarkable rocks in Derbyshire. It presents a solid wall of rock, much resembling the High Tor at Matlock, rising to a height of about three hundred feet. The rock on the opposite side is nearly the same height, and appears to be its counter-

part. Indeed, the vale looks like a huge crack in the
earth's stony crust.    The graphic description of Rhodes is
so apt that we cannot resist copying it.    " Looking down
the river," he says, " which widens as it winds round the
Tor, an islet adorned with light trees and underwood occupies the middle of the river.    On the left the view is diversified with masses of rock, piled upon each other until they
close in the prospect.    Their jutting crags are partly
covered with overhanging branches, and the hazel, the
aspen, the wild rose, and the mountain-ash, adorn their
summits.    Turning round, and looking up the dale, a different picture, but yet equally beautiful and interesting, is
displayed.    The wildest part of the dell opens immediately before you, and the river, with its innumerable
miniature cascades, is seen to greater advantage than in the
contrary direction.    Chee Tor is still the grand object, and
though it gradually loses its feature of vastness, it assumes
a greater portion of picturesque beauty.    The regularity of
its receding outline is broken with light and graceful
foliage, which, hanging like wreaths upon its brow, plays
along the rock in tasteful sportiveness, until it mingles
with the ascending branches of the ash and the elm that
decorate its base.    Almost every circumstance," he adds,
"even the most minute, in the following extract from
Sir Walter Scott's description of Loch Katrine is peculiarly
applicable to Chee Dale."

> " Here eglantine embalm'd the air,
> Hawthorn and hazel mingled there ;
> The primrose pale and violet flower,
> Found in each cliff a narrow bower ;
> Foxglove and nightshade, side by side,
> Emblems of punishment and pride,
> Grouped their dark hues with every stain
> The weather-beaten crags retain.

> With boughs that quaked at every breath,
> Grey birch and aspen wept beneath;
> Aloft, the ash and warrior oak
> Cast anchor in the rifted rock;
> And, higher yet, the pine-tree hung
> His shatter'd trunk, and frequent flung,
> Where seem'd the cliffs to meet on high,
> His boughs athwart the narrow'd sky."

LUDCHURCH, on the borders of Staffordshire, seven miles from Buxton, is one of the most beautiful and picturesque, yet least known, of the many attractive places in this neighbourhood; and visitors who desire a pleasant and romantic drive cannot do better than pay it a visit. The way is along the Leek road to Flash, and so on to Gradbach. "The Castle Cliffs," a mass of rugged rocks rising above the wood, on the north side of the road, are a sufficient guide to the place. At the cliffs there is a foot-path running southwards at the back of the wood, and this path leads into the rocky chasm called " Lud-church "— the church where, it is said, Robin Hood worshipped, " bending there with his stout yeomen, the sentinels posted at either end, with Tuck singing the service, and his sturdy congregation spread in various attitudes around." Few can go there without saying that a more appropriate place for such a service, and such worshippers, could not well be found. There are some curious legends connected with Ludchurch, tor which the visitor may be referred to the " Reliquary."

LONGNOR, a small market-town six miles from Buxton, has very beautiful scenery in its neighbourhood, and is a pleasant drive by way of Earl Sterndale and Glutton. The road crosses the river Dove about five miles from Buxton, and the limestone crags on one side, and the gritstone hills on the other, give a charming variety to the scenery, the peaky ridges of Croom and Park Hill, of High Wheeldon, and of Harley, forming conspicuous objects in the landscape. There is good accommodation at the Longnor inns.

RAILWAYS.—The railway stations are elegant and commodious, with beautifully foliated capitals, on which the fern, the ivy, and other plants, are carved with exquisite skill. They are approached by a wide and most convenient road from the Quadrant.

Buxton has now direct railway communication with Manchester by the "Stockport, Disley, and Buxton" line, which is worked by the London and North-Western Company, and with Derby, London, and the north and south of England by the "Buxton and Rowsley Extension" line, worked by the Midland Company. On this line thirteen miles of the "extension" to Buxton, though but a small proportion of the great aggregate of the railway system, presents, nevertheless, owing to the nature of the country through which it is carried, many features in construction which have called forth all the resources of the engineers and contractors, and, for its length, is perhaps scarcely anywhere exceeded in the number and variety of "works" which its construction has necessitated. In that distance there are no less than eight tunnels, through a variety of "measures," the chief of which is the limestone, which, at Chee Tor, and in some other tunnels, is of such solidity as to require no masonry. The number of bridges or viaducts, of great height and span, in crossing and recrossing the valley of the Wye, and the lightness and beauty of many of the works by which the line is carried, form a not insignificant addition to the picturesque effects of the district, and a monument of the skill and ability of engineer and contractor, pride of which is easily pardonable. The works were completed in two years and nine months, being, we believe, several months within the time specified. The engineer of the line was W. H. Barlow, Esq.—Messrs. Campbell and Champion being the resident engineers ; and the contractors, Messrs. Rennie, Logan, and Matthews. The stations on this line, from Buxton, are Miller's Dale for Wormhill ; Tideswell (here is the celebrated ebbing and flowing well), etc. ; Thornbridge, for Longstone and other places ; Hassop, where is the former seat of the Earl of Newborough, Bakewell, Rowsley, Darley Dale, Matlock Bridge, Matlock Bath, Cromford, Whatstandwell Bridge, and Ambergate, where it joins the main line north and south, having passed through one of the most truly beautiful districts in the kingdom.

The " Stockport, Disley, and Buxton " line is nine miles in length. About two miles and a half from Whaley Bridge the line crosses the head of the Coombs Valley. Here it was necessary to construct a bridge beneath which the road from Coombs to Chapel might pass. The navvies dug through scores of feet of clay resting upon sand, but could find nothing upon which to build a foundation. The earth also of which the embankment was to be made forced outward the surface of the ground, and made it bulge to a remarkable extent. Finally, the company were compelled to abandon the construction of the bridge, and to build another upon the nearest solid ground they ʀould find. In connection with this deviation, it may ʌnterest our readers to be told that all this trouble and expense is popularly believed to be ascribable to the malign influence of a skull, known as " Dickey of Tunstead " which has been for " ages " preserved in a farm-house at that place, and connected with which many curious super-

F

stitions have been given in Mr. Llewellynn Jewitt's "Ballads and Songs of Derbyshire," and in the " Reliquary," vol. viii., where the belief concerning this railway mishap is thus spoken of:—"The newly formed line of the Stockport, Disley, and Whaley Bridge 'Buxton Extension' Railway passes through the land belonging to the farm-house where the skull is deposited, and had to cross the Coombs Valley to the Chapel-en-le-Frith station by a high embankment, and an archway over the highway. The embankment was formed, and a stately arch erected ; but they were not out of the hands of the contractor before the arch rapidly sank into the earth, its walls were riven and dislocated, and the ground at each end of the archway thrown up into large mounds. Every effort was made to overcome the difficulty and restore the fabric, and a very large amount was expended for that purpose, but without avail. Either the ground was naturally a quicksand which swallowed up all the material, or (according to the neighbourhood), Dickey would not have the archway in that position. The Railway Company and contractors battled with the malign power a long time, but were eventually obliged to give way, and not only remove their bridge to some distance, but form a new highway at a great expense for upwards of a quarter of a mile. When this alteration (which made a new and very handsome road into the Coombs) was completed, Dickey appears to have been appeased ; and the new road and bridge stand a proud monument of his engineering taste, and determined opposition to the erection of the bridge upon a swamp."

Near the railway station a large and handsome hotel has been built by the " Buxton Palace Hotel Company." It is a magnificent building, containing splendid suites of apartments.

## CASTLETON.

Hotels.—*Castle*—Bed 1s. 6d., breakfast 1s. 6d. to 2s., lunch 1s., dinner 2s. 6d. to 3s., tea 1s. 3d. to 1s. 9d., supper 1s. 6d. *Nag's Head*—(charges moderate). *Bull's Head*—Bed 1s., living according to order. Furnished apartments and cottages are to be had on reasonable terms.

From Buxton 12 m.; from Chatsworth by Hathersage 14 m.; from Stoney Middleton 10 m.; from Chesterfield 21 m.; from Matlock 24 m. Coach in summer from Buxton to Castleton and back.

Population, 678.

The walk or drive from Buxton to Castleton possesses some attractions. The road passes by the village of Fairfield, which, from its elevated position, commands one of the finest and most extensive views in the neighbourhood. From Fairfield it continues along the old Roman road, the Batham Gate, past the Marvel Stones, an extensive group of limestone rocks cropping out from the surface. Immediately beyond the Marvel Stones is the hamlet of Peak Forest, with its quaint old chapel, which until late years enjoyed the same privileges as Gretna Green, and was used to no small extent for the solemnization of runaway matches. The hamlet is picturesque, and there are many curious traditions connected with it. Further on at the side of the road is the famous "*Ebbing and Flowing Well*," one of the most remarkable of any of the intermitting springs in this district. At this well, after much rain, the flow is frequently about every ten minutes, and the quantity of water poured out is very considerable. It is considered one of the wonders of Derbyshire, and is well worthy a visit. It is defended by a semicircular stone wall, under which are nine openings, through which the water flows,

It flows for about five minutes, and then gradually ebbs, and in that space of time is supposed to throw out about 120 hogsheads of water. Those acquainted with the action of the syphon will have no difficulty in accounting for the ebbing and flowing well. It is only necessary to suppose a cavity in the rock, in which to collect the rain water as it falls ; and a syphon-shaped fissure to conduct it to the well. When the internal cavity becomes filled with water beyond the level of the upper bend of the fissure, the water immediately commences to flow, and will continue until the cavity becomes empty, when of course there will be an ebb until the rain has again filled it. From this well the large and picturesque village of Tideswell (Tides Well) evidently takes its name.

The next object of interest passed on the way is the Odin Mine on the left (see page 76), and a little further along on the right is the Blue John Mine. The stage-coach which runs between Buxton and Castleton stops near the opening to the mine, to afford tourists an opportunity of visiting it, which it is well to take advantage of, as it is some distance from the village. The descent is so easy that it may be made by ladies, but the intense cold and damp, even in summer, should prevent those of delicate constitution undertaking the exploration. An hour in the bowels of the earth, with the water dripping all around, is not favourable to health. This mine is described along with the others at page 75.

THE VILLAGE OF CASTLETON lies in a dale immediately at the foot of Mam Tor, one of the highest mountains in the Peak, having an altitude of above 2000 feet above the level of the sea. It is crowned on its southern side by a steep and commanding eminence, on the summit of which are the ruins of the old Norman castle of "Peveril of the Peak," from which it takes its name. The church, which is an interesting little building with some good Norman details, contains monuments to the memory of Mawe the mineralogist, who was buried at London, but desired this monument to be erected in Castleton, where he acquired his taste for mineralogy and geology ; to the Rev. Edward Bagshaw, a clergyman much and deservedly esteemed in the Peak ; and to an attorney named Micha Hall. On the latter is an inscription in English and Latin, said to have been written by himself. It is characteristic of anything but a liberal mind. The following is the inscription :—

TO THE MEMORY OF
MICHA HALL, GENTN.,
ATTORNEY-AT-LAW,
Who died on the 14th of May 1804,
Aged 79 years.

Quid eram, nescitis ;
Quid sum, nescitis ;
Ubi abii, nescitis ;
Valete.

Which may be thus translated—

"What I was you know not—What I am you know not—Whither I am gone you know not—Go about your business."

At Castleton, too, Elias Hall, a famous native geologist, is buried.

There is an excellent library attached to the church. There are "museums" in the village for the sale of Derbyshire productions, in the same manner as at Matlock, Buxton, etc.

THE CASTLE is said to have been built by the Saxons,[*] who worked the Odin lead mine in the neighbourhood, so celebrated for its elastic bitumen. Pilkington gives an account of a grand tournament which took place here. A half-brother of William, named "Pain Peveril, Lord of Whittington, in the county of Salop, had two daughters ; one of whom, named Mellet, was no less distinguished by a martial spirit than her father. This appeared from the declaration she made regarding the choice of a husband. She firmly resolved to marry none but a knight of great prowess ; and her father, to confirm her purpose, and to

* Sir Walter Scott, in the first chapter of "Peveril of the Peak," writes the following :—

"William, the Conqueror of England, was, or supposed himself to be, the father of a certain William Peveril, who attended him to the battle of Hastings, and there distinguished himself. The liberal-minded monarch, who assumed in his charters the veritable title of Gulielmus Bastardus, was not likely to let his son's illegitimacy be any bar to the course of his royal favour, when the laws of England were issued from the mouth of the Norman victor, and the lands of the Saxons were at his unlimited disposal. William Peveril obtained a liberal grant of property and lordships in Derbyshire, and became the erector of that Gothic fortress, which, hanging over the mouth of the Devil's Cavern, so well known to tourists, gives the name of Castleton to the adjacent village. From this feudal baron, who chose his nest upon the principles on which an eagle selects her eyry, and built it in such a fashion as if he intended it, as an Irishman said of the Martello towers, for the sole purpose of puzzling posterity, there was, or conceived themselves to be, descended (for their pedigree was rather hypothetical), au opulent family of knightly rank, in the same county of Derby. The great fief of Castleton, with its adjacent wastes and forests, and all the wonders which they contain, had been forfeited, in King John's stormy days, by one William Peveril, and had been granted anew to the Lord Ferrers of that day. Yet this William's descendants, though no longer possessed of what they alleged to have been their original property, were long distinguished by the proud title of Peverils of the Peak, which served to mark their high descent and lofty pretensions."

procure and encourage a number of visitors, invited all noble young men who were inclined to enter the lists, to meet at Peveril's Palace in the Peke, and there decide their pretensions by the use of arms ; declaring at the same time, that whoever vanquished his competitors should receive his daughter, with his castle at Whittington, as a reward for his skill and valour. Guarine de Metz, a branch of the house of Lorraine, and an ancestor of the Lords Fitz-Warrine, hearing this report, repaired to the place above mentioned, and there engaged with a son of the king of Scotland, and also with a Baron of Burgoyne, and, vanquishing them both, obtained the prize for which he fought."

The castle belonged, at the time of the taking of the Domesday survey, to William Peveril, the manor having been given him by his father, William the Conqueror, and is therein described as " Terra Castelli William Peverell in Pecke fers." The Derbyshire estates, however, were not long held by the family, for William, a grandson of the first Peveril, having been concerned in the poisoning of the Earl of Chester, forfeited his estates, which were granted by Henry II. to his son John, Earl of Morteyne, afterwards King John. In the sixth year of John, Hugh de Neville was governor of the castle, and it was afterwards in the hands of the rebellious barons. In 1215 William de Ferrars, Earl of Derby, assaulted it and took it for the king, and was appointed governor. He was succeeded by the Earl of Chester. The castle then continued a royal one under different governors, and was then, by Edward II., granted to John, Earl of Warren, and Edward III. gave it, in his second year, as a part of the portion of Joan, his sister, on her marriage with David,

Prince of Scotland, and afterwards it was granted in 46th Edward III. to John of Gaunt, from whom it has descended as part of the Duchy of Lancaster.

The castle, even as it now exists, is one of the most interesting Norman fortresses in England. The keep and a portion of the walls are still standing, and are well worthy of examination. The masonry is of the most massive character, and the details of pure Norman work, including some herring-bone masonry, and other remains, are valuable examples. The situation of the fortress is commanding in the extreme, and in the height of its glory the castle of the Peak must have been one of the most powerful strongholds in the kingdom, but now

" The rampant nettle overspreads the halls,
The mournful ivy mantles on the walls ;
The portal now admits the straggling sheep,
The long grass waves about the ruin'd keep ;
The playful breezes whistle through each cell,
Where bats and moping owls, sole tenants dwell.

" Sad are the ruthless ravages of time !
The bulwark'd turret frowning once sublime
Now totters to its basis, and displays
A venerable wreck of other days."

*Wanderings of Memory,* by Rev. A. G. Jewitt.

The caverns are more interesting to ordinary sight-seers than the castle, though they miss that charm which history or romance throws around a spot.

THE PEAK CAVERN is one of the finest specimens of a chambered cave in this country. It extends 2250 feet into the mountain, and is about 600 feet below its summit. This cavern is a quarter of a mile from the village, and is gained by following a pathway, through a chasm, between two tall cliffs, with a clear rivulet by its side. Taking a turn in the road, we front a huge mass of rock, in which is the grand natural archway composing the dark mouth of the cavern. This archway, which is 42 feet in height, 120 feet in width, and 300 feet in depth, is used as a ropewalk, in which several men and boys are employed. Proceeding about thirty yards, the first compartment, through which a dubious twilight prevails, is crossed, the roof gradually becoming lower, and the excavation narrower, till a confined passage is reached, at which all trace of the blaze of day is lost. After traversing this aperture about twenty yards, the first great interior cavity is reached, and five other capacious openings follow." Here the guides light the candles, and the remainder of the journey is accomplished with their assistance. For nearly thirty yards the visitor has to walk in a stooping posture to a chamber called the BELL HOUSE, and thence he gains the margin of a subterranean lake, about fourteen feet across. Here a boat used to be put into requisition, until the present way was cut in the rock for the further exploration of the cavern. The rock in one part approaches to within a foot and a half of the water, and when the stream is swollen with a fall of rain in the uplands, even this space is entirely filled by the flood, and thus all communication between the two halls is cut off, occasionally much to the discomfiture of the visitor. M. St. Fond says, " Here we stood some time on the brink ; and as the light of our dismal torches, which emitted a black smoke, reflecting our pale visages from the bottom of the lake, we almost conceived that we saw a troop of shades starting from an abyss to present themselves before us." The water is not usually more than three feet in depth. A chamber 210 feet broad, 220 long,

and about 120 high, is next entered. Then follows an
expansion of the stream termed the SECOND WATER, and
shortly we reach ROGER RAIN'S HOUSE, so termed from
the drops of water continually trickling from the roof.
The CHANCEL, a rugged chamber, is next gained, and
through a passage the DEVIL'S CELLAR. We now descend
a passage 150 feet in length to the HALF-WAY HOUSE, and
continuing our walk, enter a cavity formerly termed GREAT
TOM OF LINCOLN, from its bell-like shape, but now the
VICTORIA DOME, after the visit of Her Majesty in 1842. The
cavern here diminishes in size until all passage is closed up,
and the stream loses itself in the earth. " Upon retracing his
steps, the visitor is usually stayed at a point of rock which
commands a view of the entrance, in order to observe the
effect of the first return to the light of day. The exterior
rocks, as seen from thence through the mouth of the chasm,
appear as if highly illuminated ; the plants and mosses,
faded with the heat, and soiled with the dust of autumn,
exhibit a vernal freshness ; and the impression produced is
that of a brilliant day reigning without, though the atmosphere may be hazy, and the sun veiled with clouds."

THE SPEEDWELL MINE, at the entrance to the
Winnats, scarcely a mile from Castleton, will well repay a
visit. This is an artificial opening excavated in search of
lead by a mining company, who, after expending £14,000,
and eleven years incessant labour, abandoned the attempt.
The excavation is about 750 yards in length, and it then
bursts into the most gigantic and extensive natural gulph
ever discovered, and which, as yet, it has been impossible
to fathom. It is in the first instance necessary to descend
by a flight of 106 steps cut in the rock, to the " level " or

subterranean stream, on which a boat is in waiting, im-
pelled by the guide, to conduct visitors to the internal
natural cavern. The portion of this "level" or stream
along which the boat, which is capable of holding a party
of about 20 persons, passes, is 750 yards, and is a passage
of 7 feet in width and 9 in height, cut through the solid
rock the entire distance. This passage is lit, as the visitor
progresses, by candles. Landing on a ledge of rock, and
ascending to a platform protected by an iron rail, we view,
by the assistance of the lights, a lofty cavern spread out
above us, and strive in vain to penetrate the deep gloom
which fills the abyss beyond ; while the wild sound of the
stream, rushing into its all but unfathomable depths,
makes us tremble as we stand. "During the further
excavation of this mine, this tremendous gulph received
upwards of 40,000 tons of material, without any impression being made upon its capacity, while into the
awful dome overhead, rockets have been projected, which
have risen to their usual height, exploded and thrown out
their beautiful coruscations as freely as if ascending simply
beneath the vault of heaven."* The passage extends to a
considerable distance beyond the gulph, but is not followed
by visitors. Charge for admission, one person 3s. ; two
persons 4s. 6d. ; and 1s. for each additional visitor above
two. Blasts 1s. 6d. extra.

THE BLUE JOHN MINE is celebrated for the quantity
of beautiful spar which it produces. Indeed few
mines in the world produce such fine specimens as this.
The entrance is effected by a series of steps, which steeply
descend. The guide generally leaves a candle a con-

* Caves of the Earth.

siderable way up, which casts a dim but beautiful light on the spar with which the cavern is adorned. A large chamber, fully 150 feet in height and 60 in width, called LORD MULGRAVE'S DINING ROOM, is soon gained, and after that the VARIEGATED CAVERN, where, standing on a ledge protected by rails, we take a survey of the deep gulph beyond. It is advisable to let off a Bengal light here, in order to form a proper idea of the beauty of the place ; stalactites and crystals mingle in admirable confusion, and the depth and gloom which even its vivid rays fail to pierce, raise a feeling of profoundest awe. Returning towards the opening, we are pleased with the gem-like lustre of the spar which everywhere prevails, and cannot help realizing the "fancy flight" of Allan, so beautifully depicted by Sir Walter Scott in his Lord of the Isles—

> "He turn'd
> To tales at which his youth had burn'd,
> Of pilgrim's path by demon cross'd,
> Of sprightly elf, or yelling ghost,
> Of the wild witch's baneful cot,
> And mermaid's alabaster grot,
> Who bathes her limbs in sunless well,
> Deep in Strathaird's enchanted cell.
> Thither in fancy wrapt he flies,
> And on his sight the vaults arise ;
> That hut's dark walls he sees no more,
> His foot is on the marble floor,
> *And o'er his head the dazzling spars*
> *Gleam like a firmament of stars.*"

*Charge of admission for one 2s., for three 4s. 6d., or for four 5s. 1s. for each additional visitor above four. Bengal lights and blasts extra.*

THE ODIN MINE, worked by our Saxon forefathers, and still worked, is rich in its veins of lead ore, and pro·

CRYSTALLIZED CAVERN—BLUE JOHN MINE.

duces lead which yields upwards of three ounces of silver to the ton.

THE BRADWELL MINE, about two miles from Castleton, and ELDONHOLE, the same distance, are worthy of a visit, though inferior to the other places described. The latter is a deep vertical cavern. Cotton endeavoured to ascertain the depth, but, from some mistake, failed.

> " But I myself, with half the Peake surrounded,
>   Eight hundred, four score, and four yards have sounded,
>   And though of these four score return'd back wet,
>   The plummet drew, and found no bottom yet ;
>   Though when I went to make a new assay,
>   I could not get the lead down half the way."

Mr. Lloyd descended and published an account in 1781. He found a bottom at sixty-two yards' depth.

THE WINNATS, before mentioned, ought to be visited. This is a deep chasm, about a mile in length, with a mountain road from Buxton to Chapel-en-le-Frith. In most places the rocks are steep and scarcely accessible, while here and there they are perpendicular. The name Winnats, originally Wind-gates, has been applied to this ravine on account, probably, of the fierce howling of the winter's wind down the vale. This chasm was the scene, some years ago, of a most mournful tragedy—the murder of a young man and woman while on their wedding trip, which has given rise to several traditions, and been a prolific theme both for the poet and the romance writer.

MAM TOR, or shivering mountain, is but a mile from the entrance to the Winnats. The hill consists of shale and grit in alternate layers. By the action of severe frosts the latter becomes disintegrated, and falls down in considerable quantities.* The view from the summit takes in the beautiful vale of Edale. On the top are still traceable the remains of a Roman encampment. This mountain is the highest in the Peak, and is one of the most singular in appearance.

CAVE DALE affords a delightful ramble, and a good view of the castle from below. The entrance is gained by a narrow street of the village. The wildness of the scene as we walk up the glen surprises one when visiting this locality for the first time. The castle, built on the extreme verge of a narrow ridge of rock, looks down upon the spectator, borrowing importance from the situation it occupies amongst rocks and precipices. At the upper end of the vale the sides again contract. Passing this portal, and gaining an eminence near the Castleton and Tideswell road, the landscape changes, embracing hill and dale, wood, cultured fields, and water, in rich variety. The geologist will be interested at finding a basaltic column, three feet high, and about a foot and a half in diameter, in the dale.

* Immediately upon the limestone is placed a bed of calcareous slate or shale, varying in thickness from three to six hundred feet. The compact strata are separated by coarse layers, which readily disintegrate, and these form the exposed face of Mam Tor, or the "shivering mountain," near Castleton.—*Mantell's Wonders of Geology,* vol. ii. p. 664.

## CHAPEL-EN-LE-FRITH.

HOTELS and INNS.—*King's Arms, Bull's Head*—Market Place.
From Buxton 6 m. ; Bakewell 14 m. ; Glossop 10 m.

CHAPEL-EN-LE-FRITH is a market-town of some considerable importance in the High Peak. It is a particularly neat, clean, and respectable-looking little town, situated on the side of a hill which slopes down into a fertile valley beneath. The Town-Hall is in Market Street, and was erected in 1851. In it the County Court is held, as well as the Petty Sessions of the district. There are several Dissenting places of worship, a National and other schools, Mechanics' Institution, Union House, and other public buildings. There are also two Railway Stations, one on the Midland, and the other on the North Western line, so that the town is now, with the lines running to Manchester, Derby, London, etc., connected with the entire railway systems of the kingdom.

The neighbourhood of Chapel-en-le-Frith is rich in antiquities and in places of interest, and the scenery by which it is surrounded is wild and remarkably grand. Within a short distance is a Roman camp, on the summit of a mountain, similar in height to the Chinley Hills, known as "Chinley Churn," and so placed as to command all the country round for many miles.

The village of HAYFIELD, a short distance from Chapel-en-le-Frith, possesses large printworks, the water from the neighbouring hills being pure and well adapted to the purposes of those establishments. It has an increasing population, and a railway from the Stockport, Disley, and Whaley Bridge line. "The ridge of hills running northward and eastward from Hayfield is the highest in Derbyshire : Kinder Scout is the summit, and commences that tract of picturesque scenery which spreads itself over Edale, the Woodlands, Hopedale, and the Valley of the Derwent. The greater part of this wild country is unknown to the traveller, as there are no roads passable by carriages ; and to see the scenery in its beauty, it must either be done on foot or on horseback. The road into the Scout may be travelled by carriages, but it terminates in a *cul de sac* at the foot of the mountain, about three miles from Hayfield. Parties (and there are many in the course of the summer) usually leave their carriages at one of the farm houses if they intend to ascend to the summit, which occupies a good part of an hour. In a propitious day the view from the top of Kinder is so extensive that in some states of the atmosphere you may descry the sea at Liverpool, nearly fifty miles distant. A mountain stream descends from the head of Kinder, and has worn its way through the granite rocks to the valley beneath. The water descends by leaps from ledge to ledge for the space of four or five hundred feet, and in stormy weather, when the wind blows hard against the "Downfall" as it is usually called, the water, blown into spray, extends a quarter of a mile in width. With the alternate blast or lull of the wind it rises and falls with fitful variation, and presents a very singular and beautiful appearance. At the very top of the fall, and before it makes its first leap, several large granite rocks have been thrown together at some very distant period (probably on the breaking up of the crust of the earth by volcanic action, as there is no higher region in the country from which the rocks could have been borne), and form an arch and ceiling above the stream, which runs sparkling over a bed of bright sand,

and is perfectly pure. The grotto will hold twenty people, and has long borne the name of "the mermaiden's well," though the tourist may probably be disappointed on finding any of those amphibia on his arrival. It is, however, a beautiful cavern, into which the sunbeams penetrate through the chinks of the rocks, and sparkle in the water, and forms a delightful apartment for refection on a hot summer's day. On the cliffs which lie adjacent to the grotto are a number of rock basins, which in all probability were used in Druidical worship. All around, the scenery is savage and sublime ; but is relieved in one place by the remains of a Druidical circle, and in another by a little cross of stone, which pointed out the way across the moors to the traveller, before any road was made for man or horse. By the cross you descend into Edale, the deepest valley in Derbyshire, guarded on the north by hills of twelve or fourteen hundred feet elevation, and on the south by the celebrated mountain Mam Tor, at the entrance of the Castleton valley. This valley (called Hope Dale) is of great beauty and fertility."

TUNSTEAD, of which place, or rather of " Dicky of Tunstead," the visitor of this neighbourhood is sure to hear, is a short distance from Chapel-en-le-Frith. "Dicky" is a skull which for many generations has been preserved in a farm house there, and concerning whose supernatural powers there are many curious stories and beliefs current among the "natives."

BRADSHAW HALL, in the parish of Chapel-en-le-Frith, the ancient patrimonial seat of the Bradshaws, of which family the too celebrated judge, John Bradshaw, was a

member. His brother, Francis Bradshaw, rebuilt the Hall
in 1620, as will be seen from the date of the inscription,
surmounting a sculptured shield, on the gateway of the
house, as shewn in the accompanying engraving. The
gateway also, on its outer side, bears the arms of Bradshaw, as shewn in the next engraving. The gateway
is an excellent example of Jacobean architecture. Bradshaw Hall is pleasantly situated on the southern slope
of Eccles Pike, and commands an excellent view of Chapel-
en-le-Frith, but more particularly of the Comb's valley,
and the beautiful sheet of water used as a reservoir to
supply the Peak Forest Canal, and which from the house
has, in every respect, the appearance of a natural lake.
The lake is nearly a mile in length by about a third of a

mile in breadth, and covers 80 acres of land. The hill
called Comb's Moss lies beyond its southern shore, and on
the top of its north-western side, which rises like a perpen-

dicular rampart from a considerable depth below, stand the remains of the Roman camp, just noticed. Bradshaw Hall was built in the form of a cross ; but one limb of it has been pulled down, and the materials taken (according to tradition) to erect one of the inns of Chapel-en-le-Frith. The house originally faced the hill, and the road from it passed through the gateway to the highway, which, according to the fashion of thĕ old time in Derbyshire, passed over the highest part of the mountain. Bradshaw Hall contains some good old-fashioned rooms, one or two of

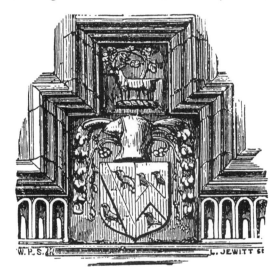

which are wainscotted with black oak ; and on the top of one of the staircases leading to the chambers above, the landing is surrounded with the following inscription :—

"LOVE GOD AND NOT GOULD."

"He that loves not mercy,
Of mercy shall miss ;
But he shall have mercy
That merciful is."

# CHATSWORTH.

*Chatsworth Hotel,* Edensor, J. Harrison, close to the Park gates at Edensor
  Omnibuses from the Hotel meet all the principal trains at Rowsley
  station.  A spacious coffee-room for ladies.  Private sitting, and well-
  appointed bed rooms.  Post-horses, carriages, etc.  Fishing tickets
  supplied at the Hotel for the river Derwent.

Chatsworth from Rowsley Station, 3½ miles ; from Hassop Station, 3 miles
  from Bakewell, 4 miles ; from Matlock, 10 miles ; from Buxton, 14·
  miles.

CHATSWORTH, the seat of the Duke of Devonshire, is
usually called the "Palace of the Peak." Whatever the
most capricious taste could desire, or the most varied art,
aided by almost countless wealth, could supply, has been
applied here to the decoration and ornamentation both of
nature and art.  A mansion fit to satisfy a king—sculpture, paintings, and articles of vertu, for the artist and

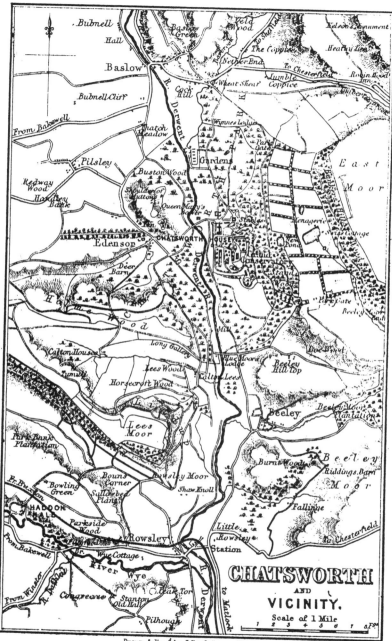

CHATSWORTH
AND
VICINITY.

Scale of 1 Mile

Drawn & Eng.ᵈ by J. Bartholomew, Edin.ʳ

Published by A. & C. Black, Edinburgh.

antiquary—tapestry and elegant furniture such as even George Villiers himself might have envied—a noble park, rich in leafy honours, in herds of deer, and myriads of birds—and not less the ornamental gardens, where the artistic skill of Sir Joseph Paxton has all but outdone nature, in chasteness of design and elegance of execution.

CHATSWORTH PARK extends over a space of upwards of eleven miles in circumference, and is richly varied in its scenery — the mountainous heights covered with forest trees of magnificent growth, the valley watered by the river Derwent and its small tributary streams, the gently-swelling eminence, the carpet-like lawn, the elegant parterres, the quiet secluded nook, and the palatial terrace— are all to be found amongst its attractions. The river Derwent divides the park into two almost equal portions — the gardens and house being situated on the eastern division, and the beautiful little village of Edensor on the western skirting of the park. Many delightful views occur in the park, particularly on the way to Rowsley, which is by a road almost parallel with the Derwent. Visitors enter the park by the lodges at Edensor ; Edensor Mill by Beeley Bridge, and at Baslow ; and there is a private lodge at Beeley.

CHATSWORTH HOUSE exteriorly presents a simple yet magnificent western façade. The base is rusticated ; on this rests a series of finely proportioned Ionic fluted pillars and pilasters, supporting a sculptured frieze, and in the centre, a pediment bearing in its tympanum the Cavendish Arms, beautifully sculptured by the celebrated Samuel Watson, who, in conjunction with Lobb and Davies, supplied the major part of the carving about Chatsworth. The elegant open balustrade which surmounts the frieze bears at intervals statues, urns, and vases. An extensive northern wing has been added from the designs of Sir Jeffrey Wyatville, and of the most chaste character ; it is an addition truly worthy of the mansion, but differs from it in style, being a compound of Corinthian, Doric, and Ionic architecture. Like the mansion, which it equals in height, the temple at the end of the wing is surmounted by an open balustrade, at the corners of which are elegant vases.

As the hour of eleven arrives, there are generally several parties outside the richly gilded gates of wrought iron, waiting for the time of admission. The first hall is termed the SUB-HALL. The corridor has a rich mosaic pavement of modern design and workmanship. The material employed is chiefly marble. The ceiling is ornamented with Guido's Aurora, by Miss Curzon. In the corridor are busts of Homer, Jupiter, Ariadne, Socrates, and others. The GREAT HALL is sixty feet by twenty-seven. The floor is mosiac work, laid by Henry Watson, son of the carver. The decorations, which illustrated the career of Julius Cæsar, are by Verrio and Laguerre. The periods chosen for illustration are—1st, The crossing of the Rubicon ; 2d, The voyage on the Adriatic, to meet his army at Brundusium ; 3d, The sacrifice before going to Senate ; 4th, His death at the hand of his friend Brutus ; and 5th (on the ceiling), His deification. The appointments of this hall display much taste and grandeur. The pillars and table of Derbyshire marble cannot fail to excite admiration. The following inscription is over the fireplace :—

Ædes has paternas dilectissimas
Anno libertatis Anglicæ MDCLXXXVIII institvtas,
Gvl. S. Devoniæ Dux Anno MDCCCXI Hæres accepit
Anno mœroris svi MDCCCXL perfecit.

The Countess of Burlington, niece of the former Duke, and whose husband is now Duke of Devonshire, died in the spring of 1840 ; hence the melancholy expression in the last line of an inscription which records the completion of the hereditary mansion. By the grand southern staircase, ornamented with paintings, and figures of Apollo, Minerva, and Lucretia, we gain the STATE APARTMENTS, the door-cases of which are of variegated Derbyshire marble. The ceilings are decorated with allegorical scenes by Verrio, Laguerre, and Sir James Thornhill, among which may be mentioned "The Judgment of Paris," "Aurora chasing away Night," " the discovery of Mars and Venus," " Phaëton taking charge of the horses of the Sun." The remainder are similar subjects from the heathen poets. The floors are of oak par-queterie. Some of these rooms are lined with fancy woods, others hung with rich tapestry, copied from the cartoons of Raphael, and others again with embossed leather. The wood carving will attract especial notice, and will recal the well-merited eulogium passed upon the principal artist by Horace Walpole. "There is no instance," says he, " of a man before Gibbons who gave to wood the loose and airy lightness of flowers, and chained together the various productions of the elements with a free disorder natural to each species." It is generally believed that Gibbons was the artist of these exquisite carvings. There is, how-ever, no proof that this was the case, whilst agreements and documents at present in existence shew that at least the greatest part were the work of Watson and his asso-ciates. That Gibbons superintended the work, and sup-plied some, is probable, but his name does not appear in any of the accounts of the expenses of the erection, which are still preserved by the Duke of Devonshire. The prin-

cipal carver was Mr. S. Watson, already mentioned as the
sculptor of the arms of the pediment. Watson was buried
in his native place Heanor, where a richly ornamented
monument bears the following inscription :—

> " Watson has gone, whose skilful art display'd,
>   To the very life whatever nature made :
>   View but his wondrous works at Chatsworth Hall,
>   Which are so gazed at, and admired by all,
>   You'll say 'tis pity he should hidden lie,
>   And nothing said to revive his memory."

It is gratifying to know that this beautiful carving, consisting of dead game, fish, flowers, fruit, shells, and other
objects, is still in perfect preservation. The most striking
piece of carving is preserved in the State Dressing-room.
This is a group consisting of a cravat of point-lace as fine
and delicate in the open-work as the lace itself, a wood-
cock, some foliage, and a medal with a bust in relief.
Another exquisite specimen of carving is the net and
game, with fish, etc., in the State Dining-room, of which a
writer has observed, " you imagine, at the first glance, that
the gamekeeper has just hung up his day's sport on the
wall, and that some of the birds are still in the death-
flutter." The suite of state rooms, occupying the upper
storey of the south front, and extending its entire length,
consists of the State Dressing-room, the old State Bed-room,
the State Music-room, the State Drawing-room, and the
State Dining-room. In this latter is the exquisite carving
of game, net, etc., already alluded to, and here too are
several busts by Nollekins, Chantrey, and others ; and a
cabinet of fine old china. On the central table are preserved, among other rare and valuable articles, the rosary
of King Henry VIII., a fine set of carved ivory chessmen,

ivory carvings, rare glass and china, and silver filigree and other ornaments. Here, too, are the malachite clock presented to the late Duke by the Emperor Nicholas of Russia, and a splendid model of the Victoria Regia. In another of these rooms is the malachite table presented by the Emperor Nicholas; and various paintings adorn the walls. In the old State Bed-room are an ancient canopy and chair embroidered by Christian, Countess of Devonshire; a wardrobe said to have belonged to Louis XVI.; the coronation chairs and footstools of George III. and Queen Charlotte, and of William IV. and Queen Adelaide, and some fine old cabinets, vases, beakers, etc. In the State Music-room, besides many other interesting objects, is a curious piece of deceptive painting, which invariably attracts the notice of visitors. This is a fiddle, so cleverly painted upon one of the doors, by Verrio, that it deceives every one.

Adjoining these State-rooms, and running the entire length of the building on the south side of the inner quadrangle, is the SKETCH GALLERY, on the walls of which are displayed a most valuable and perfectly unique collection of upwards of a thousand original drawings and sketches by the old masters, embracing the Italian, French, Flemish, Venetian, Spanish, and other schools, and including sketches by Titian, Rubens, Salvator Rosa, Raphael, Claude Lorraine, Correggio, Michael Angelo, Albert Durer, Rembrandt, Leonardo da Vinci, Poussin, the Carracci, Holbein, Vandyke, and indeed almost every well-known name.

The centre or Library storey contains the Gallery of Paintings, the Gallery of the Chapel, the Library Corridor, the Billiard or Music room, the Grand Drawing-rooms, the Libraries, the Dining-room, the Sculpture Gallery, Orangery, etc.

The Gallery of Paintings occupies two sides of the quadrangle, and, with the adjoining apartments, contains many choice art treasures,— such indeed as no other mansion can boast. Among these are Landseer's "Bolton Abbey in the olden time," and "Laying down the law;" and a number of other admirable pictures.

The CHAPEL is one of the glories of Chatsworth. It occupies the south-west angle of the mansion, and in height extends up two storeys, reaching from the ground floor up to the floor of the upper or state-room storey. At its east end, midway in height, and communicating with the gallery of paintings and with the billiard-room, is a gallery supported upon two massive pillars of black marble, with white marble ,capitals and bases. The Chapel is lighted by three windows on the upper storey. The floor is paved with marble, and the altar-piece is also of marble ; the pillar and steps of black, and the remainder of white marble. On the sides are two fine figures of Faith and Hope, by Caius Gabriel Cibber (father of Colley Cibber), who was much employed at Chatsworth from 1688 to 1690 or thereabouts, and who, besides these marble figures, carved two large Sphinxes, statues of Pallas, Apollo, a Triton, and other figures. The top of the altar-piece is exquisitely sculptured with cherubs and festoons, and at the sides are vases of flowers. In the lower pediment or recess is a dove, and there are also some charming figures of cherubs, etc., and under the recess is a chaste and beautiful bust of our Saviour. The chapel is wainscoted throughout in its lower storey with cedar, which, besides its beautiful rich colour, gives a peculiar odour to the place, which is very grateful, and accords well with the subdued light and its general effect. The reading-desk also is of cedar. The ceiling, and the upper storey of the apartment, are painted in the same remarkably fine manner as those of the state-rooms, by Verrio and Laguerre ; the subjects being "The incredulity of St. Thomas," "Christ and the woman of Samaria," "Christ healing the blind," and the "Ascension of our Saviour." There are also figures of the Christian attributes, Justice, Mercy, Charity, and Liberality.

One great interest of the chapel, and, indeed, as we have already said, of the state-rooms of this noble pile, are the splendid wood-carvings which adorn its walls and the heads of its upper doors. Between the larger panels of the cedar walls are exquisite pendants, ten in number, and others occur on either side of the altar. The pendants consist of flowers, fruit, foliage, and corn, festooned and entwined with drapery in the most free and graceful manner, and so true to nature in every detail as to be deceptive. Over the doors in the gallery are fine figures of Cupids with musical instruments.

The BILLIARD or MUSIC ROOM, and the GRAND DRAWING-ROOMS, which form one continued suite, are as well-proportioned, as chastely and elegantly decorated, and as magnificently furnished, as can well be imagined, and they contain a matchless collection of works of art. In the billiard-room, from which a door opens into the gallery of the chapel, are several remarkably good paintings, the most striking of which are an admirable full-length seated portrait of the present Duke of Devonshire, and a full-length portrait of the father of the present noble Duke. Among the treasures of art in the drawing-room (the ornaments of the ceiling and cornices of which are richly gilt), may just be named—Reynolds' celebrated portrait of " the beautiful duchess." of Devonshire, Rembrandt's grand head of a Jewish Rabbi, and picture-gems by Claude, Murillo, Bassano, Steinwyck, Salvator Rosa, Titian, Berghem, Caspar Poussin, Leonardo da Vinci, Primaticcio, Parmigiano, Watteau, Teniers, Brueghel, Guercino, Luca Giordione, Carlo Maratti, Jan Miel, and others. In the grand drawing-room, which has a splendid ceiling divided into compartments, and, with the massive panellings of the pictures let into the walls, richly gilt, are some rare and priceless full-length paintings. These are Philip II. by Titian, Admiral Capella and Antonio de Dominis by Tintoretto, the Duke of Albemarle by Dobson, Henry VIII. by Holbein, Mary Queen of Scots by Zucchero ; and Charles I. by Jansen. The furniture is of the most sumptuous character, and every elegancy which the most perfect taste can desire, or the most liberal expenditure secure, adds its endless charms to the room.

The LIBRARY, which is about 90 feet long by 23 in width, and of corresponding height, has eight windows in length on its east side, between which are presses for books, surmounted by looking-glass ; the opposite side and the ends are also lined with books ; and an elegant gallery, to which access is had by a hidden spiral staircase, runs along the ends and one side. The ceiling is white and gold, and is adorned with three large and five smaller circular paintings, of the most exquisite colouring, by Louis Charon. The mahogany book-cases are divided into presses by gilt metal columns, from which stand out the brackets supporting the gallery. The chimney-piece, of Carrara marble, has beautifully sculptured columns with wreaths of foliage, and is surmounted by candelabra, massive vases, and a magnificent mirror. In the glass-cases and table presses, as well as on the shelves, is preserved, as may well be supposed, one of the richest and rarest collections of books and MSS. which any house can boast; amongst them are the famous Anglo-Saxon MSS of Caedmon and many other MSS.; the prayer-book given by Henry VII. to his daughter, Margaret, Queen of Scotland, with the touching autograph, "Remember yr kynde and louyng fader in yor good prayers. Henry R." and other equally curious writings; the compotus of Bolton Abbey, 1287 to 1385; the "Liber Veritatis," of Claude Lorraine; a splendid collection of Wynken de Wordes and Caxtons; etc. etc.

Passing out from this splendid apartment is the ANTE-LIBRARY, formed of two exquisitely beautiful little rooms, filled with books of the greatest value and interest. From the window of the second of these rooms, which has a domed ceiling, the Italian garden, with its forest of tall pillars surmounted by busts, is seen to great advantage, as are also the wooded heights crowned with the Hunting Tower. The ceiling of the first or larger room is richly gilt, and adorned with paintings by Hayter and Charles Landseer. The smaller apartment is a perfect architectural gem, of apsidal form, the dome supported by a series of columns and pilasters with Corinthian capitals. In this room are some remarkably fine vases on pedestals.

The DINING-ROOM has full-length portraits of the first Earl and Countess of Devonshire, supposed to have been painted by Vandyke; the second Duke of Devonshire by Sir Godfrey Kneller; one of the Countesses of Devonshire and her family; Sir Arthur Godwin; Lady Wharton; and Lady Rich. The doors are surmounted with pediments, supported by Ionic columns of Siberian jasper and

African marble. Round the room is a deep' plinth of
polished marble from Hopton. The two chimney-pieces
are masses of sculpture, ornamented with life-sized figures
by the younger Westmacott and Sievier. Six extremely
beautiful slabs are fitted to the sides of the room as side-
tables. Those at the north end are of Siberian jasper, and
were presented by the Emperor Nicholas ; at the east side
are two of hornblende and calcareous spar mixed ; and on
the south are the remaining two, composed of " porphy-
ritic sienite." This apartment is 58 feet long by 30 wide
and 25 high.

The SCULPTURE GALLERY is entered through a little
ante-room, in which are two heathen deities, " from the
hill of Abor." They are cut in fine statuary marble.
The connoisseur in sculpture will find a rich treat in this
collection, while even the most heedless observer cannot
fail to be struck with the results of genius, which can give
form, attitude, grace, and all but life, to cold marble. It
is impossible to give a list of the various figures and
groups, as changes in the disposition of the statuary and
additions frequently take place ; but the following may be
mentioned as worthy of notice, and will prepare the visitor
for what he is to see.

Canova's beautiful figure of the Sleeping Endymion, with his watchful dog
　　at his feet.
A wounded Achilles, by Albicini.
Discobulus, from the chisel of Kessells. An inlaid slab in the pedestal is
　　composed of a variety of Swedish marbles. A mosaic from Hercula-
　　neum occupies another panel.
Tanerani's celebrated group of Venus, with her son Cupid, extracting a
　　thorn from her foot. Inlaid in the pedestal is a slab of Oriental
　　marble.
Trentanove's Resting Cupid.
Canova's colossal bust of Napoleon the First. The pedestal is of porphyry.
Campbell's recumbent figure of the Princess Borghese.
Gott's Venus.
Small columns, five in number, one of Giallo antico, two of Oriental por-
　　phyry ; and two of the beautiful Verd antique. They bear vases and
　　balls.

Canova's celebrated figure "the Mother of Napoleon." "It is an exquisitely finished statue, and powerfully suggests a recollection of some of the most beautiful works of art; the natural ease and grace of the figure, and the taste and disposition of the drapery, are inimitably fine; the hands and arms, particularly the left, might form studies for future sculptors."

Gott's greyhound and pups.

Rennie's colossal bust of Achilles.

Bartolini's Bacchante.

Pozzi's group of Latona supplicating Jupiter to turn the inhabitants of Caria into frogs. She is supported by her children Apollo and Diana.

Serpentine vase on pedestal of jasper, both Siberian, presented by the late Emperor of Russia.

Two lions in white marble, by Rinaldi and Benaglia. The weight of the pair exceeds eight tons. They are from Canova's monument to Clement XIV. in St. Peter's, Rome.

Two tables, the larger one of plasma verde, with scrolls and wreaths of Derbyshire marble; and the smaller Labrador feldspar and Elfdalen porphyry. They are both supported on gilt stands. On the latter stands that wonderful Derbyshire production, the Blue John Vase.

Double bust of Isis and Serapis, in Ashford black marble, which was sent to Rome, where the sculpture was executed. Copied from a bust in the museum of the Capitol.

Schadow's Spinning Girl, or Venus Filatrice, one of the gems of the collection, stands on a portion of a column from Trajan's forum.

Colossal bust of Lucius Verus, on a granite pedestal.

Wyatt's Musidora.

Thorwaldsen's Venus Genetrix.

Colossal bust of Alexander the Great, antique.

Two dogs, in bronze—from a marble in the Vatican. Allegorical figures of Famine and the river Arno, from Dante's Inferno; and a bronze alto-relievo of Count Ugolini and his sons, from Michael Angelo, on the pedestal.

Some magnificent sculptures, by Schwanthaler and others, formerly in the Duke's splendid collection at Chiswick.

Westmacott's Cymbal-player.

Two prophyry tables, bearing models in black marble, from Ashford, of the obelisk of Constantine, and that of the Vatican.

Rinaldi's busts of Ceres and a Bacchante.

Canova's bust of Laura, the mistress of Petrarch. It "has a touching expression of countenance, where loveliness, purity, tenderness, and affection, are divinely blended together. This little work (for so it may be termed in reference to the space it occupies) gave me a more exalted idea of the genius and talent of Canova than any of his more elaborate productions had previously done."

Bust of Pope Pius IX.

Canova's Hebe; if not superior in grace and beauty, at least equal to his Laura.

Pinelli's Cupid, with a butterfly in his hands.

Tadolini's Ganymede and Eagle.

Gibson's colossal group, Mars and Cupid. This sculptor was a pupil of Canova's.

Thorwaldsen's bust of the Cardinal Gonsalvi.

Four colossal busts in niches. The Duke of Devonshire by Campbell; Ariadne by Gott; Canova by Rinaldi; and an antique.

Bust of a Vestal after Canova.

Etc.        etc.        etc.

The huge Mecklenburg vase, by Canteen, occupies the

centre of the apartment. It is composed of one block of granite, and measures twenty feet in circumference.

Many other pieces of sculpture will be noticed in passing through the house.

The walls of the Sculpture Gallery are of smooth gritstone, and form an admirable background for statuary. The light is admitted at the top. The doorways are lined with Derbyshire marble, and the entablature is supported by columns of Egyptian green marble and yellow jasper.

The ORANGERY, which partakes of the double character of gallery and conservatory, is a noble apartment 108 feet in length, 27 in width, and 21 in height. Here is a fine collection of orange trees, which are at all seasons to be seen with either the fair white blossom or the juicy fruit. Many of the plants were brought from the collection of the Empress Josephine, at Malmaison. A magnificent Rhododendron (*R. arboreum*) imported from Nepaul in 1820, has been known to bear more than 2000 blossoms at a time. There is some fine sculpture in this gallery.

At the north end a door leads into the BALL-ROOM and BATHS. The BALL-ROOM, or BANQUETING-ROOM as it is sometimes called, is a magnificent apartment, 81 feet long by 30 in width, and very lofty. The ceiling is divided into compartments, each of which contains a beautiful painting set in richly-gilt framing, and the whole of the intermediate parts painted in fresco, with medallions of crest and coronet, and monogram, of the duke. Prominent among the subjects on the ceiling are Sir James Thornhill's " Perseus and Andromeda," paintings by Louis Charon, and a view of Chatsworth, with allegorical figures in the front. Over this room is the open PAVILION, from which extensive and charming views of the surrounding country are obtained.

CHATSWORTH.

The GARDENS and GROUNDS of Chatsworth are marvels of beauty, and are indeed, in many respects, matchless both for their picturesqueness, their elegance, and the skill with which they have been laid out. Leaving the mansion from the door of the Orangery, to the left is a spacious alcove, and to the right, running in a direct line for more than a quarter of a mile in length, is a broad gravel path, at the summit of which, beneath a lofty avenue of trees, is seen a gigantic vase, bearing the simple name of " Blanche," in touching memory of the late much-loved and accomplished Lady Blanche Georgiana Howard, wife of the present Duke of Devonshire.

Opposite to the Orangery is the ITALIAN GARDEN, with its forest of pillars surmounted by busts, its grand old Egyptian figures, its Chinese beakers and vases, its sculptured figures and groups, and its raised parterres ; and near this are green-houses, conservatories, and camelia and orchid houses, with their endless store of beauties ; while here and there sculptured figures, or groups of statuary, add their charms to the place.

From above this part of the gardens a broad path to the right leads on to the Great Conservatory, passing on its way the Cascade, the Willow Tree, and other interesting spots. The GRAND CASCADE, the Willow Tree, some of the fountains, and other parts of the artificial water-works, were designed and executed in the early part of last century, by M. Grillet, and added to and repaired by the late Duke, under the direction of Sir Joseph Paxton. The water supplying the works falls from the summit of the wooded heights at the back of the grounds, and is then conveyed along a lofty arched aqueduct, from the end of which it falls with considerable force, and is then carried underground to the temple, at the head of the cascade. Here it rises to the domed roof of the temple, which becomes a sheet of water, and, rushing through the various carved channels prepared for it in the groups of figures, etc., makes its way down the cascade, formed of a long series of stone steps with flats at regular intervals, and at the bottom sinks into a subterranean channel at the spectator's feet. The temple, which is open, is of circular form in its interior, with recess and niches with stone seats, the niches with carved shell-heads and festoons of flowers. Externally, an open temple supported on six pillars surmounts the dome. In front, over the central arch, is a powerfully-carved recumbent figure of Neptune holding an urn; below him, on either side, is an immense dolphin, with head downwards; and on the sides are water-nymphs with vases. On either side the open archway is a gigantic dolphin's head, and at the base are dragons. From the whole of these figures and heads the water rushes out, and, simultaneously, two beautiful fountains rise in front of the temple.

The WILLOW TREE, one of the most striking and clever of the water-works, is a weeping-willow about twenty feet in height, entirely formed of copper and lead, and coloured in imitation of a real tree. It stands in a charming little circular dell, at the entrance to which is a vase and fountain, and on the opposite side is a leaden statue of Pan. From each leaf and stem of this remarkable tree, the water, when turned on from a small hidden cave in the rock in front, rushes out in a rapid stream, and thus forms a novel kind of " shower-bath " to any luckless visitor who may happen to be beneath it. At the same time a number of jets rise up from hidden pipes all around the dell, and these streams being directed angularly upwards towards the centre, while those from the tree fall in all directions downwards, there is no way of escape without being caught in the heavy shower. Near the Willow Tree, passing on- wards towards the Grand Conservatory, is a rocky archway of wondrous construction, and a little beyond this a "rocky portal"—an immense block of unhewn stone, turning upon an axis with such ease as to be moved with the pressure of a single finger. Passing through this, one of the next most striking objects is a perpendicular rock, of great alti- tude, down whose face a stream of water is for ever falling, and this water supplies some charming little lakes filled with aquatic plants.

The GREAT CONSERVATORY, one of the wonders of Chatsworth, besides its own attraction as the finest con- servatory in the kingdom, possesses an historical interest as being the first of its kind ever erected, and from which the idea of the Great Exhibition building of 1851, and all the later exhibition buildings, including the "Crystal Palace" at Sydenham, was taken. This splendid conserva- tory was erected by Sir Joseph, at that time Mr., Paxton, in 1839, and is, in its interior, 277 feet in length, 123 feet in width, and it is no less than 67 feet in height in its centre. Its form is that of a trefoil ; the transverse section showing a semicircle 70 feet in diameter, rising from two segments of circles springing from breastwalls. The whole building is of glass, constructed on the "ridge and furrow" principle, with iron ribs. About 70,000 square feet of glass are used on this gigantic building, and the iron sash ribs alone are calculated to extend, if laid together lengthways, no less than forty miles. At each end is a large doorway, and along the centre is a wide carriage-drive, so that several carriages can, on any special occasion, as on the Queen's visit in 1843, be within the building at the same time. Besides the central drive, there are side-aisles running the entire length, and a cross aisle in the centre of the building. A light and elegant gallery also runs round the entire interior, and is approached by a staircase hidden among the rockery. Of the collection of trees and plants preserved in this giant conservatory it is not necessary to speak, further than to say that from the smallest aquatic plants up to the most stately palm-trees, and from the banana down to the papyrus and the delicate fern, every conceivable rarity and beauty is here, flourishing in native beauty and in endless profusion. Beneath the conservatory a railway runs around the entire building, for fuel and other purposes.

Not far from the conservatory, and approached by a path between tall and stately yew hedges, is a sweetly pretty circular pool of water, with central fountain, filled with water-lilies, and surrounded first by a broad circular band of grass, then by a broad encircling gravel-path, edged on half its circumference with a closely-cut yew hedge with arched entrances, and the other half planted at regular intervals with cypress trees. This, however, is but one of many charming spots which characterise the grounds of Chatsworth. Near here, too, is a sylvan slope, headed by a gigantic bust of the late Duke, mounted on a pillar composed of fragments of an ancient Greek fluted column from the temple of Minerva at Sunium. They were brought to this country by Sir Augustus Clifford, in the Euryalus. The following beautiful lines by the Earl of Carlisle are on a tablet on the base:—

" These fragments stood on Sunium's airy steep,
They rear'd aloft Minerva's guardian shrine,
Beneath them roll'd the blue Ægean deep,
And the Greek pilot hail'd them as divine.

Such was e'en their look of calm repose,
As wafted round them came the sounds of fight,
When the glad shout of conquering Athens rose
O'er the long track of Persia's broken flight.

Though clasped by prostrate worshippers no more,
They yet shall breathe a thrilling lesson here ;
Though distant from their own immortal shore,
The spot they grace is still to freedom dear."

The EMPEROR FOUNTAIN is one of the great attractions of Chatsworth, and one that to see is to remember. This marvellous fountain throws up a thick jet of water no less than 267 feet in height, which, spreading out as it falls, forms a liquid sheet of spray, on which, not unfrequently, the sunlight produces an exquisite rainbow. The quantity of metal, we are told, required in the formation of the pipes, etc., for this gigantic work, amounted to nearly 220 tons. The force of the water is so great that it is said to rush out of the pipe at the rate of a hundred miles a minute. Near the " Emperor" are other fountains of great beauty, and when all are playing the effect is beyond description.

Of the truly elegant and indeed wondrous gardens and parterres on the west and south fronts of the mansion, and of the other attractions of the place, we have not space to speak ; but there are yet two or three objects on which we must say a word. These are the trees which have been planted by royalty, and which most loyally have been tended, and grown up to a wondrous size. One of these is an oak-tree, planted in 1832 by our present beloved Queen, when, as a child of thirteen, she visited Chatsworth with her mother, the Duchess of Kent. This tree bears the label, " This Oak planted by Princess Victoria, October 11th, 1832." Near it is a Spanish chestnut thus labelled :—"Spanish Chestnut, planted by the Duchess of Kent, October 17th, 1832." Then comes a sycamore, planted when the Queen and the Prince Consort, " Albert the Good," visited Chatsworth in 1843 ; it is labelled—" This Sycamore planted by Prince Albert, 1843." In another part of the garden, opposite the west front, are a " Sweet Chestnut, planted by the (late) Emperor of Russia, 1816 ;" and a " Variegated Sycamore, planted by the Archduke Michael of Russia, 1818."

The KITCHEN GARDENS OF CHATSWORTH are situated about midway between Baslow and the mansion, being half-a-mile from each. They cover an area of twelve acres. Near the entrance is the house, long the residence of the late Sir Joseph Paxton, M.P., head gardener to the Duke of Devonshire, and the architect of the Crystal Palace. In the GARDENS, which are not shown to the public, are the NEW HOLLAND HOUSE, filled with Banksias, Grevellias, Epacrises, and other leathery-leaved plants ; the AMHERSTIA HOUSE ; and the VICTORIA REGIA HOUSE, which is right opposite. This latter building was purposely erected for the reception of the magnificent plant whose name it bears. The plant was introduced to this country from South America, where it is said to have a range of thirty-five degrees of longitude. It first flowered in Britain under the care of Sir Joseph Paxton in 1849.

The first flower was presented to Her Majesty, in honour of whom the genus was named. Those who have been accustomed to see our beautiful white water-lily on lakes and ponds, will be surprised to find one of the same family with leaves from four to six and a half feet in diameter, and rose-blushed flowers fully twelve inches across. The entire length of the house is about $68\frac{1}{2}$ feet, by $48\frac{3}{4}$ in width. The foundation is native gritstone ; on this stand the iron pillars which support the roof. The tank provided for the reception of the plant is circular and 34 feet in diameter. The ORCHIDACEOUS HOUSE, PINE HOUSE, and VINERIES, are also very fine and extensive.

On the wooded heights is the HUNTING TOWER—one of the most prominent objects in the landscape. This fine old tower, on which floats a flag whenever the Duke is at Chatsworth, was erected for the accommodation of the ladies of the house and guests, so that they might enjoy the sight of the chase. It is 90 feet in height, and has a circular tower at each angle. In the Park, near the Bridge, is QUEEN MARY'S BOWER—a small, raised, and moated enclosure, formed, it is said, for the convenience of Mary Queen of Scots while a prisoner at Chatsworth.

CHATSWORTH PARK and Grounds, from the Baslow Lodge on the north to Edensor Mill Lodge on the south, and from the East Moor on the east to Holme Wood on the west, are somewhere about ten miles in circumference, and comprise an area, in round numbers, of about 1250 acres ; and it would be difficult to find anywhere, in the same space, so great a variety of scenery, ranging from the purely sylvan to the wildly romantic, and from the luxuriant wood to the rugged and barren rock.

## EDENSOR.

The village of EDENSOR, close to the park, was, with the exception of the church and one or two houses, removed some years ago to its present position from its former site in the park. It is, indeed, a perfect model village, and the beauty of its villas—for every cottage in the place *is* a villa—the charm of its scenery, and the peace and quietness which reign in and around it, make it as near an *Eden* on earth as one can expect any place to be, and to which its name most curiously and appropriately points. Edensor is entered by a very picturesque lodge from the park, and the outlet at its upper extremity is also closed by gates, so that the only thoroughfare through the place is a highway to Bakewell. Besides the agent's house, there are in Edensor a good parsonage house and a village school.

The old church of Edensor, taken down a few years ago, consisted of a nave with side aisles and a chancel, and it had a square battlemented tower at its west end. The nave and western porch were also battlemented ; the battlements being carried over the gable of the chancel-arch, in the centre of which was a niche for a Sanctus bell. The east window was of Decorated character, as were those at the east end of the south aisle, and one near the priests' door on the south side of the chancel. Interiorly the church possessed many interesting features, including some remarkable capitals, which have mostly been preserved, with the curious monuments, in the new edifice.

The present church, completed in 1870, from the pesigns of Gilbert Scott, and erected at the cost of the Duke of Devonshire, is a remarkably fine and elegant structure, with a lofty tower and broach spire at its west end. It consists of a nave with side aisles, a chancel, and a monumental chapel opening from the south side of the chancel. The font and pulpit are of marble. In the chancel are elegant *sedilia*, and the floor is laid with encaustic tiles. In the chancel is a brass plate to the memory of John Beton, one of the household and confidential servants of Mary Queen of Scots, who died at Chatsworth while his royal mistress was a captive there, in 1570. At the head of the plate are the arms of Beton (who was of the same family as Cardinal David Beton, who took so prominent a part in the affairs of Scotland in the reign of James V. and of Mary, and of James Beton, Archbishop of St. Andrews)—quarterly first and fourth a fesse between three mascles; second and third, on a chevron, an otter's head, erased; with the crest a talbot's head. At the bottom is a figure of Beton, in plate armour, lying dead upon a pallet, his hands by his side, and his head resting on a pillow. The inscription is as follows :—

Deo Opt. Max. et posteritati sacrum.
Joanni Betonio Scoto, nobilis et optimi viri Joannis Betonii ab
Anthmwthy filio, Davidis Betonii, Illustriss S R E Cardinalis,
nepoti, Jacobi Betonii Reverendiss. S Andreæ Archiepiscopi,
et Regni Scotiæ Cancellarii digniss. pronepoti ab
inuente ætate in humanioribus disciplinis, & philo-
sophia, quo facilior ad ius Romanů. (cuius ipse
Consultiss. fuit) aditus pateret, ab optimis
quibusq3. preceptorib. & liberaliter et ingenue,
educato : omnibus morum facilitate fide pru-
dentia & constantia charo unde a Sereniss
Principe Mariā Scotorů. Gallorumq3 Regina
in prægustatoris primů, mox œconomi munus
suffecto ; ejus demq3. Sereniss. Reginæ, una cum

aliis, e vinculis truculentiss. Tiranni,
apud levini lacus castrum, liberatori fortiss.
quem Carolum 9 Gallearum Regem Christianiss.
& ad Elizabetham. Sereniss. Anglorum Reginam,
fœliciter, & non sine laude susceptas : fatis
properantibus, in suæ ætatis flore, sors aspera
immani dysenterias morbo, e numero
viventiū. exemit. Jacobus Reverendiss.
Glasguensis Archiepiscopus, & Andreas
Betonii, eiusdem sereniss. Reginæ, ille apud
Regem Christianiss. Legatus, hic vero œconomus,
in perpetuam rei memoriā ex volūtate & pro
imperio Sereniss. Reginæ heræ clemētiss frs.
mœstis posuerūt.   Obiit Anno Salutis 1570.
Vixit annos 32, menses 7, & diem dīi expectat
apud Chathworth in Anglia.

EPITAPHIUM.

Immatura tibi legerunt fila sorores
Betoni, ut summum ingenium summumq3 periret
Judicium, et nobis jucundum nil foret ultra.
Domi et Foris.

In the chapel alluded to is a large and remarkably fine
monument, entirely filling up its west side, and of somewhat remarkable character.   On either side is a massive
pedestal, supporting a life-size statue, and pilasters which
rise behind them support a pediment for the sculptured
arms, crest, and supporters of the Earl of Devonshire.   In
the centre are two inscription-tablets, with long Latin inscriptions, surmounted by a figure of Fame blowing a
trumpet, and on either side of these is a semicircular arch,
supported upon black marble columns, with foliated capitals.
In one of these arched niches is sculptured the suit of
armour, with helmet, gauntlets, etc.—hung in the niche in
natural form, but without the body, of Henry Cavendish
of Tutbury, eldest son of Sir William Cavendish of Chatsworth, by his wife, who afterwards became the celebrated
Countess of Shrewsbury ; in the other, in same manner,

are sculptured the earl's empty coronet, robes of state, and sword, the body being gone, of the first Earl of Devonshire, who was the second son of the same Sir William Cavendish and the Countess of Shrewsbury. In front stands an altar-tomb, on which rest the effigies of these two brothers ; that of the eldest (Henry Cavendish) represented as a skeleton, and the other (William Cavendish, first Earl of Devonshire) wrapped in a winding-sheet, the heads being placed at opposite ends. Over these effigies is a slab of marble, supported upon eight marble pillars.

In an inclosure at the top of the churchyard is the plain tomb, here engraved, of the late Duke of Devonshire, bearing the following inscription :—

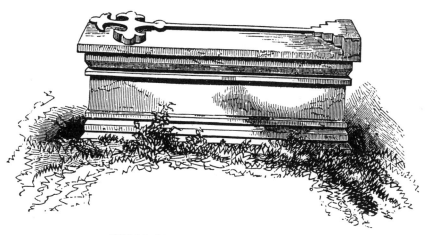

WILLIAM SPENCER CAVENDISH,
Sixth Duke of Devonshire,
Born May 21, 1790. Died 18 January, 1858.

Near this, on a coped tomb, with a plain cross standing at the head, is the following inscription to the mother of the present Duke of Devonshire :—

" In the Faith and Peace of Christ, here Resteth all that was Mortal of Louisa Cavendish, daughter of Cornelius, first Lord Lismore, widow of William Cavendish, eldest son of George Henry Augustus, first Earl of Burlington, and mother of William, seventh Duke of Devonshire. Born August 5th, 1779. Died April 17th, 1863."

" ' As in Adam all die, even so in Christ shall all be made alive.'—1 Cor. xv. 22."

And another is thus inscribed :—

" Henry George Cavendish, Born May 24, 1836. Died November 9, 1865."

In the churchyard is the heavy tomb of Sir Joseph Paxton, who was head-gardener at Chatsworth, and became the designer of the Crystal Palace, and was for some years member of parliament for the city of Coventry. The tomb bears the following inscriptions :—

" In memory of Sir Joseph Paxton, born at Milton Bryant, Bedfordshire, August iiird, MDCCCIII ; died at Rockhills, Sydenham, June viiith, MDCCCLXV, aged LXI years."

" In memory of Laura, the lamented daughter of Sir Joseph and Lady Paxton, who departed this life Jany. viiith, MDCCCLV, aged XVI years. ' Her sun is gone down while it was yet day '—Jer. xv. ix."

" In memory of William, son of Sir Joseph and Lady Paxton, who departed this life Decr. xvith, MDCCCXXXV, aged VII years. ' He shall gather the lambs with his arm, and carry them in his bosom '—Isaiah XL. XI."

In the church and churchyard are other inscriptions which will interest the visitor. Among these he will, no doubt, be glad to have the following copied for him :—

" Of stature great,
Of mind most Just,
Here lies Will Grumbold
In the Dust ;
Who died 25 May 1690."

" Here

| lieth ye body of James Brousard, who departed this life Aprill the 10th, 1762, aged 76 yrs. | Also Sarah ye wife of James Brousard, who departed this life February ye 10th, 1735, aged 77 yrs." |

" Ful forty years as Gardener to ye D. of Davenshire,
  to propigate ye earth with plants it was his ful desire ;
  but then thy bones alas brave man earth did no rest afoard,
  but now wee hope ye are at rest with Jesus christ
     our lord."

"Here lieth the Body of William Dunthin, who departed This life September the 12, 1787, aged 21 years.

  I wass like grass cut down in haste
  for fear to long should grow.  I hope
  made fit in heaven to sit, so why
  should I not go?"

## Another, to William Mather, 1818, says—

  " When he that day with th' waggon went
  he little thought his glass was spent
  But had he kept his plough in hand
  he might have longer till'd the land."

The CHATSWORTH HOTEL is close outside the park gates at Edensor. It is one of the best, most convenient, and most desirabel of houses for the visitor to stay at, and is well situated as a centre from which to make excursions to the more beautiful parts of the county. It is the only hotel at Edensor, and is admirably situated, and liberally and well conducted. At Baslow, too, which lies not far from the Baslow Lodge of the park, are one or two comfortable inns.

## CHESTERFIELD.

Hotels and Inns.—*Angel*, Wilkinson—Bed 1s. 6d., breakfast 2s.; *Scarsdale*, W. Green ; *Commercial*, G. Stevenson ; *Midland*, Station Road, etc. etc. etc. Population in 1871, 11,427. From Derby, 25 miles. From Sheffield, 12 miles.

Chesterfield, the second town in the county, is situated in the eastern end of the northern division, between two streams, the Rother and Hipper, in the rich vale of Scarsdale. It is irregularly built, with narrow streets, a spacious market-place, and an interesting church. It was a Roman station on the road from Derby to York, and its name is of Roman origin. At the time of the Domesday survey, it was only a " bailiwick belonging to Newbold, now a small hamlet, at a short distance to the north." The manor was granted by William the Conqueror to his natural son, William Peveril, and having been seized by Henry II., was afterwards granted by King John to his favourite, William de Briwere, through whom the town received a charter of incorporation, which was added to by subsequent monarchs. Until the time of Elizabeth, the government of the town was vested in an alderman and twelve brethren. By her the corporation was changed, and so continued until the passing of the Municipal Reform Act. Among the earliest mentions of the town is that of a battle fought between an army under Robert de Ferrars, Earl of Derby, and the soldiers of Henry III. in 1266. Ferrars was assisted by Baldwin Wake, Lord of Chesterfield, John D'Egville, and a few other powerful gentlemen. " They assembled a numerous force in the vicinity of Duffield, about six miles from Derby, marched to Chesterfield, and took up a military post there, with the hope of having their little army increased by the accession of some of those rebellious barons and their followers, who, in the preceding year, had been beaten and dispersed at Evesham. Their dreams of success were, however, soon over. They had scarcely established themselves in the neighbourhood of the town, when they were surprised and attacked by Henry, the eldest son of the king of Almaine. This rebel army was soon beaten, and the greater part of them were put to the sword. The Earl of Derby himself took refuge in the church, and sought a hiding-place amongst some bags of wool that had been deposited there. A woman in whom he had confided pointed out the place of his concealment to his pursuers, and he was taken prisoner. Several of the knights and barons made their escape to the forest of the Peak, where they continued for two years leading a predatory life, close hemmed around with danger, and subject to continual alarm. Robert de Ferrars, the principal in this mad scheme, was conveyed to Windsor in irons, and detained a prisoner for several years. He was at length set at liberty, but his estates were confiscated, and he was ultimately deprived of his earldom of Derby." The estates thus forfeited were granted by the king to his son Edmund Crouchback, from whom they passed to John of Gaunt, and hence became part of the duchy of Lancaster. In 1430 Thomas Beresford mustered a force at Chesterfield for the succour of the king, Henry VI.

In 1586, the dreaded plague did not spare Chesterfield ; its ravages, however, do not seem to have been so great as in Derby or Eyam. In 1642 Sir John Gell marched into Chesterfield at the head of his army, and raised an extra

force of 500 men.   In the following year Sir Thomas
Fairfax entered the town with his army

Chesterfield has several good charities, two churches,
several Dissenting chapels, a town-hall, a market-hall, free
grammar school, dispensary and hospital, theatre, union
workhouse, water-works, gas offices, savings bank, etc.
Chesterfield has a station on the main line of the Midland
Railway, which passes · on the outskirts of the town,
and lines to Sheffield, etc.    It supports two newspapers—the "Derbyshire Courier" and the "Derbyshire
Times," and gives the title of Earl of Chesterfield to one
branch of the Stanhope family.   Amongst the eminent
persons born at or resident in Chesterfield, may be named
—Ince, a poet ; Lucas, a mathematician ; the nonconfor-
mists, Wood, Oldfield, and Charles ; Billingsley, the nonconformist divine and author ; Rev. Arthur G. Jewitt,
author of "Wanderings of Memory" and many other
works ; the venerable Dr. Samuel Pegge, the well-known
antiquary and indefatigable author of numerous valuable
and important works ; Samuel Halifax, bishop of St.
Asaph ; Dr. Jonathan Stokes, author of a Botanical
Materia Medica, a Botanical Commentary, etc. ; Mrs. Blore,
the poetess ; Mrs. Stokes, a novelist ; Rev. Samuel Bromley,
the poet ; and several others of eminence.

THE PARISH CHURCH, "All-Saints"—sometimes called
"St. Mary's"—is the most striking object in Chesterfield.
The twisted or "crooked" spire, which, from whatever side
it is surveyed, seems ready to fall on the head of the
observer, has caused an endless number of speculations as
to whether it was so built, and if so, by whom, and for

what purpose ; and if not by what strange freak of wood, lead, and stone, the alteration has been brought about. The same questions have been raised to account for the leaning tower of Pisa, and with precisely the same issue. It appears nothing really wonderful that builders should even raise a steeple in such a form, ungraceful though it certainly is ; and if they desired it, there could be very little difficulty in accomplishing the task. The most generally received opinion is, that the tortuous appearance of the spire is caused by the warping of the wood. One of the supporters of this theory says—" Its crooked appearance, it is contended, is owing to its peculiar design and construction, that it was originally intended to be what it now is, and that in fact it is a display of singular skill in steeple architecture. All this is evidently incorrect ; its inclination, instead of accommodating itself, as it is reported, to do, to the situation of the spectator, is to one point only. That it was originally a straight spire there is but little doubt, but the materials of which it is constructed not being of sufficient strength and dimensions, have given way, and the structure has shrunk into something like a twisted form ; and this I presume to be the whole secret of Chesterfield church spire. No man who ever lived would voluntarily erect an object of deformity, a thing that in its form and outline was offensive to the eye, and in opposition to every principle of taste. A casual observation only is sufficient to convince any man that the spire of Chesterfield church was at one time an erect structure, and that it lost its perpendicular subsequently to its original formation." The extreme height of the spire is 230 feet.

The history of the church is involved in much obscurity ;

I

Camden, Pegge, Davies, Pilkington, and Ford, each have brought their learning to the subject, but with very little success. There was a church at Chesterfield in the 11th century, which, with its chapels, was given by William Rufus to the Dean and Chapter of Lincoln, in whom the rectorial manor has since remained. Camden states that Brampton chapel was "rebuilt and consecrated in 1253, by Brenden, Bishop of Ardfert, suffragan to Weseham, Bishop of Lichfield and Coventry, but still *continued dependant on the rectory of Chesterfield*, which belongs to the Dean of Lincoln, the vicarage not being endowed till 1268." 1232, 3, and 4, have each been stated as the date of the erection of the edifice. That it could not have been later than the period pointed at is evidenced by a receipt for six acres of land given to the church, on its dedication, by Sir Mathew de Hathersage. The receipt is in the name of Hugh of Walton, who rented the land of the Dean of Lincoln, and distinctly alludes to the gift, though it does not even hint at the date. The receipt itself is dated, "the Wednesday after the Assumption of the Blessed Virgin Mary, in the year of our Lord 1234." The present building is undoubtedly, for the most part, of the fourteenth century, with later additions. The manor passed into the hands of Edmund Woodstock, by marriage with Margaret Wake, the last of her family. So late as 1811, when Davies wrote, the arms of the Plantagenets and Wakes were represented impaled on one of the windows of the church. The glass is said to be still in preservation, and it is hoped that it may again be inserted.

"There were formerly three chantries in the church of Chesterfield; the chantry of St. Michael the archangel, founded in the year 1357 by Roger de Chesterfield, the revenues of which were valued in 1547 at £11 : 7 : 3 per annum ; that of the Holy Cross, founded by Hugh Draper, valued at £10 : 6 : 8 ; and the guild of the Alderman, Brethren, and Sisters of the Virgin Mary and the Holy Cross, endowed in 1392 by Thomas Dur and others, and valued in 1547 at £15 : 10s. per annum.

" There was formerly a chapel dedicated to St. Thomas, in Halliwell Street, the remains of which form part of a barn and stable ; another dedicated to St. Helen, which, after the Reformation, was appropriated to the use of the school ; and a third, dedicated to St. James, at Lordsmill Bridge. Of the last mentioned there are no traces."

Part of the west end of the church was erected in the reign of Henry VII. In the reign of Charles II. the vicar and curate were both expelled under the " Act of Uniformity." In 1718 the chancel was enlarged, and had new seats fitted to it. Twenty years later a gallery was erected on the north side, to correspond with one of a much older date on the south. In 1755 the tomb of Sir Gilbert Heathcote, one of the benefactors of the church, was restored by the corporation. The following copy of the receipt may be of interest to most readers :—" 1755, July 26, Work done upon Sir Gilbert Heathcote's tomb by ye Mayor and Aldermen of this town's order—52 duz. letters, at 1s. per duzn, £2 : 12 : 0d.; the Coat of Arms Cleaning, Painting, and Gilding, 11s. 8d.—£3 : 3 : 8d. Sept. ye 22, 1755, Red. the contents of this bill by mee, Wm. Fletcher." In the succeeding year the west gallery was built, and the organ, which cost £500, put up by Schnetzler of London. The north transept was almost entirely rebuilt in 1769 at a cost of £372 : 5 : 7. Additions were made to the churchyard in 1787 and 1824.

In 1820 a new peal of bells, cast by Mr. Mears, was put up in the tower. A clock, with an illuminated west face, was put up in 1836. It was made by Mr. Paine of London, and cost the sum of £352. A rate was imposed to defray the expense.

The general plan of the church is cruciform, with a tower springing from the intersection of the nave and choir with the transepts. On viewing it externally, we are struck by its motley appearance. During the alterations which have lately taken place, two recesses, one on either side of the altar, were found. That on the south presented a beautifully decorated arch of early date. The screen which separates the transept from the chancel is of oak, elaborately and curiously carved. "It is carved like the rest of the screen work except in the upper portion, along which are a series of curious figures, whose design has been found quite inexplicable, we dare say, to most persons who have examined them. Some persons have supposed that they are representations of different trades, but their position renders that explanation untenable in our opinion. We are inclined to think that they are emblems of the crucifixion; this is likely to be correct from their being placed in front of that portion of the sacred building in which the awful events of Calvary are accustomed to be commemorated. There are eight figures; and beginning from the right, we find, 1st, a man bearing a hammer and scourge: 2d, another bearing a bundle of nails and a spear; 3d, another bearing a curious device emblematic of the five wounds inflicted upon our Saviour; 4th, another figure bearing the vesture; 5th and 6th, figures bearing the cross and the crown of thorns; 7th and 8th, a lion and a bird, each bearing the end of a label, on which there was, doubtless, an explanatory legend painted ; it is, however, quite obliterated." Among the curiosities of the church is " the dun cow's rib," said, and generally believed to be, the rib of the veritable " dun cow," killed by Guy, Earl of Warwick, where, at the castle, is preserved a similar bone. It is, however, evidently the jaw-bone of a small whale. Its dimensions are, when measured along the outer curve, seven feet four inches, and in a straight line from each extremity, five feet seven inches ; its circumference is about fourteen inches. At one end is engraved, " Thomas Fletcher." It was probably deposited in the church about 1650.

Two beautiful tombs belonging to the Foljambe family are very fine, and range from the fifteenth to the beginning of the seventeenth century. One near the altar bears a well-sculptured figure of a knight in the attitude of prayer. Round the sides are canopied double niches, with figures of knights and ladies, elaborately sculptured, and highly illustrative of the costume of the period—that of the time of Edward IV. On this tomb has been placed, most absurdly, the figure of a kneeling warrior of the reign of Elizabeth or James I., the head of which having been broken off or lost, has, with equal absurdity, been replaced by a head from another effigy, thus making one of the most ridiculous mongrel monuments in the kingdom. Another is semi-vasiform, ornamented with cherubs and flowers, and bearing a recumbent figure. In the south aisle, in an arched recess, is a very early figure of an ecclesiastic, supposed to be the founder of the church. There are also many other extremely fine and interesting monuments in the church.

Until lately the chancel of the church had a flat plaster

ceiling, the pulpit was against the north gallery, and the pews and galleries were too cumbrous and inconvenient for the increasing wants of the congregation. In 1840 a movement was set on foot for the reconstruction of the interior. The old galleries were removed, and new ones of a more elegant design substituted in their stead. The ceiling was entirely changed, and from being an eyesore is now an object of great beauty. It is in the Gothic style ; the ribs are elegant and highly decorated. Escutcheons are placed on the ends of the ribs, to the number of twenty-four. As these will convey some idea of the plan of the ceiling, we give an arranged list of them, as pub-lished in the Derbyshire Courier.

### East.

| EDWARD III. HENRY III. HENRY VII. | Sovereigns in whose reign the church was built, enlarged, or restored. | WILLIAM II. EDWARD II. VICTORIA. |
|---|---|---|

| SIR H. HUNLOKE, Bart. High Sheriff in 1840. | HIS GRACE THE DUKE OF DEVONSHIRE, Lord Lieutenant. |
|---|---|
| W. EVANS, Esq., M.P. | HON. G. H. CAVENDISH, M.P. |
| GODFREY HEATHCOTE, Esq. | GODFREY FOLJAMBE, Esq. |

| BUTLER. HODGSON. SHIRLEY. | Present and two preceding Archdeacons. | Present and two preceding Archbishops of the province. | MOORE. MANNERS SUTTON. HOWLEY. |
|---|---|---|---|
| WOOD. BOSSLEY. HILL. | Present and two preceding Vicars. | Present and two preceding Bishops of the province. | RYDER. BUTLER. BOWSTEAD. |

A new east window, a testimonial of respect to the vicar, Rev. Thomas Hill, B.D., is a fine piece of workman-ship, well drawn and admirably coloured. It is in five compartments. The centre contains a representation of Ascension. The Annunciation, and Adoration of the Wise Men of the East, are lower down. Still lower, the centre compartment contains a life-size figure of the Saviour, with reduced figures of the apostles. Figures of the evangelists, also life-size, occupy compartments, two on each side of our Saviour. Along the bottom of this range is a Latin inscription in Lombardic characters. It runs as follows :—

"In Dei gloriæ observantia simul testanda gratia erga virum reverendum Thomam Hill, s.t.b., hujusce ecclesiæ vicarium, ecclesiæ Lichfieldiensis prebendarium honorarium, qui per annos, viginti et amplius pari fide ac fervore huic paræsiæ in sacris feliciter præest, pictam hanc tabulam vitream, plurimis subsidia ferentibus, honoris causa incolæ ornavere, Anno salutis, 1843."

Which may be rendered thus :—

"In observance of the glory of God, as well as in grateful testimony of the labours of the Rev. Thomas Hill, B.D., vicar of this church, honorary prebendary of the church of Lichfield, who, for upwards of twenty years, with equal faithfulness and earnestness, governed this parish in sacred matters, this window of painted glass was erected, through the subscriptions of many of the inhabitants, as a token of regard, in the year of grace 1843."

The window was designed and executed by Mr. W. Wailes of Newcastle-on-Tyne, and was to cost the sum of £600. A new font, the gift of S. Johnson, Esq., of Somersal Hall, is in the centre of the nave. The exterior is octagonal, with deep arches, and eight figures of angels. The cover is in keeping, and is suspended from the roof. The estimated expense of the whole was £60.

A tablet in the east wall records the date and object of the alterations :—

Hujusce ædis
ut amplior foret liboriorque
usus Parochianis solemniter
congregatis, communium
subselliorum novis
ordinibus instruendum eam

atque adornandam procuravere,
Privato suorum aliorumque sumptu,
Thomas Hill, s.t.b., ecclesiæ vicarius,
Johannes Clark } Æditui.
Gulielmus Booth }
A.S. MDCCCXLIII.

For the sake of those interested in such subjects, we give the dimensions of the church, copied from the same source as the table of arms on the ceiling :—

|  | Feet. | Inches. |
|---|---|---|
| Length of nave or body | 101 | 1½ |
| Breadth of do., taken from door to door at west end | 59 | 5 |
| Breadth of middle aisle | 29 | 5 |
| Length of Transept | 109 | 8 |
| Breadth of do. | 27 | 4 |
| Breadth of chancel from north to south | 47 | 7 |
| Length of do. from east to west | 39 | 9 |
| Total length of the church inside | 168 | 8 |
| Height of transept and nave | 43 | 0 |
| Length of south-west porch | 18 | 0 |
| Length of transept porch | 9 | 0 |
| Abutments at each end of church, extending | 3 | 0 |
| Total height from ground to ball of steeple | 228 | 0 |

A chime of ten bells was put up in 1820, when one of eight was removed. The latter bells had been cast at different times, from 1612 to 1774. The new chime was cast by Mr. Mears, and cost between £400 and £500.

TRINITY CHURCH, situated between the Sheffield and Newbold Roads, is a plain but substantial modern erection, with a tower at its west end. The first stone was laid in 1837, by the Duke of Devonshire. In this church is buried the celebrated George Stephenson, to whom a tablet is erected. The architect was Mr. Thomas Johnson. Adjoining the church are spacious schools.

Places of worship, belonging to the Roman Catholics are in Spencer street ; to the Unitarians, erected in 1692, in Elder Yard ; to the Independents, in Soresby Street ; to the Methodists, in Salter Gate ; to the Quakers, in Salter Gate ; to the Baptists, the Primitive Methodists, in Beetwell Street, and to the United Methodist Free Church, Elder Yard.

THE FREE GRAMMAR SCHOOL, nearly opposite Trinity Church, a picturesque and interesting looking building, was founded by Queen Elizabeth, and rebuilt in 1710, and again in 1845 at a cost of £2000. It has the presentation of two fellowships and two scholarships at Cambridge.

Among the other educational establishments in Chesterfield are—the TRINITY NATIONAL SCHOOLS, in Sorseby Street, built in 1814 ; the GIRLS' SCHOOL OF INDUSTRY, in Holywell Street, built 1819, with accommodation for 150, and conducted on the British system ; the BOYS' BRITISH SCHOOL, in Hollis Lane, erected in 1844 ; the MISSION HOUSE RAGGED SCHOOLS, in Saltergate ; the VICTORIA SCHOOL, in Vicar Lane, erected in commemoration of the visit of the Queen in December 1844 ; and Sunday schools belonging to the churches and all the principal places of worship.

The MUNICIPAL HALL, in Beetwell Street, erected by the corporation in 1849, is a large neat stone building. In it the PETTY SESSIONS for the borough are held every Monday ; and for the Chesterfield division of the county every other Saturday. The POLICE OFFICE is at the Municipal

Hall. The *County Lock-up* is in Marsden Street, and was erected in 1860, at a cost of £1300.

The MARKET COMPANY established in 1853 for the purpose of providing a suitable building for the accommodation of the merchants, factors, and farmers, who attend the market, was incorporated by Act of Parliament, with a capital of £10,000. The *Market Hall* which stands in the centre of the Market place was commenced in July 1855, and completed in about two years. It is a noble brick building, in the Roman Italian style, with stone cornice, quoins, and window dressings, 30 feet wide and 55 yards long ; including a Corn Exchange at the western end, occupying an area of 290 square feet, covered with glass ; a covered market in the centre, 25 feet high, and occupying 450 square feet ; which is surrounded on the north, south, and east sides by shops ; above which, on the south side are private offices, and on the north and east is the Public Room, which is 70 feet long, 32 feet wide, and 27 feet high. This room is lighted by five large windows and two smaller ones ; the ceiling is coved. The other accommodation provided in this splendid building are rooms set apart respectively for a Town Library, Mechanics' Institution, Magistrates, etc., each 22 feet 6 inches square and 14 feet high. The east front of the building is ornamented with a tower 100 feet high. The total cost of the building, including the requisite fittings, was upwards of £8000

The MECHANICS' INSTITUTION, New Market Hall, was established in 1841. The reading room is well supplied with London and country papers. The library contains above 2000 volumes.

The OPERATIVES' LIBRARY in Saltergate has a valuable collection of books and newsroom.

The DISPENSARY AND HOSPITAL, in Holywell Street, was established in 1800. The present building was commenced in October 1859, and is now about to be enlarged.

The CEMETERY is at Spital, and comprises 7A. 3R. 30P. of land. There are two chapels under one roof—one for the use of Churchmen, the other for Dissenters.

Chesterfield RACES are held about the end of September, on Whittington Common, about a mile from the town. The grand stand was erected in 1830.

The THEATRE, situate in a yard at the bottom of the Market-place, is a small brick building belonging to the corporation.

The *Banks* are :—Crompton, Newton, and Co. ; Robinson and Broadhurst ; Chesterfield Banking Co. ; and Sheffield Banking Co.

Chesterfield has a STATION on the main line of the Midland Railway ; and a direct line for Sheffield, to do away with inconvenience of passing through Masborough, has been opened. By means of this line, which runs through Dronfield, Sheffield is placed in direct connection with the Midland system, and a considerable saving of time is effected. Not far from Chesterfield a branch line also runs off for Trent, so as to form a more direct route for London, Nottingham, Lincoln, etc.

In the neighbourhood of Chesterfield are many interesting places. At Brampton is a most interesting church, with several curious monuments, one of which, to Matilda de Caus, has the upper part of a female figure within a quatrefoil, and others to the families of Clarke and others. The Rev. Edmund Cartwright, the inventor of the power-loom, was curate of this place. St. Thomas's Church is a large modern erection, and is a rectory. A Local Museum for the district was opened in April 1868. At WINGER-WORTH, besides the fine old church, is Wingerworth Hall, the seat of the Hunlocke family. STUBBING COURT was at one time the residence of the late Right Hon. J. Aber-crombie, Speaker of the House of Commons. At NEWBOLD is a singular little desecrated chapel, with a Norman door-way; and at WHITTINGTON is the famed " Revolution House," where the Earl of Devonshire, the Earl of Danby, and the other " conspirators," met to concoct the plan for the " Glorious Revolution" of 1688. The cottage in which they met until lately stood in its original form, and was used as a public house, under the sign of the " Cock and Pynot" (magpie) ; and in the room known as the " plotting parlour " was, until lately, preserved the old arm-chair in which the Earl of Devonshire is traditionally reported to have sat during the conference ; it is now at Hardwick Hall. The Rev. Dr. Samuel Pegge, the well-known and learned antiquary and author, was for forty-five years rector of Whittington, and is buried in the church. Sir Richard Whittington, the original of " Whittington and his Cat," was a descendant of the lords of this place.

CLAY CROSS is the centre of a large coal and iron pro-ducing district, and is, although of modern rise, a large and influential place. It has its Board of Health ; its Post Office ; its Gasworks and Waterworks ; its Mechanics' Institution and Public Hall ; and its Colliery Hospital, Church, Chapels, and other public buildings, besides many useful societies.

## CODNOR CASTLE.

CODNOR CASTLE, to which allusion has been made on page 11, may be visited by the tourist at the same time as the Codnor Park Ironworks, and is well worth a visit.

" The ruins are very considerable, and give evidence of the noble character and extent of the building as it once existed. The castle stands on an eminence of considerable altitude, overlooking the valley of the Erewash, and a broad expanse of country stretching far out into the county of Nottingham, whilst below it lie the Ironworks before described. It was formerly deeply moated, and had on its eastern side a fine avenue of majestic trees, which were cut down not many years ago, whilst on the west was a spacious court-yard, strongly fortified, some of the massive round towers of which, with the connecting curtain, are still remaining in good preservation in the garden. These towers, which were originally surmounted with battlements, are strong and massive in the extreme, and have cruciform loopholes deeply splayed in the inner side, and in one of them are the remains of a chamber with a small trefoil headed window. In other portions of the outer walls are also recessed loopholes of size sufficient for a single bow-man, and between them are the remains of means of ascent to the ramparts. The principal portion of the ruins consist of lofty outer and inner walls of the main building, containing several windows and doorways, a fine wide chimney, and the remains of a turret. One of the most interesting features of the place, however, is the venerable old dove-cote, standing at a short distance from the ruins ; the dove-cote is a circular stone building of considerable height, and of conical form, surmounted by a tiled roof, from which rises a square wood turret ; the walls are of immense thickness and solidity, and the interior, which affords accommodation for hundreds of pigeons, is honeycombed throughout its entire circumference and height with small nest-chambers. Near it is a spacious pond, concerning which there appears to be almost a superstitious feeling in the neighbourhood, as it is said that it has never, in the longest drought of dry weather, been short of water, and that although the ground has been undermined and intersected in every direction by pits and mines, they have had no effect whatever on the supply of water, which remains the same as if placed in the bottom of a deep valley, instead of as in reality on the summit of a high hill. There is an old distich which seems to have given rise to this feeling—

" When Codenour's pond runs dry
Its Lordes may say goodbye."

but if this was a true prophecy, surely the well must have ' run dry ' ages ago, for its ' lords ' have long since said ' goodbye ' to the spot.

" Codnor Castle was built in the thirteenth century, although doubtless there was even then an older erection standing. In 1211 it belonged to the family of the Greys, Henry de Grey having at that time acquired it. From him have sprung the wide-spread noble families of the Greys, from whom were descended the long line of Lords Grey of Codnor, the Lords Grey of Ruthen, Groby, Wilton, Rotherfield, of Lady Jane Grey, and of the Earls of Stamford, and the extinct families of the Dukes of Suffolk and Kent. His son Richard, who settled at Codnor, was one of the loyal Barons in the reign of Henry III., and it is related that that monarch, on his intended pilgrimage, 'called all the Londoners together, and bade the bishops excite them to take a voyage with him to the Holy Land, when but few of them would go ; this Richard, and John his brother, readily consented, and the king kissed them, and called them his brothers.' John, Lord Grey of Codnor, distinguished himself in the Scottish wars, and was in great favour with Edward III. In the 26th, Edward III., the Lord Grey of Codnor, was joined in commission with William D'Eincourt, to command all the knights in Derbyshire and Nottinghamshire in case of an invasion. In the 3d of Henry V., the king sent the Lord Grey of Codnor to bring to England Henry, the son of Hotspur, from Scotland. Henry, the last of the family, it was said, was much devoted to chemistry, and obtained a license for the transmutation of metals. Dying in the reign of Henry VIII., he left part of his lands to his two natural sons, Richard and Henry, the remainder of his estates went to his aunt Elizabeth, who was married to Sir John Zouch, younger son of William, Lord Zouch, of Harringworth. Codnor remained in the hands of the Zouches until 1622, when it was sold, and the family left the kingdom. Sir Keynshen Master, who resided here in 1712, is supposed to have been the last inhabitant of the Castle."

# CRICH.

[Principal INN : *The Bull's Head.* Population in 1871, 2705.]

CRICH is a considerable mining village in the Peak, and is approached from the Ambergate or Whatstandwell Stations; or from Matlock by way of Cromford and Lea.   Its principal attraction to the tourist is the magnificent view which is obtained from " Crich Stand," a tower built on the summit of the immense " cliff" of limestone near the village.   In the church, which is very ancient, are some interesting features ; and one or two curious monuments are quite worthy of examination.   Crich Stand is a round tower, built on the site of a former one, and is surrounded by a low wall.   Its top is gained by means of a winding staircase, and on the top is a tablet on which is engraved—

" This tower, rebuilt in 1851, is 955 feet above the mean level of the sea, according to the Ordnance Survey."

From this spot one of the finest panoramic views of the surrounding country which it is possible to obtain from anywhere, may be enjoyed ; and some idea of the breadth of landscape spread out before the eye may be gleaned from the fact, that with a telescope Lincoln Cathedral may be distinctly seen on a clear day.   Of the geological formation of the hill on which the Stand is built, the following section sketched by Dr. Mantell, the author of " Wonders of Geology," with the accompanying extract from his letter which appeared in the " Reliquary " a few years ago, will give a very tolerable idea.   Dr. Mantell says— " There is one spot, which perhaps is not equalled in England, for the lesson it teaches of some of the ancient revolutions of the globe.   It is called Crich Hill, about five miles east of Matlock. Even from a distance you see there is something extraordinary concealed in that mountain range from its mere outline. On its summit a tower has been erected, which is now (1843) in ruins. This hill consists of strata of limestone like the rocks of Dovedale and Matlock, which have been forced up into a dome, through overlying strata of quite a different character, and much less ancient. These new rocks are called 'millstone grit,' and once, of course, were horizontal and deposited on the limestone.

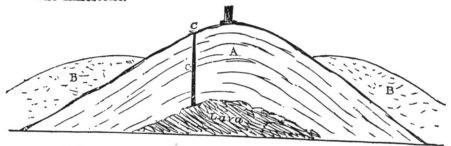

" But now the lower beds A protrude through the upper strata B in the form of a dome, while the beds are pushed on one side and shivered to pieces.

" You will ask how I know this, as there is no section through the hill ? But there are numerous quarries all round, and thus we find that the strata are lying over each other like the coats of an onion. A geologist will have no hesitation in assigning this upheaval of the rocks to volcanic action; but fortunately we are not left to supposition. The proof remains ! The very melted lava, the eruption and expansion of which occasioned the elevation of the limestone A, and forced it through the overlying strata B, occupies the heart of the mountain. A shaft C was sunk from the top of the hill in search of lead ore, and a bed of ancient lava was found in the centre of the hill."

# CROMFORD

Principal INN : *The Greyhound*, Market Place.

**From** Matlock Bath, 1¼ mile ; from Wirksworth, 1½ mile ; from Belper, 8 miles. Railway Station about ½ mile from the Market Place.

CROMFORD is mentioned in the Domesday survey as Crum-forde. It is a market town ; its market day being Saturday. It was here that Sir Richard Arkwright erected, in 1771, the first cotton mill in the county, and the largest at that time in the kingdom. The situation was well chosen for the carrying on of his undertaking ; the mills are supplied from a never-failing warm spring, which is of the highest advantage. The mills employ about 800 persons, and are still worked by the Arkwright family, whose seat is at Willersley Castle, close by. The manor, at the Conquest, belonged to the king, and after passing through the Meynells, Leches, and other families, was purchased by Peter Nightingale, Esq., in 1776, and by him sold in 1789 to Sir Richard Arkwright the founder of the cotton mills, and consequently of the town. There is at Cromford a station on the Midland Railway, and there is also a station on the High Peak line. In the lead and colour works many hands are employed. " At a perforated rock near Cromford, called Scarthin Nick, about 200 Roman coins were found some years ago."

SCARTHIN NICK is an opening between two massive limestone rocks, through which the turnpike road passes. Close to these rocks is the entrance lodge to Willersley Castle, the drive passing along between the river Derwent and the rocky boundary of the grounds, until it reaches the bridge.

CROMFORD CHURCH was begun by Sir R. Arkwright, and finished by his son. It is built of gritstone of a fine grain and quality. It was opened in 1797. By the late R. Arkwright, Esq., it was endowed with £50 per annum, besides which it has received several grants. On the south side of the communion-table is a beautiful monument to Mrs. Arkwright and her three infant children, by Chantrey. The church has recently been considerably altered and enlarged, and another chapel has also been erected in the district.

WILLERSLEY CASTLE, the seat of P. Arkwright, Esq. (*Gardens and grounds open on Mondays* from 10 A.M. till 4 P.M.) Notwithstanding the aversion with which admirers of the wild and natural view the intrusion of busy industry into secluded spots like the vale of Matlock, few men can be said to have exercised a greater moral influence in a like limited place than Sir Richard Arkwright, who founded the first cotton mill in Derbyshire. Sir Richard was a native of Preston—was the thirteenth child of a poor working man. He was put apprentice to a barber, and afterwards practised the calling for a livelihood at Wirksworth. He then became an itinerant hair dealer, and on forming the acquaintance of a clockmaker named Kay, he, conjointly with him, set about the study of machinery, and constructed the machine for which he obtained his first patent. His talent for mechanical applications was so great, and his industry so untiring, that he only required the assistance of a little capital to make his fortune. He was, however, some time before he could accomplish this end. He applied unsuccessfully to Mr. Hatherton of Liverpool, but at length the celebrated Jedediah Strutt of Derby, who was rapidly acquiring a competence by the manufacture of stockings on his newly invented " Derby Rib" machine, entered into partnership with him. From this time the success of the invention was complete, and

the fortune laid of a large and influential landed proprietary. So successful was his genius, and so accurately was his example followed by his son, that the latter, Richard Arkwright, Esq., became the richest commoner in England. Willersley Castle was built, and the grounds laid out for Sir Richard. To reach Willersley from Matlock, it is necessary to take the road to Cromford, passing Glenorchy Chapel. From the lodge, the chapel walk is gained ; or, if the visitor takes a carriage, he must enter at the further gate. The chapel walk winds considerably in its descent under the rocks, which rise at some places as much as 150 feet. Gradually this shelving rock tapers off until it becomes lost in the soft green lawn. Rock House is soon gained, an erection hid in wood, and under it is seen the Cromford Canal. The park is diversified with lime and elm trees. The Castle is seen on the left, occupying an elevated position under the "Wild Cat Tor."

STONNIS, or the "Black Rocks," or as it was originally called "Stonehouse," is a high gritstone rock, rising above Cromford Moor, between Matlock Bath and Wirksworth. To gain this point it is necessary to take the Wirksworth road, over Cromford, until the road divides. Here take the road on the left for a hundred yards, when a gate is entered, and we find ourselves at the foot of the cliff, which is easily ascended. The view from the summit is one of great beauty, and well worth the trouble of ascent.

## DALE ABBEY.

### From Derby, 6 miles.

THIS interesting ruin of what has been one of the finest monastic buildings in the county, is most picturesquely situated at an easy distance for a visit from Derby. The Abbey was founded about the year 1204, and there is a curious chronicle extant connected with it, by which it appears that it was founded in consequence of a baker of Derby having, through a vision, become a recluse, and cut for himself a hermitage in the rock here. The abbey was afterwards founded, and a grant of as much land as could be ploughed round by two deer caught from the forest was made by the king. The stained glass from the windows of this abbey, on which are depicted **a** series of representations of the events of this ploughing, etc., are preserved in MORLEY CHURCH, where are also many monuments and other interesting matters worthy of examination.

The HERMITAGE cut by the pious baker is still to be seen on the hill side, not far from the curious little chapel, and the whole place is filled with interest. It was in connection with this place that the beautiful ballad—the Legend of Dale Abbey—by William and Mary Howitt, was written.

> " The Devil one night as he chanced to sail
> In a stormy wind by the Abbey of Dale,
> Suddenly stopped and looked wild with surprise
> That a structure so fair in that valley should rise.
> When last he was there it was lonely and still ;
> And the hermitage scooped in the side of the hill,
> With the wretched old inmate his beads a-telling
> Were all could be found of life, dweller, and dwelling."

\*    \*    \*    \*

## DARLEY DALE.

From Matlock Bath, 5 miles ; from Rowsley, 2 miles ; Railway Station near the village.

DARLEY DALE is a very ancient, large, and important village in one of the most delightful districts of the Peak. The manor at the time of the Domesday Survey was parcel of the ancient demesnes of the crown. The church is a very interesting old edifice dedicated to St. Helen. In it is a fine altar tomb of a crusader, and other interesting monuments. There are also some curious inscribed monumental slabs and other remains worthy of examination. In the course of alterations made at the church a few years ago several incised slabs bearing various devices were discovered. These are now preserved in the Bateman museum, at Lomberdale. They have been described and engraved in the "Reliquary." In the churchyard is a yew tree which is always a source of attraction to Peak visitors. It is said to be the largest and oldest yew tree in the kingdom. It measures 33 feet round its stem, and although denuded of many of its branches is still in full vigour.

At Darley Dale is *Stancliffe Hall*, a seat of Sir Joseph Whitworth, Bart., the celebrated inventor of rifled cannons and maker of the "Whitworth rifle." The mansion is erected on the site of the old hall, and is one of the noblest and most commanding in the country; and his grounds, which are now being formed, will be certainly the finest, most wildly picturesque, and most romantic of any in existence. The celebrated Darley Dale stone quarries—from one very small corner of which the stone which built St. George s Hall at Liverpool was taken—are all included in his pleasure-grounds, and form natural rockeries of the most stupendous nature.

Near Darley Dale is *Stanton Woodhouse*, a delightful shooting-box of the Duke of Rutland. At Toad Hole (Two Dales) is a large flax manufactory, established long ago by the Dakeynes, who are famous as inventors of much useful machinery.

Winster (see page 273) an old market-town with interesting features; *Birchover Rocks* with their rocking stones, *Cratcliffe Rocks* with its hermitage, *Stanton Moor* with its "Nine Ladies," and *Hartle Moor* with its druidical remains, are all within approachable distance from Darley Dale or Rowsley, and may well all be visited in one day. *Stanton*, the seat of W. P. Thornhill, Esq., is also in the same neighbourhood.

# DERBY.

HOTELS.—*Royal*, Victoria Street, J. Taylor. *Midland Hotel*, W. Towle, Railway Station. *St. James's Hotel*, F. H. Plock, built by the "Derby Hotel and Improvement Company," Corn Market. *Bell*, Sadlergate, King. *County Hotel*, next the County Hall, St. Mary's Gate. *York Hotel*, near the station, etc. etc.
Population in 1871, 61,360. Inhabited Houses, 12,599.
Derby from London *via* Rugby, 131½ m., *via* Hitchen, 127 m.; from Birmingham, 42½ m.; from Bristol, 134 m.; from Manchester, 70 m.; from Liverpool, 101 m.; from York, 88 m.; from Edinburgh, 300 m.

THE county town, is situated in the southern division of the county, on the banks of the river Derwent. It was anciently styled Northworthige, a name of undoubted Saxon origin, and at a later period Deoraby, a Danish name. That the Danish name was the source of the modern appellation appears perfectly evident. It is not unlikely that the Danish title, however, may have been derived from the Celtic "*Dwr*," water, and the Anglo-Saxon termination "bye," signifying a habitation; the name Deoraby, since transformed into the more civilized title Derby, would thus be descriptive of a habitation, or of habitations, near a river or piece of water. The proximity of the Derwent fully justifies the application. Another conjecture is, that it may have been originally written Derwentby, and that in course of time the middle syllable was dropped. It is conjectured that the Britons had a station here, and the fact of the British Road, the Rykneld Street, running through the town would strengthen the probability of such being the case. Many interesting Celtic remains have from time to time been found on the line of this road in various parts of the town and in the neighbourhood. The Roman settlement was at Little Chester, on the outskirts of the present town, but Roman coins and other remains have frequently been dug up in various parts of Derby.

The earliest authentic notice of the town is in Bede, who flourished about the middle of the seventh century. He styles it " Villa Regalis." It was captured by the Danes about 918 ; they were afterwards surprised and totally defeated by Ethelfleda, daughter of King Alfred, who boldly attacked the castle and took it by storm. They returned, however, and were ultimately turned out by Edmund I. The battlefield of Hastings was the last resting-place of many of the inhabitants. In the reign of Edward the Confessor Derby was a royal borough, containing a large number of burgesses. The Conqueror, when he made away with the property of the disaffected English, granted Derby and a great part of the county to his natural son William Peveril. At this time the town was fortified, and had a strong castle, the last vestiges of which disappeared about 250 years ago. Henry I. granted the town to Ralph, Earl of Chester, and in 1204 John granted them many privileges, and confirmed their mercatorial guild. In 1665, when the plague raged with such fury in the metropolis, it was so severe in Derby that the country people refused to bring their commodities to market, and the poor sufferers were threatened with famine. To avert this additional calamity, the inhabitants erected a stone a little to the west of the town, and hither the market people came with their goods, which were exposed to the purchaser, who was not permitted, however, to touch. Having purchased the goods, 'the money was deposited in the hollow stone, containing vinegar, from whence it was not removed until the purchaser had got out of the way. This stone, called the Headless Cross, has been removed from its original situation, and placed in the Arboretum, where it is now preserved.

An interesting historical event connected with Derby, was the visit of the gallant but unfortunate Charles Edward, in December 1745. He had determinedly marched so far as the very centre of England, almost without opposition, when that party spirit which always creeps into hastily organized unions, completely overthrew the scheme, and he retreated with his devoted army to Scotland, to be finally defeated at Culloden. His army arrived in Derby on the 4th of December in two divisions. The Prince entered on foot, and took up his residence at a house in Full Street, belonging to the Earl of Exeter, and which retained the name of *Pretender's House* until 1854, when it was taken down. His artillery was planted on Nuns Green. A council of war was held both on the day of arrival, and on the succeeding one, at which it was determined to retreat to Scotland, and the Prince left Derby on horseback, "for his spirit was heavy, he could not walk, and hardly stand, as was always the case with him when he was cruelly used." Two parliamentary representatives have been returned since 1294. Derby has given title to an Earl from a very early date, having been granted in 1138 to Robert de Ferrars, then Earl Ferrars. Robert de Ferrars, his descendant, was dispossessed of the title and estates by Henry III., and the title having thus merged into the crown, was given and held by the Plantagenets, the first being Edmund Crouchback, and so on in succession to John of Gaunt, when the title again merged into the crown in the person of Henry IV. By Henry VII.

the title of Earl of Derby was given to Sir Thomas Stanley, in which family it still remains.

The borough is divided for municipal purposes into six wards, viz.—Bridge Ward, Becket Ward, Castle Ward, Derwent Ward, Friar Gate Ward, and King's Mead Ward. Derby is the chief place of election, and one of the polling places, for the southern division of the county ; the Assizes for the county are also held there, as are the Quarter Sessions. There are also Borough Sessions, as well as a Court of Record, held quarterly, and a Petty Sessions daily. The corporation consists of a mayor, twelve aldermen, and thirty-six councillors. Considerable improvements have been recently carried on in Derby. The east side of Irongate and the whole of St. James's Lane have been taken down for the purpose of widening these thoroughfares, and handsome frontages have been erected ; and the entire block of buildings, including the old " Piazzas," the shambles and the shops on the east side of Rotten Row, have been swept away, and the space thrown into the Market-Place.

The MARKET-PLACE, which is in the centre of the town, is a spacious area of square form, surrounded by shops and public buildings. The market-day is Friday, and is well attended. There is also a busy Saturday evening market. At Full Street, the corner of the Market-Place, are the Assembly Rooms, and on the south side is the Town-Hall.

The MARKET-HALL, recently erected on the site of what had before been called the New Market, at the back of the Town-Hall, was opened on the 29th of May 1866, and is allowed to be second to none in this country as regards internal arrangement and appearance ; though St. John's at Liverpool and the Birkenhead Markets are larger in area.

The Market-Hall is oblong in form, 220 feet long by 112 feet in width. The Fish-Market is 60 feet in length by 38 feet in width. The Hall will hold 6000 people (standing) It is entered from the Town-Hall end by two large doorways, built in massive rusticated stonework (with windows over each) with a bold projecting stone cornice, and surmounted by a handsome parapet and balustrade, the centre window between the doors having a sunken stone panel, with the words "Market Hall, 1864," wrought in stone. The Exchange Street entrance is built entirely in rubbed rusticated stonework, having a large door and iron traceried window in the centre, with a smaller door at each side, and windows over them, with a bold cornice and pediment : the Borough Arms and Scroll are carved on the tympanum. The other entrances are built in rubbed stonework of a massive but plainer character. The roof is formed of wrought-iron semi-ribs, springing from cast-iron columns, the clear span being 106 feet ; there are 22 columns 21 feet high, placed 12 feet from the side walls, connected and tied to the walls with ornamental cast-iron spandrills. The roof is covered with glass, galvanised iron, and slates. At each angle of the large hall is an ornamental tower 12 feet square, with stone pilasters, cornice, and windows, which give a finish to the large roof. Ample ventilation is provided in the roofs. Shops are constructed round the sides of the building, each 12 feet square, and stalls are arranged in the body of the hall. In the centre is a highly ornamental fountain. The hall is cleverly decorated by Mr. Cantrell, from the designs of Owen Jones.

THE NEW CATTLE MARKET, recently formed, is built on the "Holmes" by the Morledge. The market, which is built on the same general plan as the famous one at Pentonville, is extremely commodious, and is admitted on all hands to be one of the best arranged in the provinces. It is approached from the town by a bridge over the canal from the Morledge, and from the other side by a fine bridge over the river Derwent, and by new roadways which have been constructed. A siding for cattle has been made close to the market by the Midland Railway Company, and every possible convenience for farmers, dealers, and the public, has been provided. A convenient house for the superintendent, Mr. Austin, has been erected at the entrance. The market day is Tuesday. The CATTLE FAIRS are very numerous, and there are two extensive pleasure fairs—the Friday in Easter week and the Friday in Whitsun week. The CHEESE FAIRS are amongst the most extensive in the kingdom, and are extremely well attended. The DERBYSHIRE AGRICULTURAL SOCIETY, one of the most flourishing in the kingdom, holds its annual "shows" in the New Cattle Market.

ALL SAINTS' CHURCH is, as Hutton the historian of Derby remarks, "the pride of the place." "The Tower is extremely chaste and well proportioned, possessing a peculiar beauty of outline and detail. It is of the late perpendicular style of architecture, and consists of three storeys, the *lower* one containing on its western face the west door, with an elegant canopied and groined niche on either side, surmounted by a line of beautifully formed quatrefoil panels with shields, from which rises a majestic four-light window with an enriched label. The buttresses of this storey are enriched with canopied niches, and the western door is deeply recessed, the arches springing from semi-detached shafts. The *second* storey begins with a line of quatrefoiled panelling, alternating in octagonal and hexa gonal compartments, surmounted by battlements ; this storey consists on each face of a deeply recessed and elegant window of crocketed tracery, the lower portion of which only is pierced for light ; up the sides of the window the face of the tower is panelled in three stages with cinquefoil cusps and quatrefoils, and the spandrels at the head are likewise decorated with quatrefoils. The *third* or belfry storey commences with a course of quatrefoiled panelling in circular compartments, with a battlemented cornice ; this storey contains on each side a large four-light window of elegant proportions, with a transom ; the face of the tower being panelled on either side in two stages with return cusps and intervening quatrefoils, the spandrels having shields in the cusps ; the buttresses at this stage are again decorated with canopied niches and crocketed pinnacles. The tower is surmounted by a rich battlement, elaborately panelled in pierced tracery bearing shields, and by four lofty crocketed pinnacles and four smaller inter-mediate ones, corresponding with the terminations of the buttresses, with ogee caps and rich finials.

The lower portion of the tower has recently been re-paired, but the details have been strictly preserved through-out. It is 174 feet in height, exclusive of the pinnacles, being 21 feet higher than the celebrated tower of St. Mary Magdalene, at Taunton ; 22 feet higher than Doncaster ; 42 feet higher than that at Wrexham, and 52 feet higher than the tower of Magdalene College, Oxford ; whilst it also exceeds very considerably in height the towers of Wells, Peterborough, Winchester, Exeter, Carlisle, Chester, and Bristol cathedrals.

"On one of the string courses of the tower are the words, 'Young men and maydens,' from which popular tradition infers that the tower up to that point was built by the joint subscriptions of the maids and bachelors of the town, and that when any young woman born in the town was married, the bachelors always rang the bells in All Saints' Tower. It is however most probable that the portion of inscription now remaining is the commencement of the appropriate verse, 'Young men and maidens, old men and children, praise ye the Lord.' The tower contains a peal of ten fine-toned bells, and a set of chimes which play at various hours of the day.

"Of the ancient body of the church no portion appears now to remain, the present building having been erected in 1725, from the designs of Gibbs, the architect of the Radcliffe Library at Oxford, etc. Nothing could be more out of character with the magnificent tower, than is the general body of the church, and few towns can boast so perfect a specimen of the bad taste of the last century as a first glance at All Saints reveals. The general design of the body of the church consists of a series of plain semi-circular headed windows, with alternating pilasters, above which is a plain entablature and cornice, surmounted by a balustrade ; the whole is remarkably plain and unostentatious, and as an example of that particular style of classic architecture is well designed and executed ; but when its long unbroken surface, of an equal flatness throughout, is compared with the noble tower whose buttresses break the long monotony of lines, and whose admirable details and arches tend to carry the thoughts gradually upwards— whose elegant windows, niches, canopies, and pinnacles, each, however beautiful in itself, still becoming more so when considered as a portion of the grand whole, and each doing its part nobly in the great aim of church architecture, that of attraction to the sacred edifice and pleasure in its contemplation—it sinks into more than insignificance; and the tower standing far above it in its magnificence, looks down in silent and majestic contempt on the mean and paltry pile to which it is attached. The present body, built of freestone from the neighbourhood, was opened for public worship on the 25th of November 1725, by the Rev. Dr. Hutchinson the then incumbent, through whose personal exertions the funds for the purpose had been raised, and to whom therefore the public are indebted for this vile admixture of such incongruous styles.

" At the west end is a spacious wainscoted organ gallery, with a powerful and finely toned organ, and beneath it is the entrance from the west door. The chancel, vestry, and Cavendish chapel, are divided from the nave and side aisles by an iron screen of rich open-work design, by Bakewell. In the chancel a fine altar-piece, painted and presented by Rawlinson of Matlock Bath, representing the Resurrection, has just been removed, consequent on the alterations considered necessary for the putting up of the memorial windows to the late Prince Consort. This artist died in 1848, aged 80, and is buried in the church. Beneath the painting are a series of pilasters supporting an entablature, with the intervening spaces filled with folds of crimson drapery. The communion-table, altar-piece, and a portion of the pavement, are formed of Derbyshire marble. Adjoining the vestry is the Court of the diocese, appropriated for visitations of the Archdeacon, etc. In front of the seat used by the bishop, when a court is held, is preserved a magnificent piece of oak carving from the old church, consisting of a series of thirteen figures beneath rich canopies ; near this, and between the parish chests and the screen, is a fine incised slab of alabaster, bearing the figure of a priest holding a chalice in his left hand, and having his right hand uplifted.

"In the north aisle of the chancel is a beautiful monument to the memory of Thomas and Margaret Chambers of London, by Roubilliac ; to Mary Elizabeth Chichester, wife of the Rev. J. H. Chichester, 1830, by Westmacott to Richard Bateman, Esq., 1721, by Chantrey ; and several others. The south aisle of the chancel is the Cavendish Chapel, one of the chief points of interest in the church ; in it are several splendid monuments of the Cavendish family who are buried in the vault beneath. Against the south wall is the tomb of the celebrated Countess of Shrewsbury, of whom Lodge says, ' she was a woman of a masculine understanding and conduct, proud, furious, selfish, and unfeeling. She was a builder, a buyer and seller of estates, a money lender, a farmer, a merchant of lead, coals, and timber. When disengaged from these employments, she intrigued alternately with Elizabeth and Mary, always to the prejudice and terror of her husband. She lived to a great old age, continually flattered but seldom deceived, and died immensely rich, and without a friend.' On her tomb the Countess is represented in a recumbent attitude, and she is said to have superintended its erection some time before her death.

"Nearly in the centre of the chapel stands the monument of William, the second Earl of Devonshire, who died in 1628, and Christian his Countess, daughter of Lord Bruce, of Kinloss. The monument consists of the figures of the Earl and Countess in white marble, standing upright beneath a massive canopy, twelve feet in height, and supported upon pillars at the angles. The figures which are life size are finely executed, and the whole design is extremely bold and striking. The angles of the canopy on the outside bear the busts of their four children, William, the third Earl; Charles, Lieutenant-General of Horse in the civil wars; Henry; and Anne, wife of Lord Rich. The Countess, who was much celebrated by the literati of the period, and whose brilliant talents met with universal applause, was buried with great pomp on the 18th of February 1674-5, and at the same time the bones of her son, the brave Colonel Charles Cavendish, a distinguished Royalist officer, who was killed at Gainsborough in 1673, were, by her express orders, removed from Newark, and deposited in the same vault with herself. On the south wall is the monument of Caroline, Countess of Besborough, by Ruysbach. This lady, who was the daughter of William, the third Duke of Devonshire, died in 1760, and near her monument is that of her husband, William, Earl of Besborough, who died in 1763; on his monument is a fine bust of the Earl, by Nollekins. Amongst the other members of the noble family of Cavendish buried in the vault, is the celebrated Henry Cavendish, grandson to the third Duke of Devonshire, who was one of the most eminent chemists and natural philosophers of the age, and in the same vault also are the remains of the brave Earl of Northampton, who was killed in March 1643 at the battle of Hopton-heath, near Stafford, but who was not buried until the June following.

"In the south aisle are memorials to Thomas Rivett, 1763; Henry Hadley, 1830; Major Jordan, who was buried with military honours in 1797 ; the Osborne family ; Daniel Parker Coke, M.P., 1825 ; Captain Gilham, 1810 ; Rev. S. Willes ; the Rev. Michael Hutchinson, D.D., commending his exertions in providing subscriptions, amounting to £3249, towards the rebuilding of the body of the church ; and several others. The account of this worthy given by Hutton is sufficiently amusing to be quoted. 'The people,' he writes, 'to whom he applied were not able to keep their money ; it passed from their pockets to his own as if by magic. Wherever he could recollect a person likely to contribute to this desirable work, he made no scruple to visit him at his own expense. If a stranger passed through Derby, the Doctor's bow and his rhetoric were employed in the service of the church. His anxiety was urgent, and his power so prevailing, that he seldom failed of success. *When the waites fiddled at his door for a Christmas box, instead of sending them away with a solitary shilling, he invited them in, treated them with a tankard of ale, and persuaded them out of a guinea.* I have seen his list of subscribers, which are 589 ; and the sum £3249 : 11 : 6. But it appears he could procure a man's name by his eloquence easier than his money, for fifty-two of his subscribers never paid their sums, amounting to £137 : 16 : 6.' In the north aisle of the church are monuments and memorials to Richard Crowshaw, a native of Derby, master of the Goldsmiths' Company in London, who died in 1631, and of whom it is said, that 'In the great plague (1625), neglecting his safety, he abode in the city, to provide for the relief of the sick poor ; and left by will for charitable uses the sum of £4000, to which his executors added £900 ;' and several others ; there is also an Elizabethan monument to Sir William and Lady

Wheeler, who, flying from London to avoid the plague, died of that dreadful pestilence at Derby in 1666 ; to the Bateman family ; to William Allestrey, recorder of Derby in 1655, and several members of his family ; to the Richardsons ; to the Cox family ; to Sarah Balidon, daughter of Sir Thomas Gresley, etc., etc." The organ has been recently enlarged, and a splendid memorial window of three lights, by Clayton and Bell of London, in memory of the late Prince Consort, has been placed at the east end of the church.

St. Peter's Church, St. Peter's Street, is picturesquely situated, and nearly covered with ivy. The church is principally of the perpendicular style, but has some windows of a late decorated character, and other earlier portions. The tower is battlemented, and has lofty pinnacles at the angles, and double windows on each side of the upper stage. The church consists of a nave with clerestory, north and south aisles, and chancel, in which some modern windows have been lately introduced. In the porch are some incised slabs. The south doorway has semi-detached shafts with good capitals and mouldings. The interior of the church has recently been restored, the hideous galleries removed, and the unsightly pews replaced by open stalls. Some Norman capitals and other interesting details are to be seen in the interior, which is one of the most striking and well arranged in the town. The east window is in the perpendicular style, of five transomed lights with cinquefoil cusps ; it is filled, as are also some other windows, with well executed modern stained glass.

St. Michael's Church, Queen Street. A portion

of the chancel of the old and venerable church of St.
Michael having fallen in 1856, it was deemed advisable
to take the entire edifice down and erect a new one on its
site. This was done in 1857 at a cost of £2420. The
new building is very picturesque, and has no enclosed
ground, being open to the street on all its sides. It will
accommodate 450 persons, and is conveniently fitted with
open stalls. A drinking fountain is attached to the tower.

St. Werburgh's Church, at the bottom of Friar
Gate, is modern, with some few earlier portions retained.
The churchyard is bounded on its north side by the Markeaton brook, and owing to the floods which have occurred
from time to time, it has sustained very considerable
damage. In 1601 the tower and a considerable portion
of the church fell down, and on rebuilding, the tower, for
the sake of safety, was removed to its present position at
the south-east angle. In 1698, some of the pillars being
undermined, the body fell. The tower is Gothic, and the
remainder of the edifice in the Grecian style of architecture. The tower, which has recently been considerably
repaired, is battlemented, and has four large pinnacles and
four intermediate ones; there is a good doorway, with
semi-detached shafts on the south side, and each face of
the tower has a double belfry window. In the chancel is
a beautiful monument, by Chantrey, to the memory of
Sarah Elizabeth, daughter of Samuel Crompton, and wife
of Col. Winyate, and her infant child; there are also other
memorials to Gervase Sleigh, 1626; and to various members of the Milward, Gisborne, Hall, and Unwin families.

St. Alkmund's Church, Queen Street and Bridge Gate,

is an elegant and well-designed modern edifice, in the decorated style of architecture. It was built in 1846, from the design of Mr. H. I. Stevens of Derby, at a cost of about £9000, on the site of the picturesque old church of St. Alkmund, which was removed for that purpose. The church consists of a nave and side aisles, with a spacious chancel; a south porch with a parvise; and a lofty tower and spire at the west end. The nave is divided from the side aisles by a series of clustered columns with foliated capitals. The roof is of timber with carved bosses. In the chancel is a beautifully executed altar screen, with illuminated texts, etc.; and a carved eagle lectern. At the west end of the south aisle, against the wall, is a fine Elizabethan tomb of alabaster, of John Bullock of Darely Abbey. The sides of the tomb are highly decorated with sculptured panels and mouldings, and on the top is the effigy of Bullock, in gown and ruff, and with a close fitting cap on his head.

"The old church of St. Alkmund, which was taken down in 1845," says Mr. L. Jewitt, "was of very early foundation, and was interesting from the fact of the saint to whose honour it was dedicated having been buried within its walls. St. Alkmund was the son of Alured, the deposed king of Northumbria, and was much venerated for his meekness and humble piety. He was martyred by order of Eardulph, the usurper of his father's kingdom, on the 19th of March, A.D. 800, on which day he was commemorated in the old English calendar. The saint was buried at Lilleshall in Shropshire, but many miracles having been performed at his shrine, his body was translated to Derby, and buried in the church dedicated to his honour, with much pomp and solemnity. Here his shrine was much visited, and such was the celebrity which in a short time it obtained for the many miracles wrought by the saint, that hosts of pilgrims were constantly arriving to pay their devotions at his shrine. In the same neighbourhood Duffield Church and Darley Abbey were dedicated to St. Alkmund, and most probably possessed relics of him which claimed a portion of the devotion of pilgrims on their passage.

"During the removal of the old church, and the excavations preparatory to the erection of the present edifice, several interesting fragments of an earlier structure were discovered ; amongst these were portions of a church-yard cross, and two capitals in sandstone, of conical form, and which, from their sculptured ornamentation, consisting of figures, crosses, and interlaced foliage, have been referred to the Anglo-Saxon, or more probably the early Norman period."

St. John's District Church, Bridge Street, is in the parish of St. Werburgh. It was erected in 1826-7, from the designs of Mr. F. Goodwin of London ; it is a mixed building, principally in the Tudor style of Gothic architecture, but of a very debased character. The interior is extremely neat and convenient, and has a spacious gallery round three sides. Adjoining the churchyard are St. John's Sunday and Infant Schools.

Trinity District Church, London Road, is in the parish of St. Peter. It was built some years ago on speculation, at a cost of about £3500. It was then called St. George's Church, but the builder having subsequently become bankrupt, the church was sold for the benefit of his creditors, and after being closed for some length of time, was consecrated by its present name in honour of the Holy Trinity. It was bought for about £2000, which was raised by subscription. The Rev. Robert Simpson, author of "Collections for a History of Derby," was formerly the incumbent of this church.

CHRIST CHURCH, on the Normanton Road, is a picturesque and elegant little structure, erected in 1838-40, on the highest point in the town, and was built as a memorial to the late Bishop Ryder. It is a district church in the parish of St. Werburgh, and affords accommodation to a large and populous district. The tower, which is at the east end, is remarkably elegant, and is surmounted by a spire of good proportions.

ST. PAUL'S, Little Chester, was erected in 1850, in memory of the late Right Rev. W. A. Shirley, D.D., bishop of Sodor and Man, and formerly archdeacon of Derby. It is cruciform in its structure, with a tower in the north-east angle, in the decorated style.

ST. ANN'S DISTRICT CHURCH, Leyland Street, on the Kedleston Road, is a modern, plain, unassuming little building, with a bell-turret. It was erected in 1852, by E. S. Chandos-Pole, Esq., and is capable of accommodating about 100 persons, all free.

ST. JAMES THE GREATER, Rose Hill, is a handsome new Church, intended to accommodate the new and rapidly increasing district on the south-west of the town.

ST. ANDREW'S CHURCH, Litchurch, recently erected, is a large and elaborate Gothic building, with tower and lofty spire, situated on a convenient plot of ground near the Railway Station, where church accommodation is much needed. Adjoining the church spacious schools and parsonage-house have been erected.

St. Luke's Church has recently been erected in Parliament Street, California, as a memorial to the lately deceased and highly beloved Bishop Lonsdale of Lichfield. The temporary church was opened in March 1868, and the present edifice in 1871.

Another new church and schools is also proposed to be erected on the Ashborne Road, to accommodate the rapidly increasing district in that locality.

Roman Catholic Church of St. Marie, Bridge Gate, designed and erected under the superintendence of Mr. A. W. Pugin, was completed in 1839. The church is in the perpendicular style of architecture, and its general proportions and decorative details are remarkably chaste and fine: it consists of a nave and side aisles, a chancel, with sacristies, and all the usual offices. Its internal decoration is of the most beautiful and costly character, and it is considered to be one of the most perfect, elegant, and complete of Pugin's erections. And a tower at the south end.

The extreme length, from the entrance-door under the tower window to the sanctuary windows, is 127 feet, and the width 45 feet; the nave 80 feet long, the chancel 27 feet by 20, and the tower 20 by 14 feet. The tower is 100 feet high to the top of the embattled parapet, and 117 feet to the top of the pinnacles, and is greatly admired for its beauty, being richly ornamented with crockets, figures, niches, etc. etc. Above the doors of the tower is a large window 28 feet high by 13 feet, with mullions, admirably arranged; and above this window, in a large and highly ornamented niche, stands the ever blessed mother of our Lord. The figure is 6 feet 4 inches high, enveloped in folds of drapery of the most graceful form, and possesses extreme beauty both in design and execution, and the infant Saviour is represented reclining in her arms, having in his hand a lily, the emblem of purity. There is a gallery at the south end, in which there is an excellent organ. The ground cost £1400, the church about £7000, the houses, schools, etc., £2000, total cost upwards of £10,400. The first stone of this beautiful structure was laid on the 28th of June 1838, by the Honourable and Rev. George Spencer. The dedication took place on Wednesday, 9th October 1839. Adjoining the church are residences of the Canon, and other priests ; the convent of the Sisters of Mercy, etc. etc. The schools are situated near, in Edward Street. The building is the most capacious and well-designed of any school in the town.

The CONVENT OF ST. VINCENT OF PAUL, which, until the year 1866, stood on the site of the Old China Works, on the Nottingham Road, just beyond St. Mary's Bridge, has been taken down, and the nuns transferred to a house adjoining the Roman Catholic Church.

The CONGREGATIONAL CHURCH, Victoria Street, is an extremely large and very elegant Gothic building, with tower and spire. It was built on the enlarged site of the old chapel belonging to that denomination.

The VICTORIA MISSION HALL, in connection with this place of worship, is on the Ashbourne Road.

The BAPTIST CHAPEL, Osmaston Road, is also a remarkably elegant and elaborately decorated Gothic building, with tower and spire. Its erection is principally due to the munificence of the late Mr. Alderman Pegg. Adjoining it is the residence, in the same style of architecture, of that gentleman, and the residence of the minister, and this district is now being built with new streets and villa residences.

The NEW WESLEYAN CHAPEL, London Road, is a Gothic building, of good character, and very capacious.

Besides these, there are places of worship belonging to the Friends, in St. Helen's Street (built in 1808); the Baptists, in Agard Street (erected 170 years ago), St. Mary's Gate (originally the private residence of William Osborne, Esq., who erected it in 1751); the Congregationalists, in Chester Place (built about 25 years ago), and London Road (erected in 1841-2); the Wesleyans, in King Street (erected in 1841), at Greenhill (built in 1816), and in Cotton Lane, Litchurch; the Wesleyan Reformers, in Becket Street (erected in 1857), and Brook Street (erected in 1802 by the Baptists); The New Connection Methodists, in London Road (built in 1819); the Primitive Methodists, in Traffic Street (built in 1843), Kedleston Street (erected in 1848, and enlarged in 1850), and Abbey Street (built in 1853); the Swedenborgians, in Babington Lane; the Unitarians, in Friargate (erected in 1647); and to most of these excellent day and Sunday schools are attached.

The TOWN HALL, in the Market Place, was erected in 1842, on the site of one destroyed by fire in the previous year. It is an elegant edifice, with a lofty and well-proportioned clock and bell tower rising from its front, and supported upon massive arches, forming an entrance to the

New Market and to the Municipal Hall, and other offices.
On either side the tower the face of the Hall is decorated
with an admirable piece of sculpture in bas-relief, by Bell;
the one being emblematical of the judicial and the other of
the municipal proceedings, for which the building is designed.

The POLICE COURT is on the ground-floor, and has recently been re-fitted with raised daïs, etc. The Police
Office is also on the ground-floor on the opposite side, and
adjoining is the Town-Clerk's Office. The residence of the
chief constable adjoins the Town Hall. The NEW LOCK-
UP, a substantial stone building, recently erected, is at the
entrance of the New Market from Corn Market. It is fitted
with separate cells, and every convenience.

The COUNTY HALL, St. Mary's Gate, was erected in 1660.
It is a spacious building of freestone, with a large court-
yard in front, across which formerly an avenue of trees led
up to the entrance. The front of the building, which
is the only part remaining of the old hall, consists of two
spacious entrances and three windows, separated by pilasters. The new hall and courts were opened for public
business 1829. In the hall is a bust of the late Francis
N. C. Mundy, Esq. of Markeaton, by Chantrey. On the
right of the court-yard are the judges' lodgings. Adjoining are the COUNTY POLICE OFFICES and the Head Quarters,
with ORDERLY ROOM, of the first Battalion Derbyshire
Volunteer Rifles.

The COUNTY GAOL, at the top of Vernon Street, Friar
Gate, an extensive and commodious erection, in the Grecian

Doric style of architecture, was built in 1826, from designs by Goodwin. The POOR LAW OFFICES are in Becket Street.

The ASSEMBLY ROOMS are situated in the market-place, at the corner of Full Street. The building is extremely commodious, with a pedimented front and wings.

The THEATRE, Bold Lane (built 1773), is a small and inconvenient erection, which has of late been converted into a room for religious meetings, called " Gospel Hall." At present dramatic and operatic entertainments are given at the Corn Exchange and the Lecture Hall, where stages are fitted up for the purpose.

The RIFLE DRILL HALL, Becket Street, erected 1869, is the largest public room in Derby, and consists of a large Hall 150 feet long, and 55 feet wide, with span roof supported by iron arch-girders ; a reading, orderly, committee, and officers mess-rooms, and quarters for two sergeants. The Hall is used for concerts, balls, etc., as well as for its own special purpose.

The ATHENÆUM, etc., Corn Market and Victoria Street, is a magnificent pile of building erected in 1839, at a cost, including the purchase of the land, of upwards of £20,000. The pile of building comprises also the Athenæum and Royal Hotel, and is one of the most striking features in the town ; possessing, with the Bank, two lines of frontage, the one 185 and the other 134 feet in extent. The entrance to the Athenæum Rooms, where public meetings, lectures, concerts, etc., are held, is by the doorway in Victoria Street, opposite to Green Lane. The Athenæum is also entered by folding-doors from the Royal Hotel, it is a large and well-proportioned room, with an elegant ceiling. Over the hall is another room of equal size, which used to be appropriated to the uses of the Museum.

The NEW POST OFFICE, a building of great extent and of much architectural beauty, is in Victoria Street, at the corner of St. James's Lane. There are also Branch Offices and pillar letter-boxes in many parts of the town.

The DERBY FREE MUSEUM and LIBRARY, 5 Wardwick, is a spacious and elegant mansion, standing in extensive grounds, and is one of the noblest institutions of its kind in the midland district. The Museum, which is very extensive, was established in 1820. It contains many objects of interest in the various departments of natural history, archæology, and general knowledge. Amongst the relics from the neighbourhood are several from the Roman station at Little Chester, which have been discovered during the course of excavations at various periods ; some of the pottery is remarkably interesting. There are also from the same locality a cast of a skeleton which was exhumed in 1824, along with some rivets and other metallic fragments ; a spear-head of thirteen inches in length ; and several small objects in bronze. Amongst the other antiquities in the museum are celts from Horsley, Breadsall Moor, etc.; some Roman lamps, bells, and other relics ; three Egyptian mummies, some fine Egyptian sepulchral slabs, and a remarkably interesting and extensive collection of casts of mediæval seals. The mineralogical, geological, and natural history departments are very extensive, and

well arranged, and contain many rare and valuable specimens. The Museum also contains the saddle of the Duke
of Wellington, and a large variety of interesting relics.
The Library, established in 1820, was a few years ago
incorporated with the museum, and occupies a fine suite
of apartments in the building. The Derby Philosophical Library, founded by the celebrated Dr. Darwin,
was also incorporated with the museum. Annual subscribers used to have a special privilege of admission to
the museum for themselves, their families, and friends,
and casual visitors were admitted on payment of a small
charge ; but some years ago an offer to present the museum
to the town was made, which was renewed in 1870, when
the town accepted it, adopting the Free Libraries Act. The
collection was handed over by the authorities to the corporation, and in October 1871 was opened as a Free Library
and Museum.

The DERBYSHIRE CLUB is held in the New Club Rooms
in the Corn Market, being the first-floor front of the new
St. James's Hotel.

The MECHANICS' INSTITUTE, 4 Wardwick, is a spacious
and substantial building, with a pedimented front. Adjoining the general building is the large LECTURE HALL,
which was erected in 1836-7, at a cost of £2000, and is
used for lectures, concerts, operas, etc. The hall is 75
feet in length, 40 feet in width, and its height is 65
feet. The walls are hung with a magnificent collection
of pictures, bequeathed to the Institution by Joseph
Strutt, Esq. A spacious gallery has recently been erected
in the Hall, and new rooms added to the general

arrangement of the building.  The secretary is **Mr. W. C.**
**Watson.**

The WORKING MEN'S ASSOCIATION, Full Street, has a
good Reading Room and Library, as has also the RAILWAY
LITERARY INSTITUTE by the Station.

The PUBLIC BATHS and WASH HOUSES, erected in 1858,
are situated in Full Street.  The building is a fine and
imposing one, and contains swimming, private, and other
kinds of baths, and is replete with every accommodation
for visitors of both sexes and of every class.

The LOCAL BOARD OF HEALTH Offices, and Borough Sur-
veyor's Offices, are in the same building.

The TEMPERANCE HALL, Curzon Street, is a large and
extremely commodious building, used for lectures, concerts, etc.

The CORN EXCHANGE, in Albert Street, is a large and
extremely commodious building, with a circular entrance
tower and dome.  It was erected in 1861-2, by a company
of shareholders, from designs by Mr. B. Wilson of Derby.
The Exchange Room is very often used for meetings,
concerts, theatrical performances, etc.  The capital of the
company is £7000, in shares of £5 each.  Secretary, Mr.
C. Eddowes.  A remarkably fine drinking fountain, erected
in honour of Mr. W. T. Cox, late High Sheriff and Mayor,
is attached to the side of the building.

The ELECTRIC TELEGRAPH OFFICE is at the Post Office,
Victoria Street.

The DERBYSHIRE GENERAL INFIRMARY, London Road, founded in 1806, is one of the most convenient establishments of the kind in existence. The building, which was erected from the designs of William Strutt, Esq., is of three storeys in height, and has projecting wings at each angle, with a spacious Doric portico on the principal front. The entrance hall is terminated by a dome of elegant design, surmounted externally by a colossal figure of Æsculapius, and has a gallery running on three of its sides, and communicating with the various rooms on the upper storey. At the north-west angle, are the fever and lock wards, and the building has recently been remodelled and considerably enlarged.

The GENERAL DISPENSARY, formerly in Bridge Gate, is now conveniently located in St. Mary's Gate. It was established in 1830.

The DERBY AND DERBYSHIRE HOME FOR PENITENT FE-MALES has recently been removed from South Street to a large and convenient building specially erected for the purpose, in Bass Street, Ashbourne Road. It was established in 1859. Secretaries : Rev. J. Chancellor and R. Sale.

The GRAMMAR SCHOOL was formerly in St. Peter's Churchyard, but has been removed to the splendid mansion, St. Helen's House, in King Street, which has been purchased for its use and for residence of the head master. The school is endowed with valuable exhibitions to the

M

University of Cambridge, and is the oldest grammar school in England. It was founded by Walter Durdant, Bishop of Lichfield, in 1160, and confirmed by the charter of Queen Mary. The school is divided into upper and lower, and is governed by trustees of the corporation of Derby and others. It is one of the best schools in the kingdom, ranking along with Rugby, Repton, and others, and many leading men have received their education within its walls. The present head master is the Rev. Walter Clarke, M.A.

The DIOCESAN INSTITUTION for TRAINING SCHOOL-MISTRESSES, Uttoxeter Road, is a handsome and large Elizabethan building, with bell-turret, erected in 1851 at a cost of £6000. The grounds contain two acres, and the institution affords accommodation for forty students, with separate dormitories.

The DIOCESAN SCHOOL, Friar Gate, is also in the same style of architecture. It was erected in 1842.

Besides these, are National, British, Lancasterian, Infant, and Ragged Schools, besides those attached to the different places of worship, and a School Board has been appointed under the provisions of the Education Act of 1871.

The principal charitable institutions are the Liversage Alms-Houses, London Road, one of the richest of local charities; Larges Hospital, Friar Gate, for widows of clergymen; Wilmot's Alms-Houses, Bridge Gate; and the Devonshire Alms-House, founded by the Countess of Shrewsbury in the time of Queen Elizabeth, in Full Street, by All Saints' Church. The Union Workhouse is on the Osmaston Road.

The OLD CEMETERY, on the New Uttoxeter Road, contains four and a half acres of land, which is tastefully laid out ; cost about £3400. It has a handsome stone Gothic chapel.

The NEW CEMETERY, on the Nottingham Road, about one mile and a half from the market-place, comprises thirty-two acres of land, twenty-four acres of which are consecrated. The grounds are tastefully laid out. It has two neat chapels and entrance-lodges.

The COUNTY COURT is held in the County Hall, St. Mary's Gate. The office is at 10 Full Street.

The PROBATE COURT is a new and elegant building in St. Mary's Gate.

The DERBY GYMNASIUM and ATHLETIC CLUB, have their Gymnasium in St. Mary's Gate.

The COUNTY LUNATIC ASYLUM, one of the finest and best arranged in the kingdom, is situated at Mickleover, four miles from Derby. It was erected at a cost of £98,396, from the designs of H. Duesbury.

TRENT COLLEGE is situated near the Trent Station, a few miles from Derby. It is a large and admirable building recently erected for the purposes of a middle class college.

The MILITIA BARRACKS, erected a few years ago on the Uttoxeter Road, are large and extremely commodious, and comprise every requisite of a military building, with rifle-range and staff residences.

The BANKS are—Messrs. Samuel Smith and Co. (Smith, Payne, and Smiths); Messrs. Crompton, Newton, and Co.; Messrs. Walter Evans and Co.; the Derby and Derbyshire Banking Company (W. Turpie, Manager); and the Derby Commercial Bank, Tenant Street (T. B. Hutton, Secretary). The SAVINGS BANK is in Friar Gate, and the PENNY BANK in Full Street. ST. PETER'S PENNY BANK is in Siddals Road. POST OFFICE SAVINGS BANK, at the Post Office.

The RAILWAY STATION is a large, commodious, and elegant building, having a frontage of 1050 feet. Over the principal entrance is a window surmounted by a shield charged with the armorial bearings of Derby, Leeds, and Sheffield. On the wings are the arms of York, Nottingham, Leicester, and Birmingham. The passenger-shed, covering nine pairs of rails, has an elegant iron roof 450 feet long by 140 wide. To the south of this shed is an arrangement of rails for luggage-trains covering about fifty acres. At this station the Midland Counties, the North Midland, and the Birmingham and Derby, and North Staffordshire lines meet. A large building for the purposes of a Railway Literary Institution and Board-Room adjoins the station, and a spacious arrival and departure space for carriages and omnibuses, covered with glass, has been added. A central platform, so as to provide accommodation for the immensely increased traffic, has recently been formed. The secretary of the Midland Railway is Mr. John Noble, and the station-master Mr. J. Maxey.

The ARBORETUM is a favourite place of amusement and recreation among the people of Derby. It contains about sixteen acres of ground, splendidly laid out, and surrounded by a belt of majestic trees on its irregular sides.

The ground, which has a gentle rise, but a tolerably even surface, has been judiciously planned with a series of undulating mounds of irregular form and of considerable elevation, thus screening persons from observation from other parts, and by disguising the boundaries, materially increasing the apparent extent of the grounds. The whole is laid down with grass, and planted with every variety of shrub and tree which will bear the climate. It was a portion of the private property of Joseph Strutt, Esq., who, with the assistance of the late celebrated horticulturist Loudon, had it laid out in walks, flower-plots, shrubberies, and arbours. The value of the property thus improved was estimated at £10,000. These magnificent grounds were prepared and presented as a free gift for ever to the town of Derby by Mr. Joseph Strutt, for the purposes of exercise and recreation. In the centre of the grounds is a fountain, rising from a large basin filled with gold and silver fish. For the benefit of those who are interested in the study of plants, a catalogue was prepared by Mr. Loudon. The plants themselves are also marked by means of stoneware labels, bearing the name, natural order, native country, year of introduction into Britain, etc. The entrances are ornamented with Gothic lodges, in which are rooms for the accommodation of *pic-nic* parties and others who bring refreshments with them. On Wednesdays and Sundays the Arboretum is thrown open, free of charge, and many hundreds avail themselves of the privilege. Sixpence is charged on the other days in the week. The money thus obtained is expended in keeping the grounds in order. The Arboretum having been made over as a gift for ever, by Mr. Strutt, to the people of Derby, it was opened amid enthusiastic rejoicings on the

**16th** of September 1840.　It is under the management of the Mayor for the time being, and a Committee.　The principal entrance is at the head of Arboretum Street, and is surmounted by a colossal statue of the munificent donor of the place, Mr. Joseph Strutt.　The entrance consists of lodge rooms, etc., with a glass pavilion forming a pleasant covered promenade.　On the new grounds which have been added to the Arboretum a spacious " Crystal Palace" has been erected, in which flower-shows, concerts, etc., are occasionally held, and which forms a delightful promenade in wet weather.　In front of the palace are two Russian cannon captured in the late war.　The anniversary of the opening is held in June as a grand annual gala in Derby, and is attended by a vast concourse of people from all parts of the kingdom.

The RACE-COURSE is on the Nottingham Road, and is an excellent plot of ground, well adapted for the purpose. The grand stand is a spacious and well arranged building, erected from the design of Mr. Duesbury, the architect. Races are held twice a year, and are well attended.

The RIFLE-RANGE of the 1st Battalion Derby Volunteer Rifles is near the race-course.　It is said by Government authority to be one of the best which has been erected. The targets move on a double line of rails laid down for the purpose.　At these butts the annual conpetitions of the Derby Rifle Association take place.

The WATER-WORKS are situated near Breadsall, and the GAS-WORKS at the back of Friar Gate.

LITCHURCH, one of the outskirts of Derby, has its own local board of health, and its own local governing body.

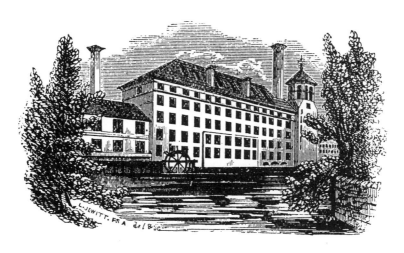

The OLD SILK-MILL, erected by John Lombe in 1718, the first silk-mill ever erected or established in England, and from which the whole of the gigantic silk-manufactures of the kingdom have sprung, is situated on the Derwent, at the bottom of Silk-Mill Lane, and is shown on the accompanying engraving. The original chest in which John Lombe brought over his models, etc., of silk machinery from Italy, is now in the possession of Mr. Llewellynn Jewitt, F.S.A. Besides this, which is now far from being the most extensive silk manufactory in the town, there are a large number of other factories in all parts of the town, and employing many thousand hands, principally females and young persons, in the different processes carried on. The principal manufactures are — silk, which is here both thrown for the purposes of manufacture into finished goods at other towns, and is also in Derby itself made into fringes, gimps, trimmings, sewing silks, ribbands, gloves, stockings, cords, etc. etc. Boot-laces, bonnet-wires, cotton, tape, iron, shot, white and red lead, procelain, spar and marble ornaments, stockings, lace, colours, etc ; chemicals, carriages, watches, clocks, and a great variety of other manufactures, are also carried on.

Six newspapers are published weekly in Derby—the *Derby Mercury,* begun in 1732 ; the *Derby Reporter,* 1823 ; the *Derby Telegraph and County Advertiser,* established in 1853 ; the *Derbyshire Advertiser,* 1846 ; the *Derbyshire Chronicle;* and the *Derby Gazette.*

Amongst the distinguished men of Derby may be named Flamstead the astronomer ; Richardson the novelist ; Joseph Strutt, the donor of the Arboretum ; the present Lord Belper ; Linacre ; Jones ; Hutton, the historian of the town ; Wright the painter ; Bourne ; the two Dethicks, Kings-at-arms ; Maw the mineralogist ; Sir Charles Fox, and others. Pilkington, the county historian ; Simpson, the author of a " History of the Town ;" Whithurst, author of a " Theory on the Formation of the Earth ;" Degge the antiquary, Fox the Quaker, and Dr. Darwin, were residents. The Earl of Macclesfield was an attorney in Derby, from which pursuit he rose to be Lord Chancellor. Flamstead was born in 1646, and being a delicate youth, had by no means a liberal education. Getting into his hand an astronomical work, he felt a strange desire to pursue the science, which he did with admirable success until the day of his death. In 1674 he was appointed Astronomer Royal, with a salary of £100. At the same time, the observatory at Greenwich was founded, and was styled Flamstead House. In 1684 Flamstead's income was increased by the living of Burstow. He died in 1719. Wright the painter, better known as " Wright of Derby," was born in 1734. He studied in London under Hudson, at the same time as did Sir Joshua Reynolds. Owing to the ill feeling which not unfrequently exists among men of talent, as well as lesser minds, Wright did not receive the title of R.A. when he was proposed ; and so deeply did he feel the slight, that, on a subsequent occasion, when Newton, secretary to the Royal Academy, visited him at Derby with the offer of a diploma from the society, he indignantly refused it. He died in 1797.

In the neighbourhood of Derby are many places of interest, and noblemen's and gentlemen's seats. *Markeaton Hall*, the seat of William Mundy, Esq., late M.P. for South Derbyshire, is one mile from Derby. Not far from it is *Mackworth Church*, and near it again *Mackworth Castle*, long the seat of the De Mackworths and of the Touchets, Lords Audley, the picturesque gateway of which is still standing. *Allestree Hall*, the seat of T. W. Evans, Esq., M.P. for South Derbyshire, is 2½ miles from Derby, the village of Allestree being passed through on the way. *Kedleston Hall*, the seat of Lord Scarsdale, of which more will be said anon, is 3 miles from Derby. *Chaddesden Hall*, the seat of Sir H. S. Wilmot, Bart, is 2 miles from the town, and adjoins the village of Chaddisden with its highly interesting church. *Radbourne Hall*, the seat of E. S. Chandos-Pole, Esq., of which family the famous Cardinal Pole was a member, is 4 miles from Derby. *Osmaston Hall*, close to the village of that name, the seat of Sir Robert Wilmot, Bart, is 1½ mile from Derby. ELVASTON CASTLE, the seat of the Earl of Harrington, with its splendid grounds, its quaint winter garden, and its thousand attractions, is 3 miles from Derby. *Spondon Hall*, the seat of T. W. Cox, Esq., M.P. for the borough of Derby, is 4 miles from Derby. And at Morley is one of the most elegant of new mansions, the seat of T. Osborne Bateman, Esq.

## DOVEDALE.

HOTELS near the Dale—the *Izaak Walton*, Prince (Ilam); the *Peveril of the Peak*, Waterfall (Thorpe); *Dog and Partridge*.
Distance from Ashbourne, 3 miles; from Matlock Bath, 17 miles; from Derby, 16 miles; from Buxton, 16 miles.

DOVEDALE, celebrated by the poets for its beauty, and a favourite resort for anglers, may be said properly to commence about Tissington. Byron says that " there are things in Derbyshire as noble as Greece or Switzerland." Cotton the poet sings of it thus :—

> " O my beloved nymph, fair Dove,
> Princess of rivers, how I love
> Upon thy flowery banks to lie,
> And view thy silver stream,
> When gilded by a summer beam ;
> And in it all thy wanton joy,
> Playing at liberty."

In the first view of Dovedale the hills are seen to stretch majestically from the river. For some time after entering the dale we continue along the margin of the Dove, whose crystal stream, now calm and placid, becomes in places turbulent and wild, and in others almost hidden by the masses of rock thrown across its channel. Its banks, and the rising slopes beyond, are luxuriantly covered with ash, hazel, birch, and drooping willow, while honeysuckles, wild roses, and brambles, tangle irregularly amongst them. Having reached that part where the dale assumes its greatest width, we take a footpath over a " broomy knowe," from the summit of which we have a totally different scene from that which we left. It was in

ascending this pathway on horseback, that the Rev. Mr.
Langton, Dean of Clogher, lost his life. He lies buried in
Ashbourne church-yard. Descending to the brink of the
Dove again, we soon near a strange mass of rifted rocks,
"closely united together below, but above indented with
deep fissures, and divided into pyramidal terminations."
This assemblage is generally termed from its appearance
DOVEDALE CHURCH. Our walk being continued for about
200 yards, we descry on the opposite side from Dovedale
Church the entrance to REYNARD'S CAVE, "one of the
most extraordinary and curious specimens of rock scenery
in any part of Derbyshire." The mouth of the cave is an
arch about 40 feet high by 20 wide. "An open court is
seen beyond, and in the distance the entrance to another
cavern appears." Great care should be taken in making
the ascent to the cave, the view from which is truly grand.
The dale soon begins to narrow, and realizes the lines of
Sir Walter Scott—

> " So high the cliffs of limestone gray,
> Hang beetling o'er the torrent's way,
> Yielding, along their rugged base,
> A flinty footpath's niggard space,
> Where he, who winds 'twixt rock and wave,
> May hear the headlong torrent rave,
> And like a steed in frantic fit,
> That flings the froth from curb and bit,
> May view her chafe her waves to spray,
> O'er every rock that bars her way,
> Till foam-globes on her eddies ride,
> Thick as the schemes of human pride
> That down life's current drive amain,
> As frail, as frothy, and as vain ! "
>
> ROKEBY, canto ii.

On the Staffordshire bank the glen is impassable, and

the path on the Derbyshire side is not over wide. The following description of this portion of the glen by an enthusiast in Peak scenery cannot fail to be acceptable :—
" About two hundred yards beyond Reynard's Cave is the termination of the second grand division of Dovedale. Here the narrow path commences, affording only a passage for the troubled waters of the Dove, and, on the Derbyshire side of the stream, a very scanty pathway beneath the rocks ; the opposite bank is totally impassable.  Here the river, as if impatient at being restrained within the limits of this contracted chasm, rushes with great impetuosity to a more open part of the dale, when its turbulence subsides, and it becomes again a placid but a rapid stream.  Through this upper division of the dale the rocks rise in perpendicular masses on both sides of the river.  In some places, imposing precipices frown over the path below, inspiring emotions of awe and terror.  Beneath these we passed in silence, as if we feared our voices would disturb the firm fixed rock above, and bring the incumbent mass, like a tremendous avalanche, upon our heads.  This, though not the most beautiful, is certainly the most terrific part of Dovedale."

Dovedale, the most charming of the many dales of Derbyshire, is, naturally, one of the greatest attractions of the county of Derby.  For its picturesque beauties, its wild passes, its gorgeous woods, its magnificent rocks, its beautiful river, and the wondrous variety of its scenery, it is unrivalled by any other in the kingdom ; but apart from all this it is rendered immortal by its association with old Izaak Walton and his " dear son," Charles Cotton, whose name is most intimately connected with the charming river from which the dale is called.  Cotton's " Beloved nymph, fair Dove," is indeed a pleasant river, and one which from its beauty and gentleness is appropriately named. It takes its rise, as do also the Wye, the Goyt, and the Dane, on Axe Edge, the huge mountain near Buxton, and from its source to its union with the Trent near Egginton, is about forty-five miles in length, and forms, throughout its extent, the boundary of the counties of Derby and Stafford. Visitors, of course, generally enter the Dale from its lower or Ashbourne end, and so rise with the river. We shall, however, commence our notes at its upper end, at the spot rendered classical by its Waltonian associations, at the veritable " fishing house," erected by the poet Charles Cotton, and dedicated, as his inscription still preserved shews, to anglers. The visitor will at once, on arriving at this spot, be ready to exclaim with Viator, in the Complete Angler, " Now, I think this is a marvellous pretty place," especially if, like Cotton, he looks at it " from the back of the hill," at the river, and " the dale it winds through like a snake, and the situation of the little fishing-house." The fishing-house is a quaint, quiet-looking little building of square form, with a lofty roof surmounted by a hip knob. Over the arched doorway is the inscription carved, as Cotton described it to his friend Viator, with the words *Piscatoribus sacrum,* and beneath them " the two first letters of my father Walton's name and mine, twisted in cypher," and which Walton saw " cut in the stone before it was set up," and which Viator described well when he said, " It stands on a kind of peninsula too, with a delicate clear river about it. I dare hardly go in, lest I should not like it so well within as without ; but by your leave I 'll try. Why this is better and better—fine lights, finely wainscotted, and all exceeding neat, with a marble

table and all in the middle." We cannot but here quote
Izaak Walton's note, in which he says, "Some part of the
fishing-house has been described ; but the pleasantness of
the river, mountains, and meadow about it, cannot, unless
Sir Philip Sidney, or Mr. Cotton's father, were again alive
to do it." This description is true to the letter, and the
sweet little building, which has been thoroughly repaired,
stands as it did in those days when the two anglers sat and
smoked their pipes, which was " commonly their breakfast."

Almost directly after leaving the fishing-house, the
visitor will come to PIKE POOL, a spot where the river,
leaving the broad meadows through which it has quietly
flowed, has forced its way through the solid rock, a spire-
shaped mass of which stands boldly in the midst, and
which made Viator exclaim, " But what have we got here ?
a rock springing up in the middle of the river ! This is
one of the oddest sights I ever saw ;" to which his host,
Cotton, replied, " Why, sir, from that Pike that you see
standing up there, distant from the rock, this is called
Pike Pool, and young Mr. Izaak Walton was so pleased
with it as to draw it in landscape, in black and white, in
a blank book I have at home, as he has several prospects
of my house also."

From here the rambler will pass on to Woscote or Wolf-
scote Bridge, where the hills close again, and the Dove
makes its way through a part called Narrowdale, a gloomy
but strikingly solemn and beautiful valley, with high
mountains on either side, from which masses of rock jut
out in every direction, a more majestic and glorious valley
cannot well be conceived. The scenery of the whole of
Dovedale is gorgeous and grand beyond conception, and

SCENE IN DOVEDALE, NEAR NARROWDALE.

the rocks, woods, trees, mountains, and river blend together in the wildest forms. Some parts of the dale are extremely narrow, so much so, in fact, that the visitor has to cross the water on stepping-stones, and in other places it is more expansive, but in every part it is truly beautiful. *Reynard's Cave, Pickering Tor,* and other parts, are usually visited by the stranger. At the Ashbourne end is the fine mountain called Thorpe Cloud, and not far off, is Ilam Hall, and the curious underground rivers (called the Swallows), the Hamps and the Mainfold.

The Dove has been a source of inspiration to poets, and a theme for prose writers innumerable. We can only now quote the following !—

" Such streams Rome's yellow Tiber cannot show,
The Iberian Tagus, or Ligurian Po ;
The Maese, the Danube, and the Rhine
Are puddle-water all, compared to thine :
And Loire's pure streams yet too polluted are,
With thine, much purer, to compare :
The rapid Garonne, and the winding Seine,
Are both too mean,
Beloved Dove, with thee
To vie priority ;
Nay, Tame and Isis, when conjoined, submit,
And lay their trophies at thy silver feet."

CHARLES COTTON.

" Harp, to the sweeter voice of waters played !
Where Ilam's fountains rise in crystal rings ;
And where with cliffs o'erhung, and leafy shade,
The stream of Dove descends on brilliant wings !
Here must thou hush to rest thy quivering strings ;
For I have seen Pike Pool's deep mirror'd cone ;
Within the marble cave have drank its springs ;
And resting now on Dove's fountain stone,
Thy music dies away—her soft pipe trills alone."

EDWARDS' " *Tour of the Dove.*"

ILAM HALL. Although situated in Staffordshire, Ilam Hall generally forms one of the places of resort for Derbyshire tourists. The hall, the seat of J. Watts Russell, Esq., being close by Dovedale, is generally seen by tourists at the same time with it, is not exhibited as a show-house, though parties furnished with a proper introduction are politely shewn round. Rhodes says of it—" It is situated on the Staffordshire side of the river Dove, and therefore not properly an object for these excursions ; but with those who visit DOVEDALE, Ilam is always a point of attraction. Thorpe Cloud, one of the highest mountains in Derbyshire, stands like a mighty sentinel over its woods, gardens, groves, and meadows, that quietly repose in the deep hollow at its base."

As we enter the village of Ilam or Ham, our attention is attracted by an exquisitely designed and beautifully executed cross, of similar character to the crosses of Queen Eleanor, which was erected in memory of Mrs. Mary Watts Russell by her husband in 1840. It is a hexagonal cross, highly decorated, and bears the following inscription :—

" This Cross and Fountain,
erected by her Husband,
perpetuate the memory of
One who lives in the hearts
of many in this Village and
Neighbourhood.
MARY WATTS RUSSELL.
1840.

Free as for all these crystal waters flow,
Her gentle eyes would weep for others' woe ;
Dried is that fount ; but long may this endure,
To be a Well of Comfort to the Poor."

ILAM CHURCH, in front of the hall, has lately been rebuilt
from the designs of Mr. Scott, and is a bald and poor-look-
ing edifice. The old church was extremely picturesque,
and was thus described :—" The tower appears to be a
structure of foliage, for the stone work is so invested with
ivy as to be almost obscured with its verdant covering ;
and the dial of the clock is half buried amongst thickly
entwined leaves. Ash, elder, and wild roses, of the most
luxuriant growth and colour, flourish close around the
walls of the church, and the adjoining burial-ground is
covered with the richest verdure, amongst which a grey
stone occasionally appears, inscribed to the memory of
those who sleep beneath." The chief attraction here, however, is the affecting monument, by Chantrey, to the
memory of D. P. Watts, which occupies a little Gothic
chapel over the family vault, to the north side of the
church. Rhodes, though the intimate friend of the sculptor, did him no more than justice when he thus described
the monument :—" In this fine work of art, the venerable
David Pike Watts is represented on his bed of death, from
whence he has half raised himself, by a final effort of expiring nature, to perform the last solemn act of a long and
virtuous life. His only daughter and her children—all
that were dearest to him in life—surround his couch, and
bend at his side, as they receive from his lips the blessings
and benedictions of a dying parent, when the last half-
uttered farewell falters upon them. Nothing can be more
affecting than this family group. The figures here committed to marble have the semblance of beings like ourselves, with passions, feelings, and affections similar to our
own. We therefore sympathize in their afflictions, and
mingle our tears with theirs. Fame, justice, wisdom.

N

fortitude, charity, religion, are all represented by certain understood modifications of the human form, and they may be bodied forth in marble with great skill and felicity of execution ; but, in comparison with the work I have described, how cold and feeble are the effects they produce !"

THE HALL, as it now stands, was erected by the present proprietor. It is in the Elizabethan style of architecture, and presents a truly noble appearance. The pictures and armoury are highly interesting.

Dr. Johnson, when he wrote Rasselas, is said to have had the scenery of the neighbourhood of Ilam in view, as the pattern of his " Happy Valley." Congreve wrote his " Old Bachelor," and part of his " Mourning Bride," in a grot near the hall, which is still known as " Congreve's Grot." The rivers Hamps and Manifold both rise within a few yards of each other, in the pleasure-grounds.

-------

*N.B.*—See also the separate *Guide to Alton Towers and Dovedale*, by the same author as this work, illustrated with several wood engravings, *price* 1s.

# DRONFIELD.

INNS, etc.—*Blue Posts* (Goodwin); *Green Dragon* (Cartledge); *Red Lion* (Radforth), etc. etc.

From Chesterfield, 6 miles.

DRONFIELD, formerly a market town, is a considerable village in the busy iron district lying between Chesterfield and Sheffield. It is pleasantly situated in a valley, and is surrounded by a very pleasant neighbourhood.

It is principally supported by the iron and coal works, and manufactories of the neighbourhood. It has large edge-tool, scythe, and sickle manufactories ; beside which it has iron foundries, chemical works, a large steam and water corn-mill, and some spindle and flyer manufactories, and in its vicinity are several coal mines. It has Gas Works. It has still an annual Cattle Fair, on April 25th ; a feast on the nearest Sunday to Midsummer-day ; and statutes for hiring servants. The manor of Dronfield belonged to the Crown till, in the reign of King John, it was granted to William de Briwere, from whom it passed successively to the families of Tateshall, Cromwell, Hastings, Selioke, and others. In 1854 the old market cross was taken down, and a monument of stone to the memory of Sir Robert Peel was erected on its site, at a cost of £30, raised by subscription. The PARISH comprises the townships of Dronfield, Little Barlow, Coal Aston, Holmesfield, and Unstone, together containing 4976 inhabitants, and 10,570 acres of land. The townships of Dore and Totley, formerly in this parish, were, by order of Council, in January 1844, united in a distinct parish for all ecclesiastical purposes. Dronfield township has 2971 inhabitants, and 2414 acres of land. The Church, dedicated to St. John the Baptist, is a large and handsome structure, consisting of nave, chancel, side aisles, tower, and spire. In 1855, it was thoroughly repaired and repewed at a cost of £1000. It contains several interesting monuments and monumental brasses. Among the former is a recumbent effigy of a knight in armour. There was formerly a chantry which stood on the site of the Green Dragon Inn, and was appropriated to Beauchief Abbey. The vicarage, worth about £224 a year, is in the gift of the Lord Chancellor, and incumbency of the Rev. W. D. B. Bertles, M.A. The Independents, Baptists, and Methodists, have each a chapel here. That belonging to the Independents is a large handsome building, erected in 1861, on the site of a more ancient edifice. The Grammar-School was founded in 1579 by Thomas Fanshawe, Remembrancer of the Court of Exchequer, in pursuance of the will of Henry Fanshawe, his predecessor in that office, who endowed it with lands, which now produce an excellent income. The school is open to all the children of the parish, thirty of whom are instructed free. The Mechanics' Institution, established in 1850, has a good library, and a well supplied news-room.

One of the most interesting things connected with Dronfield is its connection with Sir Richard Fanshawe, ambassador to Spain and Portugal, the author of " Original Letters and Negotiations," and translator of " Il Pastor Fido," and several other translations of Virgil, Camoens, Guarini, Mendoza, etc. ; and with his wife, Lady Fanshawe, the amiable and accomplished authoress of the " Memoirs," with which every reader of taste is acquainted.

Within easy distance of Dronfield are—Norton, rendered

famous as being the birth-place of Chantrey, Beauchief Abbey, and other places of interest. Of Norton, an account will be found later on. BEAUCHIEF ABBEY lies on the Yorkshire confines of Derbyshire, and is an extra-parochial district adjoining the parish of Norton. The Abbey, of which some interesting remains still exist, was founded about 1174, for an Abbot, with Canons of the Premonstratensian order from Welbeck, by Robert Fitz-Ralf, Lord of Alfreton and Norton. The Abbot was summoned to Parliament in the reign of Edward I. At the Dissolution, there were an Abbot and twelve Canons.

# EYAM.

PRINCIPAL INN.—The *Bull's Head.*

From Bakewell, 7 m. ; from Sheffield (post town), 12 m. ; from Buxton, 11 m.

THE VILLAGE OF EYAM has many claims on the notice of the tourist—the charm of its situation, its tale of the plague, the almost superhuman devotedness of its pastor called into action by that calamity, and the talent to which it has either given birth, or has nursed—one and all give it an imperishable interest in the eyes of the intelligent. The village, which is large and well-built, as usual with Peak villages, of stone, runs east and west, and, like Selborne, is built on two different strata. On the north side the houses rest on shale and sandstone, and on the south on mountain limestone. The name has been conjectured to be derived from *Ey* or *Ea*, water, and *am* or *ham*, high. In the Domesday book it is written *Aiune.* The antiquities of Eyam are numerous, though they are gradually disappearing. At a place on Eyam Moor, known as " Wet-withens," is a Druidical circle consisting of sixteen stones, enclosing a space about ninety feet in diameter. The stones are about three feet above the surface of the soil, with the exception of three, which are much smaller. A large stone until a few years ago occupied the centre of the circle. Several other smaller and less distinct circles exist in the vicinity of this. Numerous barrows were once to be found on Eyam Moor. One which formerly stood near the great circle was from 75 to 90 feet in diameter, and about 35 feet in height. When opened, an urn composed of unbaked clay was found, containing bones, ashes, wood, charcoal, and a flint arrow-head. About a mile further west, on "Hawley's Piece," stood another smaller barrow. It was 66 feet wide and 36 feet high. On the enclosure of the common in 1801 it was cleared away to make fences. A large urn was found in the interior, and carried home by an individual as a great prize; but his cow dying, he attributed the evil to the jar, and accordingly had it devoutly buried. On Eyam Edge, not far from the "Old Twelve-meers Mine," is a barrow, which measures upwards of 100 feet in diameter at the base, and nearly 30 feet high. Urns have frequently been found near Eyam, containing chiefly ashes, arrow-heads, and coins. On Riley-side, not many years ago, two barrows were destroyed. It is within the recollection of many still living, that in their vicinity there existed a circle of large stones, "surrounded by a circular ridge of earth." The most recently opened barrow was at Grindlow, where some very interesting discoveries were made in 1862, which have been described in the "Reliquary." The principal relic discovered was a fine Celtic drinking cup, of the form usual in Derbyshire barrows. Many early customs, some of them very pretty and simple, are still observed in this and the neighbouring villages.

That lead was wrought here, as in many other parts of Derbyshire, by the Romans, is evident, from pieces occasionally found on the moor. Little more than thirty years ago a conical piece weighing between thirty and forty pounds was found near Leam Hall (M. M. Middleton, Esq.) Roman coins are now and then turned up. The language of the people of this neighbourhood exhibits a rare mixture of nations and ages. Some excellent papers on the dialect of

this district of the High Peak, by the Right Hon. Lord
Denman, which have lately appeared in the "Reliquary,"
will be read with interest by the visitors to this interesting
locality. The principal entrance into Eyam is called Lyd-
gate (Saxon, Cover-gate), and here watch and ward used to
be kept until within a century back. The villagers took
the post by turns, watching the entrance from nine at
night until six in the morning. "The watchman had a
large wooden halbert, or 'watch-bill,' for protection, and
when he came off watch in the morning, he took the watch-
bill and reared it against the door of that person whose turn
to watch succeeded him." The Lords of the Manor of Eyam
are the Duke of Devonshire, the Duke of Buckingham,
and the Earl of Thanet. The village is extensive, and particularly clean and respectable looking. The houses are
built of stone, as most Peak houses are, with stone floors,
and these are kept scrupulously clean, with whitened lines
round the floors, and the door and window places coloured
either white or blue. This gives a cheerful and cleanly
appearance to the place which is quite remarkable.

CUCKLET CHURCH is situated in the dell known as the
Delf or Cucklet Dale. The rock which bears this name
stands out from the steep side of the dell. It is a large
mass of rock standing out from the top of a steep acclivity,
which rises nearly perpendicularly from the valley. It is
one of the most remarkable and picturesque rocks in the
kingdom, and is naturally hollowed out into a number of
cavities, whose natural arches give it the appearance of
a rough ecclesiastical building. In one of these rude
archways stood the worthy pastor Mompesson to read
prayers to his fear-stricken congregation, at the time when

" Contagion closed the portal of the fane
    In which he wont the bread of life to deal ;
    He then a temple sought, not made with hands,
    But rear'd by Him amidst whose works it stood
    Rudely magnificent."—ROBERTS.

And it must have been one of the most striking and solemn
pictures which the imagination can dwell upon, to see the
venerable pastor, standing in the church which Nature had
rudely formed, and addressing his parishioners—the few
who remained—while they were assembled in the sweet
valley below.   It is impossible to conceive anything more
sublime or touching than such a scene in the midst of the
desolation and death which was spread around.

At the head of the dell is a narrow little chasm called
the " SALT PAN ROCK," through which, after continued
rains, rushes a " troubled stream."   It is one of the most
exquisite spots in the whole of this charming neighbourhood, and ought to be seen by every visitor.   From this
end of the dell access to Eyam is to be had.

EYAM CHURCH, with its pinnacled tower at the west
end, stands in the centre of the village.   In the church are
some very interesting details ; amongst which are the remains of a stone altar and a remarkable squint, with piscina adjoining, attached to a shaft ; some early English
shafts and capitals, a font probably of the same period ;
some curious bosses, etc.   There is also an elegant decorated window and other matters worthy of examination.
" The chancel and tower were re-erected about the year
1600.   At the east end of the north aisle is a window of
the fourteenth century, still containing a few squares of
painted glass."   The tower, nearly sixty feet high, was
erected at the expense of a maiden lady named Stafford.

" The bells are also said to have been given by Madam Stafford; they are rich in material, and contain much silver."
They bear the following inscriptions :—

> JESVS BEE OVR SPEED. 1619. CO.
>
> GOD SAVE HJS CHVRCH. 1618. CO.
>
> JESVS BE OVR SPEDE. 1618. CO.
>
> JESWS BE OVR SPEDE. 1628.

Over the south door-way is a complex sun-dial, on which
" the parallel of the sun's declination for every month in
the year, a scale of the sun's meridian altitude, an azimu-
thal scale, the points of the compass, and a number of
meridians, are well delineated." Several monumental tablets and brasses ornament the walls and pillars of the
interior. The churchyard contains many interesting memorials. The ANCIENT CROSS, covered with interlaced
knots and figures, is of the early Saxon period ; it is somewhat of the same character as the one at Bakewell. It is
about eight feet in height, one of the stones being lost,
and greatly resembles the crosses of Ireland and Iona,
though its decorations are not so elaborate. Few village
churchyards are richer in epitaphs than that of Eyam.
Many of them were written by the Rev. Mr. Cunningham,
for many years curate of the place. Of these the following is a good example. It is from the tomb of a youth
named Froggat.

> " How eloquent the monumental stone,
>> Where blooming modest virtues prostrate lie,
>> Where pure religion from her hallow'd throne,
>> Tells man—it is an awful thing to die.
>
> " Is happiness thy aim ! or death thy fear?
>> Learn how their path with glory may be trod,

From the lamented youth who slumbers here,
Who gave the glory of his youth to God."

Another poet who contributed to beautify " God's Acre,"
was Richard Furness, the author of the "Rag Bag," etc.,
who was a native of Eyam.  His epitaph over his wife's
remains is worthy of preservation—

" Love like a pilgrim came
With Hope, and raised this urn,
Where elegy's sad muse
Long lingering shall mourn—
Shall pour ambrosial dews
T' embalm the virtuous name
Of Frances, the wife of Richard Furness, who died August 12, 1844.

Another from the same pen has an unusual mixture of
quaintness and pathos.  It marks the last resting-place of
a sick-nurse—

" In memory
of
Dorothy, wife of
Daniel White,
Who departed this life, August the sixth, 1811, aged 58 years.

Of honest memory this worthy wife,
In nature's sorrows smooth'd the way to life :
Peace to her ashes, when the lab'ring earth
Shall, groaning, heave its millions into birth,
May she, with all the children of her hand,
Receive a portion of the better land."

An epitaph on a tablet monument on the tower, written
by a young gentleman for his deceased sweetheart, will be
recognised as in part borrowed from the beautiful elegy of
Guiderius over the supposed dead body of Imogen—

"Elizth. Laugher, Ob. Feb. 4th, 1741, Æt. 24.

Fear no more the heat o' the sun,
Nor the furious winter rages ;

Thou thy worldly task hast done,
Home art gone and ta'en thy wages.
I weep thee now, but I too must,
Here end with thee, and turn to dust :
In Christ may endless union prove
The consummation of our love.
            Erected by Tho. Sheldon (Her Lover)."

Two more epitaphs may be quoted to save the tourist
the trouble of copying them in the churchyard. The first
is interesting from its peculiarity—

" Here lieth the body of Ann Sellars,
Buried by this stone—who
Died on Jan. 15th day, 1731.
Likewise here lise dear Isaac
Sellars, my husband and my right,
Who was buried on that same day come
Seven years, 1738. In seven years
Time there come a change—
Observe and here you'll see,
On that same day come
Seven years my husband's
Laid by me.
            Written by Isaac Sellars."

The other is even more peculiar, being a most astonishing tissue of contradictions—

" William Talbot, died April 16, 1817, aged 79 years.

Cold death o'ertook him in his aged years,
And left no parent's unavailing tears ;
Relations now enjoy his worldly store—
The race forgotten, and the name no more."

By far the most interesting tomb in the place is that of
the pious Mrs. Mompesson, the wife of the rector of the
parish at the time when the plague almost depopulated
the place. The tomb has plain shields on its sides, while

one end is decorated with an hour-glass between wings, and the words

CAVE

NESCITIS

HORAM,

and on the other a death's head, with the words

MIHI LUCRUM.

At each corner of the tomb, as is customary in this locality, is a stone pillar. On the slab at the top is the inscription in Latin as follows :—

CATHERINA VXOR

GVLIELMI MOMPESSON

HVIVS ECCLESIÆ RECT

FILIA RADULPHI CARR

NVPER DE COCKEN IN

COMITATV DVNELMENSIS

ARMIGERI

SEPVLTA VICESSIMO

QVINTO DIE MENSIS AVGTI

ANO DNI 1666.

THE PLAGUE AT EYAM occupies by no means an uninteresting and unimportant place in British history. In the latter end of 1664 the plague broke out in London, and in the course of a twelvemonth swept away about one-sixth of the population. So much more dreadful, were its ravages, however, in the little village of Eyam,* that in a few months in the summer of 1666, about five-sixths of

---

* For a detailed account of the history, antiquities, and general memorabilia of Eyam, the reader is referred to an interesting little work entitled "The History of Eyam," by Mr. William Wood. It is sold by the author, who resides in the village.

the population were carried away by it. Out of about 350
who inhabited the village before this dreadful visitation,
only 91 were left alive.

> " The Plague
> O'er hills and vales of gold and green,
> Pass'd on, undreaded and unseen ;
> Foregoing cities, towns, and crowds ;
> Gay mansions glittering to the clouds,
> Magnificence and wealth,
> To reach the humbler, sweeter spot,
> The village and the peaceful cot,
> The residence of health."—HOLLAND.

Tradition states that the Plague reached Eyam in a box
containing tailors' patterns in cloth, and, it is said, some
old clothes. This box was sent from London in September
1665, and was opened, it was believed, by a journeyman
named Vicars, who, noticing that the contents were damp,
held some of them before the fire. While engaged in this
act, he was suddenly seized with violent sickness, his neck
and other parts of his body began to swell, and on the
third day, " the fatal token—the plague spot—appeared on
his breast." He died in the course of the following evening. This was the first case in the village, the precursor
of an almost unheard of scourge.

> " Out it burst, a dreadful cry of death ;
> ' The Plague ! the Plague !' the withering language flew,
> And faintness follow'd on its rapid breath ;
> And all hearts sunk, as pierced with lightning through.
> ' The Plague ! the Plague !' no groundless panic grew
> But there, sublime in awful darkness trod
> The pest ; and lamentation, as he slew,
> Proclaimed his ravage in each sad abode,
> 'Mid frenzied shrieks for aid—and vain appeals to God."
> HOWITT.

Fourteen days elapsed before another victim died, and then almost every day had its death. On the last day in September no less than five fell. In October twenty-two died, in November seven, and in December nine. Even winter's severity did not seem materially to affect it, and when spring smiled, and summer bloomed upon the village they but increased its virulence. Unutterable woe spread through the village and entered every cottage. By the end of August, about four-fifths of the population were no more. The Rev. Mr. Mompesson, who held the living of Eyam, was greatly the means not only of staying the ravages of the plague, but of alleviating the agonies of those who suffered by it. "He was the priest, the physician, and the legislator of a community of sufferers; and the bond by which they were connected had a melancholy influence over the minds of his parishioners. His will, nay, even his wish but half expressed, had the force and effect of a legislative enactment; and even at a time, and under circumstances, when men usually listen to the suggestions of personal safety only, he was regarded with reverence, and obeyed with alacrity. He represented to the inhabitants the consequence of leaving their homes, and communicating to others the pestilent malady with which they were visited, and the little probability of escaping the contagion by flight. His character and example, combined with his authority, drew a circle round the village of Eyam which none attempted to pass, even though to remain within it was to hazard almost inevitable death. At his suggestion, an arrangement was made by which supplies of food and everything necessary to mitigate the horrors of the disease were deposited, from whence they were regularly removed by some of the villagers to whom this task was assigned."

The pastor's children were sent to a distance, but his wife heroically remained behind to share the dangers of his office. At length she fell, and he stood alone with the dead and dying :—

> " One lightning-winged cry
> Shot through the hamlet and a wailing grew,
> Wilder than when the plague fiend first drew nigh,
> One troublous hour—and from all quarters fly
> The wretched remnant who had ceased to weep ;
> But sorrow which had drain'd their bosoms dry,
> Found yet fresh fountains in the spirit deep,
> Wringing out burning tears that loved one's couch to steep."
>
> HOWITT.

The letters of Mompesson at this period are regarded as amongst the finest specimens in the English language. That to his children announcing the death of their mother is peculiarly touching. In a letter to Sir George Saville, written on the 1st of September 1666, he says :—" This is the saddest news that ever my pen could write. The destroying angel having taken up his quarters within my habitation, my dearest wife is gone to her eternal rest, and is invested with a crown of righteousness, having made a happy end. Indeed, had she loved herself as well as me, she had fled from the pit of destruction with the sweet babes, and might have prolonged her days ; but she was resolved to die a martyr to my interest. My drooping spirits are much refreshed with her joys, which I think are unutterable." " Sir," he afterwards writes, " I have made bold in my will with your name for executor, and I hope you will not take it ill. I have joined two others with you, who will take from you the trouble. Your favourable aspect will, I know, be a great comfort to my distressed orphans. I am not desirous that they should be great, but good ; and my next request is, that they be brought up in the fear and admonition of the Lord."

Neither his unparalleled exertions, nor the pestilential air which he was continually compelled to breathe, at all affected the health of the good man. Over the sick-bed as pastor and physician, or in the quiet recess of Cucklet Church, he was day and night employed until October 1666 when the plague ceased. It is gratifying to know that his exertions were not unrewarded even on earth. He obtained the prebends of York and Southwell, and the rectory of Eakring. The deanery of Lincoln was offered to him, but he declined it in favour of his friend Dr. Fuller. He died in 1708. Among the other great stays of the plague, the Rev. Thomas Stanley must not be forgotten, for his labours were untiring and heroic. The only other individual whose duty led him into such imminent danger, was Marshal Howe, who interred the bodies. Though his wife and son fell victims, yet he survived and lived for many years.

Scarcely a field in the vicinity of Eyam is without its graves, some marked with tombstones, but many hidden in the grass. Riley Graves, called the " Riley Stones," about a quarter of a mile to the east of the village, are frequently visited by strangers. Here the family of Hancock, which was completely swept away by the plague, was buried.

The " Riley Stones " consist of a tomb to the memory of John Hancock, Senr., August 7, 1666, and grave-stones to Elizabeth Hancock, August 3 ; John, August 3 ; Oner, August 7 ; William, August 7 ; Alice, August 9 ; and Ann, August 10 ; so that of this family of Hancock, two were buried on the 3d of August, three on the 7th, one on the

9th, and one on the 10th. Thus seven members of the same family were carried off in as many days. The tombs will be seen by the visitor, enclosed by a low wall, in the centre of a field on Riley, overlooking the village.

Eyam has been long celebrated as the abode of talent. In the fourteenth century John Nightbroder, the founder of the house of Carmelites at Doncaster, was born in the village. Anna Seward, whose father was appointed to the rectory on the death of the Rev. Mr. Bruce, was born at Eyam in 1744, and at an unusually early age evinced a strong poetical tendency. Early in life she was removed to Lichfield, her father having become canon of that cathedral ; yet so strong was her attachment to the scenes of her early youth, that she every year visited Eyam. She died at Lichfield in 1809. From her voluminous letters, which occupy six closely printed volumes, Miss Seward is perhaps as well known as a prose writer as she is as a poet. Her poems are all remarkable for their chasteness and purity of style, and for their polished language. Many of her poems were published in her lifetime, and have since gone through several editions, and they have been published since her decease, in three volumes, edited by Sir Walter Scott. Miss Seward was also authoress of a Life of Dr. Darwin, who was her intimate friend. On the occasion of a visit to Eyam in 1788, she composed an elegiac ode, three stanzas of which we quote :—

> " In scenes paternal, not beheld through years,
> Nor view'd till now, but by a father's side ;
> Well might the tender tributary tears
> From keen regrets of duteous fondness glide !
> Its pastor to this human flock no more
> Shall the long flight of future day's restore ;

Distant he droops—and that once gladdening eye,
Now languid gleams e'en when his friends are nigh.
　　　*　　　*　　　*　　　*
" Ere yet I go, who may return no more,
That sacred pile; 'mid yonder shadowy trees,
Let me revisit !—Ancient massy door,
Thou gratest hoarse !—my vital spirits freeze,
Passing the vacant pulpit, to the space
Where humble rails the decent altar grace,
And where my infant sisters' ashes sleep,
Whose loss I left the childish sports to weep.
　　　*　　　*　　　*　　　*
" But O ! thou blank and silent pulpit !—thou ·
That with a father's precepts, just and bland,
Didst win my ear, as Reason's strengthening glow
Show'd their full value ; now thou seem'st to stand
Before my sad, suffus'd, and trembling gaze,
The dreariest relic of departed days—
Of eloquence paternal, nervous, clear,
Dim apparition thou—and bitter is my tear."

The Rev. Peter Cunningham, a gentleman with a refined poetic taste, clear judgment, and liberal education, became curate under Mr. Seward, and became the intimate friend of Miss Seward. Many exquisite passages occur in his poems.

" He left the village of Eyam in 1790 ; and was under the necessity of selling all that he possessed, even his books, to enable him to encounter the expensive outset of the new life he was entering upon." He was appointed chaplain to the English factory at Smyrna, but the climate did not suit him, and he resolved to revisit his native shore. In his journey home he suffered many privations, being frequently in absolute want. Having arrived at the Hungarian frontier, he sat down by the wayside to rest. Recollecting that he had in his pocket a volume of poems which a lady had given him before leaving Smyrna, he sat down to look at one which she had recommended to his perusal, when, to his astonishment, he found "closely nestled within the leaves," a note or order for fifty pounds. On his return home he had a curacy given him, and soon after obtained a living in Devonshire. "This he did not long enjoy. Invited to preach an annual sermon to a society at Islington, to whom he had become endeared, he attended, and dined with the members, after delivering to them his last, and one of his best discourses. He appeared in perfect health and high in spirits, but, soon after the cloth was removed, while conversing with a gentleman near him, he fell back in his chair, and immediately expired without a sigh or groan: such was the end of Cunningham."

Richard Furness, a native of Eyam, and for some time schoolmaster in the village of Dore, is also favourably known as a poet. His best known productions are entitled the "Rag Bag," and "Medicus Magus," which are both talented productions. Furness died in December 1857, and a memoir of his life, with a collected edition of his poems, has been written by Dr. Holland of Sheffield. Two short passages from the latter poem will illustrate the style of the author. In the first he describes the spread of the plague, which

> "Darts on the whirlwind—floats upon the breeze—
> Creeps down the vales, and hangs upon the trees—
> Strikes in a sunbeam—in the evening cool—
> Flags on the fog, and stagnates on the pool—
> In films ethereal, taints the vital air—
> Steals through a pore, and creeps along a hair—
> Invades the eye in light—the ear in sounds—
> Kills with a touch, and at a distance wounds."

The other passage describes the recovery of a female sufferer :—.

> " But nature rallied, and her flame still burn'd—
> Sunk in the socket, glimmer'd, and return'd ;
> The golden bowl and silver cord were sound ;
> The cistern's wheel revolved its steady round ;
> Fire—vital fire—evolved the living stream,
> And life's fine engine pump'd the purple stream."

At Eyam is an old mansion which belonged to the family of President Bradshaw called " Bradshaw Hall ;" and the neighbourhood is rich in beautiful scenery and interesting localities. One interesting relic lies to the left of the roadway to Eyam Moor. It is a small well, covered with a carved stone, and is called Mompesson's Well. In this well, in the time of the plague, the villagers used to place their money, and the inhabitants of the neighbouring villages deposited their wares by it in exchange, so as to prevent the spread of the contagion.

# GLOSSOP.

Population of the Parish only, in 1871, 5933.
From Chapel-en-le-Frith, 10 m. ; from Derby, 50 m.

THE parish of Glossop, one of the most extensive in Derbyshire, lies on the extreme northern boundary of the county,
on the borders of Cheshire and Yorkshire. The town,
which, with the surrounding district, has of late been
made corporate, is inhabited by a large manufacturing
population, who are engaged in the cotton-factories and
print-works in the neighbourhood. At the time of the
Domesday Survey it belonged to the Crown. It was
granted by Henry I. to William Peverel, on the attainder of whose son it reverted to the Crown. In 1157
it was gifted by Henry II., along with the church, to the
Abbey of Basingwerk. Henry VIII. bestowed it on the
Earl of Shrewsbury, and it now belongs to Lord Edward
Howard. The town, which is irregularly built, has increased very rapidly in size, and now consists of three main
divisions, known respectively as "Old Town" (or Glossop
proper), "Howard Town" (or Glossop Dale), and "Mill
Town." It is now a great centre of the cotton trade, and
is able in size, in extent of manufactures, and in commercial
importance, to compete with many of the principal seats of
the cotton manufacture in Lancashire. There is an excellent market (Saturday being market-day), a commodious
Town-Hall and Market-House, a Temperance Hall, a Savings' Bank, Gas and Water Works, Grammar School,
Mechanics' Institution, and every other requisite public
building for a large and rapidly increasing commercial
community. It has also its parent and district churches,

and several commodious chapels for Catholics and different denominations of Dissenters, to most of which excellent schools are attached.

County Court and Petty Sessions are held regularly at Glossop Hall, for many years the seat of the lord of the manor, Lord Edward Howard, recently raised to the peerage by the title of Baron Howard of Glossop, is a remarkably picturesque old building, with extensive terraced grounds.

The *Corporation of Glossop* consists of a Mayor, six Aldermen, and eighteen Town-Councillors; with Town-Clerk, Borough Treasurer, Chief Constable, and all the usual officers.

The *Bank* is a branch of the Manchester and Liverpool District Bank.

In the neighbourhood are the Roman station of MELANDRA CASTLE, and many other interesting remains of that and of the preceding period ; CHARLESWORTH, a large and important manufacturing village ; DINTING VALE, where are the large print-works of the Messrs. Potter, and where one of the most stupendous pieces of railway engineering will be seen by the visitor ; HADFIELD, with its calico and print works ; WATERSIDE, also with factories and other cotton works, as there are also at PADFIELD, MARPLE BRIDGE, WHITFIELD, etc. ; and HAYFIELD, a romantic village, 4½ miles distant, where is a good church, with some interesting monuments.

# HADDON HALL.

From Rowsley Station, 2 m. ; From Bakewell, 3 m. ; from Chatsworth, 5½m., by way of Rowsley; from Matlock Bath, 7½ m. ; from Baslow, 7 m. May be seen by visitors and parties every day. A gratuity is given to the attendant. Accommodation for horses is provided.

HADDON HALL is situated on a natural elevated ridge of limestone, on the east bank of the river Wye, in one of the most fertile spots in the whole county of Derby. The first view of its castellated walls, as we approach it from Bakewell, is rather disappointing, but as we come into close contact with it, the magnitude of this venerable pile, its castellated form, and its embattled turrets rising above the trees, have a magnificent effect.

At the time of the Domesday survey Haddon belonged to Henry de Ferrars, of the family of the great Earls of Derby, but the whole manor was given by the Conqueror to his natural son William Peveril, the famous " Peveril of the Peak." In this family it remained until the reign of Henry II., when, from the then holder having previously taken the part of Queen Matilda, in the reign of Stephen, he fled from the approach of Henry, and his lands reverted to the Crown. It was then granted to the Avenalls. From them it passed by marriage to the Vernons, the last of whom, Sir George Vernon, styled from his princely hospitality, and sumptuous style of living, the " King of the Peak," died in 1567. He left two daughters, Margaret, married to the second Earl of Derby of the Stanley family ; and the celebrated Dorothy Vernon, married to John Manners, son of the Earl of Rutland. Thus the Derbyshire

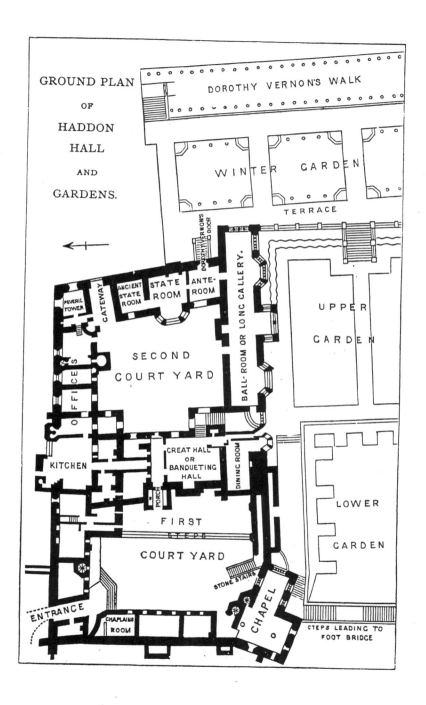

GROUND PLAN

OF

HADDON

HALL

AND

GARDENS.

DOROTHY VERNON'S WALK

WINTER GARDEN

TERRACE

DOROTHY VERNON'S DOOR

PEVERIL TOWER

GATEWAY

ANCIENT STATE ROOM

STATE ROOM

ANTE-ROOM

BALL-ROOM OR LONG GALLERY.

UPPER GARDEN

SECOND COURT YARD

OFFICES

KITCHEN

GREAT HALL OR BANQUETING HALL

DINING ROOM

PORCH

LOWER GARDEN

FIRST

STEPS

COURT YARD

STONE STAIRS

CHAPEL

ENTRANCE

CHAPLAINS ROOM

STEPS LEADING TO FOOT BRIDGE

estates passed to the Rutland family, who still hold them. The Manners, Earls and Dukes of Rutland, made it their family residence until about a century and a half ago, when it was deserted for the more splendid castle and palace of Belvoir. It is asserted, on the authority of tradition, that the fair Dorothy stole through one of the ante-rooms while the family were regaling with some friends, and eloped with her lover; and this is perhaps one of the most charming and pleasant episodes in the history of this truly interesting pile of buildings. This story has been most gracefully and beautifully told by Eliza Meteyard—so well known by the *nom-de-plume* given her by her friend Douglas Jerrold, "Silverpen"—in the "Reliquary," under the title of "the Love Steps of Dorothy Vernon," and will be read with interest and profit by the visitor. Some passages in the life of Sir George Vernon afforded William Bennet materials for his novel, "The King of the Peak."

By a small bridge we cross the river Wye, and passing the cottage of the keeper of the hall, soon gain the entrance. The scenery which surrounds Haddon on every side is beautiful. Behind rises a gentle hill covered with leafy honours, and in front flows the clear water of the Wye, amid rich pastures, shady nooks, and sedgy banks. The effect of a fine baronial hall in such a position is peculiarly pleasing.

Through a little door under a large archway we enter the first court-yard, which is surrounded by various offices and apartments. On the lower side is the "Chaplain's Room," a dark gloomy apartment, containing a number of curious relics. A singular matchlock of primitive make, a pair of huge boots, a thick "buckskin doublet," and a number of pewter plates of immense diameter, tell of fêtes on the field and by the board. Behind the wainscotting of this room a curious washing tally has recently been found. An old cradle and the chapel bell are the only other relics of note. Through a Gothic arch we enter the chapel at the south-west corner of the quadrangle. This chapel, which is one of the oldest portions of the hall, is Norman, with later additions. In it is a Norman font, and pillars of the same period. There are also some interesting remains of stained glass, an old chest, and various other curious relics. In the stained glass of the east window is this inscription :—

" Orate pro ai'abus Ricardi Vernon et Benedicite uxoris ejus, qui fecerunt Ano Dni. Milesimo ccccxxvii. '

The subjects represented on the glass are the Crucifixion and the Twelve Apostles. The roof was renewed by Sir George Manners, and bears the date 1624. Some curious wall paintings may also be seen in the chapel.

In the porch of the Great Hall is a Roman altar found in the grounds. Camden, who saw it, preserved the inscription. By other travellers it has been differently stated. The following is the inscription :—

DEO. MARTI. BRACIACAE. OS(I)TIVS. CAECILIA(NVS). PRAEF.

COH. I. AQVITANO. V. S.

The porch bears the arms of the Vernons and " Fulco de Pembridge, Lord of Tonge in Shropshire."* From it a passage leads to the other court. On the left are the kitchen with its large oaken door and buttery hatch, and other offices. The GREAT HALL, where the Vernons once lived in regal state, is one of the most interesting speci-

---

* Sir R. Vernon, Speaker of the House of Commons in 1426, married Isabella, heiress of Sir Fulk de Pembridge.

mens of the kind in existence. An oaken table on a
slightly elevated platform or dais at the upper end of the
room, is recognised as that at which the " lord of the
feast" sat with his noble guests, while those of lower degree feasted at tables round the hall. A gallery occupies

two sides of the hall. The joists of the roof are bare ;
and the huge fire-places contrast strangely with the more
elegant comforts of modern times. The hall is thirty-five
feet long by twenty-five wide. There are some curious
relics of bygone days in this hall. Fire-dogs are still retained, stags' antlers adorn the wainscotted gallery, and
against the entrance doorway in the screen is a strong
iron hook, to which it was customary to attach the hands,
high above the head, of defaulters at carousals who did

not do their full duty to their liquor, and while in this position, as a further punishment, cold water was poured down the sleeves of his doublet.

The DINING-ROOM is a magnificent apartment, erected by the " King of the Peak." The ceiling is divided by beams of wood into bays, and though now destitute of ornament, was undoubtedly both painted and gilt in the time of the builder. The oriel window of this room is richly ornamented with carving, exhibiting portraits of Henry VII. and his Queen, of " Will Somers," the king's jester, and a shield bearing the arms of the " Avenells, Pipes, Pierreponts, and Vernons." There is also a carving of the royal arms, with the motto—

" Drede God & honour the King."

The room is wainscotted throughout, and has some fine old portraits and furniture, a curious fire-place, and a splendid old wine-cooler of large dimensions.

Immediately over this room is the DRAWING-ROOM, a more cheerful apartment. In this room is the old state chair. The walls are hung with arras. A door at the upper end conducts to the apartment known as the Earl's dressing room, also hung with tapestry. The subjects here represented are various—ranging from Scripture pieces to the sports of the field. " Tapestry may certainly be classed among the finest ornaments of ancient halls and castles ; there is a cumbrous magnificence about it that no other decoration possesses, and which, in connection with the structure it is intended to adorn, assimilates with our ideas of former times, creates a species of delusion, cheats the mind of its realities, and prepares it for the reception of those visionary and sublime impressions that constitute a part of its felicity. The entire covering of the walls with loose arras was less essential to the splendour than the comfort of Haddon. The inner doors are so rudely fashioned, and in point of workmanship so ill made, that any other mode could hardly have been adopted to render the place tolerable as a winter residence ; hence the tapestry with which the principal rooms were hung served a more useful and important purpose than that of show."

Returning again to the Drawing-Room, we enter from it the BALL-ROOM or LONG GALLERY, a noble apartment " 110 feet long and 17 wide." It is wainscotted with oak, and ornamented with Corinthian pilasters. On the frieze are innumerable carved " boars' heads" and " peacocks," the crests of the families of Vernon and Manners. There is in this room a portrait of the first Earl of Rutland, and in a box at the upper end, a cast of the head of Lady Grace Manners (ninety-three years old when she died), taken immediately after death. A painting over the fireplace is supposed to represent Tomyris, the Scythian Queen, with the head of her implacable foe Cyrus.

The ANTE-ROOM, at the end of the Ball-Room, is next entered. Like the last room, the frieze is adorned with the crests of Vernon and Manners. On the walls are numerous old paintings, among which are readily recognised portraits of Queen Elizabeth, Charles I., Prince Rupert, and Prince Eugene, said to be copies from pictures by Vandyke. A good picture of birds, chiefly swans, by Schnyder, is also here. From the ante-room, a doorway, known as Dorothy Vernon's Door, leads by a short flight of steps to the terraced grounds, and Dorothy Vernon's Walk. This is one of the most charming portions of the mansion. The next room is the STATE BED-ROOM, a fine apartment hung with the costly tapestry of Gobelins, representing subjects from Æsop's Fables. A state bed, last occupied by George IV., then Prince Regent, when on a visit to the Duke of Rutland at Belvoir, was removed here some years since. It is fourteen and a half feet high and six feet long. The hangings are of green silk velvet, lined with white satin. It is said that Eleanor Roos, the wife of Sir Robert Manners, made the hangings Over the fireplace is a rough piece of plaster work in relief, representing Orpheus charming wild beasts with his heavenly music. In the raised recess of the large oriel window is a very old French looking-glass, said to have belonged to Queen Elizabeth, and a dressing-table. Behind the tapestry is a door opening into what is termed the ANCIENT STATE-ROOM, a gloomy apartment hung with Gobelins tapestry, representing the principal incidents in the life of Moses. This is undoubtedly one of the oldest parts of the hall. The windows, instead of being ample and cheerful, are reduced to the character of little better than loop-holes. The doors are of a rude style of workmanship, now seldom seen, even on out-houses; and the walls are rough and unplastered.

By a dark passage of no great length from the Ancient State Room we gain a spiral staircase (against which is a strong frame for stringing bows), ascending which we in time reach the PEVERIL TOWER, the highest point and most ancient part of Haddon. It is even supposed that this part was erected before the Conquest, though it is more probable that it is of Norman origin. In the rooms not usually shewn to visitors are some remarkably fine pieces of tapestry; and the kitchens and other domestic offices ought to be visited and examined.

The visitor to Haddon will feel a chill creep over him when he looks at its silent and deserted halls, and reflects that the " King of the Peak" kept noisy hospitality in it, with four-score servants, as merry and as prodigal as himself. The Manners had seven-score servants, and kept open house for twelve days at Christmas. One eloquent writer observes—"How changed are the fortunes of this once hospitable mansion ! The festive board at which thousands were regaled is no longer spread within its halls, nor are the sounds of mirth heard within its gates. A gloomy and solemn silence pervades its neglected apartments, and the bat and the owl are alone the inmates of its remaining splendour. Grand and imposing as Haddon is without, but little attention has been paid to convenience in its interior construction ; with the exception of the kitchen, the cellar, the dining-hall, and the gallery, it is a discordant mass of small and uncomfortable apartments, crowded together without order. The style of architecture that pervailed in England previous to the reign of Elizabeth, when it experienced considerable improvements, was but little adapted to domestic convenience ; and some of its defects are exemplified at Haddon. Those portions of this old mansion which were appropriated to the purposes of good living, and essential to that princely hospitality by which it was distinguished, when, in the days of the first Duke of Rutland, upwards of seven-score servants were maintained within it, are sufficiently ample to justify all that tradition has told of the ancient festivities of the place. The very limited capacity of the chapel, when contrasted with the magnitude of those apartments, shows that though the good people of this establishment took up a large space in which to manage their temporal affairs, they contrived to arrange their spiritual concerns within very modest dimensions."

The grounds of Haddon, the terraced gardens, the balustered walls, the groves of majestic trees, the long flights of stone steps leading from terrace to terrace, the cedars, the sombre walls, the narrow pathways leading to the foot-bridge, the lawn, the court-yards, and every part, are filled with beauty and loveliness.

> ' Haddon, within thy silent halls,
>   Deserted courts, and turrets high
> How mournfully on memory falls
>   Past scenes of antique pageantry.
>
> A holy spell pervades thy gloom,
>   A silent charm breathes all around,
> And the dread stillness of the tomb
>   Reigns o'er thy hallow'd haunted ground.
>
> King of the Peak! thy hearth is lone,
>   No sword-girt vassals gather there,
> No minstrel's harp pours forth its tone
>   In praise of Maud or Margaret fair.
>
> Where are the high and stately dames
>   Of princely Vernon's banner'd hall?
> And where the knights, and what their names,
>   Who led them forth to festival?
>
> They slumber low and in the dust.
>   Prostrate and fall'n the warrior lies,
> His falchion's blade is dim with rust,
>   And quench'd the ray of beauty's eyes."—H. B

# HARDWICK HALL.

Hardwick, 5 miles from South Wingfield station; from Bolsover 6 miles; from Matlock Bath 17 miles; from Buxton 28 miles; from Chesterfield 11 miles.

Inn near the Hall: the Hardwick Inn.

HARDWICK Hall, one of the princely seats of His Grace the Duke of Devonshire, and now belonging to his son the Marquess of Hartington, H.M. Post-Master General, lies about five miles from the Wingfield station, on the Midland Railway, from which it is an extremely pleasant drive, by way of Williamsthorpe and Stainsby. The mansion is advantageously situated on the brow of a high hill, overlooking one of the most beautiful valleys which even this district of Derbyshire can boast, and commanding a fine view of the surrounding country, embracing considerable portions of Nottinghamshire, as well as Derbyshire. The Hall is one of the most imposing looking structures in the kingdom, from its loftiness, its magnificent proportions, and its unity and beauty of design, and is surmounted by an open-work parapet of curious design, embracing the initials of the foundress, E. S., and her arms pierced in the stonework. The building is remarkable for the immense size and number of its windows, which occupy nearly its whole front. The windows of buildings of the Elizabethan period, to which this edifice belongs, were usually large, both in number and size; but those at Hardwick are even more spacious than other examples. Alluding to these large numbers, Lord Bacon said, " One cannot tell where to become to be out of the sunne."

Hardwick is one of the very few buildings of that period which remain intact at the present day, and is

P

therefore especially interesting as being a perfect specimen
of an Elizabethan mansion, both as regards the building
and the furniture which it contains, remaining in its
original state. The present building was erected by the
celebrated Elizabeth, Countess of Shrewsbury, commonly
known as "Bess of Hardwick," the old hall adjoining, and
now in ruins, being her birthplace. This lady, whose
maiden name was Elizabeth Hardwick, was heiress of the
family of that name, and was married, it is said, at
fourteen years of age, to Robert Barley of Barley, who died
soon afterwards. She then married Sir William Cavendish,
ancestor of the present Duke of Devonshire. This gentleman, by whom she had a large family, was the founder of
the palatial seat of Chatsworth. After his death she
married Sir William St. Loe, and having again become a
widow, took for her fourth husband George, Earl of
Shrewsbury, whom she survived seventeen years, and was
buried in All Saints Church, Derby. As the builder of
Hardwick, Chatsworth, and other places, this lady is justly
celebrated. It is but seldom that the erection of so fine a
series of buildings has fallen to the lot of any one person,
and it has been said, on the faith of tradition, that this
rage for building originated in a superstitious feeling, she
having been told by a fortune-teller that she would never
die so long as she continued building. This feeling she
carried so strongly in her mind, that she employed a large
portion of her wealth in building, but at last died in a
hard frost, when the workmen could not labour. It is
said that Mary Queen of Scots was imprisoned here for the
space of eight years, but this is an error, as the present
building was not commenced until four years after the
execution of that injured and ill-fated woman. That she

was occasionally, while in the custody of the Countess' family, at the Old Hall at Hardwick, is certain ; and that the furniture yet preserved as being that used by her, was removed from Chatsworth, and from the Old Hall, is also pretty certain.

In the GREAT HALL is a beautiful statue, by Westmacott, of the unfortunate Mary Queen of Scots. On the pedestal is a panel, bearing the inscription, "MARIA REGINA SCOTORUM, NATA 1542 ; A SUIS IN EXILIUM ACTA 1568 ; AB HOSPITA NECI DATA, 1587." At the end of the Hall, which is hung with tapestry, is a massive gallery with oak balustrades, supported by pillars of the same material. In the CHAPEL is a quantity of tapestry, illustrative of Scripture scenes, and some exquisite specimens of ancient needlework, in the chair-covers and altar-cloth, with figures of saints under canopies, and other kinds of embroidered ornamentation of the fifteenth century. The DINING-ROOM is wainscotted with oak, and has a number of interesting portraits, including Chancellor Pelham, Lord Walpole, Lord Treasurer Southampton, Lord Clifford, etc. Over the mantelpiece is an earl's coronet, with the initials E.S., the date 1597, and the inscription, " THE CONCLUSION OF ALL THINGES IS TO FEAR GOD AND KEEPE HIS COMMAUNDEMENTES." In the DRAWING-ROOM is some beautiful tapestry, illustrating the story of Esther and Ahasuerus, and amongst the portraits are those of Sir William Cavendish, in fur gown and flat cap, and of the Countess Spencer, mother to Georgiana, the beautiful Duchess of Devonshire. The bed-rooms are mostly hung with tapestry, and contain fine old paintings and superb specimens of ancient furniture, many of them perfectly unique. The

STATE ROOM or PRESENCE CHAMBER is a very remarkable and interesting apartment sixty-five feet long, thirty-three wide, and twenty-six high. At one end of it is a magnificent canopy of richly embroidered black velvet, underneath which are a chair and footstool covered with the same material. Within the canopy are armorial and other devices, and under this the noble owner sat in state to receive his guests on great occasions. In a recess on one side of the room is a lofty state bed, with embroidered canopy, and surmounted by ostrich plumes ; the curtains are of crimson velvet, embroidered in gold and silver tissue. In the room are some curiously inlaid tables, carved chairs and stools, splendid pieces of embroidery, curious cabinets, etc. It is hung with tapestry, representing the story of Ulysses. Over this is a frieze rudely executed in plaster, in bas-relief, representing, among other subjects, that of Diana and her nymphs. The effect of this room, with its antique furniture, its glittering embroidery, its tapestry, its pargetting frieze, its elaborate and quaint carvings, its polished floor, its exquisite inlaid work, and its many other delightful features, is one of the finest and most interesting which can be conceived. The LIBRARY is also hung with tapestry, and contains, besides a collection of books, a number of curious portraits, amongst which are Jeffrey Hudson, the Dwarf, by Vandyke, the first Duke of Devonshire, the celebrated Countess of Shrewsbury, and the Duchess of Portsmouth. In this, and in other rooms, are some remarkably curious firescreens.

The apartments of Mary Queen of Scots are interesting on account of their furniture. The bed is of black velvet, and the hangings are beautifully embroidered, it is said by the Queen's own hands, in flowers in coloured silks. This, as well as a set of chairs and other work, it is highly probable, was the work of the unfortunate captive and her attendants. It is well known that she was continually employed over embroidery, and in a letter from Mr. White to Sir Wm. Cecil, describing an interview with her at Tutbury Castle, he says, "She sayes that all daye she wrought with her nydill, and that the diversity of the colours made the work seem less tedious, and contynued so long at it till very payne made her give it over." Over the door of the bed-room are the Royal Arms of Scotland, and the Queen's cypher M.R. beautifully carved, with the inscription, "Marie Stewart, par le grace de Dieu, Royne de Scosse, Douariere de France." The PICTURE GALLERY occupies the entire eastern front of the building, with the exception of the towers, and is about 170 feet in length, 22 in width, and 26 in height. The windows, eighteen in number, are twenty feet in depth. The room is hung with tapestry, and contains upwards of 170 portraits, mostly of the family and its connections. Among these will be noticed Mary Queen of Scots, Queen Elizabeth, Stephen Gardiner, who was twice bishop of Winchester, in which office he succeeded Cardinal Wolsey; the Countess of Shrewsbury, Lady Jane Grey, Cardinal Pole, Sir Thomas More, the first Earl of Devonshire, the first Duke of Devonshire, and the eccentric poet and philosopher Thomas Hobbes. "This celebrated hall," writes Fisher, "is one of the possessions of His Grace the Duke of Devonshire; and in the sixteenth century it was part of the dower of Elizabeth, sister and heiress of John Hardwick of Hardwick, Esq., on her espousals with Sir William Cavendish. That lady, as we have elsewhere observed, afterwards became Countess of Shrewsbury, and, by her extraordinary abilities, greatly enlarged and adorned her estates, and laid the foundation of much of the wealth and honours of the illustrious family of Cavendish. This mansion was rebuilt under her superintendence, and has been noticed by Walpole, in his ' Anecdotes of Painting,' as a remarkable specimen of the noble edifices of the ' Elizabethan era,' combining the beauties and faults of a style in which magnitude was often mistaken for grandeur, and costly workmanship for taste. There was also a desire in its designers for the whimsical and elaborate, which frequently displayed itself in all intended to be ornamental ; and of this we have an instance in the towers of the edifice, which, as their summits emerge above the wide-spreading oaks of the fine park in which the mansion stands, appear to be covered with lightly-shivered fragments of battlements ; but upon attentive observation, these seeming flaws are discovered to be neatly-carved open work, in which the letters E.S. under a coronet, frequently repeated, signify Elizabeth, Countess of Shrewsbury."

The Old Hall of Hardwick, which is in complete ruin, is a most picturesque pile of building. Several of the rooms are still perfect, and are adorned with most curious and exquisite specimens of pargetting, some of the devices being extremely elaborate, and remarkably well executed. The ruin stands on one side of the open yard of Hardwick, opposite the great mansion, and overlooking the surrounding country in every direction. At the foot of the hill and at the entrance to the park is the " Hardwick Inn."

Near Hardwick is the village of HAULT HUCHNALL, in the church at which place is buried the world-celebrated philosopher "Hobbes of Malmsbury," who was tutor in the family of Hardwick, and who wrote " the Wonders of the Peak," and a whole host of works of high-class merit. At ELMTON, in the same district, is buried the celebrated calculator Jedediah Buxton, who was a native of the place, and was one of the most extraordinary mental calculators on record.

# HARTINGTON.

Principal Inn—The *Charles Cotton Hotel* (formerly the Sleigh Arms).
From Ashbourne 10 miles ; from Buxton 9 miles.

Hartington, from which the second title of the Duke
of Devonshire—the Marquis of Hartington—is taken, is a
considerable village and market town in the High Peak.
The parish comprises an immense district, divided into
" quarters " by the names of " Hartington Town Quarter,"
"Hartington Upper Quarter," " Hartington Middle Quarter "
(with chapelry of Earl Sterndale), and " Hartington Nether
or Lower Quarter." The district is rich in mines, and
contains also some excellent farms. The market, granted
to William Ferrars, Earl of Derby, in 1203, is now disused, with the exception of butter, eggs, poultry, etc. At
Newhaven, in the lower quarter, celebrated cattle fairs
are held. The Manor of Hartington belonged to the
Ferrars, Earls of Derby. On the attainder of Robert de
Ferrars it was given to Edmund Earl of Lancaster, who
had a capital mansion or castle there in the time of
Edward I., in whose reign Margaret Countess of Derby
claimed the right of having a gallows there. The manor
continued in the duchy of Lancaster till 1603, when it
was granted to Sir George Hume, then Chancellor of the
Exchequer, and afterwards to Sir George Villiers. In 1663
it was purchased of the Duke of Buckingham by the
Earl of Devonshire, and now belongs to his descendant,
the Duke of Devonshire.

Hartington is a deanery of itself, being exempt from
the authority of the bishop and the arch-deacon. The
church is a remarkably fine building with many interest-

ing architectural features. It contains some good monuments to the Bateman, Sleigh, and other families ; a memorial window to Sleigh ; some good incised slabs, and other relics.

Hartington Hall, long the patrimonial estate of the Bateman family, is a fine mansion, now used as a farm residence. It has recently been restored at a cost of several thousand pounds, by the present owner, T. Osborne Bateman, Esq., J.P. of Derby.

The chapelry of EARL STERNDALE in this parish is a prettily situated village in midst of some of the finest and wildest scenery of the Peak. It is rich in gorgeous scenery, in Celtic remains, and in everything which can make a locality interesting.

## HATHERSAGE.

PRINCIPAL INN—The *George*.
From Stoney Middleton 5 miles ; from Tideswell 8 miles ; from Hassop 7 miles ; from Castleton 5½ miles.

HATHERSAGE, as well known from its connection with the "bold outlaw" Robin Hood, or rather with his right-hand man Little John, as from its being the centre of a rich antiquarian district, and from the needles, etc., which it produces, is an extensive parish containing the townships of Hathersage, Bamforth, Outseats, and Nether Padley. It is celebrated for its manufactory of steel-wire, needles, hackle-teeth, etc., and for its millstones. In the reign of Henry IV. the manor belonged to De Hathersage, and afterwards passed into the hands of Goushill, Longford, Thorp, and Pegge. It now belongs to the Duke of Devonshire. The church is a large and highly interesting structure, with a spire. It contains some fine monumental brasses and monuments to the family of Eyre. There is a Roman Catholic chapel in the village.

In the churchyard is a grave said to be that of Robin Hood's faithful follower Little John ; and the cottage in which that worthy is said to have been born is not far away. The cottage is a very picturesque little building, and has an air of antiquity about it which seems to accord with the belief that on that spot, though in an earlier building, Little John breathed his first and last breath— for in it, it is said, he was born, and to it also it is believed he wearily returned to die. The grave of Little John is on the south side of the church. It is marked by two small stones, one at the head and the other at the

HATHERSAGE CHURCH.

foot. In 1728 it was opened, and bones of an enormous size found in it. Some years ago it was again opened, and a thigh bone measuring 32 inches taken out. It is said that within memory of "the oldest inhabitant" Little John's green cap hung in the church.

The antiquities of Hathersage and its neighbourhood have been well and carefully described by Sir Gardner Wilkinson, the learned author of the "Manners and Customs of the Ancient Egyptians," in the "Reliquary," from which we quote the following remarks, with their accompanying illustrations. "Of antiquities, Hathersage possesses its 'full share—in the camp called 'The Carl's Work,' and the less important one near the church; in the rocking-stones, and numerous rock-basins; in the circles near Longshaw and Eyam; and in the

rocks above Derwent, known as 'The Cakes of Bread,' and 'The Salt-cellar,' with others named from their peculiar forms.

"The drive from Hathersage to Derwent is highly picturesque, and derives an additional charm from the contrast of its wood and water with the moorland heights above the valley; aptly illustrating the name Derwent (*Der gwent*), 'fair water,' and fulfilling the expectations raised by an appellation of such high promise. The hope, however, of finding Druidical remains, which some might entertain from the name of the so-called 'Cakes of bread,' and other objects indicated in the ordnance survey of the hill above Derwent, is not so well repaid; these being simply

natural rocks of fantastic shape, the first of which, consisting of layers of gritstone, lying one upon the other, have
the same character as the masses of granite that composo
the Cheesewring in Cornwall, and similar irregular pillars
of rock on Mistor, and other heights of Dartmoor. Neither
these 'Cakes of Bread,' nor the other works of whimsical
shape upon the Derwent hills, in Cornwall, or on Dartmoor, are attributable to the Druids ; and it must be admitted, that if, from being in the neighbourhood of old
British remains, any superstitious feeling was attached to
them, this could only have arisen from the strangeness of
their shape, as they are evidently not formed by human
agency.

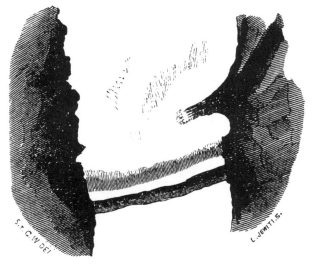

" The small earthwork called ' Camp Green,' near the
church of Hathersage, once surrounded by a ditch, is said
to be Danish ; but its position and *entourage* argue in
favour of its being British, connected as it is, in a strate-

gical point of the view, with " Carl's Work," and the command of the approaches from the eastward. ˙ For the one
would be ineffectual without the other ; and the earth-

work was necessary to watch the southern approach on
that side, at the same time that it guarded the western
valley, and communicated with the heights of Eyam Moor,
all of which were masked from ' the Carl's Work.'

"The church, with the vallum of earth enclosing the camp, the churchyard, famed as the burial-place of Little John, the companion of Robin Hood, and the surrounding scenery, present many pleasing views ; but as little remains of the camp itself, I proceed to notice the more striking peculiarities of 'the Carl's Work.'

"This bears the marked characteristics of an ancient British fort. It occupies one end of an isolated hill, rising above the plain below, and is a site admirably chosen, from its position and the nature of the ground.

"The vallum is here about 17 or 18 feet in thickness ; its outer face, or scarp, fronted with a well-built wall of masonry, of which some of the stones are 50 inches in length ; and it extends nearly in a straight line across the gorge of the hill, which is here about 150 feet in breadth. One of the most remarkable features in this fort is the gateway on its south side. It is 7 ft. 2 in. in breadth ; and as the road ascending from the valley below passed between the two curvilinear faces of the wall, which formed the entrance passage, an enemy advancing to force the gate was exposed to the missiles of the besieged on both sides ; while the portion of it to the west, projecting like a round tower, raked the face of the wall to the right and left, and formed an advanced work over the ascent."

In the neighbourhood of Hathersage are many interesting villages. DERWENT, with its fine old Hall of the Newdegates, and pleasant residences ; BAMFORD, with its cotton mills ; OUTSEATS, BROOKFIELD HALL, NORTH LEES, PADLEY, with its ancient chapel and Hall of the Eyres, etc., etc.

# HEANOR.

From Derby 9 miles

HEANOR is a somewhat important market town in the midst of a rich colliery district. Its inhabitants are principally employed in the coal and iron trades. The church consists of a nave and chancel, with a south aisle divided from the nave by a series of four arches springing from octagonal pillars, above which are the windows of the clerestory. The tower is at the west end, and internally is thrown open to the nave by means of a lofty arch, the inner mouldings of which spring from corbels ; in the south aisle are several hatchments and tablets of the Mundy family, including one to the memory of the Dowager Baroness Middleton, and in the chancel is the monument of Samuel Watson, 1715, the celebrated sculptor, with the following quaint inscription—

> " Watson is gone, whose skilful art display'd
> To the very life whatever nature made ;
> View but his wondrous works in Chatsworth Hall,
> Which are so gazed at and admired by all.
> You'll say 'tis pity he should hidden lie,
> And nothing said to revive his memory ;
> My mournful friends forbear your tears,
> For I shall rise when Christ appears."

Sir John Zouch, of Codnor, and several other members of that family, as well as John Hieron, the celebrated nonconformist divine, have also received sepulture in the church. Heanor is celebrated in modern times as being the birthplace of William and Richard Howitt, of whose writings, known to all the world, it is needless here to speak.

In the neighbourhood of Heanor are SMALLEY, LOSCO, CODNOR, LANGLEY, MARLPOOL, SHIPLEY the seat of the Mundys, etc.

# ILKESTON.

Principal Inn.—*Rutland Arms.*

Population in 1861, 3330.   Inhabited Houses, 709.

From Derby 9 miles.

ILKESTON is a considerable market town, of very ancient origin.  It is a petty sessional district, has a county court, and is one of the polling-places for the southern division of the county.  The manor belonged to Gilbert de Gaud, nephew of the Conqueror, who gave it to his steward Sir Robert de Muscham, from whom it passed through the families of Gresley, Cantelupe, Zouch, and Savage, till it was purchased by Sir John Manners, ancestor to the Duke of Rutland, in 1608, in which family it still remains.  The parish Church contains a fine monument of a crusader, and other monuments of note.  There are several dissenting Chapels, Mechanics' Institute, and other public buildings, and Gas and Water works.

ILKESTON BATHS.—A warm mineral spring was discovered here some years ago, the properties of which are said to be different from those of any other spa in the kingdom, and resemble the Seltzer water in Germany. Extensive Baths have been erected and fitted up with every convenience for plunge, shower, slipper, and vapour baths, as also the practice of the homœopathic system.  The water is an alkaline, and its analysis contains the following ingredients, as given by Dr. Thompson, of Edinburgh, and others :—

Q

*Constituents in a Pint.*

| Carbonate Acid | . | . | . | 4,189 grains. |
|---|---|---|---|---|
| Sulphuric Acid | | . | . | 1,300 ,, |
| Muriatic Acid | . | . | . | 11,678 ,, |
| Lime | | . | . | 13,323 ,, |
| Magnesia | . | . | . | 5,700 ,, |
| Soda' | | . | . | 5,860 ,, |

These Baths are gaining great notoriety for their usefulness in the cure of severe and aggravated rheumatism, gout, and other chronic affections of the joints, as also paralytic affections, muscular contractions, lumbago, sciatica, and stone in the bladder, scrofula, scurvy, leprosy, liver complaints, and spinal affections. The grounds attached to the Baths are tastefully laid out in walks, bowling green, archery ground, etc., and afford every facility for a variety of amusements.

Ilkeston has a railway station on the Erewash Valley line of the Midland Railway Company. Its principal manufactures are common earthenware, stoneware bottles, drain pipes, hosiery, etc.; and a great number of the inhabitants, who are not engaged in these branches, are employed in the collieries and ironworks of the neighbourhood.

# KEDLESTON.

HOTEL.—*The Kedleston Hotel* (Aulton).
From Derby 4 miles.

KEDLESTON HALL, the magnificent seat of Lord Scarsdale, about four miles from Derby, is situated in a very exten-sive and well wooded park. The house consists of a centre and two wings, connected by corridors of the Doric order. The length of the whole being 360 feet. A double flight of steps leads up to a grand portico supported by six mas-sive Corinthian columns ; over the pediment are statues of Venus, Bacchus, and Ceres, and within the portico are many other statues. The garden front is designed after the arch of Constantine. The ordinary entrance in the basement storey opens into a spacious apartment called Cæsar's Hall, which is adorned with busts of the Cæsars, and from thence the visitor will pass into the grand Hall, the most magnificent part of the house, and erected in the style of the ancient Greek Halls. The ceiling is supported by twenty fluted Corinthian columns, twenty-five feet in height, made of solid pieces of veined alabaster. The whole of the rooms are arranged in the purest taste, and the house is adorned by an extensive and valuable collec-tion of pictures and sculpture. The Hall, which occupies the site of a former mansion, was built from the design of the celebrated architect Adam, in 1765.

The manor of Kedleston belonged, at the time of the Domesday survey, to De Ferrars, and as early as the reign of Henry I. was held under that family by Curzon, ances-tor to its present noble possessor.

The village adjoins the park. It is one of the most

pleasant and rural little places which can be imagined, and has an air of quiet which but few places possess. The Church, which is closely adjoining the House, is a remarkably picturesque building covered with luxuriant ivy, and surrounded by lofty trees ; it has a good Norman doorway and other Norman portions, and contains several curious monuments ; of these, perhaps the most interesting are in the floor of the chancel, where upon removing two circular pieces of wood, the heads of a knight in armour and his lady in veil and whimple, appear about a foot below the surface ; the heads are in high relief, and are enclosed in quatrefoils. Besides these there are many very fine and large monuments to different members of the Curzon family, which are well deserving careful examination.

The BATHS.—In the Park is a chalybeate spring, the waters of which are much prized, and over which a neat building has been erected, containing baths and waiting rooms, etc. The entrance lodge of the park is designed from the arch of Octavia, and in the grounds is a picturesque little spot called the Gothic Temple, erected as a summer-house, but now in ruins.

Not far from Kedleston is the picturesque village of QUARN, the " Malvern of Derbyshire," as it has not inaptly been called, from its extreme salubrity. It has a famous medicinal spring, and in its church the visitor will notice a Norman doorway, and other interesting features.

KIRK IRETON, from which the family of the celebrated regicide Ireton took his name, is in the neighbourhood. MUGGINTON, with its interesting church and fine monumental brasses, is also near, as are many other places of note.

## LEA HURST.

LEA HURST, adjoining the romantic villages of Lea, Dethick, and Holloway, is situated about three miles from
Cromford, the road following the course of the river Derwent. As one of the lovely spots of the county of Derby,
Lea Hurst stands naturally high, but as the home of Florence Nightingale, it possesses an historical interest which
will always remain. Of Miss Nightingale herself we will
not now stop to speak, for her noble actions live in the
hearts of all. Of Lea Hurst, the home of her childhood,
we will quote a descriptive passage or two from a little
work, " A Stroll to Lea Hurst, the Home of Florence
Nightingale," by Mr. Llewellynn Jewitt, F.S.A. He says :—
" Lea Hurst, the seat of William Edward Nightingale, Esq.,
is beautifully and romantically situated on rising ground

in the midst of one of the most charming and extensive of
the Derbyshire valleys, and surrounded on every side with
hills and mountains, rocks and woods, of majestic and
gigantic proportions, and watered by the winding Derwent
and its tributary streams. The park and grounds in which
the hall is situated, extending along the conjoined hamlets
of Lea Mills and Holloway, form a conspicuous feature in
the landscape from any of the surrounding eminences.

" The hamlet of Lea or Leyghe, which is usually joined
with Dethick and Holloway, is partly in the parish of Ash-
over, partly in Wingfield, and partly in Crich, and is of
considerable antiquity. In the reign of King John, the
manor belonged to Roger de Alveley, one of whose heir-
esses brought a portion of it by marriage to the Ferrars,
and from them it passed successively to the Dethicks and
Babingtons ; the other portion of the manor passed from
the De la Leas, who had acquired it by marriage, to the
Frechevilles, of whom in the fourteenth century it was
purchased by the Rollestones : from them it descended by
marriage and purchase through the Pershalls, Spatemans,
and others, to the family of Nightingale, in which it is
still vested. At Lea, a chapel was erected in the reign of
King John, by the Alveleys, and a chantry founded in the
reign of Henry IV. by Roger de Wingerworth ; of this
chapel some remains were converted into a barn.

" Lea Hurst Hall, erected in the Elizabethan style, is
most enchantingly situated on an expansive sloping lawn
on the outer edge of an extensive park, and is surrounded
and overhung with luxuriant trees. It is built in the form
of a cross, with gables at its extremities and on its sides,
surmounted with hip-knobs, with ball terminations ; the
windows, which open beneath the many gables, are square-

headed, with dripstones and stone mullions, and the general contour of the building is much heightened by the strongly built clustered chimney stalks which rise from the roofs. At the extremities of the building large bay windows stand out into the grounds, and are terminated with balustrades and battlements. The hall, with its out offices, gardens, and shrubberies, etc., is enclosed from the general park by a low fence, and is approached by a gateway, whose massive posts are terminated by globes of stone.

" The whole place, embosomed as it is amongst a profusion of beautiful trees, in an extensive park raised upon a kind of table land in the midst of one of nature's choicest valleys, and from which a long series of exquisite views of the surrounding country are obtained, surrounded by its gardens and shrubberies, and the walls covered with a profusion of ivy and creeping plants, is one of the most charming and poetical spots we have ever visited."

# MATLOCK BATH.

HOTELS AND INNS.—*New Bath Hotel* (Ivatts and Jordan). *Temple* (W. Evans). *Walker's Terrace Hotel* (Walker). *Hodgkinson's Hotel*, Museum Parade (Parkin). *Prince of Wales Hotel* (Gordon). *Devonshire Arms* (Robinson). *Rutland Arms, Clarence Hotel, Roberts*, etc.

Matlock Bath from Derby 16 miles ; from Buxton 22 miles ; from Bakewell 10 miles ; from Ashborne 12 miles ; from Chatsworth 10 miles.

THE rivers Derwent and Wye in their course from the Peak unite their strength and beauty in a vale beginning about Rowsley, after which the Derwent retains more or less of its romantic features until it passes Derby, twenty-two miles distant. In the whole valley no spot exhibits more romantic scenery than that overlooked by the High Tor ; and certainly no more desirable site for a village could be found than that occupied by Matlock Bath. The drive into the village from any side is striking. The valley, here narrowed almost into a ravine, walled with rich verdure and rough projecting rocks ; the High Tor, like some huge bastion, lifting its grey head to the sky ; the silver Derwent making sweet music as it flows ; and the Swiss-like cottages, peering out of green clusters, or crowning craggy steeps,—give the place an air, if not of romance, at least of genuine picturesqueness. And yet this romantic village has sprung up in somewhat less than a century and a half. The appearance of the dale at this point previous to 1698, when the springs were discovered, must have been very different from its modern aspect. The inanimate forms of nature, it is true, would be pretty nearly the same ; the rocks, trees, and river would be as fascinating as now, if indeed they would not appear more so, from the absence of the pruning hand of man ; but everything would have a wilder and a colder aspect ; the absence of even a human habitation, unless it were the miserable hut of the poor miner ; the trackless nature of the woods and heights, at that time destitute of roads ; the rough, almost wild, herds of sheep and cattle, finding abundant sustenance, and tasting unrestrained liberty, on the heights and by the river banks ; the happy choir of birds, pouring their " wood notes wild" in fearless security, must have rendered a visit to Matlock Dale in the latter end of the seventeenth century an event to be long and fondly remembered. The dale as it now exists bears a striking contrast to this picture. Here, under the frown of the Tor, runs a street with hotels ; and above and around, tier upon tier, rise cottages of every form and material, clothed with evergreens, and flanked by smiling gardens. The stream, as it slowly sweeps round the wooded hill in the front of the Museum Parade, sparkles with the vivid reflections of the white houses and the lofty trees that here adorn its banks ; carriages rolling along the road, and ladies and gentlemen perambulating the dale in various groups, give animation to the scene. The scenery of this exquisite dale is thus graphically described by Mr. Llewellynn Jewitt in his " Nooks and Corners of Derbyshire :"—

" On entering the dale from the south the road gradually rises and winds its way at a considerable height above the river, in many places the descent being almost perpendicular ; from this road many beautiful glimpses of scenery are obtained on the way, but on arriving at the summit the gorgeous beauty of the whole place bursts on the view. Immediately in front, but considerably lower, lies the village of Matlock Bath. in front of the most pro-

minent feature of which, the Museum Parade, the Derwent
is seen winding its way around the wooded base of the
gigantic rocks to the right ; to the left, rising abruptly
from the cheerful cream-coloured row of houses on the
' Parade,' is the pine-crowned Heights of Abraham, studded
here and here with fantastically-built villas, relieving the
sombre mass of foliage with which it is covered, and surmounted by a lofty prospect tower ; beyond this again is
the summit of the glorious hill Masson, towering over the
landscape in infinite majesty, and rearing his proud head
nearly to the skies, whilst through the opening towards the
extremity of the dale rises, in all his huge proportions, the
solemn Tor.    It is difficult to tell at what period the view
from this point is most charming.   We have seen it in the
spring, when the young foliage has scarcely burst from the
bud, and when the brilliant green of the unfolding leaf
has been relieved by the strongly defined outline of the
branches, and we have thought that nothing could exceed
the beauty of the scene ; we have seen it in the summer,
when the whole slope of the mountain-side has been but
one broad mass of thick luxurious foliage, and we have
compared the deep green and brown tints of the wooded
heights with the greyness of the jutting masses of rock,
and thought the effect gorgeous in the extreme ; we have
seen it in the autumn, when the almost impenetrable
masses of trees have arrayed themselves in their richest
and most varied tints and colours, and we have glanced
upwards from the solemn darkness of the river, the whitened roads and houses, the cold and mottled greyness of
the rocks mapped in every direction by clinging ivy, the
sombre brown of the stems and branches of the trees, the
dark green shades of some of the foliage, and the brilliant

reds, oranges, and purples of the others, up to the dark
fringe of heavy pines standing out in bold array against
the warm tints of the autumnal sky, and we have felt,
even then, that there were beauties which we had not
before noticed ; we have seen it in the cold winter, when
Masson's proud head has been encased in snow, and when
the trees have been festooned in ice, and the streams con-
gealed, and we have felt that there was more grandeur,
more majesty, more wildness and romance, in the scene,
than we felt in any other season."

" On leaving the point from which we have been describing the scenery of Matlock, the road gradually
descends at a little distance from the river bank, to the
Museum Parade, the only approach to town-like appearance in the place, where shops, and houses, and museums
for the sale of the natural productions of the neighbourhood, are ranged in regular street-like order ; opposite the
houses are small gardens sloping down to the water's edge,
and from them a glimpse of one of the finest bits of rock
scenery imaginable is obtained ; the river, here still and
placid as a lake, spreads out its broad surface as if anxious
to reflect the full height of the ponderous tors that tower
above it, on its glassy bosom, its bank overhung with
luxuriant trees, whose rich and delicate verdure here and
there hang down to the water's edge, as if in contemplation of their own beautiful image which is there reflected,
or in silent admiration of the music produced by the
rippling of the waters whilst flowing amongst their projecting roots. Beyond the Parade, the road, still winding
round the foot of Masson, proceeds onwards by the river
side to the stupendous High Tor, rearing aloft its bold
front of grey limestone, mottled and chequered with mosses

and lichens, and with luxuriant ivy. The Tor, which here rises nearly perpendicular from the river's edge to a height of upwards of 400 feet, has its sloping base covered with tangled underwood, from which rise tall elms, ashes, and sycamores, whose branches afford shelter for myriads of rooks and daws, while their rich foliage, mixed with the light and elegant verdure of the birch and aspen, but tend to heighten the effect of the tremendous cliff above them ; the Derwent winds rapidly round its base, murmuring over the pebbly bed, and thus unconsciously adding to the solemnity of the scene, in which the mighty rock stands out so prominent a feature."

The MEDICINAL SPRINGS, to which Matlock Bath owes its prosperity, were first introduced to notice about the year 1698, being more than a hundred years later than the discovery of the " Old Spa," at Harrogate.

" Matlock, fortunately for the benefit of its visitors, is blessed with three excellent bathing establishments— one at the Old Bath Hotel, another at the New Bath Hotel, and the third at the Fountain Gardens, to the north of the Museum Parade ; and at each of these the visitor will find every accommodation he can require. At the first is a spacious tepid bath, and other warm and shower baths ; at the second a fine natural tepid swimming bath, and other conveniences ; and at the third are plunging and other hot, cold, and shower baths. The waters are, in temperature, about 14° Fahrenheit below those of Buxton, and 8° below those of Bristol, which they much resemble. They are said to be particularly valuable as curatives in rheumatism, consumption, gout, and pulmonary and nervous disorders."

The following analysis by Sir Charles Scudamore, M.D., published in Turner's Chemistry, gives but a faint idea of the ingredients of the water, and it is to be regretted that a more recent and careful analysis has not been made.

"Temperature, 68 degrees ; specific gravity, 1.003.

Free Carbonic Acid.

Muriates and Sulphates of Magnesia, Lime, and Soda, in very minute quantities not yet ascertained."

MATLOCK BATH CHURCH was commenced in 1841, the foundation stone being laid by the late Walter Shirley, then Archdeacon of Derby, afterwards Bishop of Sodor and Man. It was consecrated in 1842. The church, which is in the Decorated style of architecture, is cruciform, with a handsome tower and crocketed spire, 129 feet high, at its north-west end. The communion table is surrounded by wood carving of an elegant design, and the east window, which is of five lights, is filled with elegant tracery. The ceiling is spanned by three arches, the spandrels of which are filled with tracery. The tower is octagonal, with battlements, flying buttresses, and pinnacles. Messrs. Weightman and Hadfield of Sheffield were the architects. The church cost only £2250. LADY GLENORCHY'S CHAPEL was originally built as a dwelling-house by Sir Richard Arkwright for his partner Mr. Need in 1777. By Mr. Need's son-in-law, Mr. Abney, it was converted into a chapel. The property was for sale when the pious and benevolent Lady Glenorchy, who was visiting Matlock Bath, became the purchaser, and "had it opened in connection with the Presbyterians or Independents."

MATLOCK BATH CHURCH.

CAVERNS.—The charge to each of the Caverns at Matlock is a shilling, exclusive of Bengal or other lights, which are almost essential in order to form a proper idea of their interiors.

The RUTLAND CAVERN, on the Heights of Abraham (approached from the Museum Parade by the way of Hodgkinson's Hotel), is the largest in Matlock, and has the advantage of having the finest openings. This mine was successively worked by the Romans, Saxons, and Danes, as well as in later times. In what is styled the ROMAN HALL, the traces of Roman work are readily recognised. " Jacob's Well," a basin of clear water, attracts universal attention from its beauty and purity, and from the clearness with which its brilliant sparry bottom is seen. This cave is large enough to contain 10,000 men. The entrance at present used was blasted out some seventy years ago, and the refuse from the working of the mine removed, and used for the formation of the terrace, from which the most magnificent view of Matlock is obtained. Ores of zinc occur plentifully. This mine is dry and easily penetrated, and is extremely rich in fossils and minerals. The spars are mostly extremely fine and brilliant.

The CUMBERLAND CAVERN, also situated on Masson, is approached either by a path from near Walker's Hotel, or by the Upper Wood Road from the Romantic Rocks. It is entered by a small doorway close to a mine, which is still occasionally worked, and the view from this spot is one of considerable grandeur and beauty, embracing most of the choice bits of scenery with which the place abounds. On entering the cavern, the pathway—formed originally for mining operations, and by which the stupendous natural cavern was first discovered—descends somewhat abruptly by means of steps and shews the first and second clay measures of the superior measures very strikingly,— that which separates the Dunstone beds occurring lower down, in the large gallery. After descending to some depth, and again rising, the visitor enters a wide and ex- pansive gallery-like opening, which is one of the most per- fectly marvellous places which can possibly be conceived. Unlike most other caverns, this terrific opening, and the other cavernous places leading from it, is in the rough and rude state in which nature left it—a place which has been untouched and unspoiled by the hand of man, and is just as it was

formed by man's Maker. The gallery is about 111 yards
long and about 20 feet wide, and has almost perpendicular
walls of solid rock on either side, about 18 feet in height,
which support the superincumbent mountain for a roof,
perfectly flat and naturally level on its surface. This
cavern has been exhibited for about 80 years.

The DEVONSHIRE CAVERN, also on Masson, is approached
from the same road which leads to the Heights of Abraham.
" This cavern, which was discovered in 1824, is not so
large as either of the preceding ones, but is eminently
beautiful and interesting—its principal characteristic being
an immense opening covered with an even and smooth
natural roof, 200 feet long, and 40 feet wide, dipping at
an angle of forty-five degrees, and resting on the solid rock
forming almost perpendicular walls on either side. In one
portion the scene, when lighted up by the guide, is truly
marvellous—the strange appearance of the slooping roof,
its smooth surface, the rocks rising perpendicularly on
either side, the masses of fallen rock thrown about in every
direction and nature-piled one upon another in the most
astonishing manner, and the vastness and immensity of
the whole cavity—combine to make it one of the most
impressive pictures which the eyes of the visitor to Matlock can rest upon. The Devonshire Cavern is easy of
access, and there is egress in the upper part of the mountain."

The SPEEDWELL MINE, situated on Masson, not far from
the Romantic Rocks, is full of interest and beauty. " The
crystallization is extremely fine, the dog-tooth spar and
the cubic fluor spar being spread about in the utmost

beauty and profusion. The mine, after passing through narrow passages in some parts, opens out very magnificently, and forms a wonderful picture of cavernous grandeur, the effect of which, when lit up by the guides, is truly wonderful. The stalactites in this mine are among its most interesting features, and the visitor will be struck with their extreme beauty. The water may be seen here slowly dropping through the rocks in the same unceasing and monotonous manner as it has done for unnumbered centuries."

The OLD NESTALLO MINE, another remarkably fine Cavern, has recently been made available to visitors, and has become one of the prominent attractions of the place. It is situated above the Rutland Cavern, and near to the Prospect Tower, where a new entrance has been made ; a convenient exit having also been formed on Masson. The Mine is well worth the careful inspection of the geologist and mineralogist, containing as it does some fine calcareous and fluor spars, veins of metal, and interesting fossil remains. The views from the entrance and exit are remarkably fine, and the Cavern itself is dry and perfectly safe.

The HIGH TOR GROTTO, situated at the base of the High Tor, is approached by a rustic wooden bridge crossing the river Derwent, with the huge tor towering up tremendously above head, and the river rushing wildly below from the weir. Having crossed the Derwent, the visitor will pass a paint mill, and then cross a side stream before arriving at the entrance to the Cavern, which opens in the solid rock at the foot of the Tor. From the entrance, the

view of the curious strata opposite, and the wooded slope
of the mountain, is truly beautiful. One great peculiarity
of the Grotto is its crystallisation, which extends throughout its entire length.

HIGH TOR WALKS, etc.—The summit of this stupendous
rock is now approachable for visitors with a degree of ease
which seems almost incredible. The summit of the Tor
is approached by crossing the railway bridge, turning to
the left, and then passing under the line on the right,
when the Lodge will be seen to the left of the road.

PETRIFYING WELLS.—In these wells the various objects
intended to become "Petrifactions," as they are called
by the natives, are arranged on stands, various teirs in
height, and a pipe or spout conveying the water runs
along the roof. From this the water falls gently down
upon the objects, and in time encrusts them. The ROYAL
PETRIFYING WELL belongs to Mr. W. Pearson. It is opposite the Fish Pond, by the road-side. The ORIGINAL
PETRIFYING WELL, the property of Mrs. Boden, is situated
nearly opposite the post-office in Woodland Terrace.
SMEDLEY'S PETRIFYING WELL, belonging to Mr. T. Smedley, is situated at the back of, and beneath, his spar shop,
nearly opposite Walker's Hotel. And another PETRIFYING
WELL is by the river-side, near the Boat-House.

The HOTELS in Matlock Bath afford every accommodation. *The Old Bath Hotel,* the oldest building in the town,
has been taken down, and a splendid hotel and hydropathic establishment is being erected by a company on its
site. *The New Bath Hotel,* kept by Ivatts and Jordan, was

erected at the time when the second hot spring was discovered. The buildings of which it is composed are large
and very conveniently arranged, and stand in their own
grounds. Attached to the house is a tepid bath. In the
garden behind the house is a fountain for the use of those
who desire to drink the water. In this garden is a fine
lime tree, believed to be upwards of 200 years old. It is
of a great size, and when covered with its fresh green
foliage and light coloured bracts, cannot fail to be viewed
with delight ; while the abundant shade which it affords
is peculiarly grateful in a warm summer afternoon. It
covers an area of more than 100 feet in diameter. The
stream of water from the tepid spring, running beneath
the roots, is believed to account for its extraordinary
growth and vigour. The view from the lawn and terrace
includes Cat Tor, the woods of Willersley, Harp Edge,
a portion of Masson, Cromford Moor, and the cliff of
Stonnis.

The TEMPLE HOTEL was originally designed as a super-
numerary establishment to the Old Bath Hotel. It is 150
feet above the level of the valley ; and a number of terraces variegate the descending bank.

WALKER'S TERRACE HOTEL, situated at the north end of
New Bath Terrace, near the church, is an excellent establishment, replete with comfort, and arranged to meet every
requirement of the visitor. Being placed somewhat pro-
minently on the same ridge as the New Bath Hotel, and
consequently nearer to the road and the river, some truly
exquisite views of the valley are obtained from the windows and grounds.

HODKINGSON'S HOTEL, kept by Mr. Parkin, is a comfortable house on the Museum Parade, and combines tavern accommodation with hotel requirements.

The MUSEUMS for the sale of the beautiful spars and productions of the place are numerous and extremely good. The following is a list of these establishments :—

> DAKIN'S (late Walker's and Vallance's) CENTRE MUSEUM, Museum Parade.
> BUXTON'S ROYAL MUSEUM, Museum Parade.
> HARTLE'S MUSEUM, near Walker's Hotel.
> SMEDLEY'S, Museum Parade.
> BODEN'S SPAR SHOP, near the Toll Gate.
> W. SMEDLEY'S, near the New Bath Hotel.
> Mrs. SMEDLEY'S, New Bath Terrace.
> T. SMEDLEY'S, nearly opposite the Church.
> ODGEN'S, opposite the Old Bath Hotel Obelisk, and Derwent Parade.
> WOODFIELD'S, Derwent Parade.
> PEARSON'S, Temple Walk.
> KING'S, Waterloo Road.
> GREGORY'S, Albert House.

The HIGH TOR claims attention from the broad crag which it presents to view from the vale. " If there be any object that possesses a paramount interest over every other in this enchanting dale," says Mr. Jewitt in his Matlock Companion, " that object is the High Tor. Matlock is never mentioned but the High Tor is associated with the idea—it is never seen but the High Tor forms a portion of the view ; it has furnished the subject of many a picture, and even in our school-boy days has been used as an arithmetical question. In the lapse of years since it was first noticed, it has lost none of its interest, and it continues at the present time as undiminished a source of attraction, as if it had only just emerged from the overflowing waters. It is 396 feet in height, but being composed of solid limestone, looks massive in the extreme." Rhodes justly remarks—" No part of Matlock Dale is equal

in grandeur to the HIGH TOR, yet it everywhere abounds in picturesque beauty. The wood-crowned eminence in front of the Museum Parade is a fine object, and the view from thence down the river includes one of the best pictures in the dale ; the parts are few and well combined. Nearly opposite the New Bath Hotel, a broken rock, fringed with light foliage, rises majestically out of a group of trees that adorns its base ; its topmost pinnacle is denominated Wild Cat Tor, and from its craggy summit a noble landscape is displayed."

MASSON, THE HEIGHTS OF ABRAHAM, AND THE ROMANTIC ROCKS. At the octagon lodge admission is to be had to the zigzag walks which lead to the summit of Masson and to the Rutland Cavern. Sixpence is charged for the admission.* The views during the ascent are varied and beautiful. From the summit are visible the vale of Derwent, the Derby Rail and Canal, Axe Edge (near Buxton), Crich Chase, Cromford Moor, Middleton Moor and a world of other places of less note, but not less beauty. From the summit the view is extensive and interesting. Portions of five counties are visible.

"One of the great attractions of Matlock," says Mr. Ti. Jewitt, in "Nooks and Corners of Derbyshire," " is the wooded slope called Heights of Abraham, and the gigantic mountain Masson towering above it. The heights are ascended by a zigzag walk amongst the trees with which the whole hill side is covered, and affording magnificent glimpses of the valley below in different parts ; the ground itself is covered with a rich variety of wild flowers, mosses, and lichens, and from the midst of them, and of the ferns and brackens with which they are intermixed, tall pines and firs spring up, and masses of projecting rock jut out in every direction. On arriving at the summit the scene is truly grand, and seems to strike the mind with awe ;

* Parties visiting Rutland Cave pay 1s., which frees the walks.

the view from this point embraces five counties, and the
eye ranges over the immediately surrounding district in
an unobstructed gaze, and sees the solitary moorland, the
gigantic mountain, the deep valley and ravine, the rocky
heights, and the lowly river, the woods and meadows, and

the abodes of man, spread out before it, until it wearies
with the task of tracing them singly, and retains only the
vastness and immensity of the view upon its recollection.

" On the side of this steep are the extensive caverns
which attract so much interest, and on the same slope is
one of our favourite little nooks, the Romantic Rocks, as

they are termed. This singular assemblage of rocks, although comparatively small, is, perhaps, from that very fact, and its utter exclusion from the outer world, one of the most lovely spots which even Matlock can boast ; it is formed of masses of gigantic rock, boldly jutting out from the side of the hill, and by a number of obelisk-shaped stones thrown wildly about in various directions, and beautifully covered with the richest coloured lichens and mosses. The whole assemblage is embosomed in the surrounding foliage of the trees, which grow from out the interstices of the rock, and in a profusion of shrubs and wild plants, which cast a deep gloom and shadow over the spot ; while the constant dripping of the water as it percolates through the mountain gives a coldness and sepulchral feeling to the place, which is still more heightened by the long waving leaves of the fern and hart's-tongue, which grow in great luxuriance and profusion. We could visit this little spot at all hours, and sit and listen to the monotonous dripping of the water, and watch the waving of the long dark leaves of the unearthly-looking hart's-tongue, as drop by drop the moisture fell upon them from above, and see it pass from leaf to leaf, until, with a sullen plash, it fell upon the rock beneath ; and we could peer into the darkness of the recess until our minds were lulled and soothed with the contemplation, and our very soul estranged from earthly objects."

———————Proud Masson rises rude and bleak,
And with misshapen turrets crests the Peak,
Old Matlock gapes with marble jaws beneath,
And o'er scar'd Derwent bends her flinty teeth ;
Deep in wide caves below the dangerous soil,
Blue sulphurs flame, imprison'd waters boil.
Impetuous streams in spiral columns rise

Through rifted rocks, impatient for the skies :
Or o'er bright seas of bubbling lavas blow,
As heave and toss the billowy fires below ;
Condensed on high, in wandering rills they glide
From Masson's dome, and burst his sparry side :
Round his grey towers, and down his fringed walls,
From cliff to cliff the liquid treasure falls ;
In beds of stalactite, bright ores among,
O'er corals, shells, and crystals, winds along ;
Crusts the green mosses and the tangled wood,
And, sparkling, plunges to its native flood.—DARWIN.

Masson rises more than double the height of High Tor.
From it issue the warm and petrifying springs alluded to
by Dr. Darwin in the above passage.

LOVERS' WALKS. "Another truly delightful part of
Matlock," remarks Mr. L. Jewitt, "is the Lovers' Walks,
on the opposite side of the river from the village and
Masson. These walks are entered from the ferry, and
embrace nearly the whole of the eastern side of the dale.
On leaving the boat a path to the left leads to the sloping
road and steps, whence the summit of the rocks is attained ;
this path winds slowly in a zig-zag direction up the face
of the thickly-wooded and almost perpendicular rock, the
distance of the ascent being relieved by alcoves and rustic
seats. On reaching the summit, a walk leads along the
very verge of the rocks, from which some of the most
exquisite bits of scenery burst in rapid succession on the
view, on the one side embracing Matlock, enclosed by
high hills, and watered by the 'gentle Derwent,' and on
the other the surrounding country, including the High
Tor, Riber, and other points of attraction ; from the path,
a lawn-like field slopes gently down to the valley below,
where may be seen a few cottages and the railway station ;

while the Tor, and the bare open moorland beyond it, form such a background as assimilates well with the romantic scenery with which the foreground is more immediately surrounded. The views from the points of the rock are not so extensive as, from its greater elevation, are obtained from the Heights of Abraham, but they are, on that very account, more pleasing; the views are divided and cut up by the trees of the foreground in such a manner that the eye takes in at a glance all the picture before it, instead of having to wander from object to object over the broad expanse of country which is spread out beneath it from the elevated points on Masson."

The BANK, a branch of the Derby and Derbyshire Bank, is open daily.

The POST-OFFICE is by the Bank, about midway between Museum Parade and the Railway Station.

The GAS-WORKS are situated by the railway station, near the High Tor tunnel.

WATER-WORKS have been established, whose operations are intended eventually not only to supply Matlock Bath, but also the Bank and Bridge. Matlock Bath has also its *Board of Health.*

The RAILWAY STATION is situated on the opposite side of the river Derwent from the village, and is approached by a bridge not far from the High Tor. The station, built from the designs of Sir Joseph Paxton, is small, but picturesque, and commands a fine view of the exquisite scenery of the place.

MATLOCK VILLAGE, about a mile from Matlock Bath, at the time of the Domesday survey was part of the Manor of Metesford. By grant it became the property of William de Ferrars, Earl of Derby, but it again passed to the Crown on the rebellion of his son Robert. Edward I. gave it to the Earl of Lancaster. In the reign of Charles I. it was transferred to Ditchfield and others, who sold it to several individuals. The church is an ancient structure, with a square tower ; the nave and aisles have been rebuilt. An ancient custom until lately prevailed in this village, in common with other places in the Peak, of suspending funeral garlands, carried before the corpses of young unmarried females, from the cross beams of the church. Some of these garlands still hang in the Church. There is a monument in the church to Anthony Wooley and his wife Agnes. The former died in 1578.

MATLOCK BRIDGE, between Matlock Bath and Matlock Bank, is so called from the bridge which here crosses the Derwent. It is a thriving village, well supplied with excellent shops. It has a Post-Office, a Board of Health Office, and other public buildings. The new *Market Hall*, opened in 1869, is a chaste and prettily designed Gothic building, and is conveniently arranged with internal shops and stalls. The *Assembly Rooms* are over the Market Hall. The *Matlock Bridge Station* on the Midland Railway is close to the bridge, and is conveniently arranged for the rapidly-increasing traffic of the place.

At MATLOCK BANK, a rapidly-increasing locality, there are several large and excellently conducted hydropathic establishments. Among these may be mentioned Mr. SMEDLEY'S, one of the largest and best conducted establishments of its kind in the kingdom. It is capable of accommodating some hundreds of patients, and no greater proof of its excellence can be adduced than to say it is always full, and constantly being enlarged. A large and handsome Congregational chapel of Gothic design, with tower and spire, has recently been erected here, as has also a spacious chapel, also with tower and spire, belonging to Mr. Smedley's establishment. The view from Matlock Bank is truly charming. " In the distance, Masson, that huge mountain, rises up from the valley, and towers above its neighbours in gigantic massiveness. At the foot of the mountain, in the bottom of the valley, rolls the river Derwent, crossed by the bridge which gives the name to the railway station beyond. To the right the eye traverses the country of the High Peak on towards Darley Dale, and to the left the High Tor, Matlock Dale, Matlock Church, and the Druid-crowned Riber, skirt the view."

RIBER CASTLE, an enormous building, in course of erection by Mr. Smedley, is on the summit of Riber, and, commanding the most extensive and varied views of the neighbourhood, forms a prominent object in the landscape from almost every side.

In a neighbourhood so rich in natural beauties, and in objects of interest of every kind, the visitor will find amply enough to occupy his attention, and amply sufficient strolls and journeys around the district. It is not necessary here to specify these places, as all the information concerning them will be found in the " Matlock Companion," and other guide-books published in the place

# MELBOURNE.

Population 2800.

Principal Inns.—*White Lion, King's Head, New Inn, Roebuck, Three Tuns,* etc. etc.

From Derby 8 miles.

MELBOURNE, from which place Lord Melbourne derived his title, and from which, through that Premier, Melbourne in Australia takes its name, is a considerable and important market town on the southern confines of the county. It is situated in midst of rich and highly productive land, and is noted for its market gardens, which produce abundance of fruit and vegetables of the finest description. The church, one of the finest specimens of a Norman building in existence, is a very large cruciform structure, with massive central tower, and two minor towers at the west end. It has recently been restored at considerable cost. Its western doorway is remarkably rich in sculpture, and around the interior runs a massive triforium. It contains some good monuments to the Hardinges, the Cokes, and others. The church, which has quite a cathedral air about it, is open on all sides to the roadway and green.

The manor of Melbourne belonged to the Crown, and was granted by King John to Hugh Beauchamp. Having reverted to the Crown, Henry III. gave it to Philip de Marc. It afterwards belonged to the Earl of Lancaster, and with the castle—a magnificent building—remained attached to that duchy till 1604, when it was given to the Earl of Nottingham, who conveyed it to Hastings,

Earl of Huntingdon, from whom it passed down to his successor, the late Marquis of Hastings. Melbourne Castle was for many years the prison of John, Duke of Bourbon, who was taken at the battle of Agincourt. It was dismantled in 1460. The bishops of Carlisle had a palace at Melbourne, with a park, and here they occasionally resided. Near the church is the palace, now Melbourne Hall, which was for a long time the seat of the Cokes, afterwards of the Lambs, Lords Melbourne, then of Lady Palmerston in her own right, and it now belongs to her son the Earl Cowper. It is a fine old building, with extensive grounds, including sheets of water and covered avenues. The gardens are shown to the public weekly during the summer season, and are well worthy a visit.

In the town are an Athenæum, and many Dissenting churches and schools. The principal trade is in silk-gloves; market-day Saturday. A new cemetery, with chapels, has been formed on the Derby Road. By means of the Melbourne and Worthington Branch of the Midland Railway, which has a station at Melbourne, that town is placed in connection with the entire railway system of the kingdom.

KING'S NEWTON, a little distance from the river Trent, nearly adjoining Melbourne, is a large village with an air of "gentility" about it which but few villages possess. It is full of interest, both archæological and literary, and can boast of giving title to Lord Hardinge, who was created by the style of Lord Hardinge of King's Newton. The Hall, the ancient seat of the Hardinges, which stands in the village, was destroyed by fire a few years ago, and now forms a most picturesque ruin, as shewn in the following engraving. But King's Newton has other attractions in its gifted sons. It seems ever to have been the abode of genius. Thomas Hall, author of "Wisdom's

Conquest," resided here ; William Speechly, author of many horticultural works, also resided in the village : as did also F. N. C. Mundy, the charming writer of "Needwood Forest," and the "Fall of Needwood ;" and Mrs. Green, authoress of "John Gray of Willoughby." James Orton, the poet, who wrote "The Enthusiast," "Excelsior,"

"The Three Palaces," and numberless other books, was born there ; as was also his brother Henry, whose writings under the nom-de-plume of "Philo" are well known; and last, though far from least, John Joseph Briggs, the historian of Melbourne, the author of "The Trent," and other poems, and "The Naturalist" of "The Field," and other publications, is a native, and still resident, of its soil.

Henry Kirk, the author of "Thurstan Meverel," has also been a resident of the place. Few villages can boast so brilliant an assemblage of names as this, and few can boast so pleasant and so healthy a situation. The gardens of the old ruined Hall are now used for pleasure parties, and, being only so short a distance from Derby, are much frequented.

CALKE ABBEY, the magnificent seat of Sir John Harpur Crewe, Bart., is about two miles from Melbourne. It is one of the finest and most sumptuous mansions in the county, and is surrounded by a deer park of several miles in circumference.

DONNINGTON PARK, the seat of the late Marquis of Hastings, is near Melbourne, but now of his sister the Countess of Loudoun. It is a splendid mansion, and has recently been thoroughly restored and refitted, in a style commensurate with the rank of its noble owner.

KNOWLE HILLS, a place much resorted to by pleasure parties, is a few miles from Melbourne. It is a truly romantic spot, and is well worthy a visit.

SWARKESTONE, long the abode of the Harpurs, the remains of whose mansion still exist, is on the road from Derby to Melbourne. Here is the famous Swarkestone bridge, nearly a mile in length, over the river Trent and the lowlands adjoining it. At Swarkestone, Bancroft, the Elizabethan poet, was born. In the church are many fine monuments, including one of Judge Harpur and his lady, Jane Fynderne, the last of her race and family.

## MONSAL DALE,

MILLERS DALE, CRESSBROOK DALE, and CHEE TOR, may be visited either in a walking excursion from Bakewell, or by rail from that place or Buxton. The nearest way from Bakewell is by Ashford, famous for its black marble, which is not surpassed, perhaps not equalled, in any part of the world ; its deep unvaried colour, and the compactness of its texture, fit it to receive a high polish ; a mirror can hardly present a clearer or a more beautiful surface. From this village we ascend the Wye, which is here a bright merry rivulet, bubbling sweetly over stones and moss. The character of these three dales is that of a rich spot in the midst of desolation. " Monsal Dale may with peculiar propriety be termed the Arcadia of Derbyshire." At the base of Great Finn, the river Wye forms a beautiful cascade over an abrupt shelving of the rock.

TIDESWELL is a small market-town in the High Peak about three miles from the Millers Dale Station. In the church, which is a large and fine cruciform building with many good features, are monuments to Bishop Pursglove, 1579 ; Sir Sampson Meverell, 1462 ; Thomas Foljambe, 1358 ; and many others of note. The " Grammar-School of Jesus " was founded by Bishop Pursglove. There are also Dissenting chapels and other public buildings in the place.

## NORTON.

From Chesterfield 8 miles ; from Sheffield 4 miles.

INNS.—*Mag o' th' Hay*, etc.

NORTON, chiefly celebrated as being the birth and burial place of Chantrey the sculptor, is a truly pleasant village on the Yorkshire borders of Derbyshire, near the busy town of Sheffield, and is a place of favourite resort with the inhabitants of that place. The manor of Norton, in the time of Edward the Confessor, belonged to Godeva and Nada, and afterwards passed through the families of De Busli, Fitz Ralph, Chaworth, Ormond, Dynham, Babington, etc., till it came into the hands of Shore. In the Church, which is a very large and interesting building with a tower at its west end, are many monuments to the memory of the Blythes, one of whom was bishop of Salisbury, and another bishop of Lichfield ; Eyre, Bullock, Morewood, Selioke, Bagshaw, and others. The old residence of the Blythes at Norton Lees, a fine old timbered building, is still standing, and there are many interesting spots around the place which are worth a visit. Norton Hall, the residence of Mr. Cammell, was formerly that of the Shores, and besides this there is Norton House belonging to Mr. Holy, and the Oaks long the residence of the Bagshaws.

CHANTREY'S BIRTH-PLACE.—" But we must pass on to a spot which, to the stranger at a distance, or to the Norton visitor, is more attractive than Hall or Park, Church or lime-trees—the humble cottage at Jordanthorpe, where England's greatest sculptor first saw the light, on the 7th of April 1781. It is only across a few fields beyond the village, very pleasantly situated ; but owing to modern alterations, is most *un*picturesque as a building. Chantrey's grandfather, of both his names, lived on this small farm at Jordanthorpe, as tenant to the Offleys of Norton ; and there he died, Oct. 25, 1766, at the age of 56. Concerning him even local tradition is silent : nor have I been able to learn where he came from, or whom he married. In the cultivation of the farm at Jordanthorpe, consisting of forty-five acres, the first Norton Chantrey was succeeded by his son Francis, who was also brought up a carpenter, his workshop in later years being the old priest's house in the 'Chantrey Croft,' whence probably arose the speculations on the local origin of the family name. He married, in 1780, Sarah, one of the four daughters of Martin Leggitt, of Okeover, Staffordshire, a man of some property, who died in the house of his son-in-law, and lies buried in Norton churchyard. Francis—father of the sculptor, upon whose 'depression of spirits,' as arising from the departure of ancestral property, so much stress has been laid—is described to me in very different terms by several persons who knew him well. He was, indeed, regarded as no ordinary man in his own sphere of life. He sung a song, told a tale, or bandied a joke but too cleverly for his own welfare. The public-house was not far off ; and still nearer was the hospitable residence of 'Squire Newton,' among whose eccentricities was a too frequent preference of the hilarious frankness of persons in a grade of life below his own, to the more formal intercourse of the neighbouring gentry. With him 'Frank Chantrey' was a great favourite. He died on the 21st March, 1793, at the age of forty-five, leaving a widow and one son, twelve

years of age. Sir Francis Chantrey—the third and last of
the name at Norton—was born at Jordanthorpe, in the
southern precinct of that pleasant village, ' on the 7th of
April 1781, about seven in the morning,' says his mother,
in a memorandum before me ; and he was baptized at the
Parish Church on the 27th of May following."

Chantrey went to the village school at Norton, kept by
Fox the village schoolmaster. The school, shewn in the

accompanying engraving, remains exactly as it was when
the boy " Frank Chantrey " sat on one of its rough forms.
It is a plain building, outside the village, by the lane
leading to Hazlebarrow and Coal Aston. Chantrey afterwards became a " Sheffield Milk-Lad "—that is, he carried
milk from the farm at Jordanthorpe to Sheffield, for sale,
on the back of an ass, daily, and afterwards became ap-
prenticed in Sheffield. It is needless here to trace the

circumstances of his brilliant career in art. It is only necessary to say that he was buried in the churchyard of his native place, in a grave of ample size and of stout masonry, covered with a ponderous slab of gritstone, measuring 18 feet by 8 feet, and 10 inches in thickness, bearing the following inscription :—

M.

FRANCIS CHANTREY,

DIED MVCCLXVI. AGED LVI.

FRANCIS CHANTREY,

DIED MVCCXCIII. AGED XXXXV.

SARAH, HIS WIFE,

DIED MVCCCXXVI. AGED LXXXI.

SIR FRANCIS CHANTREY,

SCULPTOR,

R. A.—F. R. S.

BORN IN THIS PARISH

VII. APRIL,

MVCCLXXXI.

DIED IN LONDON

NOV. XXV.

MVCCCXXXXI.

This tomb, prepared by Sir Francis himself, is enclosed within iron railings. Besides this a small neat marble tablet has been placed in the chancel: it bears no ornament, with the exception of a medallion likeness, carved by Heffernan, in the centre of the cornice, and is thus inscribed—

SIR FRANCIS CHANTREY, R. A.

SCULPTOR,

H.D.C.L.—F.R.S.—M.A.

Born Apl. VII. MDCCLXXXI. Died Nov. XXV. MDCCCXLI.

To these local memorials was added, a few years since, by means of a public subscription, laudably promoted by the Rev. H. Pearson, the vicar, a handsome granite obelisk, of the form shewn in the annexed engraving. It is erected on

" the green," nearly opposite the Parsonage, and forms at once a striking object in itself ; an appropriate memorial of " CHANTREY," whose name it bears ; and a feature that combines harmoniously with those of the scene immediately surrounding it.

## REPTON.

Principal Inn.—The *Mitre*.
From Derby 7 miles; from Burton-on-Trent 4 miles; from the Willington
Railway Station 1½ mile.

Repton, formerly the capital of the kingdom of Mercia, and the burial-place of its kings, is a large and important village, rich in historical associations and in remains of antiquity. Repton Priory, some small remains of which still exist, was one of the richest and finest in the kingdom. At the dissolution its revenues were estimated at £118 : 8 : 6 clear. It was given to Thacker. The church is a remarkably fine and interesting building, with a lofty and particularly elegant spire. Underneath the chancel is a perfect Saxon crypt, well worthy of examination, with a groined roof supported by twisted columns, and one of the most perfect pieces of architecture of that early period anywhere existing. In the church are several interesting monuments to the Thacker family and others, and to different head-masters of the school.

The school at Repton, which ranks next to Eton and Rugby, was founded by Sir John Porte in 1556, and has been considerably increased in size and importance. The buildings are remarkably firm and good, and the arrangements of the most perfect description. *

One side of the residence of the head-master (which adjoins the school) exhibits one of the finest and most curious pieces of early brick-work in the kingdom. Near

---

* A highly interesting discovery of a mediæval encaustic tile kiln has recently been made in the school-grounds. The tiles are of the 13th century. A fully-illustrated account of this discovery has been given in vol. viii. of the " Reliquary."

the church and schools is a noble archway belonging to the old conventual buildings, and in the village street are the remains of a cross. Repton supports a literary institution, and is altogether a most desirable and pleasant village either for a residence or a visit. It is lit with gas, and has Petty Sessions held weekly.

WILLINGTON, a rural village, near Repton, has a church with a good Norman doorway.

ETWALL is a large and important village with a most interesting church, in which are many fine monuments and monumental brasses to the Portes and others, and the famed "Hospital" for a certain number of pensioners. This village, with its church, its old Hall, and its hospital, is well worth the attention of the tourist.

FINDERN, three miles from Repton, was long the residence of the De Fynderne family, whose Hall has long since disappeared. The old church has recently been taken down, and a new one erected on its site. In the course of its removal some highly interesting slabs of the Fyndernes were brought to light, and have been fully described and illustrated by Mr. Jewitt in the "Reliquary." The new church is a picturesque little building erected from the designs of Mr. Stevens.

MICKLEOVER, six miles from Repton, is an important village with a fine old church. The Hall or Manor House, recently rebuilt, is the seat of C. E. Newton, Esq. At Mickleover is the Derby County Lunatic Asylum, a splendid and convenient building.

BRETBY CASTLE, the splendid seat of the Earl of Chesterfield, is three miles from Repton.

ANCHOR CHURCH, an interesting hermitage by the Trent,

is also at a short distance, and will well repay the trouble of a stroll thither.

FOREMARK HALL, long the residence of the celebrated Sir Francis Burdett, is two miles from Repton. It is now the residence of Henry Alsopp, Esq., the eminent brewer.

## RIPLEY.

Principal INN—The *Thorn Tree.*
From Derby 8 miles ; from Belper 3 miles.

RIPLEY is a market town in midst of a busy iron and coal district. It has a church and several dissenting places of worship. The inhabitants are principally employed in the coal and ironstone pits, and at the ironworks in the neighbourhood, and at the silk-lace manufactory. Ripley is under a *Local Board of Health,* and Petty Sessions are held weekly. The *Bank* is a branch of the Nottingham Joint-Stock Bank. There are also a *Cemetery* and *Burial Board.* A Newspaper, the *Ripley Advertiser,* is published weekly.

The BUTTERLEY IRONWORKS, to which allusion has been made under the head of Codnor Park and Ironville, are near Ripley, and employ several hundred people.

At DENBY are Bourne's potteries and manufactories of their stoneware bottles, etc. These works find employment for a large number of hands. In the same neighbourhood are immense ironworks, recently founded, and several extensive collieries. Denby is said to have been the birthplace of Flamstead the astronomer.

At KILBOURNE are the celebrated Kilbourne collieries.

# ROWSLEY.

Hotel—The *Peacock* (Cooper) family hotel. From this hotel conveyances
for Chatsworth, Haddon Hall, and all the places of interest in the
neighbourhood can be had. Parties staying at the hotel have privilege
of fishing in the Wye and Derwent.

Rowsley is a quiet and very delightful little village on
the line of railway between Matlock and Buxton. Being 4
miles from Chatsworth, 1½ from Haddon Hall, 4 from
Bakewell, 4 from Youlgreave, 1 from Darley Dale, and 7
from Matlock, it forms a desirable centre for the tourist.
The principal building in the village is the celebrated
" Peacock at Rowsley," so well known to anglers all the
world over ; and a most comfortable and enjoyable place
it is for the tourist or the sojourning family.

A new church has of late years been erected at Rowsley.
It is a very chaste and elegant little building, and in its
interior contains one of the most exquisitely beautiful
monuments which modern times have produced. This is
an altar tomb to the young and amiable wife of Lord
John Manners, and their infant. Lady John Manners died
on the 7th of April 1854, aged twenty-three. The style of
the monument partakes of the Middle Pointed Gothic, and
the materials used are all from Derbyshire. It principally
consists of stone known as " Darley Dale stone," with russet
marble columns—the carved capitals, the panels, and the
figure being of alabaster from Chellaston near Derby. The
monument is fixed in a mortuary chapel in the church,
which Lord John Manners has caused to be erected for its
reception. The floor is inlaid with rich marble mosaics,
on the centre of which the monument is fixed. The effect

is beautiful and striking, and altogether may be considered a good specimen of nineteenth century art. The whole of the works were designed and carried out under the superintendence of Mr. A. Salvin jun. The figures were executed by Calder Marshall, R.A.; and the sculpture and architectural part of the monument was by Mr. James Forsyth, of Edward Street, Hampstead Road. The recumbent effigy of Lady John Manners, with her infant by her side, is one of the most chaste and purely designed figures which it is possible to conceive. The drapery is easy and graceful in its folds, the contour of the figures perfect in every respect, and the air of repose faithful to nature.

The village is situated between the rivers Wye and Derwent, where the former falls into the latter, and the Derwent is here spanned by a fine stone bridge, near which the roadway is crossed by the line of railway.

The railway station, about 200 yards from the "Peacock," is commodious and well arranged, with platforms covered in with glass.

## STONEY MIDDLETON.

INNS.—*Moon ; Lover's Leap ; Grouse ; Miners' Arms.*
From Bakewell, 6 m. ; from Castleton, 10 m. ; from Haddon Hall, 9. m.

STONEY MIDDLETON is a large mining and agricultural village in the High Peak. The manor belonged at an early period to the Chaworths, under whom it was held by Bernake, who sold it to Furnival, from whom it passed to the Cavendishes. The church, a curious octagonal building, contains memorials to Finny and others. There are also dissenting places of worship and schools.

The HALL, the seat of Lord Denman, is a picturesque building near the church. It was long the residence of Chief Justice Denman, who was raised to the peerage by the title of **Baron Denman.**

The BATHS are near the church, and are said to be of Roman origin, and to have been dedicated to St. Martin. The water is tepid, and the baths are beautifully situated in a quiet sylvan spot, shaded by trees, and the grounds intersected by winding paths. " That this bath was established by the Romans may not be easily established at this remote period of time ; but when we consider that they long occupied this part of the kingdom, and that the use of the tepid bath was probably introduced by them into this country, the opinion appears not altogether groundless."

The village is remarkably picturesque. " About the centre of the village is the toll-gate, a characteristic little modern Gothic octagonal building, resting upon arches, beneath which the stream, after running the entire length of the dale, empties into a large mill-dam. The village mill, worked by a ponderous overshot water-wheel, has recently been rebuilt apparently in such a style of superiority and convenience as is but seldom seen. The view from the centre of the village near the toll-bar is picturesque in the extreme ; immediately in front of us is a steep rough ascent leading to the upper part of the village, on each side of which the cottages are seen rising tier above tier in the wildest confusion, and built in such nearly inaccessible places as would almost seem to preclude the possibility of their being approached. In some places the solid rock has been cut away to admit of room on which the buildings might be erected, while in others, outhouses have literally been scooped out of the immense stony masses, and the doors of some of the residences may be seen opening above the chimney tops of others. Intermingled with the houses are projecting masses of rock, from which tall trees in some places grow out in wild profusion. To our left is the toll-gate, where two roads converge ; the one leading by the village cross to Baslow, etc., and the other to the lower part of the village and the church. Immediately behind the house from which we are examining this striking view the rock rises perpendicularly above the roof to a considerable height, and frowns down upon the valley below in majestic silence, bearing on its crest, immediately over our heads, two chapels and several cottages, between which a rugged and steep path ascends to the top of the cliff, while to our right the wild majestic dale opens its rocky portals, beneath which the houses appear to nestle for shelter and warmth, to receive us."

MIDDLETON DALE is a long narrow vale with a rapid stream running through it. " The glory of Middleton," says Mr. L. Jewitt, in " Nooks and Corners of Derbyshire," " is its Dale, at the opening of which the rocks gradually rise in all their nakedness, on the right towering above the houses, whilst on the left the rugged slopes are thickly wooded between the habitations. On entering the Dale, the first grand object which attracts attention is the celebrated rock called the Lover's Leap, rearing its bold blackened front perpendicularly to a prodigious height above a substantial inn bearing the same name, kept by ' mine host' Mason, romantically situated at its base. The circumstance which gave rise to the singular name—the Lover's Leap—by which this rock is known, occurred in about the year 1760, when a love-stricken maiden, named Hannah Baddeley, finding that her affections were not returned by a young man to whom she was madly attached, and who instead treated her with coldness and disdain, in a moment of deep despondency and despair threw herself from its summit, in the hope of destroying her life, which had become so burdensome to her. Her fall was, however, fortunately broken by some small trees which grew out of the crevices, and she fell into a sawpit in an insensible state, where she was found, and having been removed home, gradually recovered from the serious injuries she had received ; and although she was crippled ever afterwards in consequence, lived a single and most exemplary life for about two years, when she died. In the church-yard a mutilated and almost worn-out gravestone shews the place of her burial ; and although the inscription is now nearly obliterated, the spot is well remembered by the villagers,

who almost seem to venerate the memory of this melancholy love-martyr.

" From here masses of rock jut out one above the other
all the way up the dale on the right hand side, while on
the left the steep ascent is for the most part covered with
herbage, with here and there circular masses of solid
masonry, used as lime kilns, and whose strong archways
and tower-like fronts give them a castellated appearance,
and remind us of the strongholds of a race of giants. A
little way above the Lover's Leap are the Barytes Works,
where that material, having been ground, washed, and
afterwards bleached with vitriol, is converted into white
paint ; and adjoining is the lower Cupola, or smelting
works, for extracting the lead from the ore. Opposite this
is the ' Grip,' an opening between the rocks, leading by a
steep and dangerous ascent to the cliffs above.

" Close to the Grip a giant Tor rises perpendicularly to
an immense height, towering above the dale in absolute awe
and majesty, and, unlike most of the rocks in the dale, its
broad front is almost unbroken, and appears as one compact and solid mass ; one portion being thickly overgrown
with ivy, seems but to render the appearance of the rest
more sterile and bare, and, contrasting with its cold grey
front, seems to add to its solemnity and grandeur ; up its
sides grow tolerable trees, while tufts of grass fringe the
ledges formed by the almost horizontal lines of strata, and
thousands of martens flit to and fro, and keep up a continual chirping as they light on their suspended nests.
From here the chain of rocks continues forward to the glory
of the dale, the Castle Rock, standing out in front of the
rest, the intermediate space being crowned by sloping
greensward, through which enormous pinnacles of the

massive rock rise up perpendicularly towards the sky. The Castle Rock is of immense height, and is not inappropriately named, for its front is flanked by two tower-like projections, spreading gradually out to their base like natural buttresses. About mid-way up its front is a narrow shelf of rock, leading to a sort of natural alcove, called the rock garden, which venturesome people sometimes visit. Above this, growing out of a small cleft in the face of the rock, is a large ash tree, spreading out its branches, and affording shelter for numberless birds, whilst below a portion of the bold projections are overgrown with luxuriant ivy.

" From this point the strata of the rock is very distinctly seen lying, layer above layer, almost horizontally, and seeming to the eye as though, in the first formation of the earth, the great hand of a giant builder had carefully spread out one course of liquid stone, and having levelled it, and smoothed its surface, had, after it had become hardened, again poured over it course upon course, and thus continued his work until the enormous pile of rock was complete ; or like layer upon layer of lava, as if it had flowed out in a stream from some gigantic crater on successive eruptions, burying in its course the thousands of living animals which still remain petrified on the surface and sprinkled over the broad front of this piece of regular natural masonry. Beyond this the rocks again fall back from the roadway, and one turret or pinnacle rises high up in the air far above the rest, like the watchtower on a castle wall, and so completely is it detached from the rest of the rock, that the clear blue sky can be distinctly seen through the cleft on its side. On this point of rock more than one daring person has, with consummate foolhardiness, we are told, stood on his head :

and it is related that one of the villagers, in a drunken frolic, having enlisted into the army, was, in a more sober mood, desirous of withdrawing his rash promise ; upon this, the officer offered that if he would stand on his head on this frightful pinnacle he would give him his discharge ; this, to the astonishment of all, he did, and having descended in safety, was rewarded by having his liberty granted.

" Under this rock the stone has been quarried very considerably, and large mounds of the waste material, overgrown with grass, now cover up its base, and in one portion of it is a cavern, which, if at money-making Matlock, would be made quite a fortune to the owner. A little beyond this point a deep chasm or cleft separates the rock from crown to base, as though cracked in two by some mighty convulsion, and in front. a clump of luxuriant trees contrasts strongly with the whiteness of the rocks and adds in appearance much to their imposing altitude. A little farther on is a cavern, known by the names of " Carl's Work," and " Scotchman's Hole," in the lower part of the solid perpendicular face of the rock. In this cavern the water sometimes rises to a considerable height, and rushes out into the open dale ; this circumstance was the cause of the discovery of a murder committed here about a century ago, for the torrent which rushed out carried into the dale a human foot with a shoe, on which was a silver buckle. On the subsiding of the waters a careful search was made, and other remains of the unfortunate man discovered ; the finding of the buckle, and other circumstances, led to the identification of the body, which proved to be that of a well-known rich old Scotch pedlar, who was in the habit of passing through the place,

T

and who, it appeared, had been murdered at one of the inns of the village where he was staying ; this is one of the current traditions of the village. Above this the bleached crest of the rock rises, tier above tier, to an immense height, its summit fringed with shrubs and grass, and a little higher up the dale crested with a fine clump of lofty fir and other trees, which skirt the surface for some distance, until the bold crest of ridge rocks rise above them. A little farther stands the Golden Ball, a quaint, solitary road-side inn, at the corner of Eyam Dale, behind which the rocks rise one above another, and form an acute angle of tower-like proportions, of the most sublime character. The opposite side of the entrance to this beautiful dale is also rocky, but of much less altitude, and completely covered and hidden by a thick plantation of trees. From here Middleton Dale continues towards Castleton, while opposite Eyam Dale a road winds up the steeps to Middleton Moor, and at this point are ranged a series of limekilns, of immense size, the smoke which arises from them curling upwards, and forming itself into light blue vapoury-looking clouds, wreathing fantastically about the rocks, and adding much to the gorgeous effect of the whole picture. A little higher on the right a sweet valley, with rocky posterns and wooded heights, opens up to that holy and classic spot in village history, the Delph, at Eyam, which we have before described.

"Passing this spot the dale becomes more contracted, the sides sloping steeply and precipitately, and covered with grass and small trees, while from the top, on the right, masses of rock jut out and rise at almost regular intervals, and are fringed on their summits with forest trees, amongst whose branches hundreds of rooks and daws congregate.

Here the road winds around the base of the rocks, and after passing the upper cupola, or lead-smelting works, where hundreds of tons of pig-lead may be seen piled up around the picturesque and quaint-looking buildings, follows its onward course through the beautiful valley, winding and threading its way amongst rocks and woods, and keeping up a close companionship with the rippling stream, which runs sparkling by its side."

BASLOW, a pretty village, is pleasantly situated on the banks of the Derwent, about two miles from Stoney Middleton, and one mile from Chatsworth Hall; the population is little above a thousand. The church is a neat and commodious building, standing on the edge of the river. In the churchyard are some interesting ancient slabs and stone coffins. Much of the moorland property in the neighbourhood belongs to the Duke of Rutland, who formerly spent about a week annually at the village. The park lodges of Chatsworth are at the east end of the village.

CALVER is principally noted for its large cotton-mill, called CALVER MILLS. We cross the river, and enter Calver, two miles from Baslow, a small village of lime-burners and cotton-spinners. A church has recently been erected in this place, near the mills.

BUBNELL is near Baslow. It is a small hamlet, the old hall of which is now used as a school.

## WINGFIELD MANOR.

About half a mile from the Wingfield Station of the North Midland
Railway.

WINGFIELD MANOR, one of the most charming ruins in
the kingdom, is delightfully situated on the brow of a hill
overlooking the surrounding country on all sides, and
forming a conspicuous object for many miles. The Manor
House was erected, on the site of a more ancient building,
in the reign of Henry VI. by Ralph, Lord Cromwell, and
was dismantled in the civil wars. It is one of the most
perfectly beautiful of all the ruins of the period now remaining, and from its many historical associations is indeed one of the most interesting Here Mary Queen of
Scots was confined for several years ; here the conspiracy
to liberate her, which, unfortunately, was unsuccessful, was
formed, and here some of the terrible scenes of the civil
wars were enacted. The building was first garrisoned for
the Parliament, afterwards taken by the Royalists, and
then retaken by Sir John Gell in a terrible engagement in
which the governor was killed. It was then dismantled
and allowed to fall into decay, and has thus formed the
charming ruin which the visitor to Derbyshire ought on
no account to omit visiting. The unfortunate Mary Queen
of Scots was confined at Wingfield in November and December 1584, as well as several times previously, and she
was removed from there to Tutbury Castle, on the 13th of
January in the following year, 1585. In November 1584,
no less than two hundred gentlemen, yeomen, officers, and
soldiers, were employed in the custody of her person at

Wingfield. Her domestic establishment at that time consisted of five gentlemen, fourteen servitors, three cooks, four boys, three gentlemens' men, six gentlewomen, two wives, and ten wenches and children.

The building consisted of two main courts, with a remarkably fine entrance gateway. Most of the building, though of course entirely in ruins, still remains, and attests to its former extent and magnificence. In its interior is a farm-house, and the visitor will find no difficulty, by aid of a gratuity, in getting permission to examine these interesting remains.

In South Wingfield Church are some monuments to the Halton family and others. The inhabitants are principally employed in stocking-making.

# WINSTER.

Principal INNS.—*The Angel* (W. Burton); *The Crown* (J. Burton).
From Matlock Bath, 6 m.; from Chatsworth, 6 m.; from Wirksworth 6 m.;
Bakewell, 6 m.; from Darley Dale Station, 2¾ m.

WINSTER is one of the oldest market-towns in the county, though the market is now disused. At the time of taking the Domesday Survey, Winster belonged to Henry de Ferrars. The manor afterwards belonged to the Mount-joys, and after them to the Meynells, by whom it was sold to the freeholders in the reign of Queen Elizabeth.

The CHURCH, dedicated to St. John the Baptist, is situated at the end of the town, and embosomed in trees. It was rebuilt some years ago, and is devoid of any remarkable architectural features. It contains a fine and very curious Norman font. There is a peal of five bells. Besides the church, Winster contains three other places of worship—viz., one chapel belonging to the Wesleyan Methodists, one to the Primitive Methodists (Winster being the head of a circuit), and one to the Reform Methodists. The Post-Office is in the High Street.

In the market-place is a curious and highly picturesque old market-house, which has originally been open beneath and the building itself supported on arches.

The NATIONAL SCHOOLS, recently erected at a short distance outside of the town on the Matlock road, are very commodious and well arranged. They are built in the Gothic style of architecture, with a central bell-turret. The residences for the master and mistress are attached.

Winster is one of the polling places for North Derbyshire, and it is also a Telegraph station. A public newsroom has been established, and quite recently a good supply of water has been brought into the town as a free gift to the inhabitants.

The principal seats are those of Miss WORSLEY, pleasantly situated at the east end of the town, and ODDO HOUSE, at the west end. Near this is the vicarage, recently erected, which is the residence of the Rev. H. Milnes.

The HALL, in the centre of the town, stands back from the main street, and is approached by a pair of gates with massive old posts. The Hall itself is an imposing looking old mansion, with pillars, decorated with roses and fleurs-de-lis, up its front. It was built by the family of Moore. It is now the residence of Mr. Llewellynn Jewitt, F.S.A., the editor of this volume and of the "Reliquary," and author of several antiquarian works.

The inhabitants are principally engaged in lead-mining and agriculture. The neighbourhood is highly picturesque and beautiful, the principal attractions being Robin Hood's Stride, Rootor Rocks, and Cratcliffe Rocks. The view from Winster Tor and the ridge of hills on which it is situated is remarkably fine and extensive.

# WIRKSWORTH.

Population 8600.

HOTELS and INNS.—The *Red Lion*; *Crown*; *Spread Eagle*; *George*; *Wheat Sheaf*, etc. etc. etc.

From Cromford Station 2¼ miles; from Derby 13 miles; from Matlock Bath 3 miles.

WIRKSWORTH is an ancient market town, and gives name to the Wapentake in which it is situated. It lies in a hollow two miles from Cromford, and three from Matlock Bath. Lead was wrought here in the time of Hadrian, and after him by the Saxons. The brass dish called the Miners' Standard Dish, used for measuring the lead ore, is still preserved in the Moot Hall, this being the place where all mining cases for the Wapentake are tried. It belongs to the time of Henry VIII., and has an interesting inscription engraved on its sides. The township of Wirksworth contains two manors besides the chief manor, which belonged to Repton Priory, but afterwards became vested in the crown. It was granted by King John to William de Ferrars, Earl of Derby, and afterwards by Edward I. to Edmund Earl of Lancaster, in which duchy it has since remained. Courts Baron for this manor, Courts Leet for the Wapentake, and Barmote Courts for the mining concerns of the Wapentake, are held. The inhabitants are chiefly employed in the lead mines.

The CHURCH, dedicated to St. Mary, and lately altered and restored by Mr. Gilbert Scott, is a handsome Gothic structure, built in cathedral style, and contains several ancient monuments. It consists of a nave with side aisles and transepts, a choir with side aisles, and a square tower, supported by four large pillars in the centre. It is a large cruciform building capable of seating 2000 persons. It has 200 free seats, and the organ is endowed with £1000, three per cent consols, for defraying the salary of the organist. The vicar is entitled by custom to every fortieth dish (of fourteen pints) of lead-ore raised in the parish, but the quantity of late years has been very small. In the north aisle of the church is a fine piece of ancient sculpture representing various events in the life of our Saviour. It is of the Norman period, and, from its having been buried for ages, is well preserved. There are also some interesting brasses and slabs to the Vernons of Haddon, the Blackwells, and monuments to the Gells, including the great Parliamentary officer, Sir John Gell; the Wigleys, Lowes, Hurts, etc.; and a fine memorial window, in remembrance of Francis Hurt, Esq., has recently been erected. The vicarage adjoins the churchyard. The MOOT HALL, where mining cases are tried, was erected in 1814 by the Hon. Charles Bathurst, at that time chancellor of the duchy. On its front are sculptured the miners' arms. A Barmote Court, and Court Leet, and Baron are held here twice a-year.

MARKET DAY is Tuesday, and there are several good fairs in the course of the year.

A BRANCH LINE of the Midland Railway from Wirksworth to Duffield, where it joins the main line, and connects it with the entire railway system of the kingdom, is now in operation.

The COUNTY COURT is held at the Moot Hall monthly. Petty Sessions are held weekly in the Moot Hall.

The Independents, Baptists, Wesleyans, Primitive Methodists, and Reform Methodists, have each a place of worship here ; and the Independents also worship in the Temperance Hall. The General Cemetery, North End, was consecrated in 1856. It occupies about three acres of ground, and has two neat chapels, for Churchmen and Dissenters, with a residence for the sexton. The cost was upwards of £1500. The Free Grammar School is a handsome Gothic building, re-built in 1828 at a cost of £1664. The present rental of the charity estates is £295, out of which £170 is paid in salaries to the masters. It is managed by governors or trustees. The National School, North End, erected in 1851, is a handsome stone building in the Elizabethan style, with residence for the master and mistress attached. A parochial library, established in 1846, is kept at the Grammar School. The Mechanics' Institute, in the Market Place, established in 1852, has a good library, and the reading-room supplied with periodicals and newspapers. The Temperance Hall at Beeley Croft was built in 1860 at a cost of £600. The Cricket Ground is near Millers' Green. The Savings' Bank, St. John's Street, is a handsome structure, erected in 1842. The bank was established in 1818, and is open on Tuesday from eleven to one o'clock. The Gas Works, erected in 1848, are at Warmbrook, and Messrs. Arkwright and Company have a bank in the town. The Barmote Courts, for the Wapentake, are held twice a year, at the Moot Hall.

At Whitsuntide the annual custom of " Tap Dressing " —somewhat like the Well Dressing at Tissington and Buxton—is here observed.

BONSALL is two miles west of Matlock Bath. A very pleasant excursion of five miles may be made from the latter place, through Cromford to Bonsall. By extending the walk to the length of nine miles, Wirksworth and

Hopton Hall may be included. The church is an old structure, situated on a rock above the dale. The village cross is ancient. The population, which numbers about 1500, is employed in stocking-making, making combs, and in mining.

HOPTON HALL may be visited from Bonsall by traversing the " Via Gellia," a road so called, by the late Philip Gell, Esq., by whom it was formed. High sloping acclivities covered with hazel, and sparingly sprinkled with dwarf oak and ash, mark each side of the road. As we near Hopton the country loses much of its wildness ; the limestone hills and crags have become softened down into gently sloping eminences, covered with trees and herbage, rich in the ore hidden beneath its verdant surface. The hall has been the family-seat of the Gells for above two centuries, who received it from its more ancient owners, the De Hoptons. John Gell, the then representative, was created baronet by Charles I. in 1642, notwithstanding which he did not scruple to take up arms in the cause of the Parliament. With the third baronet, Sir Philip Gell, who died in 1719, the title became extinct.

Not far from Hopton, on the route to Dovedale, are the villages of Carsington and Brassington, provincially pronounced " Carson" and " Brasson."

## YOULGREAVE.

Principal INN.—*The Bull's Head* (Winson).
From Bakewell 5 miles ; from Rowsley 5 miles.

YOULGREAVE is an extensive mining village in the High Peak, in midst of a district rich in the most glorious scenery which even Derbyshire can boast. At the time of the Domesday survey the manor belonged to Henry de Ferrars. In the reign of Henry I. it was held, under the Earl of Lancaster, by Ralph de Shirley, from whom it passed successively to the Rossingtons, Knivetons, Barnesleys, and Buxtons, by whom it was sold to the Earl of Rutland, in 1685, and now belongs to the Duke of Rutland.

The Church, which has lately been thoroughly restored, is a very large and fine building, with a massive battlemented tower. In it are Norman remains; a singular font ; and monuments to the families of Gilbert, Cokaine, Rossington, etc. In the village are several Dissenting places of worship, and an excellent national school.

MIDDLETON BY YOULGREAVE is a delightful little village about a mile from Youlgreave, unlike which, it is profusely and beautifully wooded. Middleton Hall, a seat of T. W. Bateman, Esq. (now a minor), is a fine substantial building, surrounded by extensive grounds. Fulwoods Castle, the site of which is still to be seen near the road, was formerly an extensive building belonging to the Fulwoods, one of whom was shot in a rock called " Fulwood's Rock " during the Civil Wars, by some Parliamentary soldiers under Sir John Gell. The manor belonged to the Herthills, and afterwards to the Cockaines, from whom it passed to the Fulwoods, then to the Curzons, Sanders, and

Howe, and was purchased from Lord Howe by the late Thomas Bateman, Esq., and now belongs to his great-grandson. A new church, erected in the village, was opened on the 15th of June 1865, but has been closed almost ever since that time ! There are Independent and Primitive Methodist chapels. The Inn is the *Bateman Arms.*

LOMBERDALE HOUSE, the residence of the late Thomas Bateman, Esq., the eminent antiquary, is situated between Youlgreave and Middleton. In it is located the magnificent Bateman Museum of Antiquities, collected by that gentleman and his father. Mr. Bateman was author of " Vestiges of the Antiquities of Derbyshire," and " Ten Years' Diggings in Celtic Grave-Mounds." The museum one of the finest private collections in existence, is now closed to the public.

BRADFORD DALE, one of the most exquisite valleys in the county, lies below Youlgreave, the village being built on the summit and side of one of the mountains which forms it. The dale may well be entered at Alport, and followed to Middleton, the visitor then returning by Middleton Dale, through the village, and past Lomberdale House back to Youlgreave.

LATHKILIN DALE is also a charming dale, and the visitor will do well to follow it from Alport to Oneash, returning by the roadway over Middleton Moor to Youlgreave.

ARBOR LOW, a splendid Druidical circle, next in extent and importance to Stonehenge, is about four miles from Youlgreave, and ought to be seen by every visitor who takes an interest in remains of antiquity.

# INDEX.

U

# BLACK'S
# GUIDE BOOK ADVERTISER
# 1873.
### (*Hotels arranged Alphabetically according to Locality.*)

# GLASGOW & THE HIGHLANDS.

### (*Royal Route* via *Crinan and Caledonian Canals.*)

#### THE ROYAL MAIL STEAMERS—

| | | | |
|---|---|---|---|
| IONA, | CHEVALIER, | GONDOLIER, | STAFFA, |
| MOUNTAINEER, | PIONEER, | EDINBURGH, | LINNET, |
| CLANSMAN, | CLYDESDALE, | CYGNET, | PLOVER, |

#### MARY JANE, AND INVERARAY CASTLE,

Sail during the season for Oban, Fort-William, Inverness, Staffa, Iona, Glencoe, Tobermory, Portree, Gairloch, Ullapool, Lochinver and Storno-way; affording Tourists an opportunity of Visiting the Magnificent Scenery of Glencoe, the Coolin Hills, Loch Coruisk, Loch Maree, and the famed islands of Staffa and Iona.

\*\*\* These vessels afford in their passage a view of the beautiful scenery of the Clyde, with all its Watering-Places—the Island and Kyles of Bute—Island of Arran—Moun-tains of Cowal, Knapdale, and Kintyre—Lochfyne—Crinan—with the Islands of Jura, Scarba, Mull, and many others of the Western Sea—The Whirlpool of Corryvreckan—the Mountains of Lorn, of Morven, of Appin, of Kingairloch, and Ben Nevis—Inver-lochy—The Lands of Lochiel, the scene of the wanderings of Prince Charles, and near to where the clans raised his Standard in the '45—Lochaber—the Caledonian Canal—Loch Lochy—Loch Oich—Loch Ness, with the Glens and Mountains on either side, and the celebrated FALLS OF FOYERS. Books descriptive of the route may be had on board the Steamers.

Time-Bills, with Maps, sent post free on application to the Proprietors, DAVID HUTCHESON and Co., 119 Hope Street, Glasgow.

GLASGOW, 1873.

A

# ABERFELDY.
# BREADALBANE ARMS HOTEL,

*(One minute's walk from the Railway Station)*

Containing First-class accommodation, is beautifully situated on the river Tay, in the County of Perth, close to the splendid Falls of Moness (Birks of Aberfeldy), Taymouth Castle, and the unrivalled scenery of Glen Lyon.

Parties leaving Edinburgh and Glasgow in the morning, and arriving in Aberfeldy by the first train, can enjoy a five hours' drive through the finest scenery in the Highlands (including Pass of Glen Lyon, Taymouth Castle and grounds from the "Fort"), and return south by the last train.

*Orders for Horses and Conveyances punctually attended to.*

**The Hotel 'Bus awaits the arrival of all the Trains.**

ABERFELDY, *April* 1873.

---

# WEEM HOTEL, ABERFELDY.

One Mile from Aberfeldy Station.    Omnibuses await all Trains.

## JAMES WATERS, PROPRIETOR.

THIS Hotel, beautifully situated at the foot of Weem Rock and gate of Menzies Castle, so well known for its excellent accommodation for First-Class Families, Tourists, &c., has been fitted up with Plunge, Shower, and Douche Baths, supplied with magnificent water from a height of 700 feet, and well adapted for Hydropathic practice. Male and female Bath attendance for families wishing to practise the Hydropathic system, free of charge.    Self-acting hot water apparatus to supply the Baths.

Episcopal Church, Rev. E. Tollinach.

Posting complete.    Every kind of Carriage.    Fishing on River Tay.

The Hotel has a dry southern exposure, protected from north and east winds.

---

# ABERGELE, NORTH WALES.
# THE CAMBRIAN HOTEL,

## PENSARN, ABERGELE.

---

## R. HUMPHREYS, PROPRIETOR.

---

Close to the Station, and within two minutes' walk of the Beach, for Boarding or Private Apartments, Posting, etc.    Wines and Spirits of the best quality.

A spacious Billiard Room has lately been added to the Hotel, with a first-class new Billiard Table, by the eminent makers Burroughes and Watts.

# ABERYSTWITH.

# THE QUEEN'S HOTEL.

### 𝔄 first-class Family Establishment.

THIS Hotel stands on the best part of the Marine Terrace, facing, and is within fifty yards of the sea at all times of the tide. It is open to the south-west, and is effectually sheltered on the north and east by the Craig-lâs mountain range. The building being of stone embedded in hydraulic lime, a residence has been secured which is cool in summer and warm in winter. It contains, in addition to noble public rooms, Ladies' Drawing-Room, Assembly Room, Billiard Rooms, numerous private Sitting Rooms, and upwards of one hundred Bed-Rooms.

BOARD, RESIDENCE, AND ATTENDANCE (inclusive terms),
£4 : 4s. PER WEEK.

### TABLE D'HOTE at Seven o'clock.

Tariff, with Heywood's "Aberystwith Guide," free, on application to "The Mid-Wales Hotel Company, Aberystwith."

*Omnibuses await the arrival of every Train.*

# BANGOR, NORTH WALES.

## BRITISH HOTEL.

### T. H. PHILLIPS, PROPRIETOR.

HANDSOME Coffee-Room, Private Sitting-Rooms, and Large Airy Bed-Rooms. Near the Station. Bus free, and attends all the day trains. Charges moderate.

BILLIARD ROOM.

## BEAULY HOTEL

*(Ten Miles North of Inverness, on the Highland Railway.)*

THE Proprietor of this HOTEL has much pleasure in informing Sportsmen, Tourists, Anglers, Commercial Gentlemen, and the Public, that this newly-erected, large, and commodious Establishment has now been opened for some time, and is situated in the midst of scenery the loveliest in the north of Scotland, in the neighbourhood of which are the beautiful Grounds of Lovat and Beaufort Castle, Belladrum Gardens and House. The famous Falls of Kilmorack, the Dhreim, the wild and romantic river and mountain scenery of Strath-Glass, Ealenegus, the unrivalled Glen Affrick, the Chisholm's Pass, Glen-Strathfarar, Guisachan, and other beautiful localities, frequented by tourists, sportsmen, anglers, artists, and lovers of nature, are all within easy reach of this Hotel. Salmon and Trout Fishing on the Beauly River in connection with the Hotel. Omnibuses attend all trains for the Hotel. The Posting Department the most efficient in the north of Scotland. D. ROBERTSON, *Proprietor.*

## BIDEFORD, DEVONSHIRE.

TANTON'S Family Hotel, Bideford, has been long and favourably known as being most comfortable and inexpensive. It is situated on the banks of the river Torridge, and commands an extensive view of the surrounding scenery.

A good Coffee and Billiard Room. An Omnibus from the Hotel meets every train. Private Omnibuses and Carriages can be had to meet any train on the shortest notice.

# BLAIR-ATHOLE.

# ATHOLE ARMS HOTEL.

THIS Hotel, which has been recently added to, and entirely re-furnished, will be found most complete and well appointed in every department.

Blair-Athole is the most central point from which to make Excursions to Killiecrankie, Loch Tummel, Rannoch, Glen Tilt, Braemar ; the Falls of Bruar, Garry, Tummel, and Fender ; the grounds of Blair Castle, &c.; and is the most convenient resting-place for breaking the long railway journey to and from the North of Scotland.

Orders by Post or Telegraph for Apartments or Carriages carefully attended to.

D. & P. T. MACDONALD, *Proprietors.*

## BLAIRGOWRIE.

# ROYAL HOTEL.

FAMILIES, Tourists, and Commercial Gentlemen will find every endeavour being made to render this Hotel equal to its long known reputation.

**Families Boarded Weekly by Agreement.**

Spacious Billiard Room with a Cox & Yeaman Champion Table.

*A 1 Stud of Horses and Vehicles.*

Coach to Braemar every Tuesday, Thursday, and Saturday ; seats secured by post or telegram. 'Bus meets all trains.

JOHN ANDERSON, *Proprietor.*

# THE GREAT WESTERN HOTEL
## (SNOW HILL STATION),
## BIRMINGHAM.

"One of the most elegant, comfortable, and economical hotels in the three kingdoms."—*The Field*, July 31, 1869.

"From experience gained by repeated visits, we are happy to be able to testify to the exceeding comfort of this hotel. We have much pleasure in recommending it."—*The Engineer*, October 14, 1870.

"An establishment remarkable for its able management, reasonable charges, and general comfort."—*Bell's Life*, June 17, 1871.

# BLAIRGOWRIE.

## QUEEN'S  HOTEL

### ESTABLISHED UPWARDS OF FORTY YEARS.

PARTIES visiting Blairgowrie will find in the Queen's Hotel every comfort and attention. It is on the shortest and most direct route to Balmoral Castle and scenery of the Dee. Superior Post-Horses. Carriages of every description, and careful drivers. An Omnibus awaits the arrival and departure of the trains.

D. M'DONALD, *Proprietor.*

## BRAEMAR.

# FIFE ARMS HOTEL,
## BRAEMAR, BY BALMORAL.

MR. MACNAB begs respectfully to inform the Nobility, Gentry, and Tourists, that the extensive additions to the Hotel are now completed, and which comprise 30 extra Bedrooms, a Dining Saloon (one of the largest and most elegant in Scotland), Ladies' Drawing-Room, and Bath-Rooms. Great care has been taken in the construction, that everything should be made of the most modern design, and include all recent improvements in ventilation, &c.

Mr. MACNAB trusts, by the most careful management and attention to visitors, to retain the reputation of this house as a first-class Hotel. The charges are strictly moderate. Letters or telegrams for conveyances or apartments will receive the most careful attention. Posting in all its varied departments. Coaches during the season to Ballater and Blairgowrie stations.

*Note.*—Gentlemen staying at the Hotel can have excellent Salmon and Trout Fishing free of all charge.

## BRISTOL.

# ROYAL HOTEL, COLLEGE GREEN.

FIRST-CLASS, Central, and pleasantly situated. Very spacious Coffee, Dining, Reading, Smoking, and Billiard Rooms. Private Apartments *en suite.* One Hundred and Twenty Bed-Rooms. Steam Lift and Laundry. Hot and Cold Baths. Telegraph Office and Post-office in the Hotel. Fixed Charges. All Omnibuses pass the door. Night Porter kept.

W. SWANSON, *Manager.*

## BRISTOL.
# CLIFTON DOWN HOTEL,

FACING THE SUSPENSION BRIDGE.    FOR FAMILIES AND GENTLEMEN.

THIS Hotel contains all the appointments found in First-Class Establishments. Its situation is unrivalled. Visitors will find all the comfort and attention of home, with fixed moderate charges. Omnibuses meet all trains.

N.B.—From this Hotel the following TRIPS are easy, returning to the Hotel the same day:—

To Chepstow Castle, the Wynd Cliff, Tintern Abbey, Wells Cathedral, Glastonbury Tor, Bath, Weston-super-Mare, Clevedon Portishead, the River Avon, and Channel Docks.

*Clifton Hotel Company (Limited).*    D. H. GITTINS, *Manager.*

---

## BRIDGE OF ALLAN.
# QUEEN'S HOTEL.

## A. ANDERSON, PROPRIETOR.

### HOT, COLD, AND SHOWER BATHS.
#### HORSES, GIGS, DROSKIES, &c.

This first-class Hotel affords excellent accommodation for Families, Tourists, and Visitors.

---

## CALLANDER.
# THE M'GREGOR HOTEL,

### JAMES M'DERMONT, PROPRIETOR.

PATRONISED BY THEIR ROYAL HIGHNESSES THE PRINCE AND PRINCESS OF WALES.

TOURISTS and Families visiting the above long-established and First-Class Hotel (so long conducted by the late Mr. M'Gregor) will have every comfort and attention, and the Charges moderate in comparison with other Hotels in the Highlands.

Posting complete. 'Bus awaits all the trains.

N.B.—Parties beware of being misled from this Hotel by porters and others on the various routes to Callander.

## CALLANDER.

# DREADNOUGHT HOTEL.

## D. M'GOWAN, Proprietrix.

THIS large and commodious Hotel, so long conducted by the late Mr. M'Gregor, and which has recently undergone extensive alterations and improvements, is beautifully situated at the west end of the village, and commands a magnificent view of the Vale of the Teith, Ben Ledi, and surrounding district, and is within a short distance of

### THE ROMAN CAMP,
### THE FALLS OF BRACKLINN,
### LOCH VENNACHAR, LOCH LUBNAIG, THE PASS OF LENY,
### BEN LEDI, etc. etc.

Tourists will find Callander very central for visiting those places mentioned in Sir Walter Scott's "Lady of the Lake"—viz., the Lake of Menteith, Clachan of Aberfoyle, Loch Ard, the Trossachs, Loch Achray, Loch Katrine, Strathyre, Clachan of Balquhidder (where Rob Roy M'Gregor is buried), Loch Voil, Lochearnhead, etc.

During the Summer Season STAGE COACHES in connection with this Hotel and Mr. Blair's Hotel at the Trossachs run several times each day, to suit the arrival and departure of trains at Callander and steamer on Loch Katrine.

*Omnibuses run to and from each Train.*

☞ Posting in all its Branches.—Letters for Carriages, Coach Seats, or Hotel Accommodation, carefully attended to.

**Lake and River Fishing to be had in the immediate neighbourhood.**

## CAMBRIDGE.

# BULL HOTEL

(Patronised by their Imperial Majesties the
Emperor and Empress of Brazil),

SITUATE in the most central part of the town, and near to the principal Colleges and places of interest to visitors. Families and Gentlemen will find this Hotel complete with every comfort. Spacious Coffee-Room, private Sitting and Bed Rooms *en suite*. Omnibus and Flys to meet all trains.     J. A. MOYES, PROPRIETOR.

## CARLISLE.

# THE COUNTY HOTEL,

WHICH affords every accommodation for Families and Gentlemen, is Fire-proof, and connected with the Platform of the Central Railway Station by a covered way. Porters in attendance on arrival of Trains.

### A Ladies' Coffee-Room.

CARNARVON, NORTH WALES.

# ROYAL HOTEL (LATE UXBRIDGE ARMS),

FIRST-CLASS FAMILY AND COMMERCIAL ESTABLISHMENT.

Beautifully situated on the Banks of the Menai Straits, and in close proximity to the Railway Station.

## EDWARD HUMPHREYS

*(Late of the Dolbadarn and Padarn Villa Hotels, Llanberis).*

AN Omnibus will regularly attend the arrival of each Train at the Railway Station. Billiards in detached premises. Daily Coaches during the Season to Beddgelert.

On and after June 19th, a Coach round Snowdon, after the arrival of the 9·45 A.M. Train, *via* Beddgelert, Vale of Gwynant, and the Pass of Llanberis, arriving at the Hotel for Dinner, and in time for the Train for Llandudno, Rhyl, &c.

---

COLWYN BAY, NORTH WALES.

# POLLYCROCHON HOTEL,

(Late the Residence of Lady Erskine).

THIS First-class Family Hotel is most beautifully situated in its own finely-wooded park in Colwyn Bay, commanding splendid land and sea views, and miles of delightful walks in the adjacent woods. It is within ten minutes' walk of Colwyn Station, and a short drive of Conway and Llandudno.

Sea-Bathing, Billiards, Posting.

J. PORTER, *Proprietor.*

# CHELTENHAM.
# BELLE VUE HOTEL
## FOR FAMILIES AND GENTLEMEN.

This Hotel is delightfully situated in the healthiest part of the town.

*TERMS MODERATE.*

**G. ROLPH, Proprietor.**

---

# CORK.
# STEPHENS' COMMERCIAL HOTEL
### (*Opposite the General Post Office, Cork*),

POSSESSES first-class accommodation for Tourists, Commercial Gentlemen, and Families.

It is very centrally situated, being opposite the General Post Office—close to the Bank, Theatre, &c. &c.

*Charges extremely Moderate.*

### WILLIAM D. STEPHENS, Proprietor,
#### *From the West of England.*

EXTRACT from a "Tour through Ireland," published in the *North Briton*, 1864:—

"When we arrived in Cork we took up our quarters at Stephens' Commercial Hotel, where we obtained excellent accommodation.

"What this Hotel lacks in external show is amply compensated by unremitting attention on the part of the Proprietors and their attendants to the comfort of their Guests."

---

# DINGWALL.
# AUCHNASHEEN HOTEL,
## AUCHNASHEEN.
### BY RAILWAY FROM DINGWALL.

M. M'IVER begs to inform the Public that he has now Removed from the Old House, and has Opened the NEW HOTEL at the Auchnasheen Station, which is much larger and more convenient than the old one.

The Coaches for Lochmaree and Gairloch leave Auchnasheen daily on the arrival of the Morning Trains from Dingwall; the Gairloch Coaches arrive at Auchnasheen in time for the Evening Trains to Dingwall and Strome Ferry.

# DINGWALL.

## DINGWALL AND SKYE, LOCH MAREE AND GAIRLOCH.

## "FRASER'S"
# NATIONAL AND STATION HOTEL—FIRST,

Is a very Large and Commodious First-Class Hotel, situated at the Junction of the Highland and Skye Railways.

The following places of interest may be conveniently visited from this Hotel between Breakfast and Dinner :—The whole of the Famed Scenery along the Skye Railway—Golspie and Dunrobin—Ben Wyvis—The Black Rock—The Famed Strathpeffer and its Mineral Wells—Falls of Rogie — Loch Achilty—Falls of Conon—Loch Garve—Falls of Kilmorack.

The following can be visited by being absent from here One Night only, viz.—Loch Maree, Gairloch, and the Isle of Skye.

A LARGE COFFEE-ROOM.

PRIVATE PARLOURS AND SUITES OF ROOMS.

### Posting, and Job Horses and Carriages.

---

## JURY'S HOTEL,
# COLLEGE GREEN, DUBLIN.

WELL known for cleanliness, good attention, and moderate charges.

TABLE D'HOTE AT THREE AND HALF-PAST SIX.

---

## DUBLIN.
# SALTHILL HOTEL,
### MONKSTOWN, COUNTY DUBLIN.

TOURISTS and FAMILIES visiting Dublin will find the above replete with every convenience, combined with moderate charges and the advantage of a seaside residence ; within easy access to Dublin ; by rail twenty minutes.

The Hotel has been re-decorated, and is now ready for the reception of visitors. From its situation, surrounded by its own grounds, facing the Bay of Dublin, it possesses unquestionable advantages as a family residence.

First-class Livery and Carriage Department—the whole under the personal superintendence of the Proprietor.

For terms apply to WILLIAM PARRY.

:DINBURGH, opposite the Scott Monument, and commanding the best views of the Gardens, Castle, and Arthur's Seat.

# THE ROYAL HOTEL,

## 53 PRINCES STREET, EDINBURGH,

### 𝔐𝔞𝔠𝔊𝔯𝔢𝔤𝔬𝔯, Proprietor and Manager.

THE above has been entirely remodelled within the last two years. It has numerous suites of apartments overlooking Princes Street, one of the finest streets in Europe.

The magnificent Coffee-Room for Families and Gentlemen is a hundred feet long and twenty feet high. The Drawing-Room and Library all *en suite*, fronting Princes Street. The most complete in Britain.

*The Royal is within a few minutes' walk of the Railway Stations.*

SPACIOUS SMOKING AND BILLIARD ROOMS FRONTING PRINCES ST.
**A Night Porter.**

# THE WATERLOO HOTEL,

## WATERLOO PLACE, EDINBURGH,

DESIGNED and built for the express purpose, in the most commodious and elegant style, and in a most beautiful situation, is always replete with everything conducive to the comfort and convenience of Families, Tourists, Commercial Gentlemen, and other Visitors, and is specially worthy of the attention of such.

# KENNEDY'S HOTEL,

## 8 PRINCES STREET, EDINBURGH,

ALSO merits particular notice as an Old-established, Commodious, and popular House. It has excellent accommodation for Families and Commercial Gentlemen. The view from it to the west is at once comprehensive, grand, and striking.

*Both Hotels adjoin the General Post Office and Railway Termini.*

WM. KENNEDY,
*Proprietor.*

**Ladies' Coffee-Room at both Hotels.**

# EDINBURGH.

# CALEDONIAN HOTEL,

## 1 CASTLE STREET AND PRINCES STREET.

### (Exactly opposite the Castle.)

LATE J. BURNETT. R. B. MOORE.

# ALMA HOTEL,

## 112, 113, and 114 PRINCES STREET, EDINBURGH.

### (*Opposite the Castle.*)

COMBINING all the comforts of a Home with the convenience of a Hotel. Ladies' Coffee-room and Drawing-room.
Charges strictly moderate.

A. ADDISON, *Proprietor.*

# THE BALMORAL HOTEL,

## 91 PRINCES STREET, EDINBURGH.

THIS old-established Hotel, re-constructed and re-furnished throughout in the most elegant manner, from designs by the best artists, and under the personal direction of John Grieve of St. James' Hall, London (the Lessee), is now open for reception of visitors.

In devising many necessary alterations, and in entirely re-furnishing the house, Mr. Grieve, while he has been careful to maintain the high character which the BALMORAL has always maintained as an elegant and comfortable residence for the Nobility and Gentry, is desirous of calling attention to the fact that he has very carefully studied the requirements of Gentlemen visiting Edinburgh on law and other business. Besides adding to the Hotel several *suites* of luxuriously-furnished apartments for Family use, he has added Thirty Single Rooms, with commodious self-contained Wardrobes, for the use of professional or business men.

The Public Dining and Drawing Rooms, furnished by London and Edinburgh tradesmen (unequalled in their several departments), are specially elegant and commodious, commanding fine views of Princes Street Gardens, Edinburgh Castle, and other interesting features of the " Modern Athens ; " whilst a snug Smoking-room, convenient Lavatories, and unlimited Water Supplies throughout the establishment, add largely to the comfort of the Visitor.

Kitchens, constructed by Benham & Sons of London, administered by Foreign and English Cooks of ability, leave nothing to be desired in the art of satisfying the most fastidious palate.

The Wine Cellars are stocked with Vintages obtained from Merchant and Shipping Houses, with which Mr. Grieve has done a large business for many years ; and, though aware of the difficulty of pleasing the British public, he confidently refers to his newly-revised Wine Carte, and to the very moderate prices therein quoted—from the 3s. bottle of "Medoc" upwards.

The Charges of the Balmoral will compare favourably even with those of minor hotels. Lists of Prices will be forwarded on application to the Manager.

Ladies and Gentlemen passing through the city are respectfully invited to visit the Balmoral, and judge of the accommodation and charges for themselves.

**Hot, Cold, Shower, Douche, Turkish, and Plunge Baths on the Premises.**

*⁎* *Wholesale Wine List on application.*

# EDINBURGH.
## PHILP'S COCKBURN HOTEL,

*Immediately adjoining the Terminus of the Great Northern Trains.*

THIS commodious and well-appointed Hotel is beautifully situated, over-looking Princes Street Gardens, and commanding some of the finest views in the city.

A large and elegantly-furnished Saloon—admitted to be the finest in Scotland—set apart for Ladies, Gentlemen, or Families, wishing to avoid the expense of Sitting-Rooms.

The views from the immense windows of this Saloon are, without exception, the finest in Edinburgh.

Private Suites of Apartments, Bath-Rooms, Coffee and Smoking Rooms, and every accommodation for Gentlemen.

### PIANOS IN ALL THE PARLOURS AND SALOONS.
*Charges, including Attendance, strictly Moderate.*

*P.S.*—Mr. Cook (of London) makes this Hotel his headquarters when in Scotland, where every information may be obtained of his Tourist arrangements.

*Cook's Hotel Coupons accepted at the Cockburn.*

ON PARLE FRANÇAIS.        MAN SPRICHT DEUTSCH.

*First-Class Turkish Baths in connection with this Hotel.*

ROBERT MIDDLEMASS,
PROPRIETOR OF THE EDINBURGH HOTEL, PRINCES STREET,
has the honour of announcing that he has
entered on a Lease of

# THE DOUGLAS HOTEL,
## SAINT ANDREW SQUARE,

which has for many years been distinguished by the Patronage of the *Royal Families of Great Britain and Europe.*

It is situated in the principal Square, from which picturesque views are obtained, within a short distance of all the Railway Stations; and while it commands perfect quietude, is in the vicinity of the various Public Buildings and Places of Interest for which the City is so justly famed.

The moderate tariff which has given such universal satisfaction to visitors at the Edinburgh Hotel has been adopted at the Douglas.

---

# DARLING'S REGENT HOTEL,
## 20 WATERLOO PLACE, EDINBURGH.
*Nearly opposite the General Post-Office.*

Situated in the Principal Street of the City, in the immediate vicinity of the Calton Hill and Public Buildings. Large comfortable Coffee-Room for parties with Ladies, free of charge. Also Private Parlours. *Turkish and other Baths can be had on the premises.* This is admitted to be one of the best Temperance Hotels in Scotland.
CHARGES STRICTLY MODERATE.

---

# ENNISKILLEN.—ROYAL HOTEL.
## E. MONAGHAN, PROPRIETOR,

Begs to announce to his numerous Friends and the Public in general that in addition to the above he has added a large house, fitted up with all the modern improvements, with a view to give additional space and comfort; also a Billiard Table of Daniel Harris's best and improved make.

*Posting in all its branches turned out in best style.*

The Hotel Omnibus attends all Trains. Ladies' Coffee-Room free of Charge.

B

# CARRICK'S ROYAL HOTEL,
## 50 GEORGE SQUARE, GLASGOW.

*(Opposite the General Post-Office.)*

This Old-established Family Hotel is delightfully situated for Gentlemen and Families.

The Charges are Fixed and Moderate.

JAMES CARRICK, Proprietor.

---

## GLASGOW.
# BEDFORD HOTEL,
### 54 ST. GEORGE'S PLACE, GLASGOW.
### JOHN CHARLES, Proprietor.

*(Corner of Buchanan Street.)*

Well situated for Parties on pleasure, Families, and Commercial Gentlemen.

*Elegant Coffee-Room.*     *Smoking and Billiard Rooms.*

---

# HANOVER  HOTEL,
## HANOVER STREET, GEORGE SQUARE, GLASGOW.
### MERTON R. COTES, *Proprietor.*

"The Editor of '*BRADSHAW*' highly recommends this Hotel for its Superior Arrangements, Excellent Management, and Domestic Comforts."—Sept. 7, 1871.

"First-Class Hotel for Families and Gentlemen, replete with the comforts of Home."—*Murray's Guide to Scotland*, 1871.

"Quiet Family Hotel, combining excellence in every department."—*Black's Guide to Scotland*, 1871.

---

# ROYAL ALBERT HOTEL.
## RESTAURANT ATTACHED.
### 63 WILSON STREET, GLASGOW.
*Situation Central, Healthy, and Quiet.*

Opposite the new Court-Houses and County Buildings, and in convenient proximity to all the Railway Termini. WM. PATON, PROPRIETOR.

Visitors at this Hotel having the benefit of the Restaurant will find it the most economical, combined with comfort and attention. The Liquors and Viands A1. Commercial Room, Parlours, and Bedrooms large and airy. All charges strictly moderate. Bed, Breakfast, and attendance, from 3s. 6d. *Hot, Cold, and Shower Baths. Night Porter.*

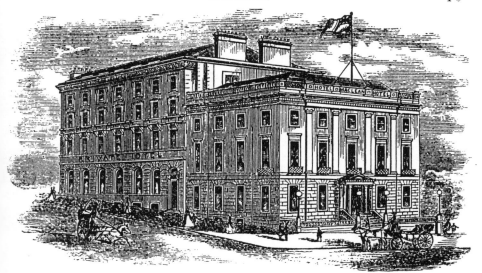

# MACLEAN'S HOTEL,
## 198 ST. VINCENT STREET, GLASGOW.

FOR Families and Gentlemen, in the immediate neighbourhood of Blythswood Square, and within five minutes of the termini of the various Railways and Steamboat Wharves. JAMES MACLEAN, Proprietor.

# CITY COMMERCIAL DINING ROOMS,
## 54 & 60 UNION STREET, AND 35 MITCHELL STREET, GLASGOW.

ONE of the most Extensive and Comfortable Dining Establishments in Scotland, capable of accommodating upwards of 2000 Visitors daily.

Breakfasts, Dinners, and Teas, served with comfort, economy, and despatch.

Bill of Fare—EXTRA MODERATE.

LADIES' PRIVATE DINING-ROOM.
GENTLEMEN'S LAVATORY.

*No Gratuities to Waiters.*

MATTHEW WADDELL, Proprietor.

# CROW HOTEL,
## GEORGE SQUARE, GLASGOW.

THIS House is situated in the very centre of the City. For Tourists and Families it is unsurpassed for Comfort and Moderate Charges.

## D. DEWAR, Proprietor.

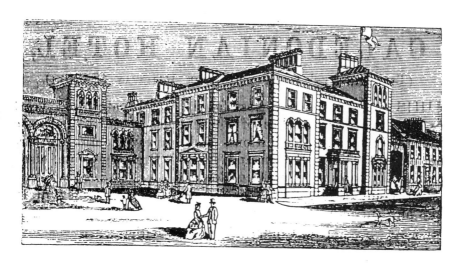

# MACDONALD'S STATION HOTEL,

## INVERNESS.

*Patronised by their Royal Highnesses the Prince and Princess of Wales, and other Members of the Royal Family, and by most of the Nobility of Europe.*

PARTIES travelling from South to North, and *vice versa*, will find this very large and handsome Hotel adjoining the Station, whereby they can arrive at, or depart from, the Hotel under cover. The house was specially built for a Hotel, is elegantly furnished with all modern improvements, and contains numerous suites of Private Rooms, includes

## LADIES' AND GENTLEMEN'S COFFEE-ROOM,

*SMOKING-ROOMS, BILLIARD-ROOMS, BATH-ROOMS, &c.*

Over 100 beds can be made up.

Parties leaving this Hotel in the morning can go over the grand scenery along the Skye Railway, or visit either Lochmaree, Gairloch, Dunrobin, or Golspie, and return same day.

Table d'Hote at 5.30 and 7.30.

French, German, and Italian Spoken.

*An Omnibus attends the Steamers. Posting.*

## INVERNESS.

# CALEDONIAN HOTEL,

(TWO MINUTES' WALK FROM THE RAILWAY STATION).

THIS well-known first-class family Hotel, patronised yearly by the best families of Europe, has recently undergone extensive alterations, additions, and improvements. A large and elegant Dining-Saloon and Ladies' Drawing-Room, also a spacious Billiard and Smoking Room.

In point of situation this Hotel has the best view of the Ness and surrounding scenery in Inverness.

Hot, Cold, and Shower Baths.

TABLE D'HOTE DAILY, AND DINNERS À LA CARTE.

An Omnibus attends all the Canal Steamers.

JOHN MENZIES,
*Proprietor.*

---

## INVERNESS.

# THE ROYAL HOTEL, INVERNESS.

*Opposite the Railway Station.*

J. S. CHRISTIE has the honour to announce that the additions and improvements on the Royal Hotel are now completed. The additions include a spacious and lofty Coffee-Room, with Drawing-Rooms *en suite*, as well as several handsome Parlours and Bedrooms, commanding magnificent views of the Moray and Beauly Firths, Fort-George, and the mountains of Ross-shire, Strathglass, &c. No other Hotel in the capital of the Highlands commands such varied and extensive views of northern scenery.

J. S. C. desires to take this opportunity of tendering the thanks of Mrs. CHRISTIE and himself to the numerous families and others who patronised them while in the Station Hotel, and to assure them that they have spared no effort to make the Royal Hotel attractive and comfortable. It has been entirely refurnished in the most modern style, and every improvement that experience could suggest has been taken advantage of in its arrangement.

Though immediately *opposite* and within a *few yards* of the Railway Station entrance, the *quietness* and comfort of the Hotel is not thereby affected.

*Table d'Hôte at 5.30 and 7.30.*

" Boots " attend all Trains. An Omnibus meets the Steamers.

Posting.

ISLE OF WIGHT.

# THE MARINE HOTEL,

## PARADE, WEST COWES.

## JAMES DROVER, PROPRIETOR.

*PLEASANTLY SITUATED, FACING THE SEA.*

*The comfort of Visitors studied in every way.*

## RYDE.

# BELGRAVE FAMILY HOTEL,

### RYDE—ISLE OF WIGHT.

Excellent Accommodation at Moderate Charges.

**W. SALTER & SONS, Proprietors.**

WHEN YOU ARE

IN

# THE HIGHLANDS

VISIT

# MACDOUGALL & CO.'S,

## JERSEY.

# STOPFORD PRIVATE HOTEL.

## 33 and 35 DAVID PLACE, ST. HELIER'S.

This establishment is situated in the most fashionable part of St. Helier's, and has been successfully conducted for upwards of THIRTY YEARS under the name of BREE'S BOARDING-HOUSE. It is specially recommended to persons who intend spending the winter in Jersey. Tariff on application. E. BREE, *Proprietor.*

## KESWICK.

# TOWER HOTEL,

## *LAKE DERWENTWATER, PORTINSCALE.*

THIS New Hotel is now open. It is surmounted by a Tower 120 feet high, the views from which are unsurpassed in the district, comprising Lake and Mountain Scenery of the most varied description.

One mile from Keswick, and near the Lake. Handsome Spacious Coffee Room and Ladies' Drawing-Room. Private Sitting-Rooms, Hot and Cold Baths. Boats on the Lake, with Private Landing-Place. Horses, Carriages, and Mountain Ponies for Hire. An Omnibus from the Hotel meets the principal Trains at Keswick Station.

A. L. OLDFIELD, PROPRIETOR.

ALSO OF THE

HEN AND CHICKENS HOTEL, BIRMINGHAM.

## KILKEE—LOWER SHANNON.

# MOORE'S HOTEL.

TOURISTS purposing to visit the Delightful scenery of the Western Coast are respectfully informed that this Establishment has been fitted up in a style that will insure them all the accommodation and comfort of a City Hotel. A magnificent Public Drawing-room for Ladies. Billiard and Smoking Room. Every exertion is used by the Proprietor to secure from each individual a confirmation of the character his house bears.

### Table d'Hote during the Season.

*Hotel Omnibus and Porter attend the Steamers.*

Kilkee has high recommendation as a Route from KILLARNEY to CONNEMARA.

MOORE'S HOTEL, WELLINGTON SQUARE, KILKEE.

# KILLARNEY RAILWAY HOTEL,

## P. CURRY,

LATE TRAVELLERS' CLUB, LONDON, AND
KILDARE STREET CLUB, DUBLIN.

---

*The Continental Languages spoken by the Manager.*

---

THIS well-known Establishment, admitted to be one of the finest in Europe, possesses everything requisite to promote the comfort and convenience of Tourists. It contains one hundred Bedrooms, a magnificent Coffee-room, a Drawing-room for ladies and families, and several elegant and handsomely furnished Sitting-rooms, Billiard and Smoking rooms, Baths, &c. &c., and is surrounded by an extensive and well-kept Flower Garden.

The Charges will be found moderate.

The Boating and Carriage Accommodation is specially attended to by the Manager, who personally arranges the formation of Boating Parties, &c., with a view to economy.

The Porters of the Hotel await the arrival of each Train, for the removal of luggage, &c.

Table d'Hote at half-past Six o'clock.

All Attendance charged.

A Room is established for the convenience of Commercial Gentlemen.

Parties taken as Boarders at Three Guineas per week, from 1st November to the 1st of June.

# KILLARNEY LAKES.

*By Her Most Gracious Majesty's Special Permission.*

# THE ROYAL VICTORIA HOTEL,

Patronised by H.R.H. THE PRINCE OF WALES ; by H.R.H.
PRINCE ARTHUR, on his recent visit to Ireland ; and
by the Royal Families of France and Belgium, &c.

THIS HOTEL is situated on the Lower Lake, close to the
water's edge, within ten minutes' drive of the Railway
Station, and a short distance from the far-famed Gap of Dunloe.

## TABLE D'HOTE DURING THE SEASON.

## KILLIN, LOCH TAY, PERTHSHIRE.

# KILLIN HOTEL,

### BY RAILWAY FROM CALLANDER,

*(One of the Finest Lines in Scotland for grandeur of Scenery.)*

THIS Hotel is situated amongst some of the finest scenery in the Highlands, including
Finlarig Castle, the burial-place of the Breadalbane Family ; Inch Buie, the burial-
place of the old Clan M'Nab ; the Falls of Lochay, Auchmore House, Kennel House, the
romantic Glenlyon, Glenlochay, Glendochart, Benlawers, and Benmore.

Salmon Fishing now open on Loch Tay.

☞ AN OMNIBUS RUNS TO AND FROM ALL THE TRAINS.
*The Posting and Hiring Establishment is complete.*

JOHN M'PHERSON, *Proprietor.*

## LIMERICK.

# CRUISE'S ROYAL HOTEL,

### J. J. CLEARY, PROPRIETOR.

THIS long-established and well-known FIRST-CLASS HOTEL is now conducted under
the sole superintendence of the Proprietor, and possesses everything requisite to promote the comfort and convenience of the NOBILITY, GENTRY, and TOURISTS, and affords
particular facilities to Commercial Gentlemen, having first-rate SHOW-ROOMS, together
with MODERATE CHARGES.

Omnibuses attend all Trains, Steamers, etc. etc. etc. ; also a 'Bus attends the Night
Mails for the convenience of Gentlemen coming by the late Trains.

*N.B.*—This is the PRINCIPAL HOTEL IN THE CITY, and is capable of accommodating over 150 persons, together with a splendid Suite of Drawing-Rooms.

HOT, COLD, AND SHOWER BATHS.

# LANARK.

# CLYDESDALE HOTEL.

FAMILIES, Tourists, and others visiting the Falls of Clyde, and other romantic scenery around Lanark, will find every comfort and attention at this old-established and first-class Hotel.

Suites of Apartments for special parties. Large well-aired Bedrooms. A spacious Hall, suitable for accommodating large Excursion Parties. A 'Bus in attendance on all trains at Lanark Station.

### Posting in all its Branches.

Orders by letter or telegram for conveyances to meet parties at Carstairs or Lanark Stations, who wish to be taken direct to the Falls, punctually attended to.

*Tickets of Admission to the Falls, on either side of the River, supplied.*

# LANCASTER
### (HALF WAY BETWEEN LONDON & SCOTLAND).

*Parties holding Tourist Tickets to and from the Lake District and Scotland, may break their Journey at Lancaster, both going and returning.*

# SLY'S
# KING'S ARMS AND ROYAL HOTEL
## And General Posting Establishment,

FOR Families, Commercial Gentlemen, and Tourists. Visitors will find this old-established Hotel equally as economical as minor establishments, with the certainty of comfort and attention.

The Hotel is teeming with ancient works of art, including pictures, china, elaborately-carved oak furniture, Gobelins tapestry (acknowledged to be inferior to none in the United Kingdom), and which have elicited the admiration of all visitors, including the late Mr. CHARLES DICKENS, who stated that in all his travels he had never met with so remarkable a house, and such an interesting collection. See his "Lazy Tour of Two Idle Apprentices," in *Household Words.*

### Omnibuses from the Hotel meet the Trains.
JOSEPH SLY, *Proprietor.*

# THE IMPERIAL HOTEL,
## LLANDUDNO,

Has been built with a view to meet the deficiency of first-class Hotel accommodation at Llandudno, increasingly felt during past seasons. It is situated on the Parade, near the centre of the Bay, and commands the surrounding scenery of Mountain and Sea, in every direction. The Apartments are spacious, well ventilated, and light. Studious attention has been given in design, arrangement, and furnishing, to the comfort and convenience of its patrons ; and by the application of a perfect system of ventilation to the drainage, the health of the inmates has been, as far as possible, insured.

*Tariff on application.*      J. CHANTREY, PROPRIETOR.

## LOCH AWE.

# DALMALLY HOTEL, NEAR INVERARY,
## GLENORCHY.

D. FRASER begs to intimate to the Nobility and Gentry that he has re-fitted and furnished the above Hotel in the most approved style for the accommodation of his visitors, and hopes that by strict attention and careful superintendence to merit a continuance of public patronage.

The Hotel is beautifully situated on the main road between Oban, Inverary, and Killin, and commands unrivalled views of mountain scenery, which are unsurpassed for grandeur by any in Scotland. Amongst the places of interest in the immediate neighbourhood are Kilchurn Castle, Falls of Orchy, Pass of Brander (where M'Dougal of Lorne attacked King Robert the Bruce), Fraoch Ellan, Loch Awe, Ben Cruachan and Ben Luie, &c.

Excellent salmon and trout fishing on Loch Awe and river Orchy, *free* of charge to parties staying at the Hotel. Boats and experienced boatmen provided for visitors. Posting establishment complete. Coaches pass daily to and from Tyndrum Railway Station, Oban, Inverary, and steamer on Loch Awe. Letters by post punctually attended to.

## KINROSS.

# LOCHLEVEN BRIDGE-END HOTEL.

Now greatly enlarged and improved, is the only Hotel situated close to Lochleven, adjoining the Railway Station, and is the favourite resort of anglers. Excellent Sitting-rooms and Bed-rooms overlooking the loch. Stabling accommodation. Conveyance on hire.

W. WOOD, LANDLORD.

*UNDER ROYAL PATRONAGE.*

**PERTHSHIRE**  **BALQUHIDDER**

# LOCHEARNHEAD HOTEL,

## BY RAILWAY FROM CALLANDER.

FIRST-CLASS accommodation for Families.   Every comfort and quiet. This Hotel, lying high and dry, placed at the head of the Loch, commands fine views, and is in the neighbourhood of many places of interest ; the Scenery of the Legend of Montrose, Rob Roy's Grave, Old Church of Balquhidder, several Lochs, and fine Walks and Drives.

BOATS FOR FISHING FREE OF CHARGE.

Omnibus to and from the Hotel for every Train during the Summer Months.

*Letters by Post immediately attended to.*

R. DAYTON.

## LOCHLOMOND.

# INVERARNAN HOTEL,

## HEAD OF LOCHLOMOND.

THIS is the only landing-place on the Lake for the Coaches to Glencoe, Ballachulish, Fort-William, Killin, Kenmore, and Aberfeldy ; the nearest starting-point for the Dalmally and Oban Coaches—all of which start daily from the Hotel, where seats are secured, maps of routes, and all necessary information, supplied.   Parties intending to proceed by either of the above routes would do well to be at Inverarnan the previous evening, so as to secure seats.   The comfort and attention afforded at this Hotel, which is newly furnished, are equal to what can be enjoyed at any Lake or other Hotel in the Highlands.   The Hotel is situated in the midst of mountain scenery which for grandeur and beauty cannot be surpassed. It has convenient and easy access to Loch Katrine and the Trossachs ; and adjacent are the Falls of Falloch, Rob Roy's Birthplace and Cave—all so much admired by Tourists.

**Posting in all its Branches.**

*A 'Bus waits the arrival of the Steamers during the Season.*

Fishing on the Falloch ; Boats for the Lake.

EDWARD M'CALLUM, PROPRIETOR.

# LOCHLOMOND.
# TARBET HOTEL,

(OPPOSITE BEN-LOMOND)

## A. M'PHERSON, Proprietor,

IS the finest and most commodious Hotel on the Lake, and commands the best View of Ben-Lomond.

Coaches direct for the far-famed Glencroe, Inverary, and Oban, will commence running early in June, leaving this Hotel immediately on arrival of the 10.15 A.M. Steamer, in connection with the 6.15 A.M. Train from Edinburgh, and the 7.35 A.M. from Glasgow.

The Coaches from Oban and Inverary also arrive at this Hotel in time for the 5 P.M. Steamer down Lochlomond for Edinburgh, Glasgow, and the south. Tourists *en route* for Trossachs and Callander can leave per 10.15 A.M. Steamer, next morning, in connection with the Steamer down Loch Katrine.

Small Boats on the Lake, and Guides to Ben-Lomond, to be had at the Hotel.—*May* 1873.

# LOCHLOMOND.

INVERSNAID HOTEL is situated in the most central and picturesque parts of the banks of Lochlomond, and is the landing-place for tourists and others visiting the delightful scenery of Loch Katrine, the Trossachs, Clachan of Aberfoyle, &c. Coaches and other conveyances are always in readiness for parties crossing to the Stronachlachar Hotel, for the Steamer plying on Loch Katrine from Coalbarns Pier to the Trossachs.

# LOCHLOMOND.
# ROWARDENNAN HOTEL,

## FOOT OF BEN-LOMOND.

B. JARRATT having taken a new lease of the above Hotel, begs to return his sincere thanks to Tourists and others who have so kindly patronised him for the last five years. Rowardennan is the best and shortest road to Ben-Lomond, and the only place where Ponies can be had, by which parties can ride with ease and safety to the top ; the distance being only four miles to the very summit.

The Lochlomond Steamers call at the Rowardennan Wharf six times a-day on their route up and down the Loch.

# OXFORD.

*In the Best and most Central part of the City.*

---

# RANDOLPH HOTEL

(OPPOSITE MARTYRS' MEMORIAL),

# OXFORD.

Within a few minutes' walk of the Railway Stations, and surrounded by the Principal Colleges.

---

# FIRST-CLASS ACCOMMODATION.

## CHARGES MODERATE.

## HANDSOME LADIES' COFFEE-ROOM.

## BILLIARD-ROOMS, BATHS, &c. &c.

---

GOOD STABLING, LOOSE BOXES, &c.

*OMNIBUSES TO AND FROM EVERY TRAIN.*

## PENZANCE—SEA-SIDE.
# QUEEN'S HOTEL.
*(On the Esplanade.)*
PATRONISED BY H. M. THE QUEEN OF HOLLAND.

THIS magnificent Hotel has recently been greatly enlarged, entirely re-arranged, and handsomely furnished, having a frontage of over 170 feet, all the rooms of which overlook the sea. It is the only Hotel that commands a full and uninterrupted view of Mount's Bay. Penzance stands unrivalled for the variety and quiet beauty of its scenery, whilst the mildness of its climate is admirably adapted to invalids. Apartments *en suite*. Ladies' Coffee-Room, Billiard-Room. Hot and Cold Baths. An Omnibus meets every train. Posting in all its branches. Yachts, &c.

HENRY BLACKWELL, *Proprietor.*

## PENRITH.
# CROWN HOTEL,
*(Opposite the Post Office).*
See Anthony Trollope's last work, "Sir Harry Hotspur."

THE best Family and Commercial Hotel in the North district, containing Ladies' Coffee-Rooms, Billiard-Room, and the largest Concert-Room in the County. *Viâ* Penrith is the best route to the whole of the Lake District. Ullswater Lake, one of if not the most beautiful and picturesque, being distant only six miles, to which a Coach runs twice daily during the season from this Hotel, meeting the Lake Steamboat and Trains. In the immediate vicinity of the town are Lowther Castle, the magnificent seat of the Earl of Lonsdale; Brougham Hall, the seat of Lord Brougham, &c. &c.; and amongst other antiquities are Long Meg and her Daughter, the extensive and fine ruins of Brougham Castle, King Arthur's Round Table, &c. &c. Hawes Water and Airey Force are also within easy distance.

**Post Horses, Carriages, &c.**    **An Omnibus meets every Train.**

J. WAGSTAFF, *Proprietor.*

## PENZANCE.
## Seaside Family Hotel and Superior Lodging-House.
# MOUNT'S BAY HOUSE,
### ON THE ESPLANADE.

NO expense or labour has been spared by the Proprietor. The house is furnished in the most modern style, is well supplied with Hot and Cold Baths, and replete with every accommodation suitable for Tourists to West Cornwall. All the Drawing-Rooms command an *uninterrupted* and *unsurpassed* View of St. Michael's Mount, and the whole of the magnificent bay. Invalids will find in MOUNT'S BAY HOUSE the comforts of a home, while the beauty and salubrity of the situation, and its nearness to the charming walks on the Sea-shore, render it a healthy and delightful residence.

## Suites of Apartments for Families of Distinction.
## Post Horses & Carriages.
## CHARGES MODERATE.

E. LAVIN, Proprietor.

## PORTREE, SKYE.
# THE CALEDONIAN HOTEL.
### F. MURCHESON, Lessee.

Tourists visiting Skye will find the above Hotel, which has recently been enlarged, very comfortable.

*Good attendance. Charges very moderate.*

## RAMSGATE.
# ROYAL ALBION HOTEL.
Patronised by HER MAJESTY and the ROYAL FAMILY.

THE above old-established Family Hotel, facing the Harbour, and commanding fine sea views, is acknowledged to be unrivalled for situation and comfort. Charges moderate. A spacious and elegant Coffee-Room for Ladies. Tariff sent on application.

EDWARD TOMKINS,
*Proprietor.*

# PITLOCHRIE.

## FISHER'S HOTEL.

---

# FIRST-CLASS FAMILY HOTEL

AND

## POSTING ESTABLISHMENT.

---

PARTIES wishing to see the magnificent Scenery in this part of the Scottish Highlands will find this Hotel (to which large additions have been made) most convenient; for in one Drive they can visit the Falls of Tummel, the Queen's View on Loch Tummel, the far-famed Pass of Killiecrankie, Glen Tilt, the Falls of Bruar, etc.

Pitlochrie is on the direct route to Balmoral Castle, by Spital of Glenshee and Braemar, and to Taymouth Castle and Kinloch-Rannoch, by Tummel-Bridge.

Salmon and Trout Fishing on the Rivers Tummel and Garry, and on the Lochs in the neighbourhood.

JOB AND POST HORSES, AND CARRIAGES OF EVERY KIND, BY THE DAY, WEEK, OR MONTH.

**Orders by Telegraph for Rooms or Carriages punctually attended to.**

# THE ROYAL HOTEL, PLYMOUTH.

S. PEARSE, Proprietor.

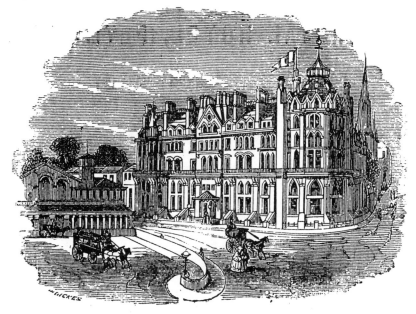

# DUKE OF CORNWALL HOTEL,

*(Opposite the Railway Station.)*

POSTAL TELEGRAPH OFFICE,

## PLYMOUTH, DEVON.

---

## FIRST-CLASS FAMILY HOTEL,

CONTAINING

A HANDSOME GENERAL COFFEE ROOM,
LADIES' DRAWING ROOM.
SMOKING AND READING ROOMS.
LARGE BILLIARD ROOM (*Two Tables.*)
SUITES OF APARTMENTS.
HOT AND COLD BATHS.

---

*TABLE D'HOTE DAILY.*

Address to the Manager.

## SALISBURY.

# WHITE HART HOTEL,

A N Old-established and well-known First-class Family Hotel, within half-a-minute's walk of the Close and Cathedral, Salisbury.

A large and well-appointed Ladies' Coffee-Room is provided. A spacious Coffee-Room for Gentlemen. Hot and Cold Baths.

Posting-master to Her Majesty. Carriages and Horses of every description.      H. WARD.

---

## SALISBURY.
### THE
# THREE SWANS FAMILY HOTEL.
### A LADIES' COFFEE-ROOM.
### A Commodious Gentlemen's Coffee-Room.

There is no Commercial Room in this Hotel, neither is it a Limited Liability Company.

HENRY FIGES, *Proprietor.*

---

# STIRLING—GOLDEN LION HOTEL.
### CAMPBELL'S, LATE GIBB'S.

D. CAMPBELL begs to return his best thanks for the liberal patronage he has received during the many years he has been Proprietor of this old-established Hotel, and respectfully intimates that many improvements have been effected in the House, rendering it complete in every department, as a residence for Families, Tourists, &c.

☞ *A large Coffee-Room for Ladies and Gentlemen.*

The Hotel is in the principal Street, near all the Public Offices and the Railway Station. A Conveyance awaits the arrival of all Trains and Steamers.

D. C.'s Posting and Carriage Establishment is complete, and parties writing for conveyances or apartments may depend on the order being carefully attended to.

☞ *Hot, Cold, and Shower Baths.*

APRIL 1873.      D. CAMPBELL, *Golden Lion Hotel, King Street, Stirling.*

☞ **See Shearer's Illustrated Guide to Stirling, 1s.**

## STIRLING.

# ROYAL HOTEL.

THIS Old-established First-Class Hotel is conveniently situated, being within three minutes' walk of the Railway Station, and is patronised by their Royal Highnesses the Prince and Princess of Wales, and other members of the Royal Family.

☞ Please address Letters in full to

A. CAMPBELL, ROYAL HOTEL, STIRLING.

## STRANRAER.

# MEIKLE'S HOTEL

## (LATE KING'S).

STRANRAER and GLASGOW Through Booking, per Coach and Rail, *via* Ayr, Girvan, Ballantrae, and along the Coast, passing through the Vale of Glenapp, giving a fine prospect of the delightful scenery of that Glen.

The "Commercial" Coach leaves Stranraer at 7.55 a.m., leaving Glasgow at 7 a.m. from Bridge Street Station. Through Ticket—First Class, 12s. 6d. ; Second Class, 10s. 6d. ; Third Class, 8s. 6d. *Dinner at 4 o'clock on arrival of the Coach from Glasgow.*

DRUMORE COACH, from Meikle's Hotel, every lawful day, leaving Stranraer at 4 p.m., and Drumore at 8 a.m. Fares—2s. Outside, and 2s. 6d. Inside.

The POSTING DEPARTMENT is complete in Horses and every description of Carriages.

A 'Bus from the Hotel attends the arrival and departure of every Train.

## TAUNTON.

# TYACK'S LONDON HOTEL,

## FOR FAMILIES AND GENTLEMEN,

Contains all the Appointments of a First-Class Establishment.

Moderate Charges. Omnibuses meet all Trains.

## THE TROSSACHS HOTEL,
### LOCH KATRINE.
#### A. BLAIR, Proprietor.

## TROSSACHS.

# STRONACHLACHAR HOTEL,
# LOCH KATRINE.

ALEXANDER FERGUSON begs to return his sincere thanks to Tourists and others for their liberal support for the last twenty-one years (since the above Hotel was opened). It is beautifully situated at the head of Loch Katrine, and commands the most extensive view of the Lake. The Hotel is comfortably fitted up, and Tourists may depend on receiving every comfort and attention combined with moderate charges. Parties staying here will find it very central for visiting the following places of interest—Trossachs, Helen's Isle, Clachan of Aberfoyle, Loch Ard, Loch Chon, Ben Lomond, &c.; the distance to the Trossachs being ten miles, to Loch Lomond five miles, and to Aberfoyle twelve miles. There is excellent Trout-fishing to be had in Loch Katrine from May to the end of September, and Fishing Boats, with experienced Boatmen, are always kept in readiness. During the season Coaches run to and from Inversnaid in connection with all the Steamers on Loch Katrine and Loch Lomond.

CARRIAGES AND OTHER CONVEYANCES KEPT FOR HIRE.
APRIL 1873.

# TORQUAY.

## VICTORIA AND ALBERT HOTEL COMPANY (LIMITED),

### FOR FAMILIES AND GENTLEMEN.

SUPPLIED with every modern accommodation. Its situation is unsurpassed. Extensive Sea Views ; South aspect. Five minutes from Railway Station. Suites of Private Apartments. Ladies' Drawing-Room, Reading and Table d'Hote Rooms, Billiard and Smoking Rooms. Hot and Cold Baths. The Hotel Omnibus meets each Train. All communication by telegram or post to be addressed to .

SOUTHAM CASH, *Manager.*

# HARKER'S YORK HOTEL,

## ST. HELENS SQUARE, YORK.

THIS long-established, First-Class Family Hotel is most conveniently situated, being within five minutes' walk of the Railway Station, and close to the Minster, the Ruins of St. Mary's Abbey, and other places of interest. This Hotel is largely patronised by American visitors.

P. MATTHEWS, *Proprietor.*

# WINDERMERE.

# CLOUDSDALE'S CROWN HOTEL.

*Patronage—Royalty, American Presidents, etc.·*

Government Postal Telegraph Office in the Hotel, close to the Lake and Steamer piers.

**NINETY BEDS.**
Table d'Hote Daily at 6 p.m.

---

**Inverness and the North, via Aberdeen.**

# GREAT NORTH OF SCOTLAND RAILWAY.

PASSENGERS are booked between LONDON, EDINBURGH, GLASGOW, and other Through Booking Stations in England and Scotland, and Inverness and the North, *via Aberdeen,* at the same Through Fares as *via Dunkeld.*

*Ask for Tickets* via *Aberdeen, and see Luggage labelled by that Route.*

# THE CALEDONIAN RAILWAY COMPANY

## RUN A FULL SERVICE OF TRAINS BY THEIR NEW DIRECT ROUTE
BETWEEN

# EDINBURGH AND GLASGOW,
(West Princes Street.)          (Buchanan Street.)

ALSO, TO AND FROM

## *PAISLEY, GREENOCK AND WEMYSS BAY*

IN CONNECTION WITH THE

## "IONA" and other Steamers,

TO AND FROM THE

## WATERING PLACES ON THE FIRTH OF CLYDE,
## WEST HIGHLANDS OF SCOTLAND, AND
## BELFAST AND DUBLIN.

RETURN TICKETS between EDINBURGH, GREENOCK, WEMYSS BAY and the COAST, are available for going or returning any day, and Passengers have the option of travelling either by the Through trains or *via* Glasgow (*but in the latter case the Company does not provide conveyance through Glasgow*).

## NEW DIRECT ROUTE BETWEEN
# GLASGOW (Buchanan Street.), STIRLING AND THE NORTH.

A full Service of Trains is being run to and from GLASGOW (Buchanan Street), and STIRLING, CALLANDER, PERTH, DUNDEE, ABERDEEN, INVERNESS, and the NORTH HIGHLANDS of SCOTLAND.

## ROYAL MAIL ROUTE BETWEEN
## SCOTLAND AND ENGLAND,
Via Carlisle and the West Coast,

To and from EDINBURGH (*West Princes Street*), GLASGOW (*Buchanan Street*), GREENOCK, STIRLING, PERTH, DUNDEE, ABERDEEN, and all Stations in the NORTH of SCOTLAND, AND
CARLISLE, PRESTON, BRADFORD, LEEDS, MANCHESTER, LIVERPOOL, BIRMINGHAM, LONDON (EUSTON) and all other Stations in ENGLAND and WALES. *The Carriages are of the most improved description, and specially Constructed for the Comfort of Through Passengers.*

Tourist Tickets are issued to the North and West Highlands, Oban, Isle of Skye, &c. &c.

**For particulars see Company's Time Tables and Programme of Tours.**

*Glasgow,* 1873.          JAMES SMITHELLS, *General Manager.*

# MIDLAND RAILWAY.

## BELFAST,

### BY THE NEW AND SHORT SEA ROUTE VIA BARROW.

THE capacious New Docks of Barrow, situated within the ancient Harbour of Piel, under shelter of Walney Island, being now open for Traffic, the Swift and Powerful First-class Paddle Steam Ships "ANTRIM," "ROE," "TALBOT," and "SHELBURNE," will sail between Barrow and Belfast (weather permitting) in connection with through Trains on the Midland and Furness Railways, and through Tickets to Belfast, in connection with the Boat, will be issued from London, Northampton, Leicester, Nottingham, Bristol, Birmingham, Derby, Sheffield, Leeds, Bradford, and principal Stations on the Midland Railway—Return Tickets being available for One Calendar Month.

Passengers to and from London, and other Stations south of Leicester, may break the journey at Furness Abbey, Leeds, Derby, Trent, or Leicester; and Passengers to or from Stations west of Derby, at Furness Abbey, Leeds, or Derby, taking care that from any of those places they proceed by Midland Trains.

The attention of Passengers is particularly directed to the sheltered situation and safety of the Harbour at Barrow, where the Waggons are taken alongside the Steamers into a covered Warehouse, from which the Goods are transferred direct into the Vessel. These advantages, together with the Swift Steamers of this Line, the short sea passage, moderate Fares, and regular Daily Sailings, render the Barrow Route the most desirable communication between England and the North of Ireland.

### BUXTON AND DERBYSHIRE.

First, Second, and Third Class Tourist Tickets are issued during the Summer Months from principal Stations on the Midland Railway, and Lines in connection, to Matlock and Buxton—Tickets being available for One Calendar Month.

Passengers holding Tickets to Buxton are allowed to break the journey at principal places of interest on the Line between Matlock and Buxton.

#### Excursions to Matlock and Buxton on Saturdays.

RETURN TICKETS at the following Low Fares will be issued to MATLOCK and BUXTON, by any of the Through Trains, on Saturdays, from May 31st to October 11th, available for Return by any Train up to the TUESDAY EVENING after date of issue.

| STATIONS. FROM | To Matlock | | To Buxton. | | STATIONS. FROM | To Matlock | | To Buxton. | |
|---|---|---|---|---|---|---|---|---|---|
| | 1st Class | 2d Class | 1st Class | 2d Class | | 1st Class | 2d Class | 1st Class | 2d Class |
| | s. d. | s. d | s. d. | s. d. | | s. d. | s. d. | s. d. | s. d. |
| Leicester . . . . | 10 0 | 8 0 | 14 0 | 10 0 | Cudworth . . . | 10 0 | 7 0 | 10 0 | 7 0 |
| Rugby . . . . . | 12 6 | 10 0 | 16 6 | 13 0 | Normanton . . . | 11 0 | 8 0 | 11 0 | 8 0 |
| Nuneaton . . . . | 12 6 | 10 0 | 14 6 | 11 0 | Wakefield (Westgt. | | | | |
| Hinckley . . . . | 11 6 | 9 6 | 14 6 | 11 0 | & L. & Y.) . . | 11 0 | 8 0 | 11 0 | 8 0 |
| Loughboro' . . . | 7 6 | 5 6 | 12 0 | 8 6 | Leeds . . . . . | 11 0 | 8 0 | 11 0 | 8 0 |
| Nottingham . . . | 6 0 | 4 6 | 10 0 | 7 6 | Bradford . . . . | 11 0 | 8 0 | 11 0 | 8 0 |
| Newark . : . . | 9 0 | 7 0 | 13 0 | 10 0 | Liverpool (Bruns- | | | | |
| Lincoln . . . . | 10 6 | 8 0 | 16 0 | 11 6 | wick) . . . . | 15 0 | 12 0 | 11 0 | 8 0 |
| *Birmingham . . | 10 6 | 8 0 | 16 0 | 11 6 | Warrington . . . | 12 0 | 8 6 | 7 6 | 5 0 |
| Tamworth . . . | 8 0 | 6 0 | 12 0 | 9 0 | Stockport (Tev. Dl. | 8 6 | 6 0 | 5 0 | 3 6 |
| Burton . . . . | 6 0 | 4 6 | 10 0 | 7 6 | *Manchester . . | 9 6 | 7 0 | 6 0 | 4 6 |
| Derby . . . . . | 4 0 | 3 0 | 7 6 | 5 6 | Staley Bridge . . | 9 0 | 6 6 | 5 0 | 3 6 |
| Chesterfield . . . | 5 0 | 4 0 | 9 0 | 6 0 | Guide Bridge . . | 9 0 | 6 6 | 5 0 | 3 6 |
| Sheffield . . . . | 7 0 | 5 0 | 10 0 | 7 0 | Glossop } via Guide | 10 6 | 7 6 | 6 6 | 4 6 |
| Masboro' . . . . | 7 0 | 5 0 | 10 0 | 7 0 | Dinting } Bridge. | 10 6 | 7 6 | 6 6 | 4 6 |
| Rotherham . . . | 7 0 | 5 0 | 10 0 | 7 0 | Stafford, via Uttox- } | | | | |
| Doncaster . . . | 10 0 | 7 0 | 10 0 | 7 0 | eter and Derby } | 9 0 | 7 0 | 11 0 | 8 0 |
| Barnsley . . . . | 10 0 | 7 0 | 10 0 | 7 0 | | | | | |

* In Manchester Tickets are issued at Cook's Excursion Office, 43 Piccadilly, and at the Midland Booking-Office, London Road Station. In Birmingham at Cook's Excursion Office, 16 Stephenson Place, and at the Midland Booking-Office, New Street Station.

# MIDLAND RAILWAY.

# ENGLISH LAKES.

DURING the Summer Months 1st, 2d, and 3d Class Tourist Tickets, available for One Calendar Month, are issued from Principal Stations on the Midland Railway to WINDERMERE, AMBLESIDE, GRANGE, FURNESS ABBEY, PENRITH, KESWICK, TROUTBECK, and MORECAMBE.

For Fares and further particulars see Tourist Programme, inserted in the Time-Tables ; or to be obtained loose, at the Principal Stations on the Line.

Every Saturday, from May 31st to October 11th, Cheap Excursion Tickets to Morecambe will be issued from Leicester, Nottingham, Derby, Sheffield, Masboro', Barnsley, Normanton, Leeds, Bradford, Keighley, and principal intermediate points, available to return up to the Tuesday Evening after date of issue.

For Fares and further particulars see Tourist Programmes and Special Hand-Bills.

## PLEASURE PARTIES.

### *From 1st MAY to 31st OCTOBER 1873,*

# CHEAP RETURN TICKETS

Will be issued to parties of not less than SIX First Class, or TEN Second or Third Class Passengers, desirous of taking Pleasure Excursions to places on or adjacent to this Railway.

The Tickets will be available for Return the **same day only,** and parties can only proceed and return by the Trains which stop at the Stations where they wish to join and leave the Railway.

To obtain these Tickets, application must be made at the Stations, or by letter "To the Superintendent of the Midland Railway, Derby," not less than three days before the Excursion, stating the following particulars, viz. :—

> That it is exclusively a Pleasure Party ;
> The Stations from and to which Tickets are required ;
> For which Class of Carriage ;
> The Date of the proposed Excursion ; and
> The probable Number of the Party.

The power of refusing to grant any application is reserved ; and if granted, an authority will be sent to the applicant in course of Post, on the delivery of which to the Booking-Clerk at the Station, the Cheap Return Tickets will be issued.

If the Party is numerous, Notice must be given the day previous to the Trip to the Clerk at the Station the Party will start from, so that sufficient accommodation may be provided.

These Tickets will be issued to and from London, and Stations not more than 30 miles distant from London ; and for School Parties to and from London, and any Station, irrespective of distance.

# GREAT NORTHERN AND NORTH EASTERN RAILWAYS.

## ADDITIONAL SPECIAL EXPRESS TRAINS AND IMPROVED SERVICE
## BY EAST COAST ROUTE
### BETWEEN
## SCOTLAND AND ENGLAND.

### FROM SCOTLAND.

| THIRD CLASS TICKETS by all Trains except 10.25 a.m. from Edinburgh. | 1 2 3 D A.M. | 1 2 3 E A.M. | 1 2 3 F A.M. | 1 2 3 G P.M. |
|---|---|---|---|---|
| Helmsdale ............................ dep. | | 5 10 | .. | 2 10 |
| GOLSPIE ................................. ,, | .. | 5 56 | .. | 2 52 |
| Tain ................................... ,, | .. | 7 38 | 10 0 | 4 33 |
| Invergordon ............................ ,, | .. | 8 13 | 10 45 | 5 20 |
| Strome Ferry (from Stornoway) ......... ,, | | .. | 8 30 | 3 0 |
| Dingwall ............................... ,, | .. | 8 50 | 11 24 | 6 0 |
| Beauly ................................. ,, | .. | 9 18 | 11 48 | 6 26 |
| Inverness .............................. ,, | .. | 10 18 | 12 40 | 7 30 |
| Blair-Athole ........................... ,, | 8 0 | 2 0 | 5 17 | 3 0 |
| Dunkeld ............................... ,, | 9 5 | 2 50 | 6 15 | 4 5 |

| | P.M. | | | |
|---|---|---|---|---|
| Ballater ............................... ,, | 4 55 | 7 25 | .. | .. |

| | A.M. | P.M. | A.M. | A.M. |
|---|---|---|---|---|
| | | | | 1 & 2 \| |
| Aberdeen .............................. ,, | 9 0 | 12 23 | 4 10 | 1 & 2 \| .. |
| Arbroath .............................. ,, | 10 7 | 1 42 | 5 18 | .. \| 6 5 |
| Dundee via Stirling .................... ,, | 9 30 | 3 3 | 6 30 | .. \| 7 55 |
| ,, via Fife ..................... ,, | 9 40 | 3 20 | 6 30 | .. \| .. |
| Perth via Stirling ..................... ,, | 12 5 | 4 4 | 7 40 | .. \| 8 40 |
| ,, via Fife ..................... ,, | 10 25 | 4 10 | 7 25 | .. \| .. |
| Stirling ............................... ,, | 1 6 | 5 3 | 8 42 | 8 55 \| 9 30 |
| Balloch, from Loch Lomond .......... ,, | 10 45 | 3 48 | 7 0 | 7 25 \| 7 25 |
| Helensburgh ....................... ,, | 10 45 | 3 45 | 7 0 | 7 25 \| 7 25 |
| Glasgow (Queen Street) ............ arr. | 11 55 | 5 6 | 8 10 | 8 40 \| 8 40 |
| Glasgow (Queen Street) ........... dep. | 1 0 | 5 0 | 9 0 | 9 0 \| 9 0 |
| EDINBURGH (from Glasgow) .......... arr. | 2 25 | 6 25 | 10 18 | 10 15 \| 10 15 |
| ,, (from North) ............... ,, | 2 25 | 6 25 | 9 55 | 10 10 \| 10 40 |
| ,, (for South) .............. dep. | 2 50 | 7 30 | 10 30 | 10 25 \| 10 45 |
| Berwick ............................... ,, | 4 30 | 9 5 | 12 14 | 11 53 \| 12 20 |
| Newcastle ............................. ,, | 7 8 | 11 23 | 2 5 | 1 30 \| 2 15 |
| York .................................. ,, | 9 45 | 2 5 | 4 35 | 3 40 \| 4 45 |
| LONDON ⎰ KING'S CROSS STATION.. arr. | 3 15 | 6 45 | 9 40 | 7.55 \| 9 30 |
| ⎱ Moorgate Street ,, ,, | .. | .. | 9 53 | .. |
| ⎱ Victoria (L. C. & D.) ,, ,, | .. | .. | 10 35 | .. |
| | A.M. | A.M. | A.M. | P.M. \| P.M. |

**D** does not run on Sundays north of Berwick. **E** runs on Sundays from York to London, but does not run from York to London on Monday mornings. **F** Runs on Sundays from Edinburgh to King's Cross. **G** does not run on Sundays.

*Passengers from Scotland are particularly urged to ask for Tickets by the East Coast Route, via Berwick and York, and to see that such Tickets are supplied to them. A Conductor in charge of Through Luggage travels with the Express Trains between Edinburgh and London. Passengers are conveyed to and from Scotland in Through Carriages of the most improved description, which have been constructed for the special accommodation of Traffic by the East Coast Route. The morning Expresses from London and Edinburgh are each allowed 25 minutes at York for Passengers to dine. Hot Dinners provided at 2s. 6d. each. No fees.*

**Great Eastern Railway.**

# EAST COAST WATERING PLACES.

TOURIST Tickets are issued to Yarmouth, Lowestoft, Hunstanton, Aldborough, Dovercourt, and Harwich, from London, and other Stations on Great Eastern Railway; also from the principal Stations on the London and North-Western, Midland, Great Northern, Manchester, Sheffield, and Lincolnshire, Great Western, and North-Eastern Railways.

*For particulars see Tourist Programme.*

## THE ROYAL ROUTE.

# FORT-WILLIAM AND KINGUSSIE.

THE Royal Mail Coach leaves Fort-William at 5 A.M. for Kingussie *via* Loch-Laggan, &c., arriving at 11.30 A.M., in time for Trains to the North and South, and returning at 1.15 P.M. Daily throughout the year (Sunday excepted). Fares, 12s. 6d. and 15s. Driver's fee, 1s.

Seats secured, and information given, at the Coach Office, Fort-William.

JAMES MILLAR, *Agent.*

"We were delighted with the scenery, which is singularly beautiful, wild, and romantic."—*From Her Majesty's Life in the Highlands.*

### Glencoe and Glenorchy Coaches

From Fort-William and Ballachulish, through the far-famed Pass of Glencoe and Earl of Breadalbane's Deer Forest, and from Oban by the Pass of Awe and Loch Awe to Glasgow, Edinburgh, Aberfeldy, &c., *via* Lochlomond or Killin, and *vice versa*. Daily during the Tourist Season.

For particulars see the June, July, August, and September numbers of Bradshaw, Murray, &c. &c. ; or apply to the Proprietor, Coach Office, Ballachulish.

## ABERDEEN AND LONDON STEAMERS.

The undernoted, or other of the Aberdeen Steam Navigation Company's Steamships will be despatched (weather, &c., permitting) every Wednesday and Saturday from each end—"Ban-Righ," "City of London," "City of Aberdeen" (new). Passage Fares (including steward's fees)—Single Tickets—First, 30s. ; second, 15s. ; children under 14 years, 15s. and 10s. Return Tickets, available for 28 days—45s. and 25s. ; children, 25s. and 15s. Passengers will please observe that from 4th June until end of September one of the Woolwich Steam Company's Boats will start from the Temple Pier (Thames Embankment) one hour before the advertised times of sailing, conveying Passengers and their Luggage alongside the Aberdeen Steamers free of charge. Porters in the Company's service will assist with the Luggage. For further particulars apply to CHARLES SHEPHERD, Agent, 257 Wapping, London ; or to JOHN SMITH, Manager, Waterloo Quay, Aberdeen.—*April* 1873.

## PORT OF SILLOTH.

COMMUNICATION BETWEEN

# DUBLIN and DOUGLAS (Isle of Man)

AND THE

# NORTH of ENGLAND and SCOTLAND.

FIRST-CLASS Passenger Steamers (in connection with North British Railway trains) leave Dublin for Silloth every Monday and Thursday, and Silloth for Dublin every Tuesday and Saturday, calling off or at Douglas Harbour each way.

The "Silloth Route" is the shortest sea-passage between Dublin or Douglas and the North of England and Scotland, and is in direct communication with the North British Railway trains for the Cumberland Lakes, Carlisle, Kelso, Jedburgh, Melrose, Edinburgh, Hawthornden, Roslin, St. Andrews, Loch Leven, Perth, and all the popular Tourist Routes through Scotland.

For information as to starting of Trains and Steamers, see the North British Railway Company's monthly Time Tables, or apply to A. NICHOLL, 20 Eden Quay, Dublin, G. BARRY, Neville Chambers, Newcastle-on-Tyne, JAS. BRUCE, Carlisle Station, or to R. DARLING, North British Steam Packet Company's Office, 4 Princes Street, Edinburgh.

# SCOTLAND & IRELAND.

## ROYAL MAIL LINE.

## DAILY SERVICE.

### GLASGOW, BELFAST, DUBLIN, LONDONDERRY, &c.

## *Via GREENOCK (Princes Pier).*

### Royal Mail Steamships.

RACOON, BUFFALO, CAMEL, LLAMA, FERRET, AND HORNET.

From GLASGOW every Day (Sunday excepted) at 4 P.M., and from Prince's Pier, Albert Harbour, GREENOCK, at 8.45 P.M., on arrival of the 8 P.M. Mail Train from Dunlop Street Station, Glasgow.

From BELFAST, every evening (Sunday excepted) at 8 P.M., for GREEN-OCK and GLASGOW.

### *Return Tickets available for One Calendar Month.*

### FARES (Including Steward's Fee),

|  | Single Journey. | Return. |
|---|---|---|
| Between GLASGOW or GREENOCK and BELFAST— | | |
| First Class and Cabin | 12s. 6d. | 20s. |
| Third Class and Steerage | 4s. | — |
| Between GLASGOW or GREENOCK and DUBLIN— | | |
| First Class and Cabin | 25s. | 40s. |
| Third Class and Steerage | 11s. | — |
| Between GLASGOW or GREENOCK and LONDONDERRY or PORT RUSH (Giant's Causeway Station)— | | |
| First Class and Cabin | 22s. 6d. | 35s. |
| Third Class and Steerage | 9s. | — |

*Cabin Berths secured at the Steam Packet Offices in Glasgow and Belfast.*

**Tickets can be procured at the principal Railway Stations in Scotland and Ireland.**

For further particulars apply to A. G. S. M'CULLOCH & SON, DONEGAL QUAY, BELFAST, or to    G. & J. BURNS, 30 JAMAICA STREET, GLASGOW.

DURING THE SUMMER MONTHS THERE WILL BE AN

## ADDITIONAL SERVICE.

*For days of Sailing, see Time Tables and Daily Papers.*

# "ANCHOR" LINE.

### REGULAR STEAM COMMUNICATION BETWEEN

## GREAT BRITAIN AND THE UNITED STATES, NEW BRUNSWICK, NOVA SCOTIA, FRANCE, PORTUGAL, SPAIN, ITALY, SICILY, EGYPT, THE ADRIATIC, AND INDIA,

By the First-class Powerful Clyde-Built Screw Steam Ships

| | | | | |
|---|---|---|---|---|
| ACADIA | Capt. Hillcoat. | ISMAILIA | Capt. J. Ovenstone. |
| ALEXANDRIA | Capt. M'Kay. | ITALIA | Capt. Greig. |
| ALSATIA | ............ | NAPOLI | Capt. Edwards. |
| ANGLIA | Capt. Small. | OLYMPIA | Capt. Young. |
| ASSYRIA | Capt. Smith. | ROMA | Capt. Donaldson. |
| AUSTRALIA | Capt. Hedderwick. | SCANDINAVIA | Capt. Harvey. |
| BOLIVIA | ............ | SCOTIA | ............ |
| CALEDONIA | Capt. D. Ovenstone. | SHAMROCK | Capt. Livingstone. |
| CALIFORNIA | Capt. Craig. | SIDONIAN | Capt. Henderson. |
| CASTALIA | Capt. Butler. | TRINACRIA | Capt. Thomson. |
| COLUMBIA | Capt. Higgins. | TROJAN | Capt. M'Queen. |
| DORIAN | Capt. Taylor. | TYRIAN | Capt. Lawson. |
| ELYSIA | ............ | UTOPIA | ............ |
| ETHIOPIA | ............ | VALETTA | Capt. Sidey. |
| EUROPA | Capt. Campbell. | VENEZIA | Capt. Gordon. |
| INDIA | Capt. J. R. Mackay. | VICTORIA | Capt. Munro. |
| IOWA | ............ | | |

---

## ATLANTIC SERVICE.

STEAMERS leave GLASGOW for NEW YORK (calling at Moville, Lough Foyle, to embark passengers only) every WEDNESDAY and SATURDAY.

From NEW YORK for GLASGOW every WEDNESDAY and SATURDAY.

From GLASGOW, LIVERPOOL, and LONDON, for HALIFAX, N.S., and ST. JOHN, N.B., ONCE A MONTH from March till September.

RATES OF PASSAGE for New York—Saloon Cabin, Saturday's Steamers, £13 : 13s. and £15 : 15s. ; Wednesday's Steamers, £12 : 12s. and £14 : 14s., according to accommodation and situation of Berths. Return Tickets, Twenty-Two and Twenty-Four Guineas. For Halifax, N.S., and St. John, N.B.—Saloon Cabin, £13 : 13s.